CRIMINAL LAW

STEVEN L. EMANUEL

Harvard Law School
J.D. 1976

The CrunchTime Series

Aspen Law & Business
A Division of Aspen Publishers, Inc.
New York   Gaithersburg

Printed in the United States of America.

ISBN 0-7355-2724-5

This book is intended as a general review of a legal subject. It is not intended as a source of advice for the solution of legal matters or problems. For advice on legal matters, the reader should consult an attorney.

About Aspen Law & Business
Legal Education Division

Aspen Law & Business is proud to welcome Emanuel Publishing Corporation's highly successful study aids to its list of law school publications. As part of the Aspen family, Steve and Lazar Emanuel will continue their work on these popular titles, widely purchased by students for more than a quarter century. With the addition of the Emanuel titles, Aspen now offers the most comprehensive selection of outstanding publications for the discerning law student.

ASPEN LAW & BUSINESS
A Division of Aspen Publishers, Inc.
A Wolters Kluwer Company
www.aspenpublishers.com

SUMMARY OF CONTENTS

FLOWCHARTS 1

CAPSULE SUMMARY 47

EXAM TIPS 153

SHORT-ANSWER QUESTIONS 203

ANSWERS TO SHORT-ANSWER QUESTIONS 225

MULTIPLE-CHOICE QUESTIONS 247

ANSWERS TO MULTIPLE-CHOICE QUESTIONS 260

ESSAY EXAM QUESTIONS & ANSWERS 271

TABLE OF CASES 283

SUBJECT MATTER INDEX 285

TABLE OF CONTENTS

FLOWCHARTS

ACTUS REUS AND MENS REA 3

CAUSATION 9

SELF-DEFENSE 14

ATTEMPT 18

CONSPIRACY 23

ACCOMPLICE LIABILITY 27

HOMICIDE 31

THEFT CRIMES 38

CAPSULE SUMMARY

ACTUS REUS AND MENS REA 49

CAUSATION 60

RESPONSIBILITY 66

JUSTIFICATION AND EXCUSE 72

ATTEMPT 91

CONSPIRACY 98

ACCOMPLICE LIABILITY
AND SOLICITATION 109

HOMICIDE AND OTHER CRIMES
AGAINST THE PERSON 118

THEFT CRIMES 136

EXAM TIPS

ACTUS REAS AND MENS REA 157

Duty to act 157
Statutory Language (as to both
    Actus Reus and Mens Rea) 158

CAUSATION. 160

Cause In Fact 160
Proximate Cause 161

RESPONSIBILITY. 163

Insanity 163
Intoxication 165

JUSTIFICATION AND EXCUSE 167

Self-defense 167
Defense of property 169
Fleeing Felons and Law Enforcement 169
Entrapment 171
Duress 171

ATTEMPT. 172

Mental State 172
Requirement of Act 173
Impossibility 173
Merger, and Convictions of Both Attempt
    and the Underlying Crime 175

CONSPIRACY 176

Agreement and Intent 176
Overt act 178
Vicarious liability for substantive crimes by
    other conspirators 178
Abandonment 179
Wharton's rule 180
Conspiracy vs. the Substantive Crime 180

ACCOMPLICE LIABILITY AND SOLICITATION 181

Accomplice Liability, Generally 181
Solicitation 183

**HOMICIDE & OTHER CRIMES
    AGAINST THE PERSON** 183

    Homicides Generally 183
    Intent in Homicide Cases 184
    Felony-murder 186
    Voluntary manslaughter ("v.m.") 188
    Involuntary manslaughter ("i.m.") 189
    Battery 191
    Assault 192
    Rape / Sexual Assault 192
    Kidnapping 193

THEFT CRIMES 193

    Larceny 193
    Robbery 197
    Embezzlement 197
    False pretenses 198
    Burglary 199
    Receiving stolen property 201

**SHORT-ANSWER
QUESTIONS** 203

**ANSWERS TO
SHORT-ANSWER QUESTIONS** 225

**MULTIPLE-CHOICE
QUESTIONS** 247

**ANSWERS TO
MULTIPLE-CHOICE QUESTIONS** 260

**ESSAY EXAM
QUESTIONS & ANSWERS** 271

TABLE OF CASES 283

SUBJECT MATTER INDEX 285

Preface

Thank you for buying this book.

The *CrunchTime* Series is intended for people who want Emanuel quality, but don't have the time or money to buy and use the full-length *Emanuel Law Outline* on a subject. We've designed the Series to be used in the last few weeks (or even less) before your final exams.

This book includes the following features, some of which have been extracted from the corresponding *Emanuel Law Outline*:

- *Flow Charts* — We've reduced most principles of *Criminal Law* to a series of 8 Flow Charts, created specially for this book and never published elsewhere. We think these will be especially useful on open-book exams. The Flow Charts begin on p. 1.

- *Capsule Summary* — This is a 100-page or so summary of the subject. We've carefully crafted it to cover the things you're most likely to be asked on an exam. The Capsule Summary starts on p. 47.

- *Exam Tips* — We've compiled these by reviewing dozens of actual past essay and multiple-choice questions asked in past law-school and bar exams, and extracting the issues and "tricks" that surface most often on exams. The Exam Tips start on p. 153.

- *Short-Answer* questions — These questions are generally in a Yes/No format, with a "mini-essay" explaining each one. They've been adapted from our *Law in a Flash* Series. The questions start on p. 203.

- *Multiple-Choice* questions — These are in a Multistate-Bar-Exam style, and were adapted from a book we publish called *The Finz Multistate Method*. They start on p. 247.

- *Essay* questions — These questions are actual ones asked on law school exams. They start on p. 271.

We hope you find this book helpful and instructive.

Good luck.

Steve Emanuel

FLOWCHARTS

TABLE OF CONTENTS
to
FLOWCHARTS

Fig.

1   Actus Reus and Mens Rea   3

2   Causation   9

3   Self-defense   14

4   Attempt.   18

5   Conspiracy   23

6   Accomplice Liability   27

7   Homicide   31

8   Theft Crimes.   38

Figure 1

Actus Reus and Mens Rea

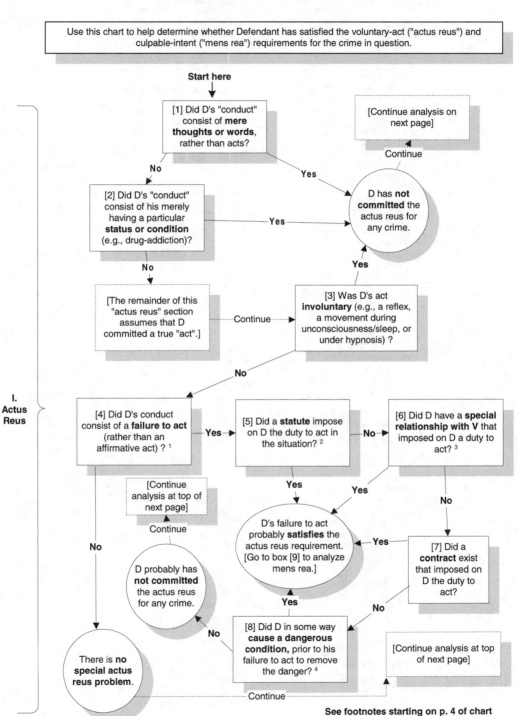

Use this chart to help determine whether Defendant has satisfied the voluntary-act ("actus reus") and culpable-intent ("mens rea") requirements for the crime in question.

Start here

I. Actus Reus

[1] Did D's "conduct" consist of **mere thoughts or words**, rather than acts?

[Continue analysis on next page]

Continue

[2] Did D's "conduct" consist of his merely having a particular **status or condition** (e.g., drug-addiction)?

D has **not committed** the actus reus for any crime.

[The remainder of this "actus reus" section assumes that D committed a true "act".]

Continue

[3] Was D's act **involuntary** (e.g., a reflex, a movement during unconsciousness/sleep, or under hypnosis) ?

[4] Did D's conduct consist of a **failure to act** (rather than an affirmative act) ? ¹

[5] Did a **statute** impose on D the duty to act in the situation? ²

[6] Did D have a **special relationship with V** that imposed on D a duty to act? ³

[Continue analysis at top of next page]

Continue

D's failure to act probably **satisfies** the actus reus requirement. [Go to box [9] to analyze mens rea.]

D probably has **not committed** the actus reus for any crime.

[7] Did a **contract** exist that imposed on D the duty to act?

[8] Did D in some way **cause a dangerous condition,** prior to his failure to act to remove the danger? ⁴

There is **no special actus reus problem.**

[Continue analysis at top of next page]

Continue

See footnotes starting on p. 4 of chart

Figure 1 (Cont.)

Actus Reus and Mens Rea (p. 2)

This page and the next will help you analyze mens rea (mental state).

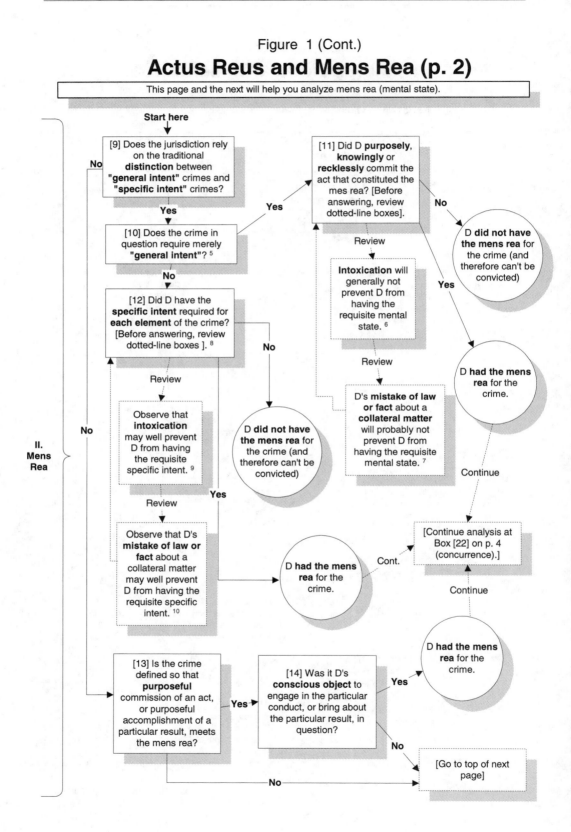

Figure 1 (Cont.)
Actus Reus and Mens Rea (p. 3)

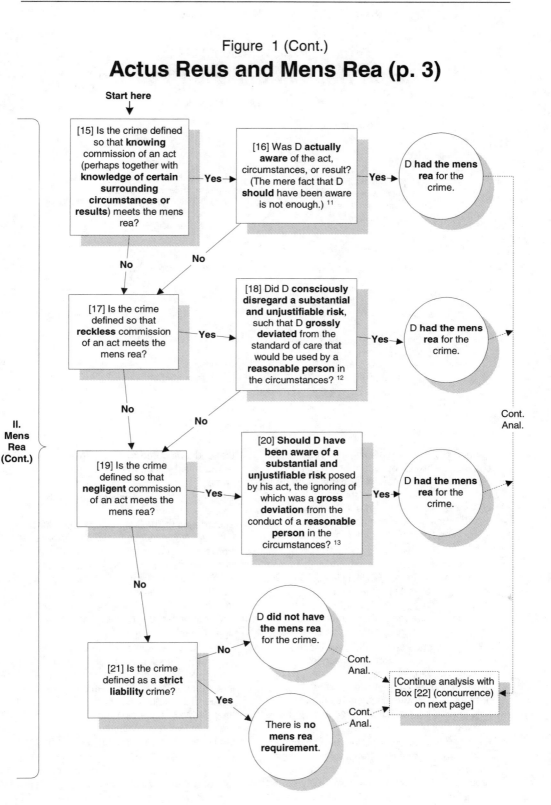

Figure 1 (Cont.)
Actus Reus and Mens Rea (p. 4)

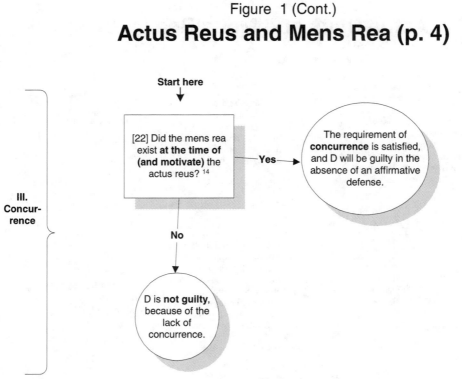

Notes

[1] Example: D sees V drowning in a pond. D continues walking, even though he could easily have thrown V a life preserver that he sees on the ground next to the pond. Here, the only "conduct" on the part of D that could possibly be considered culpable is D's failure to act -- he has not committed any affirmative act.

As a general principle, one who simply fails to act incurs no criminal liability. Unless D falls into one of several special categories (represented by boxes [5]-[8]), D's failure to act will therefore mean that D has failed to commit the actus reus for any crime.

[2] Example: A state statute provides that if a person witnesses a crime of violence against a child, the witness commits a misdemeanor if she does not report that crime to the authorities. If D witnesses such a crime and fails to report it, her failure is the actus reus of a crime.

[3] Example: In virtually all states, parents have a duty to supply medical attention to their minor children. If D, a Christian Scientist, fails to provide medical attention to V, his 10-year-old daughter who is dying of a rare blood disorder that could be cured by a transfusion, D's failure to act will be the actus reus of a crime.

[4] Example: D has a swimming pool on his property. D maintains the pool in accordance with all regulations (e.g., for fencing). Nonetheless, V, a 10-year-old child from the neighborhood, falls in. D is aware of the accident, but does nothing to help V. Because D has in some way "caused" the accident -- by creating, however non-negligently, the condition that made the accident possible -- D has an affirmative duty to render assistance.

[5] Example: In jurisdictions following the general-intent/specific-intent distinction, battery is usually classified as a general-intent crime. Thus if D is found to have intended the actus reus for battery (i.e., D intended to bring about a harmful or offensive bodily contact) the fact that D didn't necessarily intend any serious bodily injury to V is irrelevant.

[6] Example: D, while drunk, takes out his knife and puts it up against V's face, intending just to make V feel fear from cold steel against

Notes (cont.) to
Figure 1 (Actus Reus / Mens Rea)

his cheek. Because D's motor control is poor due to his drunkeness, the knife slips, gouging V's face. Even though D did not intend to harm V, the fact that D intended to make an offensive contact with V means that D meets the general-intent requirement for battery, since the actus reus for battery is the making of a harmful or offensive contact and D has intended to make such a contact.

7 Example: D is slightly hard of hearing. While drinking in a tavern one night (D is not drunk), he mis-hears something that V says to him, and thinks that V has insulted D's mother. D therefore takes a swing at V in the jaw and hits him in the jaw. Battery is a general-intent crime (in jurisdictions making the general/specific distinction); therefore, as long as D intended to make a harmful or offensive bodily contact (which he did), the fact that D was motivated by a mistake of fact will be irrelevant -- he's met the mens rea for battery. (It's true that certain mistakes -- like a reasonable but mistaken belief in the need for self-defense -- may block liability even for a general-intent crime like battery; but these are rigidly-controlled affirmative defenses. The general point is that mistakes don't count as long as they don't nullify -- as they usual don't -- the very general mental state needed for a general-intent crime.)

8 Example: In jurisdictions following the specific-intent / general-intent distinction, burglary is almost always a specific-intent crime. That is, in addition to having the intent to commit the actus reus (breaking and entering a dwelling at night), D must be shown to have had, at the time of the entry, the specific intent to commit a felony inside the dwelling. So it's not enough for the prosecution to show that D intended to break-and-enter.

9 Example: D is found very drunk inside V's house. The prosecution shows convincingly that D, although he was very drunk, formed the intent to break into V's house. However, the facts indicate that D was so drunk that he was incapable of planning to commit any particular crime inside the house -- all he wanted to do was sleep once he got inside. On these facts, D's intoxication will prevent

him from having the required specific intent (intent to commit a felony inside the dwelling), so the intoxication will result in D's acquittal.

10 Example: D mistakenly (and unreasonably) believes that V has stolen D's Trek bicycle and is keeping it in V's house. D breaks into V's house, and takes V's bicycle (also a Trek), thinking he's merely reclaiming his own bike. D's mistake of fact about whose bike it was -- even though that mistake was unreasonable -- prevented D from having the specific intent to commit a felony inside V's house (since it's not larceny to take property that one mistakenly believes to be one's own, no matter how unreasonable the mistake is). Therefore, D's mistake will result in his acquittal on burglary charges.

11 Example: D, an art dealer, sells a painting to V that D describes as a Rembrandt. D has previously been warned by two experts that the painting is almost certainly a 20th century forgery. A reasonable art dealer in D's position would believe the experts, but D honestly believes that the painting is a genuine Rembrandt. Assume that the crime of selling counterfeit property requires a showing that D has "knowingly" sold property that is not as described. On these facts, D does not satisfy the mens rea, because he did not have an actual awareness of the painting's counterfeit nature even though he "should" have had such an awareness.

12 The view stated in the box -- that the test for recklessness is whether D consciously disregarded a large risk -- is the view followed by the MPC and by most courts. Some courts, however, apply an "objective" (rather than the MPC's "subjective") approach, under which D can be deemed reckless if he failed to recognize a huge risk that a reasonable person in his position would have recognized.

Example: D, a factory owner, padlocks all but one door to the factory, while 200

Notes (cont.) to
Figure 1 (Actus Reus / Mens Rea)

workers are working. D does this because many of his workers have been sneaking out of work early without detection. D fails to recognize that the padlocks are creating a huge risk in case of fire. (He simply never thinks about the issue of fire at all.) A fire breaks out, and 100 workers are burned to death when they can't get out through the one open exit. Suppose that D is prosecuted for depraved-indifference murder, which requires a reckless disregard of the value of human life. Under the MPC (and probably majority) view, D will be found lacking in recklessness, because he has not consciously disregarded a large known risk -- he has instead failed to recognize a risk. (But a minority of courts would find him reckless merely for his failure to recognize the large risk.)

[13] Example: D drives at 30 mph in a 30-mph zone. However, the road is very slick with rain, and D's tires are worn down. A reasonably-prudent driver in these conditions would have reduced her speed to 20 mph. D's 30 mph speed causes her to lose control on a turn, and to hit V, a pedestrian, killing her. Even if D was unaware the 30 mph was dangerously fast to be travelling on a slick road with worn tires, D can be convicted of negligent homicide. That's because criminal negligence is universally judged by an "objective" standard (would a reasonable person have taken the risk?), not a subjective standard (did D recognize the risk). On the other hand, as illustrated by the prior footnote, D would have been acquitted of a crime requiring reck-lessness.

[14] Example: One morning, D decides to murder V at 6 pm later that day, the murder to take place by a rifle shot that D will fire into V's house. While D is driving to the gun store at 9 am to buy the rifle that he plans to use later, he exceeds the speed limit, and fatally runs over V by accident. D is not guilty of murder, because although he intended to kill V and did kill V, his intent did not "motivate" (cause) the actual killing.

Figure 2
Causation

Even if D committed the appropriate actus reus for the crime and did so with the appropriate mens rea, the prosecution must still show that D "caused" a particular sort of harmful result. (At least, that's so where the crime is defined to require some sort of harmful result; this is true of crimes like homicide, rape, arson, etc.) To make that showing, the prosecution must typically show two things: (1) that D's act was the **"cause in fact"** of the harm; and (2) that that act was the **"proximate"** or **"legal"** cause of the harm. This chart will help you evaluate whether the prosecution can make this showing. "V" stands for victim.

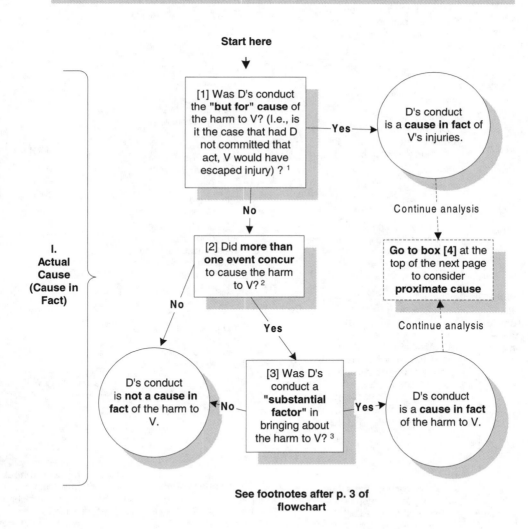

Start here

[1] Was D's conduct the **"but for"** cause of the harm to V? (I.e., is it the case that had D not committed that act, V would have escaped injury) ? [1]

— Yes → D's conduct is a **cause in fact** of V's injuries.

No

[2] Did **more than one event concur** to cause the harm to V? [2]

No →

D's conduct is **not a cause in fact** of the harm to V.

Yes

[3] Was D's conduct a **"substantial factor"** in bringing about the harm to V? [3]

← No

— Yes → D's conduct is a **cause in fact** of the harm to V.

I.
Actual Cause (Cause in Fact)

Continue analysis

Go to box [4] at the top of the next page to consider **proximate cause**

Continue analysis

See footnotes after p. 3 of flowchart

Figure 2 (cont.)
Causation (p. 2)

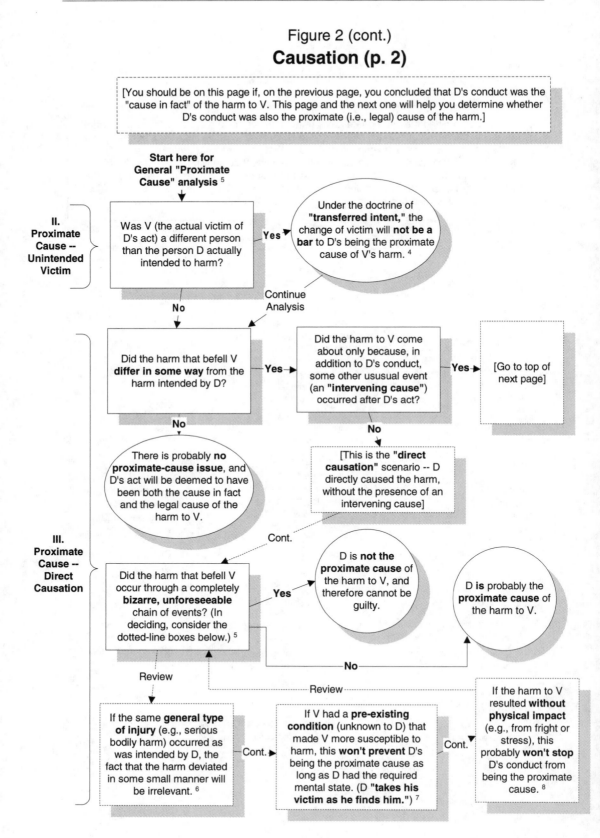

Figure 2 (cont.)
Causation (p. 3)

[You should be on this page if, on the previous page, you concluded that an intervening act or event contributed to the harm to V. This page will help you determine whether the intervening act is "superseding," i.e., prevents D's act from being the proximate cause of V's harm.]

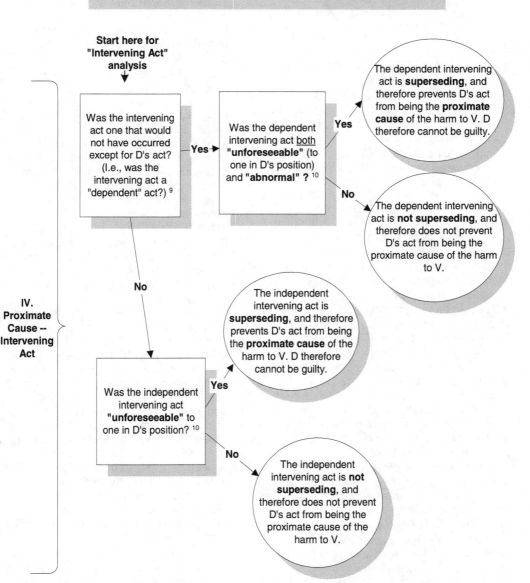

Notes to
Figure 2 (Causation)

[1] A common scenario in which the "but for" requirement is not satisfied involves a victim who is not alive at the time of D's act. Example: D, driving carefully, nonetheless inadvertently hits V, a pedestrian. Unbeknownst to D, V dies immediately upon impact. D, believing that V is still alive, throws the body into a nearby lake to cover the evidence. If D is charged with murder, the prosecution will not be able to satisfy the "but for" requirement, because the only act D committed with a wrongful mental state -- the act of throwing the body into the lake -- did not cause the death. (It's true that D's act of driving and hitting V did cause the death, but that act was not done with a wrongful state of mind, so it doesn't count.)

[2] Example: D beats V up. V summons an ambulance to take him to the hospital. The ambulance gets in a terrible accident while rushing V to the hospital, and V dies in that accident. On these facts, more than one event (the beating, plus the accident) have concurred to cause the harm to V.

[3] The most important scenario in which you have to worry about the substantial-factor test is where one person mortally wounds V, and another finishes the task. Example: X injures V, in such a way that V will definitely die soon from the injuries. D then gives V additional injuries, causing V to die sooner than had D not done this. Even though D is not the "but for" cause of V's death (V would soon have died anyway), D has shortened V's life, so he'll be deemed to have been a "substantial factor" in V's death, making D a "cause in fact" of the death. (X is probably also a substantial factor, and thus a cause in fact, of the death.)

[4] Example: D tries to shoot X to death. His bullet misses X, and hits V, killing him. Under the doctrine of transferred intent, D is guilty of murdering V -- his intent is deemed to be transferred from X to V.

The transferred-intent doctrine is often combined with the doctrine under which the mens rea for a more serious crime may suffice for conviction for a related, but less serious, crime. Example: Same facts as above Example. Now, however, assume that the bullet intended to kill X hits V but merely injures him. The court will combine transferred-intent and the "greater mens rea used to cover the lesser, related crime" doctrine to make D guilty of battery -- the mental state for murder (intent to kill) will be transferred from X to V, and that intent will suffice to meet the mental-state requirement for battery, a less-serious crime related to murder.

A related problem is the "mistaken identity" problem. Here, the fact that D has made a mistake about who the victim is will not shield D. Example: D hates V. He sees a person who looks just like V, shoots at him, and kills him. The person is really X, V's identical-twin brother, who D actually likes. D is still guilty of murder -- as long as he intended to kill the person he was shooting at, the fact that there was a mistaken identity won't make any difference.

[5] Example: D, a con man, defrauds V of $100 in a street game of 3-card monte. V becomes distraught at his own gullibility and falls into a depression. Because of the depression, V ignores headaches that he had begun having recently (before the monte game). He therefore fails to get medical attention. (Had he not been depressed, he would have seen a doctor almost immediately.) The headaches turn out to be a brain tumor, and by the time V gets medical help it's too late -- V dies from the tumor. On these facts, it can be said that D's defrauding of V "directly caused" V's death (V would not have died from the tumor otherwise). However, it's very unlikely that a court would conclude that D's fraud is the proximate cause of V's death -- the sequence of events is just too bizarre and unforeseeable for that. (Therefore, D is unlikely to be held criminally responsible for the death.)

[6] Example: D intends to poison her husband, V, to death. She puts arsenic in V's coffee. V drinks the coffee, then feels faint. While faint, he falls, hits his head on a side table, and dies from the impact.

Notes (cont.) to
Figure 2 (Causation)

The poison itself would not have been concentrated enough to kill V. Nonetheless, D will probably be held to have proximately caused V's death, because the poisoning caused the same general type of harm (serious bodily injury) as that intended by D.

[7] Example: V gets into a fight with D, through no fault of V's. D hits V in the chin, hoping to hurt V seriously (put him in the hospital) but not to kill him. The blow knocks V unconscious. Unbeknownst to D, V is a serious epileptic. While V is unconscious from the blow, V suffers an epileptic seizure (caused in part by the blow). The seizure causes V to swallow his tongue. The tongue blocks V's airway, and V dies of suffocation before an ambulance can arrive. On these facts, D will almost certainly be held to have proximately caused V's death, because: (1) he has directly brought that death about and (2) D will be deemed to "take his victim as he finds him" -- in other words, the fact that V had a hidden condition that made a blow more dangerous to him than to an average person is irrelevant. (Since D had one of the mental states that will suffice for murder -- intent to do serious bodily harm -- he'll probably be guilty of murder.)

[8] Example: D walks into a convenience store operated by V. D is wearing a mask, and points a gun at V, saying, "Empty the cash register, or I'll give you a third eye in your forehead." V, terror-sticken, drops dead of a sudden heart attack. (D had no way to know that V had previously-undiagnosed heart disease.) The gun was in fact a toy pistol, and D never intended to cause any physical harm to V. Nonetheless, he'll be deemed to be the proximate cause of V's death. Therefore, under the felony murder rule, he'll be guilty of murder (since D "caused" a death during the commission of a dangerous felony.)

[9] Example 1 (dependent act): One winter's day, D beats V up, leaving him wounded at the side of the road. V recovers enough to use his cellphone to call for an ambulance. The ambulance drives up to V at great speed, brakes, skids on some ice, and runs V over, killing him. The ambulance accident will be held to be a dependent act, since it would not have occurred but for V's injury and

subsequent call for help.

Example 2 (independent act): Same basic facts as Example 1. Now, however, V, instead of phoning for help, limps to a nearby subway station. He gets on the next train, intending to take it to the nearest hospital. Due to a suicide on the tracks, the train is delayed for 1 hour, during which time V cannot get off (the train is in a tunnel) even though V knows he's losing blood. V eventually dies of internal bleeding. Had the train not been delayed, V would have gotten to the hospital in time to be saved. The train delay will be held to be an independent act, since it would have occurred even had D not committed the beating.

[10] Notice that the dependent event will not be superseding unless it's both "unforeseeable" and "abnormal", whereas the independent event will be superseding as long as it's merely "unforeseeable". This may make the independent event a bit more likely to be superseding than the dependent event.

Thus on the facts of Example 1 in note 9, the "dependent" ambulance accident might well be held to be not "abnormal" (even though unforeseeable), since it resulted from humans responding in predictable ways. By contrast, on the facts of Example 2 in that note, the "independent" train accident (and subsequent trapping of V) might be held to have been unforeseeable to one in D's position (with no additional requirement of abnormalness). So the train accident might end up being superseding, while the ambulance accident probably would not be.

Note that many courts consider the dependent/independent distinction to be senseless. These courts usually apply just the simple "unforeseeability" standard. In such a court, D in Example 1 would probably escape being the proximate cause of the death, on the theory that the ambulance accident was truly a new (and very unlikely) cause of injury.

Figure 3
Self-Defense

A person has a general right to defend herself against the use of unlawful force. If all of the requirements for self-defense are met, the defense is a complete one, leading to acquittal. This chart helps you determine whether the requirements have been met. "D" is the defendant, charged with the crime. "V" is the "victim," i.e., the person against whom the allegedly self-defensive force is used.

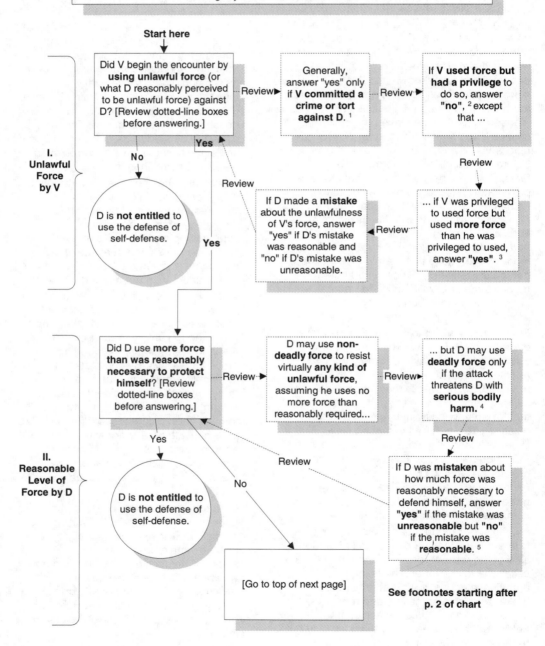

Start here

I. Unlawful Force by V

Did V begin the encounter by **using unlawful force** (or what D reasonably perceived to be unlawful force) against D? [Review dotted-line boxes before answering.]

◄Review► Generally, answer "yes" only if **V committed a crime or tort against D**. [1]

◄Review► If **V used force but had a privilege** to do so, answer **"no"**, [2] except that ...

No → D is **not entitled** to use the defense of self-defense.

Yes

Review → If D made a **mistake** about the unlawfulness of V's force, answer "yes" if D's mistake was reasonable and "no" if D's mistake was unreasonable.

◄Review ... if V was privileged to used force but used **more force** than he was privileged to used, answer **"yes"**. [3]

Review

Yes

II. Reasonable Level of Force by D

Did D use **more force than was reasonably necessary to protect himself**? [Review dotted-line boxes before answering.]

◄Review► D may use **non-deadly force** to resist virtually **any kind of unlawful force**, assuming he uses no more force than reasonably required...

◄Review► ... but D may use **deadly force** only if the attack threatens D with **serious bodily harm**. [4]

Yes → D is **not entitled** to use the defense of self-defense.

No

Review

Review

If D was **mistaken** about how much force was reasonably necessary to defend himself, answer **"yes"** if the mistake was **unreasonable** but "no" if the mistake was **reasonable**. [5]

[Go to top of next page]

See footnotes starting after p. 2 of chart

Figure 3 (Cont.)
Self-Defense (p. 2)

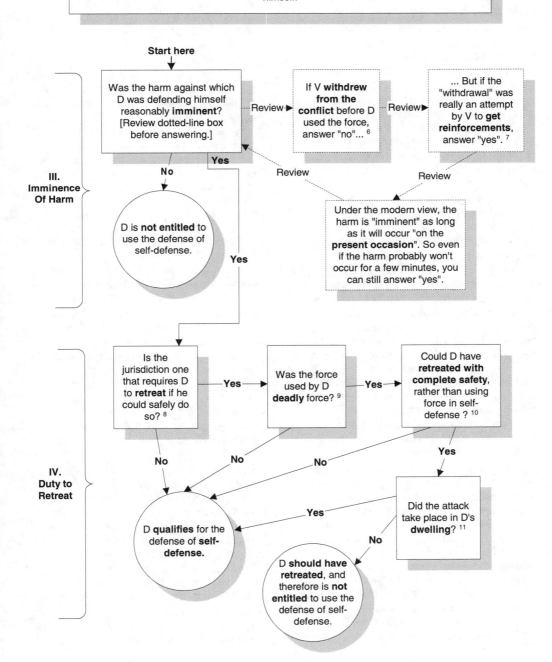

You should be on this page only if you've already determined that: (1) D was resisting unlawful force; and (2) D used no more force than was reasonably necessary to protect himself.

Start here

III. Imminence Of Harm

Was the harm against which D was defending himself reasonably **imminent**? [Review dotted-line box before answering.]

— Review ▶ If V **withdrew from the conflict** before D used the force, answer "no"... [6]

— Review ▶ ... But if the "withdrawal" was really an attempt by V to **get reinforcements**, answer "yes". [7]

No

Yes

Review   Review

D is **not entitled** to use the defense of self-defense.

Under the modern view, the harm is "imminent" as long as it will occur "on the **present occasion**". So even if the harm probably won't occur for a few minutes, you can still answer "yes".

Yes

IV. Duty to Retreat

Is the jurisdiction one that requires D to **retreat** if he could safely do so? [8]

— **Yes** ▶ Was the force used by D **deadly** force? [9]

— **Yes** ▶ Could D have **retreated with complete safety**, rather than using force in self-defense ? [10]

No   **No**   **No**

Yes

D **qualifies** for the defense of **self-defense**.

Yes

Did the attack take place in D's **dwelling**? [11]

No

D **should have retreated**, and therefore is **not entitled** to use the defense of self-defense.

Notes to
Figure 3 (Self-Defense)

[1] Example: V pulls out a pistol and aims it at D. Assuming that V did not have a privilege (e.g., self-defense) entitling him to do this, V has committed the crime (and tort) of assault against D, even if V didn't intend to fire. On these facts, you'd answer "yes."

[2] The most important result of this box is that if D was the initial aggressor, V's response will normally not be unlawful. Therefore D will not be privileged to respond with defensive force.

Example: After an argument, D pulls a knife out and brandishes it at V. V pulls out a knife of his own, and swings it wildly at D. On these facts, D was the initial aggressor. Therefore, V probably had a privilege (self-defense) to pull and swing the knife. If so, you'd answer "no" -- V's force is not unlawful.

However, if D was the initial aggressor but V escalated the confrontation by using a needlessly high level of force to resist, then V's response is unlawful and you would answer "yes" (as in the next example).

[3] Example: After an argument, D starts swinging his fist at V. V could simply block the blow. But instead, he pulls a pistol and starts to aim it. On these facts, you'd answer "yes" -- V had a privilege to use the degree of force reasonably required to repel D's fist-swinging, but by instead pulling and aiming the pistol V has gone beyond the degree of force he was privileged to use. In other words, this is an exception to the general rule that D can't use self-defense if he was the initial aggressor -- the aggressor can use self-defense if the other party escalates the confrontation and the aggressor's response is a reasonable way to defend against the escalated threat.

[4] Example: V and D get into a verbal dispute in a bar. Without any physical provocation by D, V repeatedly swings his fist at D. D is larger than V, and D has no reason to believe that V's fists will inflict serious injury on D. However, D is not a good fist-fighter, and realizes that he cannot, by using his fists, prevent V from inflicting at least some minor injuries on D. D therefore pulls a knife, and swings it at V's throat, cutting it so that V is seriously injured and needs to be hospitalized. Assume that D correctly reasoned that no form of force then available

to him other than the knife would have sufficed to prevent at least some of V's blows from landing.

On these facts, D does not have a valid self-defense defense. That's because he was not threatened with serious bodily harm, and a person may not use deadly force except in response to a threat of serious bodily harm.

[5] Example: Same basic facts as the prior example. Now, however, suppose that D mistakenly believes that: (1) V is a better fighter than V in fact is, and (2) V's fists may well cause D serious bodily injury. If D's mistake was reasonable (and the knife is no more force than D reasonably believes is needed to repel V's attack), you'd answer "no," and D would be treated as if he used no more force than necessary. But if D's mistake was unreasonable (e.g., a reasonable person in D's position would have realized that V was very unlikely to seriously injure D), then you'd answer "yes", leading to the conclusion that D was not entitled to use self-defense in the way that he did.

[6] Example: V and D are friends. They get into a verbal argument. V takes a swing at D, and D responds by swinging back. V then stops swinging and says, "Wait a minute, let's stop the fighting, and not ruin our friendship." D, however, keeps fighting. In these circumstances, D initially had a right to use force in self-defense, but lost that right once V withdrew. Consequently, D's further blows were not privileged.

[7] Example: V attacks D in a bar. D starts to fight back, and quickly begins getting the better of the contest. V backs off and says, "I'll be back." D reasonably believes that V is going outside to get three of his friends, and that all four will return to attack D. On these facts, D would be justified in keeping up his attack on V even as V is heading out the door, so as not let V leave to summon his friends.

[8] Courts are roughly split: a bit more than half hold that if D is otherwise entitled to use self-defense, he never loses that

Notes (cont.) to
Figure 3 (Self-Defense)

right merely because he could avoid the necessity of defending himself by retreating. The remainder hold that there are at least some circumstances in which D must, instead of using self-defense, retreat if he could do so safely. The questions that follow this box are only relevant in the latter states.

[9] Even jurisdictions imposing the retreat requirement hold that D <u>need not retreat before using non-deadly force</u>. <u>Example</u>: V starts punching D in a bar. D knows that he could, with perfect safety, leave the bar, get in his car, and drive home. Nonetheless, D fights back with his fists. (D is not a particularly expert fighter, and has no reason to think that his fists will do serious injury to V). Even in a jurisdiction that under some circumstances imposes an obligation to retreat rather than use force, D's fighting back is privileged, because D is responding with non-deadly force.

[10] <u>Example</u>: Without provocation, V draws a knife and attacks D in a bar, leading D to believe that if he does nothing, he will be severely injured. D realizes that he could just leave the bar and drive home, but he fears that this would cause onlookers to brand him a coward. Instead, he whips out a pistol and shoots V in the knee, making him crippled for life. (Assume that D correctly believed that his only options were to leave the bar, use the pistol to seriously injure V, or be seriously injured himself.) On these facts, you'd answer "yes". (And, in fact, in a jurisdiction imposing a duty to retreat, the present scenario would require such a retreat.)

[11] Even courts requiring retreat in some circumstances virtually never require it where D is in his own dwelling, on the theory that "a man's home is his castle." However, note this important clarification:

If D was the <u>initial aggressor</u>, he <u>won't</u> have the right to use deadly force in his dwelling, not because of the requirement of retreat, but because of the more general rule that the aggressor normally has no right to use self-defense at all -- this general rule is not suspended merely because the incident occurs in the defendant's home.

Figure 4
Attempt

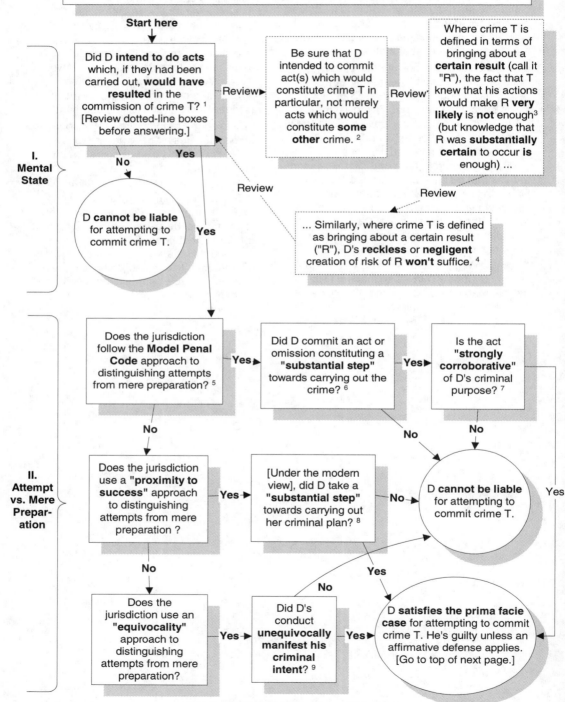

This chart will help you determine whether D is guilty of attempting a particular target crime (called crime "T"), under a general attempt statute. You should take a separate trip through the chart for each target crime you're analyzing.

Start here

Did D **intend to do acts** which, if they had been carried out, **would have resulted** in the commission of crime T? [1] [Review dotted-line boxes before answering.]

Be sure that D intended to commit act(s) which would constitute crime T in particular, not merely acts which would constitute **some other** crime. [2]

Where crime T is defined in terms of bringing about a **certain result** (call it "R"), the fact that T knew that his actions would make R **very likely** is **not** enough[3] (but knowledge that R was **substantially certain** to occur **is** enough) ...

►Review◄   ►Review◄

I. Mental State

No   **Yes**   Review

D **cannot be liable** for attempting to commit crime T.   **Yes**

Review

... Similarly, where crime T is defined as bringing about a certain result ("R"), D's **reckless** or **negligent** creation of risk of R **won't** suffice. [4]

II. Attempt vs. Mere Preparation

Does the jurisdiction follow the **Model Penal Code** approach to distinguishing attempts from mere preparation? [5]   **Yes►**   Did D commit an act or omission constituting a **"substantial step"** towards carrying out the crime? [6]   **Yes►**   Is the act **"strongly corroborative"** of D's criminal purpose? [7]

No   **No**   **No**

Does the jurisdiction use a **"proximity to success"** approach to distinguishing attempts from mere preparation ?   **Yes►**   [Under the modern view], did D take a **"substantial step"** towards carrying out her criminal plan? [8]   **No►**   D **cannot be liable** for attempting to commit crime T.   **Yes**

No   **Yes**

No

Does the jurisdiction use an **"equivocality"** approach to distinguishing attempts from mere preparation?   **Yes►**   Did D's conduct **unequivocally manifest his criminal intent**? [9]   **Yes►**   D **satisfies the prima facie case** for attempting to commit crime T. He's guilty unless an affirmative defense applies. [Go to top of next page.]

See footnotes starting after p. 2 of chart

Figure 4 (Cont.)
Attempt (p. 2)

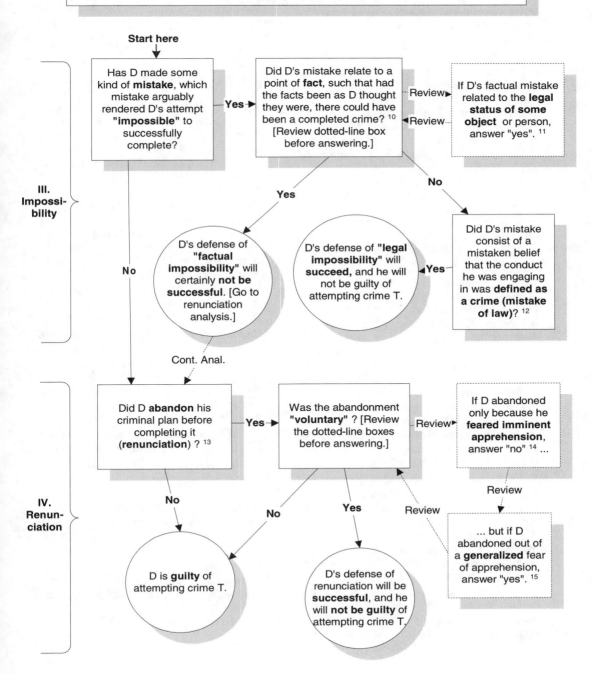

You should be on this page only if you've already determined that: (1) D had the requisite mental state for attempting crime T; and (2) D's conduct went beyond "mere preparation." This page helps you analyze two possible affirmative defenses that D might raise: (1) impossibility; and (2) renunciation.

Start here

III. Impossi- bility

Has D made some kind of **mistake**, which mistake arguably rendered D's attempt **"impossible"** to successfully complete?

Yes → Did D's mistake relate to a point of **fact**, such that had the facts been as D thought they were, there could have been a completed crime? [10] [Review dotted-line box before answering.]

Review → If D's factual mistake related to the **legal status of some object** or person, answer "yes". [11]

◄ Review

No (down from first box)

Yes (down-left) → D's defense of **"factual impossibility"** will certainly **not be successful**. [Go to renunciation analysis.]

D's defense of **"legal impossibility"** will **succeed,** and he will not be guilty of attempting crime T.

Yes ← Did D's mistake consist of a mistaken belief that the conduct he was engaging in was **defined as a crime (mistake of law)**? [12]

No (right side)

Cont. Anal.

IV. Renun- ciation

Did D **abandon** his criminal plan before completing it **(renunciation)** ? [13]

Yes → Was the abandonment **"voluntary"** ? [Review the dotted-line boxes before answering.]

Review → If D abandoned only because he **feared imminent apprehension**, answer "no" [14] ...

Review

No (down from abandon box)

No → D is **guilty** of attempting crime T.

Yes → D's defense of renunciation will be **successful**, and he will **not be guilty** of attempting crime T.

Review

... but if D abandoned out of a **generalized** fear of apprehension, answer "yes". [15]

Notes to
Figure 4 (Attempt)

[1] In the most-common case of a crime defined in terms of intentionally bringing about a certain result, this means that if D intended to bring about that result, he meets the mental requirement for attempting that crime. Example: Intent-to-kill murder is defined as intentionally killing another. If D intends to kill V, he meets the mental-state requirement for attempted murder.

[2] Example: D hits V in the jaw, intending only to slightly injure him. Instead, V slips after being hit, slams his head on the curb, and slips into a life-long coma. D will not be liable for attempted murder, even though he came close to killing V. This is so because D is liable for attempted murder only if he had the mental state needed for actual murder (in this case, either an intent to kill or an intent to do *serious* bodily injury), and he didn't. The mere fact that D had the mental state required for battery (intent to do some sort of bodily harm) won't suffice. (But if V had avoided the punch, D would be guilty of attempted *battery* -- that's so because his intent-to-do-minor-bodily-harm met the mental-state requirement for battery.)

[3] Example: As a prank, D uses his bow to shoot an arrow just to the side of V's head. D is not in fact a very good archer (and knows it), but on this occasion, he gets it right -- the arrow goes into the wall just next to V's head. Assume that in the jurisdiction, battery is defined (solely) as the intentional infliction of a bodily injury upon another, and reckless or negligent infliction of such injury cannot suffice. On these facts, D is not guilty of attempted battery -- the fact that D may have been aware that bodily injury to V was very likely won't suffice to create the mental state needed for attempted battery (only an intent to commit bodily injury could do that).

[4] Example: Same facts as above example. Assume that D is recklessly imposing a large risk of killing or seriously injuring V. Assume further that the jurisdiction defines manslaughter to include the reckless causing of death, and defines battery to include the reckless causing of bodily injury. D shoots the arrow and (as planned), misses V. D is not guilty of attempted murder (even though had he hit and killed V he would have had the mental state for recklessly-killing murder), and is not guilty of attempted battery (even

though had he hit and wounded V he would have had the mental state for recklessly-injuring battery).

[5] Under the MPC, D does not satisfy the act requirement for attempt unless he commits an act or omission that both: (1) constitutes a "substantial step in a course of conduct planned to culminate in [D's] commission of the crime"; and (2) is "strongly corroborative of [D's] criminal purpose."

[6] Example: D decides to rob the Scarsdale, N.Y., 7-11 store. He arrives at the store and hides in the bushes while he cases the place. He's arrested before he can commit the robbery. On these facts, you'd answer "yes": D's act of reconnoitering the place to be robbed suffices as a "substantial step" towards commission of the robbery.

[7] Example: Same facts as the above example, except that assume further that when D is arrested while hiding in the bushes, he is found to have a mask and gun. D's combined acts -- lying in wait, with gun and mask -- point so unequivocally to D's intent to burglarize the store that they almost certainly meet the "strongly corroborative" requirement.

[8] Under older decisions, it's not enough that D took a substantial step -- what was required was that D achieved a "dangerous proximity to success." But the modern view, in courts using a "proximity to success" approach, is that a substantial step is all that is required.

For an example of an act that constitutes a substantial step, see footnote 6 above.

[9] For an example of a set of acts that almost certainly meets the equivocality test, see footnote 7 above. By the way, most courts say that in evaluating whether the act was unequivocal, any confession by D must be disregarded.

[10] Example: D points his gun at V and presses the trigger. D intends to shoot V to death. Unbeknownst to D, the gun is not loaded. D is charged with attempted murder. Any claim of "impossibility" D might make will certainly fail,

Notes (cont.) to
Figure 4 (Attempt)

because had the facts been as D thought they were (loaded gun) his act would (or at least might) have succeeded in its objective.

[11] In other words, a mistake relating to "the legal status of some object or person" is to be treated like any other fact-based mistake, and won't be the basis for a successful impossibility defense.

Example: State X defines the crime of "receiving stolen goods" as buying stolen goods with the knowledge or belief that they are stolen. The police in State X have heard through an informant that D, a jeweler, traffics in stolen goods. They therefore arrange a "sting" operation: they send Y, an undercover officer, to visit D's store. Y brings with him several pieces of jewelry that he tells D were recently stolen in a residential burglary and offers to sell the jewelry to D. D buys the jewelry. Unbeknownst to D, the pieces are not stolen at all -- they're pieces that belong to a collector who is helping the police. D is charged with attempted receipt of stolen goods. D might raise the defense of impossibility -- since the goods were not in fact stolen at all, and since he was entitled to buy them, how can this be attempted receipt of stolen goods? But this defense will lose -- D is arguing that a mistake about the legal status of a thing (whether the jewelry was stolen or not) should be treated differently from other kinds of factual mistakes (e.g., whether the gun in the prior footnote was loaded), and courts nearly always reject this argument.

[12] Example: D witnesses a murder, and knows who did it. During the subsequent police investigation, D tells a police investigator, X, that he has no idea who committed the murder. D believes that lying to a police investigator during an investigation constitutes perjury. However, under state law perjury is defined to apply only to statements made under oath, and D's statement to X was not made under oath. D cannot be charged with "attempted perjury" -- the fact that D believed he was committing a crime (because of a misunderstanding about the definition of a crime) does not transform D's innocent conduct into a criminal attempt. (This rule is the corollary of the rule that "ignorance of the

law is no excuse" -- just as one who commits a crime can't defend on the grounds that he didn't know that particular conduct was outlawed, one who commits what he falsely thinks was a crime can't be convicted of attempt.)

[13] Example: D decides to rob the neighborhood 7-11. He purchases a mask and, the day before the anticipated robbery, cases the store to determine what its security precautions are. On the evening he's earmarked for the crime, D decides that the risks of substantial jail time outweigh the benefits of any loot he might get, so D decides to abandon his plan. On these facts, you'd answer "yes". (And, indeed, on these facts D's renunciation would negate his guilt of attempted robbery, even if his earlier conduct met the mental-state and substantial-step requirements for attempt liability in the jurisdiction.)

[14] Example: Same basic facts as the prior Example. Now, however, assume that D arrives at the store at the originally-contemplated time, puts his mask on in the car, draws his revolver, and is about to enter the store. At that moment, through the front window, he sees a man, X, whom he recognizes as an off-duty police officer. D is frightened of being caught (or, worse, shot) during the robbery, and therefore changes his mind about the robbery (at least for tonight). As he's walking back to the car, X spots him and arrests him, charging him with attempted robbery. On these facts, you'd answer "no" -- D's abandonment was not "voluntary," since it was the result of D's fear of imminent apprehension. (Therefore, D would be guilty of attempted burglary despite his abandonment of his plan.)

[15] Example: Same basic facts as prior two examples. Now, however, assume that as D is walking up to the front door of the store, with mask on and pistol in hand, he has a sudden flash, in which he remembers paying a prison visit to his boyhood friend Y, who is serving a 10-year sentence for robbery. D decides that

Notes (cont.) to
Figure 4 (Attempt)

the risk of getting caught and ending up like Y makes the robbery a bad idea, and turns around. At that moment, he's arrested by X (the officer, whom D did not recognize as such because X was in plain clothes) and charged with attempted robbery. On these facts, you'd answer "no" -- D's abandonment of his plan will be deemed voluntary, because it was the product of a generalized fear of being caught, not a response to a particular present threat of apprehension.

Figure 5
Conspiracy

This chart will help you analyze whether a defendant is guilty of conspiracy to commit a Target crime (called crime "T"). Make a separate pass through the chart for each potential defendant, and for each plausible target crime T. The chart follows the Model Penal Code's "unilateral" approach to conspiracy. "D1" refers to the person whose possible guilty is being analyzed. "D2" is some other possible co-conspirator, whose guilt is not being analyzed.

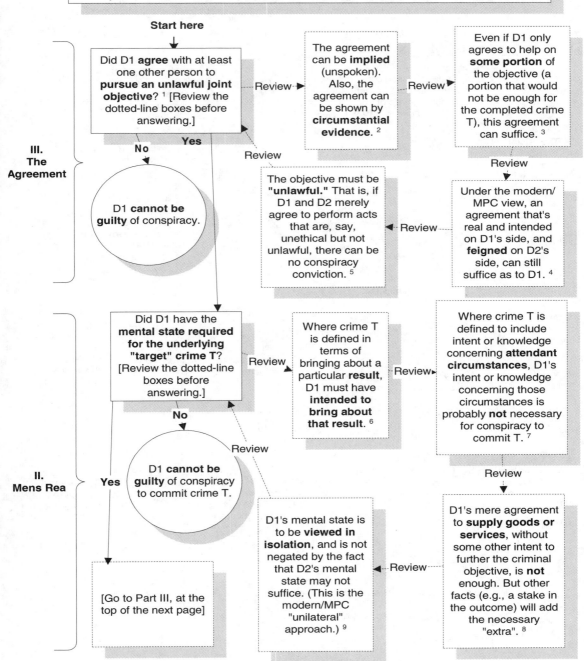

See footnotes starting after p. 2 of chart

Figure 5 (Cont.)
Conspiracy (p. 2)

You should only be on this page if you've concluded that: (1) D1 agreed with some other person to pursue a possibly-unlawful joint objective; and (2) D1 had the mental state required for the underlying target crime. This page will help you determine whether: (3) the "overt act" requirement (if applicable) has been satisfied; and (4) D1 is guilty of the underlying substantive crime T.

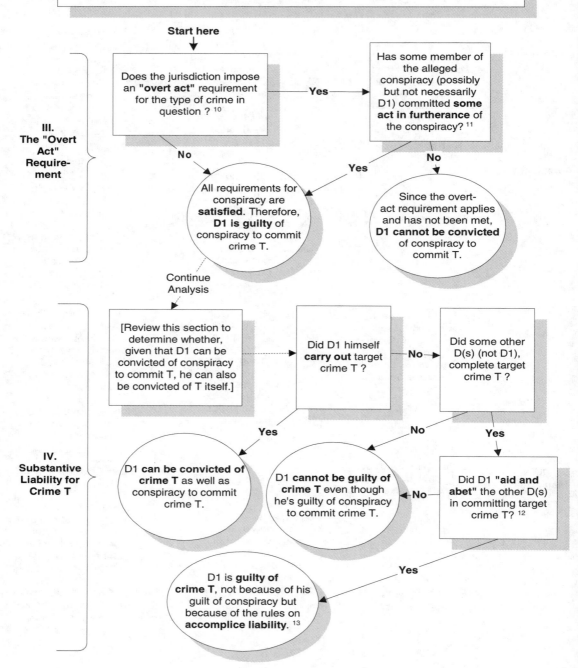

III. The "Overt Act" Requirement

Start here

Does the jurisdiction impose an **"overt act"** requirement for the type of crime in question ? [10]

Has some member of the alleged conspiracy (possibly but not necessarily D1) committed **some act in furtherance** of the conspiracy? [11]

Yes

No

Yes

No

All requirements for conspiracy are **satisfied**. Therefore, **D1 is guilty** of conspiracy to commit crime T.

Since the overt-act requirement applies and has not been met, **D1 cannot be convicted** of conspiracy to commit T.

Continue Analysis

IV. Substantive Liability for Crime T

[Review this section to determine whether, given that D1 can be convicted of conspiracy to commit T, he can also be convicted of T itself.]

Did D1 himself **carry out** target crime T ?

No

Did some other D(s) (not D1), complete target crime T ?

Yes

No

Yes

D1 **can be convicted of crime T** as well as conspiracy to commit crime T.

D1 **cannot be guilty of crime T** even though he's guilty of conspiracy to commit crime T.

Did D1 **"aid and abet"** the other D(s) in committing target crime T? [12]

No

Yes

D1 is **guilty of crime T**, not because of his guilt of conspiracy but because of the rules on **accomplice liability**. [13]

Notes to
Figure 5 (Conspiracy)

[1] For the meaning of an "unlawful" objective, see the box containing footnote 5.

[2] Example: D1 and D2 are prisoners in the same prison. At precisely 8:41 PM, D1 steals keys from a guard, and D2 simultaneously yells "Fire." Both then rush for the prison gates, before they are apprehended. These facts alone would probably support the conclusion that D1 and D2 conspired to escape: the acts by D1 and D2 are so unlikely to have happened simultaneously by coincidence that they furnish strong circumstantial evidence that D1 and D2 must have planned their activities together.

[3] Example: D2 and D3 want to rob a bank. D1 agrees to meet D2 and D3 after the robbery in a car, and to drive them to safety. D1 does not agree to do anything else in connection with the robbery. Because D1 has agreed to help D2 and D3 in their illegal plan, he meets the agreement requirement, even though he has only agreed to help with part of the plan (and even if his after-the-fact assistance was not enough to make him guilty of the robbery itself under an accomplice theory).

[4] Example: D1 asks D2 to help murder D1's husband, H. Unbeknownst to D1, D2 is horrified by the plan and goes to the police. The police advise D2 to play along by feigning agreement to the murder plan. D2 does so, and D1 is arrested before any further steps are taken. Under the modern/MPC "unilateral" approach, D1 meets the agreement requirement, even though D2 wasn't really agreeing to what D1 was proposing -- it's enough that D1 intended to make an agreement, and thought she was making an agreement, with D2 for an illegal objective.

[5] Example: In a particular jurisdiction, it is not illegal to make verbal attacks on racial groups. D1 and D2 agree that the next day, they will make and carry signs saying, "All niggers, go back to Africa." Because the ultimate objective -- publicly insulting a racial group -- is not illegal, D1's and D2's concerted action cannot be conspiracy, however unethical or distasteful it may be.

[6] Example: D1 and D2 agree that as a prank, they will remove a stop sign at a busy intersection. D1 and D2 think that perhaps a minor traffic crash may result (and they desire to cause this result), but they do not think about the possibility that a fatal crash may result. Assume that on these facts, the Ds' disregard of the risk of death to drivers amounts to wanton indifference to the value of human life (so that if a fatal crash were to occur, the Ds could be convicted of depraved-indifference murder). The Ds are arrested after they steal the sign, but before any crash occurs. The Ds cannot be convicted of conspiracy to commit depraved-indifference murder -- since murder is defined as bringing about a particular result (death), only by <u>intending to bring about that result</u> can they be convicted of conspiracy to murder.

[7] Example: D1 and D2 agree that D2 will spread a false rumor that XYZ Corp. is about to receive a takeover offer at a higher-than-market price; then, D1 will sell his XYZ holdings at a profit, before the rumor is shown to be false. D2 spreads the rumor by use of the phone and Internet. The Ds are then charged with conspiracy to commit wire fraud, since the phone and Internet are "wires" under the federal statute. Even if D1 shows that he thought D2 would use in-person rather than phone/computer methods of pumping up the stock, D1 still probably meets the mental-state requirement, because knowledge of the "attendant circumstances" (i.e., that phone and computer would be used by D2) will probably be held not to be part of the mental state for the target crime of wire fraud.

[8] Example: D2 buys a (legally-sold) lock-picking set from D1, a locksmith. D1 knows that D2 will probably use the set to burgle someone's premises. Without more, D1 has probably not met the mental-state requirement for conspiracy to commit burglary, because the mere supplying of a lawfully-sold item with knowledge that the purchaser will probably use it in a crime does not suffice. But if D1 gave D2 a reduced price

Notes (cont.) to
Figure 5 (Conspiracy)

in return for D2's promise to pay D1 10% of the profits, this "stake in the venture" would be enough to give D1 the required mental state. Similarly, if D1 charged D2 a much higher-than-usual price in return for agreeing not to list D2 on D1's usual customer records as having bought the tools, this would probably give D1 the required mental state.

[9] See footnote 4 above for an illustration.

[10] About half the states have an overt-act requirement for some or all crimes. Some states (and the MPC) only impose the requirement in the case of non-serious crimes.

[11] The overt act may be any act that is taken in furtherance of the conspiracy. It does not have to be an act that is criminal in itself. Thus mere acts of preparation (not criminal in themselves) will suffice. Example: D1 and D2 agree to rob a liquor store. D1 goes to the store to verify its hours of operation and to assess its security. In a state with an overt-act requirement for conspiracy to commit robbery, D1's act of "casing" the store will meet the overt-act requirement (both as to himself and D2), even though the act was not itself illegal.

[12] A person "aids and abets" another when he encourages and assists the other in accomplishing the crime. "Aiding and abetting" is covered more completely in Figure 6 on Accomplice Liability.

The main point is that (at least under the modern/MPC view) A won't be liable for acts committed by B in furtherance of the conspiracy merely because A and B are co-conspirators. That is, unless A can be said to have directly helped B carry out target crime T (in which case A is an accomplice), A is not guilty of B's substantive crime T even though A and B are co-conspirators as to some other crime.

Example: D1 and D2 agree to rob a bank. D1 is to drive D2 to the site, and drive him away afterwards; D2 will do the actual robbery. On the appointed day, D1 knows that D2 is carrying a gun, but believes (mistakenly but reasonably) that the gun is unloaded and just for show. D1 drives D2 to the bank, and waits outside. D2 enters, draws the gun on X (a teller), is given money, and then mistakenly believes that X is calling the police. D2 therefore fires, killing X in an attempt to stop the call.

Under the modern view, the fact that D1 and D2 were co-conspirators in bank robbery won't be enough to make D1 guilty of the substantive crime of murder, even though the murder occurred in furtherance of the conspiracy's objectives. Unless D1 can be said to have "aided and abetted" D2 in the killing (and this is probably not the case here, given D1's ignorance of the loaded gun), D1 won't have vicarious liability for the killing based merely on his being a co-conspirator with D2.

[13] Example: Same basic facts as prior example. Now, however, assume that: (1) beforehand, D1 knows that D2 is carrying a loaded gun, and (2) both have agreed that D2 will fire if and only if firing seems reasonably necessary to avoid being caught. D2 again believes that X is phoning the police, and fires, killing X. Now, D1 will be guilty of murder, along with D2. But (at least under the modern/ MPC view), this is so not because of the mere fact that D1 and D2 were co-conspirators to bank robbery, but because D1 actually aided and abetting D2's act of killing (by agreeing with D2 that the gun should be fired if needed to prevent either from being apprehended). So the fact that D1 and D2 were co-conspirators to bank robbery adds virtually nothing to the equation -- either D1 aided and abetting the actual killing, in which case he's guilty of murder, or he didn't (as in the prior example), in which case he's not guilty of murder despite being D2's co-conspirator in robbery.

Figure 6
Accomplice Liability

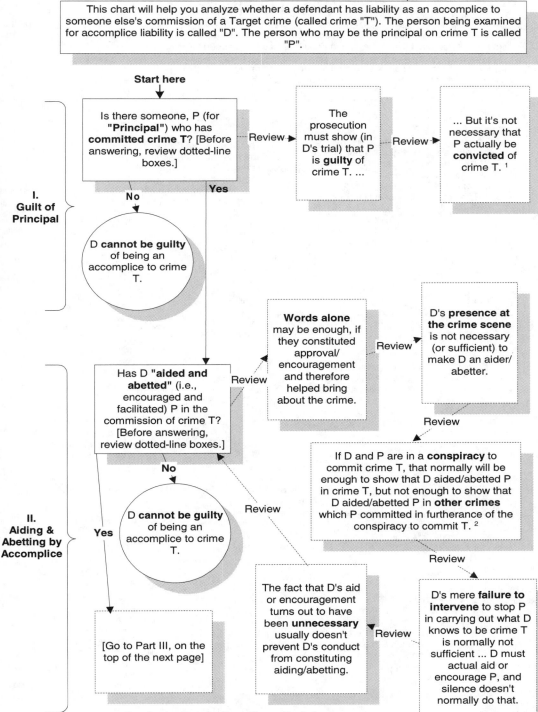

This chart will help you analyze whether a defendant has liability as an accomplice to someone else's commission of a Target crime (called crime "T"). The person being examined for accomplice liability is called "D". The person who may be the principal on crime T is called "P".

Start here

**I.
Guilt of
Principal**

Is there someone, P (for **"Principal"**) who has **committed crime T**? [Before answering, review dotted-line boxes.]

The prosecution must show (in D's trial) that P is **guilty** of crime T. ...

... But it's not necessary that P actually be **convicted** of crime T. [1]

Review ▶   Review ▶

No   **Yes**

D **cannot be guilty** of being an accomplice to crime T.

**II.
Aiding &
Abetting by
Accomplice**

Has D **"aided and abetted"** (i.e., encouraged and facilitated) P in the commission of crime T? [Before answering, review dotted-line boxes.]

Words alone may be enough, if they constituted approval/ encouragement and therefore helped bring about the crime.

D's **presence at the crime scene** is not necessary (or sufficient) to make D an aider/ abetter.

Review

Review

Review

If D and P are in a **conspiracy** to commit crime T, that normally will be enough to show that D aided/abetted P in crime T, but not enough to show that D aided/abetted P in **other crimes** which P committed in furtherance of the conspiracy to commit T. [2]

No   **Yes**

Review

D **cannot be guilty** of being an accomplice to crime T.

Review

The fact that D's aid or encouragement turns out to have been **unnecessary** usually doesn't prevent D's conduct from constituting aiding/abetting.

D's mere **failure to intervene** to stop P in carrying out what D knows to be crime T is normally not sufficient ... D must actual aid or encourage P, and silence doesn't normally do that.

Review

[Go to Part III, on the top of the next page]

See footnotes starting after p. 2 of chart

Figure 6 (Cont.)
Accomplice Liability (p. 2)

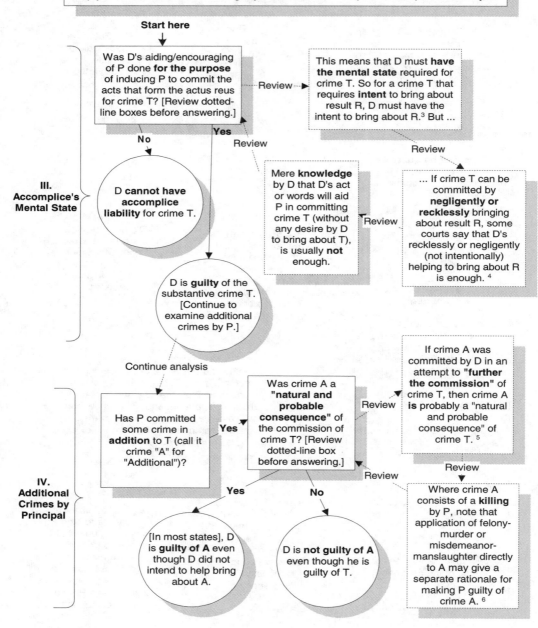

You should be on this page only if you've already determined that: (1) P (the principal) is guilty of the substantive crime T; and (2) D has aided and abetted P in committing crime T. On this page, you'll examine whether D meets the final requirement for accomplice liability: (3) that he did the aiding/abetting for the purpose of bringing about crime T. This page will also help you decide whether D can be guilty of additional crimes (other than T) committed by D.

Start here

III. Accomplice's Mental State

Was D's aiding/encouraging of P done **for the purpose** of inducing P to commit the acts that form the actus reus for crime T? [Review dotted-line boxes before answering.]

- - - Review - - - ▶ This means that D must **have the mental state** required for crime T. So for a crime T that requires **intent** to bring about result R, D must have the intent to bring about R.[3] But ...

No

Yes

Review

D **cannot have accomplice liability** for crime T.

Mere **knowledge** by D that D's act or words will aid P in committing crime T (without any desire by D to bring about T), is usually **not** enough.

- - Review - - ▶ ... If crime T can be committed by **negligently or recklessly** bringing about result R, some courts say that D's recklessly or negligently (not intentionally) helping to bring about R is enough.[4]

D is **guilty** of the substantive crime T. [Continue to examine additional crimes by P.]

Continue analysis

IV. Additional Crimes by Principal

Has P committed some crime in **addition** to T (call it crime "A" for "Additional")?

Yes ▶ Was crime A a **"natural and probable consequence"** of the commission of crime T? [Review dotted-line box before answering.]

- - Review - - ▶ If crime A was committed by D in an attempt to **"further the commission"** of crime T, then crime A **is** probably a "natural and probable consequence" of crime T.[5]

Review

Yes

No

Review

[In most states], D is **guilty of A** even though D did not intend to help bring about A.

D is **not guilty of A** even though he is guilty of T.

Where crime A consists of a **killing** by P, note that application of felony-murder or misdemeanor-manslaughter directly to A may give a separate rationale for making P guilty of crime A.[6]

Notes to
Figure 6 (Accomplice Liability)

[1] Example: In a trial in which D is the only defendant, the prosecution charges D with bank robbery on the theory that D was an accomplice to P. The prosecution says that D drove P to the bank, waited while P physically carried out the robbery, then drove P away. D cannot be convicted of bank robbery (on an accomplice theory) unless the prosecution proves in D's trial that, beyond a reasonable doubt, P physically robbed the bank while being assisted by D. But D <u>can</u> be convicted even though P is not charged or convicted in this (or any other) trial.

[2] Example: P robs a jewelry store with a gun procured for him by D. P is charged with the robbery, on an accomplice-liability theory. The prosecution shows that before the robbery, P and D had a meeting at which P asked D to line up a fence who would be ready to buy the stolen jewels, and agreed to pay D 10% of the gross proceeds from the robbery in return. The fact that P and D would be guilty of conspiracy to rob on these facts will by itself probably be enough to demonstrate that D aided and abetted P's commission of the robbery.

But now suppose that unbeknownst to D, P carried a loaded gun into the store. Assume further that P shot the storeowner to death while at the store. On these facts, the mere conspiracy to rob probably won't be enough to show that D aided and abetted the killing (and if he didn't, then he probably can't be guilty of the shooting on an accomplice theory.) However, direct application of the felony-murder doctrine might make D guilty of murder on these facts -- see footnote 6 infra.

[3] Example: D is a bodyguard for a famous (and rich) singer, P. They go to a bar together. At the bar, V, another singer, throws money in P's face, saying, "If you think your money makes you better than anyone else, think again, you a_ _ _ _ _ _." D says to P, "Are you going to let him diss you like that, or are you going to be a man?" P, responding in part to this remark, takes out his pistol and shoots V to death. D is tried for murder, on the theory that by encouraging P to shoot, he, D, was an accomplice to the shooting.

The prosecution will have to prove that D intended for P to kill V (or at least seriously injure him -- this is an alternative mental state that will suffice for murder). If the prosecution proves merely that D intended to induce P to scare V, or to injure him slightly, D must be acquitted. In other words, because murder requires (putting aside the felony-murder doctrine) an intent to kill or to seriously injure, to be an accomplice to murder D must be shown to have had the intent-to-kill or intent-to-seriously injure mental state needed for murder.

[4] Example: D, a car owner, lends his car to P, while knowing that P is drunk. P kills a pedestrian. P is charged with manslaughter (which requires recklessness). D is charged with being an accomplice to manslaughter, and therefore with being guilty of manslaughter himself. Some (but not all) courts will hold that as long as D recklessly disregarded the possibility that P might kill or maim someone, he can be convicted of manslaughter on an accomplice theory even though he, D, did not desire to hurt anyone.

[5] Example: Same basic facts as footnote 2 above (jewelry store robbery). Now, assume that P and D agree beforehand that both P and D will take whatever steps are necessary to avoid being apprehended, including shooting their way out of any attempt to arrest them. While P is in the store, the owner appears to be about to trip a police-alarm button. P shoots the owner in order to prevent the alarm from being tripped.

On these facts, P's shooting of the owner was in furtherance of the objectives of the robbery as both D and P imagined those objectives. Therefore, the additional crime of murder would probably be viewed as a "natural and probable consequence" of the robbery, in which case D would be guilty of murder (on an accomplice theory), not just robbery.

Notes (Cont.) to
Figure 6 (Accomplice Liability)

[6] Same basic facts as prior footnote. Now, however, assume that P shoots the owner by accident (the gun goes off when dropped), not on purpose. Assume further that D knew that P would be carrying a loaded gun. A court might well find D guilty of murder on the following syllogism: (1) D is an accomplice to robbery, and thus guilty of robbery; (2) the shooting, though accidental, occurred during the course of the robbery; (3) the felony-murder rule, under which a person who commits a dangerous felony that leads to death is deemed to be guilty of murder, applies. On this analysis, it's not really even necessary to figure out whether the shooting was a "natural and probable consequence" of the robbery -- as long as the shooting occurred "during the course of" that robbery, felony-murder applies to all participants in the robbery, including accomplices.

Figure 7
Homicide

This chart will help you analyze whether D is guilty of one of the varieties of homicide. This page and the next cover murder; the remaining two pages cover voluntary and involuntary manslaughter, respectively. Note that for murder, there are four different mental states that may suffice, and that you must therefore go through all four before concluding that a defendant who has caused another's death is not guilty of murder.

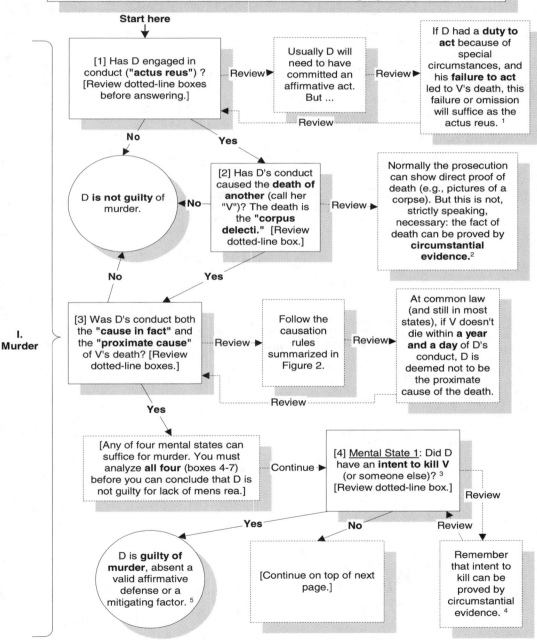

See footnotes starting after p. 4 of chart

Figure 7 (Cont.)
Homicide (p. 2)

You should be on this page only if you've already concluded that D: (1) engaged in conduct
that (2) proximately and as a matter of fact caused (3) the death of another. Also, you should
be here only if you concluded that D did not intend the death (the first possible mental state
for murder.) This page will help you determine whether D has one of the other 3 mental
states that will suffice for murder.

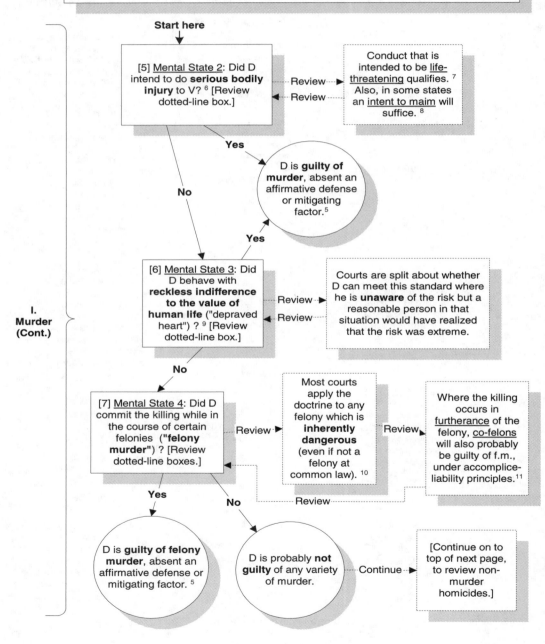

Figure 7 (Cont.)
Homicide (p. 3)

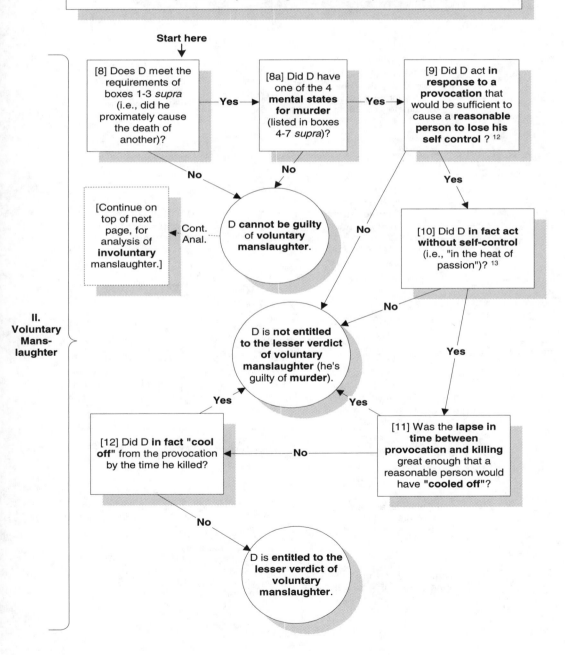

You should be on this page only if you've concluded that D is not guilty of murder. This page and the next will help you determine whether D is guilty of a form of homicide less than murder (i.e., voluntary manslaughter or involuntary manslaughter).

Start here

[8] Does D meet the requirements of boxes 1-3 *supra* (i.e., did he proximately cause the death of another)?

—**Yes**→

[8a] Did D have one of the 4 **mental states for murder** (listed in boxes 4-7 *supra*)?

—**Yes**→

[9] Did D act **in response to a provocation** that would be sufficient to cause a **reasonable person to lose his self control** ? [12]

No (from box 8)
No (from box 8a)

[Continue on top of next page, for analysis of **involuntary** manslaughter.]

←**Cont. Anal.**—

D **cannot be guilty** of **voluntary manslaughter**.

Yes (from box 9)

[10] Did D **in fact act without self-control** (i.e., "in the heat of passion")? [13]

No

II. Voluntary Manslaughter

D is **not entitled to the lesser verdict of voluntary manslaughter** (he's guilty of **murder**).

No

Yes (to box 10)

Yes **Yes**

[12] Did D **in fact "cool off"** from the provocation by the time he killed?

←**No**—

[11] Was the **lapse in time between provocation and killing** great enough that a reasonable person would have **"cooled off"**?

Yes

No

D is **entitled to the lesser verdict of voluntary manslaughter**.

Figure 7 (Cont.)
Homicide (p. 4)

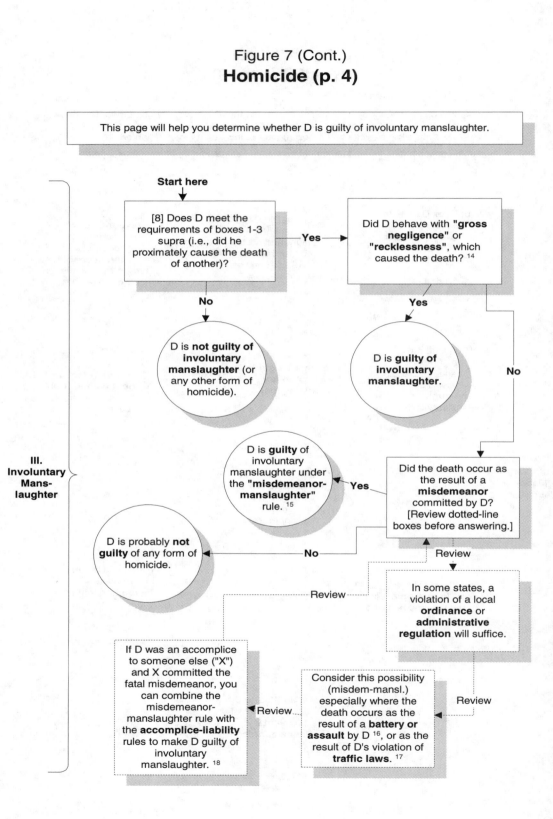

This page will help you determine whether D is guilty of involuntary manslaughter.

Start here

[8] Does D meet the requirements of boxes 1-3 supra (i.e., did he proximately cause the death of another)?

Did D behave with **"gross negligence"** or **"recklessness"**, which caused the death? [14]

Yes

No

Yes

D is **not guilty of involuntary manslaughter** (or any other form of homicide).

D is **guilty of involuntary manslaughter**.

No

III. Involuntary Manslaughter

D is **guilty** of involuntary manslaughter under the **"misdemeanor-manslaughter"** rule. [15]

Yes

Did the death occur as the result of a **misdemeanor** committed by D? [Review dotted-line boxes before answering.]

D is probably **not guilty** of any form of homicide.

No

Review

Review

In some states, a violation of a local **ordinance** or **administrative regulation** will suffice.

If D was an accomplice to someone else ("X") and X committed the fatal misdemeanor, you can combine the misdemeanor-manslaughter rule with the **accomplice-liability** rules to make D guilty of involuntary manslaughter. [18]

Review

Consider this possibility (misdem-mansl.) especially where the death occurs as the result of a **battery or assault** by D [16], or as the result of D's violation of **traffic laws**. [17]

Review

Notes to
Figure 7 (Homicide)

[1] See the discussion of omissions, and the special duty to act, on p. 1 of Figure 1 *supra*.

Example: D is the mother of V, a 6-year-old boy. D stands by without interfering as D's boyfriend X beats V to death. Given that a mother has a special duty to protect her children, D's inaction can constitute the actus reus for homicide.

[2] Example: Suppose the prosecution proves: (1) that D and his wife V quarrelled for years; (2) that D was the last person to see V alive; (3) that D was a private pilot who flew his plane out to sea shortly after V disappeared, and loaded baggage on the plane that weighed enough to contain V's body; (4) that D later told conflicting stories to girlfriends about how V died; and (5) that V has never been heard of again, and has never contacted her parents, to whom she was very devoted. These facts might well be sufficient to constitute proof that D caused V's death, even though no body was ever found. (Indeed, in a 2000 murder case, substantially these showings were enough to convince a N.Y. jury to convict Dr. Robert Bierenbaum of murder.)

[3] The doctrine of transferred intent can apply, in murder cases as in other crimes. Example: D shoots at X, intended to kill him. The bullet instead hits V, whom D does not even see. D has the requisite mental state (intent to kill) for murder.

[4] Example: D forges the signature of her husband, V, on an application for a policy on D's life, naming D the beneficiary. The day after the policy is issued, D puts a dose of arsenic in V's morning coffee. The dose is one that would be fatal about half the time in an adult male of D's size. D dies. On these facts, a jury would be easily justified in concluding, beyond a reasonable doubt, that D desired to kill V. That's true even though there is only circumstantial evidence that D had this desire.

[5] Most-likely affirmative defense: self-defense. Most-likely mitigating factor: extreme provocation, which might entitle D to a lesser verdict of voluntary manslaughter. (See p. 3 of chart for a review of what D must establish to be entitled to a voluntary manslaughter verdict.)

[6] A beating that is intended to be serious enough to put V in the hospital, for instance, probably qualifies. Example: D, a loanshark, beats V with a lead pipe. D does not desire to kill V, just to frighten him into paying back the loan and 50% weekly interest. D swings the pipe a little too hard, and V dies. D's mental state qualifies for intent-to-do-serious-bodily-harm murder.

[7] Example: D stabs his girlfriend V several times. D desires to hurt V fairly badly (certainly badly enough that she'll be hospitalized and will need surgery). However, D does not actively desire to kill V, though he recognizes that V may die. This state of mind will suffice for intent-to-seriously-injure murder.

[8] Example: D hacks off V's leg with a knife, intending mere to render V leg-less (not to kill him). V unexpectedly dies because of the blood loss. D has a mental state (intent to seriously injure) sufficient for homicide, even though D intended only to maim, not kill.

[9] Example 1: From 2 blocks away, D fires a rifle into a crowded commuter train. Example 2: D puts arsenic into 3 random bottles of Tylenol on drug-store shelves. D then sends an extortion note to the manufacturer of the Tylenol in which he offers to tell them which stores have the bottles if they pay him $1 million.

In both of these situations, a jury could properly find that D behaved with depraved indifference to the value of human life, giving him a mental state that is sufficient for a murder conviction. And that's true even if there's no evidence that D affirmatively desired to kill or even injure anyone.

[10] In the courts following the majority view (limiting the f.m. doctrine to "inherently dangerous" felonies), there are two different sub-views about how to judge inherent dangerousness: (1) some courts test the dangerousness of a felony in the abstract (e.g., is larceny in general a dangerous felony, without regard to the facts of the particular larceny committed

Notes (cont.) to
Figure 7 (Homicide)

by D?); (2) other courts test dangerousness by looking at the particular instance of the crime before them (e.g., was the particular larceny committed by D one that could be judged dangerous on the facts known to D at the time he committed it?

[11] Example: D1 and D2 agree that D1 will steal a car, drive D2 to First Bank, wait for D2 while D2 robs the bank, then drive them both to safety. D1 and D2 agree that D2 will carry a loaded pistol and use it if necessary to avoid apprehension. At the bank, D2 realizes that V, a guard, is about to call the police. D2 tries to fire a shot near (but not at) V, to scare him so he won't call the police. Unfortunately, the bullet strikes V and kills him. Since D1 committed robbery (under accomplice-liability principles, he's substantively guilty of robbery because he aided and abetted D2's actual commission of the robbery), and since the killing occurred in furtherance of robbery, most courts will view D1 as having "killed in the course of a dangerous felony [robbery]", and will convict him even though he didn't fire the shot or desire that V die. For more about accomplice-liability, see Figure 6 *supra*.

[12] The classic illustration is D's discovery of a spouse's infidelity. Example: D comes home unexpectedly early from work one afternoon and finds his wife V1 in bed with her lover, V2. D, enraged, immediately pulls a gun from a drawer, and kills both V1 and V2. At least traditionally, the discovery of spousal infidelity has been held to be a provocation that would or might cause a "reasonable person" to lose self control. If so, D would meet this first requirement for a lesser verdict of voluntary manslaughter rather than murder.

Another common context for provocation-reasonably-causing-loss-of-self-control is the "imperfect self-defense" scenario, in which D honestly but unreasonably believes that he needs to use deadly force to defend himself. Example: D believes that the person walking down the street in the town of Podunk towards him is his enemy, Will, who has sworn to kill D. (As D knows, Will lives 2,000 miles away from Podunk.) However, the person is in fact Phil, Will's identical twin brother, who lives in Podunk. When Phil puts his hand in his pocket, D believes that Phil is about to draw a pistol and shoot at D. D therefore shoots first, killing Phil. Assume that: (1) a reasonable person in D's position would know that there was a substantial likelihood that the person walking towards him was Phil, not Will, and (2) D's mistaken belief that it was Will was therefore not reasonable. In this situation, you would answer "yes," and D would probably be entitled to a verdict of voluntary murder (on an "imperfect self-defense" theory) rather than murder. The same would be true if D's error was that he unreasonably believed that only deadly force would suffice to repel a real threat when less-than-deadly force, or words alone, would have sufficed.

[13] Example: Same basic facts as the first example in note 12 above (D finds his wife V1 in bed with V2). If D in fact acted in the heat of passion, you'd answer "yes". But now suppose that D had long had suspicions of V1's infidelity, and was not all that surprised at finding V2 in bed with her. He cooly took out the pistol and methodically shot V1 and V2, each with a single well-calibrated shot. On these facts, you'd probably conclude that D was not in fact acting in the heat of passion (in which case he would be guilty of murder, not voluntary manslaughter).

[14] Example: D gets very drunk at a restaurant, then insists on driving home even though the restaurant owner offers to call him a cab. On the way home, D, while speeding, strikes and fatally injures a pedestrian, V. D's behavior -- not the getting drunk, but the driving while knowing he was drunk -- is clearly "grossly negligent" or "reckless" (whichever formulation is used in the state). Therefore, D is guilty of involuntary manslaughter even though he did not desire to harm V, let alone kill him.

[15] Under the misdemeanor-manslaughter rule, when a death occurs accidentally during the commission of a misdemeanor (or in some states any unlawful act, such as a regulatory violation), the

Notes (cont.) to
Figure 7 (Homicide)

misdemeanant is guilty of involuntary manslaughter -- the unlawful act is treated as a substitute for criminal negligence.

[16] Example 1: D gets into an argument with V. D punches V in the nose -- not hard enough to cause serious injury in most people (and not with the intent to cause serious injury), just enough to give most people a bloody nose. V happens to be a hemophiliac, and bleeds to death. D is guilty of battery (a harmful or offensive touching), a misdemeanor. The misdemeanor-manslaughter rule will apply to "bootstrap" D's conduct into involuntary manslaughter.

Example 2: Same basic facts as the above Example. Now, however, assume that V is not a hemophiliac. Instead, V falls from the blow, hits his head on the curb, and dies of head trauma from the curb impact. Again, D will be guilty of misdemeanor-manslaughter.

[17] Example: D drives his car at 50 mph in a 35-mph zone. He hits a pedestrian, V, killing him. Even if D's conduct does not amount to gross negligence or recklessness, he can be guity of manslaughter -- the violation of the speed limit will supply the culpable state of mind.

[18] Example: D and X are at a bar. X gets into a verbal dispute with V. D says to X, "You should teach him not to disrespect you -- why don't you give him a straight right to the jaw." X takes this advice -- he hits V in the jaw. V falls, hits his head on a sharp edge of the bar, and dies from head trauma. (The blow from X's fist would not by itself have been enough to kill or even seriously injure V.) X has clearly committed the misdemeanor of battery. D is an accomplice to this battery -- he's aided and abetted X in carrying out the battery. Consequently, D is himself guilty of battery. Therefore, D, like X, is guilty of manslaughter under the misdemeanor-manslaughter rule.

Figure 8
Theft Crimes

This chart begins by helping you analyze which of the three main theft crimes (larceny, embezzlement and false pretenses) D is guilty of. It then covers burglary and robbery. In all cases, the chart assumes that the common-law definition of the crime is in force, unless otherwise noted.

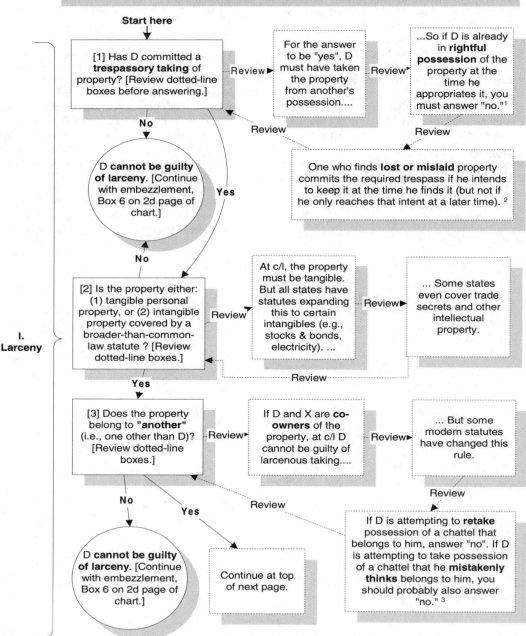

Start here

[1] Has D committed a **trespassory taking** of property? [Review dotted-line boxes before answering.]

◄Review► For the answer to be "yes", D must have taken the property from another's possession....

◄Review► ...So if D is already in **rightful possession** of the property at the time he appropriates it, you must answer "no."[1]

Review

Review

One who finds **lost or mislaid** property commits the required trespass if he intends to keep it at the time he finds it (but not if he only reaches that intent at a later time). [2]

No

D **cannot be guilty of larceny**. [Continue with embezzlement, Box 6 on 2d page of chart.]

Yes

No

[2] Is the property either: (1) tangible personal property, or (2) intangible property covered by a broader-than-common-law statute ? [Review dotted-line boxes.]

◄Review At c/l, the property must be tangible. But all states have statutes expanding this to certain intangibles (e.g., stocks & bonds, electricity). ...

◄Review► ... Some states even cover trade secrets and other intellectual property.

Review

I. Larceny

Yes

[3] Does the property belong to **"another"** (i.e., one other than D)? [Review dotted-line boxes.]

◄Review► If D and X are **co-owners** of the property, at c/l D cannot be guilty of larcenous taking....

◄Review► ... But some modern statutes have changed this rule.

Review

No

Yes

Review

If D is attempting to **retake** possession of a chattel that belongs to him, answer "no". If D is attempting to take possession of a chattel that he **mistakenly thinks** belongs to him, you should probably also answer "no." [3]

D **cannot be guilty of larceny**. [Continue with embezzlement, Box 6 on 2d page of chart.]

Continue at top of next page.

See footnotes starting after p. 6 of chart

Figure 8 (Cont.)
Theft Crimes (p. 2)

If you've concluded that D meets the first 3 requirements for larceny (a trespassory taking of personal property of another), go to box [4] at the top of this page, to examine the asportation element. If you've concluded that D fails to meet at least one of these first 3 requirements, go to box [6] in the middle of the page, to examine embezzlement.

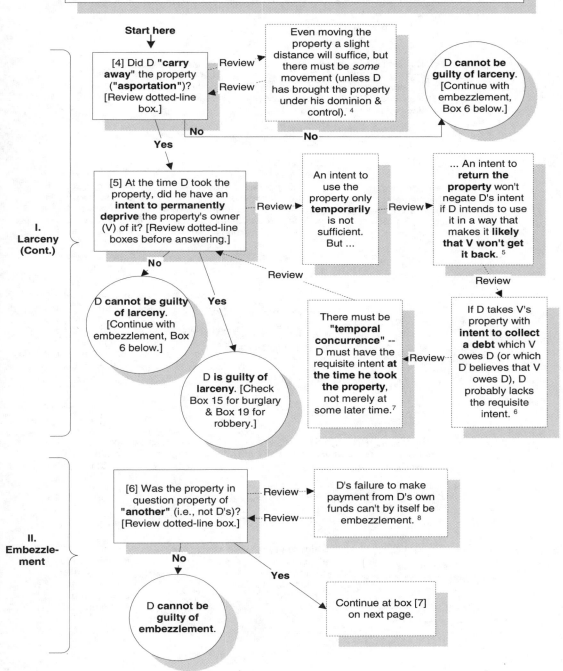

I. Larceny (Cont.)

II. Embezzlement

Figure 8 (Cont.)
Theft Crimes (p. 3)

You should only be on this page if you have concluded that: (1) D is not guilty of larceny (pp. 1 & 2 of chart); and (2) D has met the first requirement for embezzlement (property belonging to "another"). This page completes the analyis of embezzlement.

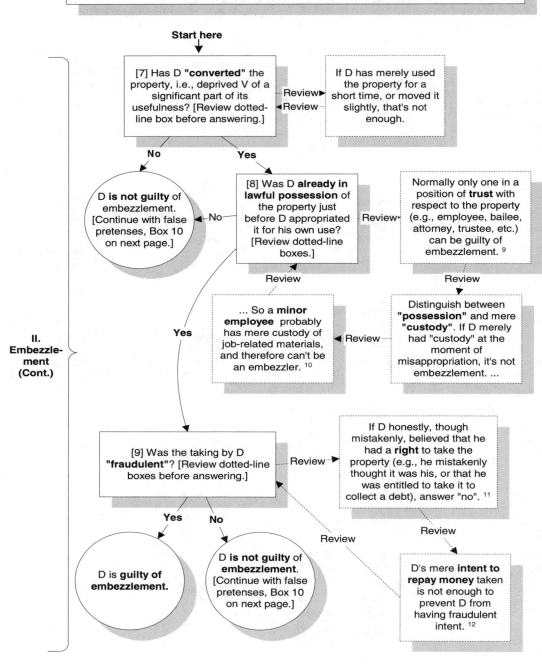

Start here

[7] Has D **"converted"** the property, i.e., deprived V of a significant part of its usefulness? [Review dotted-line box before answering.]

◄ Review ►
◄ Review ┄

If D has merely used the property for a short time, or moved it slightly, that's not enough.

No — D **is not guilty** of embezzlement. [Continue with false pretenses, Box 10 on next page.]

Yes

[8] Was D **already in lawful possession** of the property just before D appropriated it for his own use? [Review dotted-line boxes.]

No ◄

┄ Review ┄

Normally only one in a position of **trust** with respect to the property (e.g., employee, bailee, attorney, trustee, etc.) can be guilty of embezzlement. [9]

Review

... So a **minor employee** probably has mere custody of job-related materials, and therefore can't be an embezzler. [10]

◄ Review ┄

Distinguish between **"possession"** and mere **"custody"**. If D merely had "custody" at the moment of misappropriation, it's not embezzlement. ...

II. Embezzle-ment (Cont.)

Yes

[9] Was the taking by D **"fraudulent"**? [Review dotted-line boxes before answering.]

┄ Review ►

If D honestly, though mistakenly, believed that he had a **right** to take the property (e.g., he mistakenly thought it was his, or that he was entitled to take it to collect a debt), answer "no". [11]

Yes — D is **guilty of embezzlement.**

No — D **is not guilty** of embezzlement. [Continue with false pretenses, Box 10 on next page.]

Review

Review

D's mere **intent to repay money** taken is not enough to prevent D from having fraudulent intent. [12]

Figure 8 (Cont.)
Theft Crimes (p. 4)

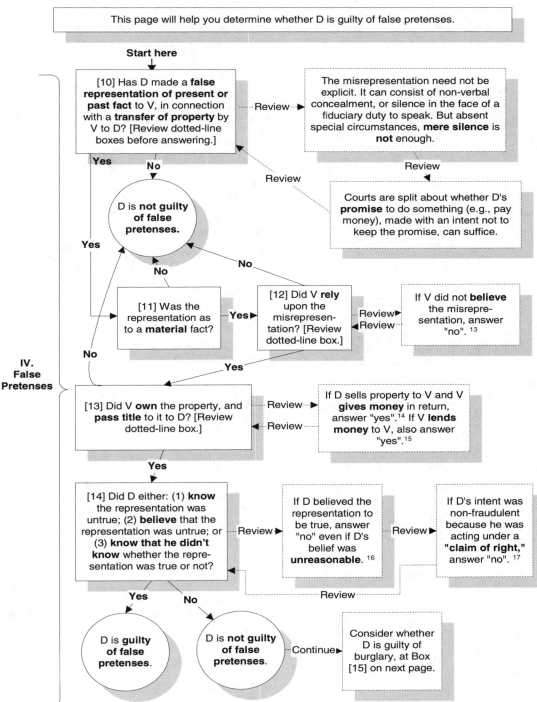

This page will help you determine whether D is guilty of false pretenses.

Start here

[10] Has D made a **false representation of present or past fact** to V, in connection with a **transfer of property** by V to D? [Review dotted-line boxes before answering.]

···Review··· The misrepresentation need not be explicit. It can consist of non-verbal concealment, or silence in the face of a fiduciary duty to speak. But absent special circumstances, **mere silence** is **not** enough.

Review

Courts are split about whether D's **promise** to do something (e.g., pay money), made with an intent not to keep the promise, can suffice.

Yes   **No**

D is **not guilty of false pretenses.**

Review

Yes

No   **No**

[11] Was the representation as to a **material** fact?   **Yes▶**   [12] Did V **rely** upon the misrepresentation? [Review dotted-line box.]   ◀Review   If V did not **believe** the misrepresentation, answer "no". [13]

No

Yes

[13] Did V **own** the property, and **pass title** to it to D? [Review dotted-line box.]   ···Review···▶ ◀Review···   If D sells property to V and V **gives money** in return, answer "yes". [14] If V **lends money** to V, also answer "yes". [15]

Yes

[14] Did D either: (1) **know** the representation was untrue; (2) **believe** that the representation was untrue; or (3) **know that he didn't know** whether the representation was true or not?   ···Review▶   If D believed the representation to be true, answer "no" even if D's belief was **unreasonable**. [16]   ◀Review   If D's intent was non-fraudulent because he was acting under a **"claim of right,"** answer "no". [17]

Review

Yes   **No**

D is **guilty of false pretenses**.   D is **not guilty of false pretenses**.   ◀Continue▶   Consider whether D is guilty of burglary, at Box [15] on next page.

IV. False Pretenses

Figure 8 (Cont.)
Theft Crimes (p. 5)

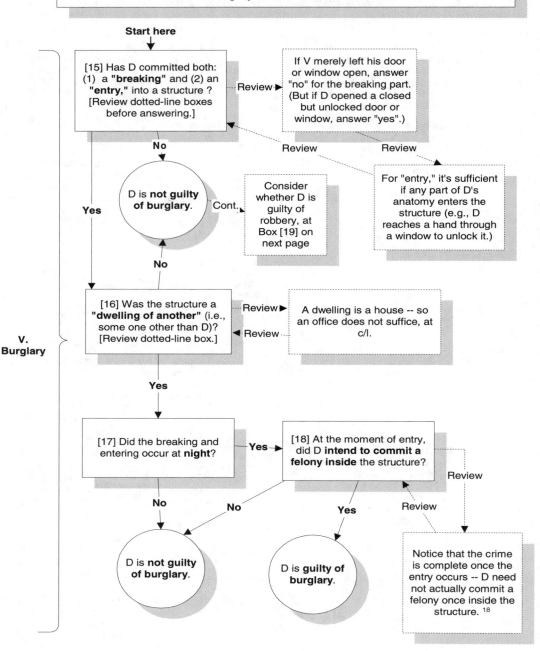

Figure 8 (Cont.)
Theft Crimes (p. 6)

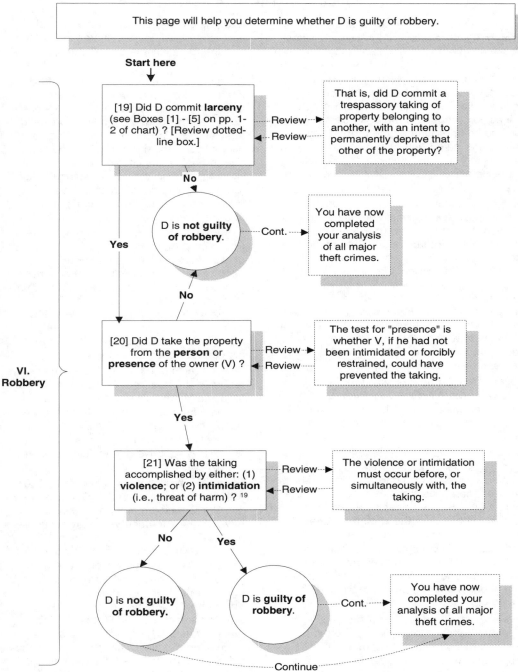

Notes to
Figure 8 (Theft Crimes)

[1] <u>Example</u>: D rents a car from V, and promises to return it in three days. At the time D signs the rental agreement, he intends to return the car as scheduled. After one day, D decides to "sell" the car, and therefore transfers possession to X for $200. On these facts, you'd answer "no" -- since D was in rightful possession (under the rental agreement) at the time he appropriated the property by making the "sale," he has not committed a "trespassory taking." (Instead, these facts fit embezzlement -- conversion of property at a time when it's in D's lawful possession).

[2] <u>Example</u>: D finds a watch on the beach, notes an inscription (which would probably be sufficient to identify the owner), and intends to return it to the rightful owner. But one day later, D instead gives the watch to his girlfriend X. This conduct does not satisfy the "trespassory taking" element of larceny, because at the time D first came into possession, he did not have the requisite intent-to-wrongfully-take. (But if D had formed the intent to wrongfully keep the property at the moment he found it, then D *would* satisfy the trespassory taking requirement.)

[3] <u>Example 1</u>: D lends a bicycle to V, who refuses to return it. One year later, D comes onto V's premises, sees the bicycle, and carries it back to D's own house. You would answer "no" on these facts -- the property is D's own, not property of "another".

<u>Example 2</u>: D's bicycle is stolen by persons unknown. Three days later, D is walking down the street near where the theft occurred and spots a bike that he honestly (though unreasonably, under the circumstances) believes to be the stolen bike. He takes the bike back to his own house. In most courts, you'd answer "no" -- this does not meet the "property of another" requirement due to D's honest belief that the property is his. (But some courts would disagree.)

[4] D walks up to V's bicycle and sits on it, with an intent to steal it immediately. At that moment, he's arrested. At common law, D is not guilty of larceny, because he has not yet "carried away" the property. But if D took an additional step of "dominion and control"

(e.g., he cut V's lock off the bike), that probably would, in most states today, be enough to satisfy the asportation requirement.

[5] <u>Example</u>: D "borrows" V's bicycle. If D intends to keep it for just a spin around the block, this is not an intent to permanently deprive the owner, so you'd answer "no". But if D intends to keep the bike all summer and return it in the fall, then probably this anticipated usage is so likely to result in V's never getting it back (or in V's being deprived of a such a major part of its useful life) that you'd answer "yes".

[6] <u>Example</u>: D works for V, a merchant, who fires him. D honestly (though unreasonably) believes that under applicable law, V owes D $300 in unused vacation pay. D takes exactly $300 from V's cash register and walks off with it. Probably D lacks the requisite intent to permanently deprive V of V's property, because D is acting under a belief that his conduct is legally authorized.

[7] See the facts of Example 2 above (watch found on the beach) -- since D lacked the requisite intent-to-permanently-deprive at the time he first took possession of the watch, he doesn't meet the intent requirement even though he later forms an intent-to-deprive (by deciding to keep the watch).

[8] <u>Example</u>: D's mother, X, gives D $1,000, with the understanding that D will use it to pay D's rent next month to V, D's sister. D never intends to use the money for this purpose, and doesn't. Since the money was D's own, he hasn't taken property "of another" even though X wouldn't have given it to him had she known he wouldn't use it for the specified purposes. Therefore, D can't be guilty of embezzlement. (But if D had received merely "custody" -- as where he agreed to hold the money for his mother until she asked for it back -- his failure to give it back *would* be appropriation of the property of "another").

Notes (cont.) to
Figure 8 (Theft Crimes)

[9] Example: D, an attorney, settles an accident lawsuit for V, his client. The settlement proceeds are paid over to D, who puts them in his escrow account. Instead of paying over the funds to V, D gambles them away. You'd answer "yes" on these facts -- D was in lawful possession of the funds before misappropriating them. (This is a classic embezzlement scenario).

[10] Example: D is a cashier at a grocery store, earning the minimum wage. During the day, she takes $10 from the cash register. A court would probably hold that D was merely given temporary "custody", not "lawful possession", of the cash in the register. Therefore, she would not meet the "lawful possession" requirement, and this would not be embezzlement. (It would be larceny instead).

[11] Example: D works for V, a bank, as Treasurer. V fires D, and fails to pay D $1,000 severance pay that D honestly (though unreasonably) believes is due to D under the bank's severance policies. D takes $1,000 from the bank's vault (to which he has access as part of his job). D probably does not have the requisite "fraudulent" intent, since his claim was made pursuant to an honest claim of right. (The fact that the mistake was unreasonable would probably not change this, though it would obviously affect the trier of fact's conclusion about whether D's claim really *was* an honest one.)

[12] Example: Same facts as the Example in footnote 9 above (lawyer who misuses client trust funds). Even if D honestly intended to replace the funds as soon as he doubled the money at the dog track, D has the requisite fraudulent intent and is guilty of embezzlement. (Indeed, this is true even if D *does* replace the money after winning at the track.)

[13] Example: D, while offering to sell his house to V, says that the house has never had termites. (D knows that this statement is false.) V hires an engineer to inspect the house. The engineer finds evidence of massive previous termite infestation. Nonetheless, V signs a contract to buy the house, reasoning that even if V has to spend money on termite-proofing it, the house is still a bargain. On these facts, D is not guilty of

false pretenses, because V has not relied on the misrepresentation.

[14] Example: D, a jeweller, sells a stone to V for $15,000 that D says is a 3-carat near-flawless diamond. In reality (as D knows) the stone is an almost-worthless cubic zirconium. On these facts, you would answer "yes" -- V owned property (the $15,000) and has passed title to that property to D based on D's misrepresentations. (Indeed, D is guilty of false pretenses.)

[15] Example: D, the owner of a money-losing Internet business, borrows money from V, a bank. D procures the loan by furnishing the bank with false financial statements (which indicate that the business breaks even). On these facts, you'd answer "yes" -- V's loan to D constitutes the passing of title to the money to D. (Indeed, D is guilty of false pretenses.)

[16] Example: D is an art dealer. He offers a painting to V, a collector, saying that the painting is by Rembrandt. D has previously hired two experts to examine the painting, and they have told D that the painting is almost certainly a 20th-century forgery. Nonetheless, D honestly (though unreasonably) believes that it is by Rembrandt. On these facts, you'd answer "no" -- D's firm belief in the truth of what he is saying prevents him from having the requisite state of mind for false pretenses, since he doesn't know or believe that the representation is false, nor does he "know that he doesn't know" that it's false.

[17] Example: D, an art professor, is the child of Holocaust survivors. He knows that a particular painting his family owned until 1939 was seized by Nazis in that year. In 2001, D sees the painting for sale in an art gallery owned by V. D asks V to let D borrow the painting for an exhibition that D is planning at his university. V agrees. D then refuses to return the painting. Even if D's belief that he has superior title to the painting is incorrect (indeed, even if his belief is unreasonable), D will not be guilty of false pretenses because he has acted under a claim of right.

Notes (cont.) to
Figure 8 (Theft Crimes)

[18] Example: D decides to enter the residence of his former girlfriend, V, late one night. He intends to rape her once he is inside. At 2:00 a.m., he climbs a ladder outside her bedroom, and enters through her window. Once inside, he immediately changes his mind about rape, and leaves. D is guilty of burglary -- he has broken and entered another's dwelling at night, with intent to commit a felony therein. The fact that D never actually committed the intended (or any) felony inside the structure does not change this result.

[19] Example: D, riding a motor scooter, comes up behind V, a pedestrian. D snatches V's purse and drives away with it before V is even aware of D's presence. On these facts, you'd answer "no" -- although D has taken V's property from her person, he has not used violence or intimidation to do so. Therefore, D is not guilty of robbery (though he is, of course, guilty of larceny).

CAPSULE SUMMARY

SUMMARY OF CONTENTS
OF CAPSULE SUMMARY

ACTUS REUS AND MENS REA 49

CAUSATION 60

RESPONSIBILITY 66

JUSTIFICATION AND EXCUSE 72

ATTEMPT 91

CONSPIRACY 98

**ACCOMPLICE LIABILITY
AND SOLICITATION** 109

**HOMICIDE AND OTHER CRIMES
AGAINST THE PERSON** 118

THEFT CRIMES 136

CAPSULE SUMMARY

Numbers in brackets refer to pages in the full-length
Emanuel Law Outline on Criminal Law, 6th Edition.

CHAPTER 1

ACTUS REUS AND *MENS REA*

I. GENERAL

1. **Four elements:** All crimes have several basic common elements: (1) a *voluntary act* ("*actus reus*"); (2) a *culpable intent* ("*mens rea*"); (3) *"concurrence"* between the *mens rea* and the *actus reus*; and (4) *causation* of harm. [1]

II. *ACTUS REUS*

A. **Significance of concept:** The defendant must have committed a *voluntary act*, or *"actus reus."* Look for an *actus reus* problem anytime you have one of the following situations: (1) D has not committed physical acts, but has "guilty" *thoughts*, *words*, states of *possession* or *status*; (2) D does an *involuntary act*; and (3) D has an *omission*, or failure to act. [1]

B. **Thoughts, words, possession and status:** *Mere thoughts* are never punishable as crimes. (*Example:* D writes in his diary, "I intend to kill V." This statement alone is not enough to constitute any crime, even attempted murder.) [1]

1. **Possession as criminal act:** However, mere *possession* of an object may sometimes constitute the necessary criminal act. (*Example:* Possession of narcotics frequently constitutes a crime in itself.) [1-2]

   a. **Knowledge:** When mere possession is made a crime, the act of "possession" is almost always construed so as to include only *conscious* possession. (*Example:* If the prosecution fails to prove that D knew he had narcotics on his person, there can be no conviction.) [46]

C. **Act must be voluntary:** An act cannot satisfy the *actus reus* requirement unless it is *voluntary*. [3-5]

1. **Reflex or convulsion:** An act consisting of a *reflex* or *convulsion* does not give rise to criminal liability. [3]

   Example: D, while walking down the street, is striken by epileptic convulsions. His arm jerks back, and he strikes X in the face. The striking of X is not a voluntary act, so D cannot be held criminally liable. But if D had known beforehand that he was subject to such seizures, and unreasonably put himself in a position where he was likely to harm others — for instance, by driving a car — this initial act might subject him to criminal liability.

2. **Unconsciousness:** An act performed during a state of *"unconsciousness"* does not meet the *actus reus* requirement. But D will be found to have acted "unconsciously" only in rare situations. [3-4]

   Example: If D can show that at the time of the crime he was on "automatic pilot," and was completely unconscious of what he was doing, his act will be involuntary. (But the mere fact that D has *amnesia* concerning the period of the crime will *not* be a defense.)

3. **Hypnosis:** Courts are split about whether acts performed under *hypnosis* are sufficiently "involuntary" that they do not give rise to liability. The Model Penal Code (MPC) treats conduct under hypnosis as being involuntary. [4]

4. **Self-induced state:** In all cases involving allegedly involuntary acts, D's *earlier voluntary act* may deprive D of the "involuntary" defense. [4]

   Example: D, a member of a cult run by Leader, lets himself be hypnotized. Before undergoing hypnosis, D knows that Leader often gives his members orders under hypnosis to commit crimes. D can probably be held criminally liable for any crimes committed while under hypnosis, because he knowingly put himself in a position where this might result.

D. **Omissions:** The *actus reus* requirement means that in most situations, there is no criminal liability for an *omission* to act (as distinguished from an affirmative act). [5-9]

   Example: D sees V, a stranger, drowning in front of him. D could easily rescue V. D will normally not be criminally liable for failing to attempt to rescue V, because there is no general liability for omissions as distinguished from affirmative acts.

1. **Existence of legal duty:** But there are some "special situations" where courts deem D to have a *special legal duty to act*. Where this occurs, D's omission may be punished under a statute that speaks in terms of positive acts. [6-8]

   a. **Special relationship:** Where D and V have a *special relationship* — most notably a *close blood relationship* — D will be criminally liable for a failure to act. (*Example:* Parent fails to give food or water to Child, and Child dies. Even if there is no general statute dealing with child abuse, Parent can be held liable for murder or manslaughter, because the close relationship is construed to impose on Parent an affirmative duty to furnish necessities and thereby prevent death.) [6]

      i. **Permitting child abuse:** Some courts have applied this theory to hold one parent liable for child abuse for *failing to intervene* to stop affirmative abuse by the other parent.

   b. **Contract:** Similarly, a legal duty may arise out of a *contract*. (*Example:* Lifeguard is hired by City to guard a beach. Lifeguard intentionally fails to save Victim from drowning, even though he could easily do so. Lifeguard will probably be criminally liable despite the fact that his conduct was an omission rather than an act; his contract with City imposed a duty to take affirmative action.) [7]

    c. **D caused danger:** If the ***danger was caused*** (even innocently) by ***D himself***, D generally has an affirmative duty to then save V. [7]

        Example: D digs a hole in the sidewalk in front of his house, acting legally under a building permit. D sees V about to step into the hole, but says nothing. V falls in and dies. D can be held criminally liable for manslaughter, because he created the condition — even though he did so innocently — and thus had an affirmative duty to protect those he knew to be in danger.

    d. **Undertaking:** Finally, D may come under a duty to render assistance if he ***undertakes*** to give assistance. This is especially true where D leaves V ***worse off*** than he was before, or effectively dissuades other rescuers who believe that D is taking care of the problem. [8]

        Example: V is drowning, while D and three others are on shore. D says, "I'll swim out to save V." The others agree, and leave, thinking that D is taking care of the situation. Now, D will be criminally liable if he does not make reasonable efforts to save V.

III. *MENS REA*

A. **Meaning:** The term *"mens rea"* symbolizes the requirement that there be a *"culpable state of mind."* [11]

    1. **Not necessarily state of mind:** Most crimes require a true *"mens rea,"* that is, a state of mind that is truly guilty. But other crimes are defined to require merely "negligence" or "recklessness," which is not really a state of mind at all. Nonetheless, the term *"mens rea"* is sometimes used for these crimes as well: thus one can say that "for manslaughter, the *mens rea* is recklessness." There are also a few crimes defined so as to require no *mens rea* at all, the so called "strict liability" crimes. [11]

B. **General vs. specific intent:** Court traditionally classify the *mens rea* requirements of various crimes into three groups: (1) crimes requiring merely *"general intent"*; (2) crimes requiring *"specific intent"*; and (3) crimes requiring merely ***recklessness*** or ***negligence***. (Strict liability crimes form a fourth category, as to which there is no culpable mental state required at all.) [12-13]

    1. **"General intent":** A crime requiring merely *"general intent"* is a crime for which it must merely be shown that D ***desired to commit the act which served as the actus reus***. [12]

    2. **"Specific intent":** Where a crime requires *"specific intent"* or "special intent," this means that D, in addition to desiring to bring about the *actus reus*, must have desired to do ***something further***. [13]

    Example of general intent crime: Battery is usually a "general intent" crime. The *actus reus* is a physical injury to or offensive touching of another. So long as D intends to touch another in an offensive way, he has the "general intent" that is all that is needed for battery. (Thus if D touches V with a knife, intending merely to graze his skin and frighten him, this will be all the (general) intent needed for battery, since D intended the touching, and no other intent (such as the intent to cause injury) is required.

Example of specific intent crime: For common-law burglary, on the other hand, it must be shown that D not only intended to break and enter the dwelling of another, but that he also intended to commit a felony once inside the dwelling. This latter intent is a "specific intent" — it is an intent other than the one associated with the *actus reus* (the breaking and entering).

3. **Significance:** The general/specific intent distinction usually matters in two situations: (1) where D is *intoxicated*; and (2) where D makes a *mistake* of law or fact. [13]

   a. **Intoxication:** *Intoxication* rarely negates a crime of general intent, but may sometimes negate the specific intent for a particular crime. (*Example:* D breaks and enters, but is too drunk to have any intent to commit larceny or any other felony inside; D probably is not guilty of burglary.) [13]

   b. **Mistake:** Similarly, a *mistake* of fact is more likely to be enough to negate the required specific intent. [13]

      Example: D breaks and enters, in an attempt to carry away something which he mistakenly thinks belongs to him; D will probably be acquitted of burglary, where mistake will generally not negate a general intent (e.g., the intent to commit the breaking and entering by itself).

4. **Abandonment of distinction:** However, many modern codes, and the Model Penal Code, have *abandoned* the general/specific distinction, and instead set forth the precise mental state required for each element of each crime. [13]

C. **"Purposely" as mental state:** Many crimes are defined to be committed only where a person acts *"purposely"* with respect to a particular element of a crime. Other crimes are defined to require the similar, but not identical, mental state of *"intentionally."* [14-16]

   1. **Definition of "purposely":** A person acts "purposely" with respect to a particular element if it his *"conscious object"* to engage in the particular conduct in question, or to cause the particular result in question. [14-15]

   2. **Not the same as "knowingly":** In modern statutes, "purposely" is not the same as "knowingly." If D does not desire a particular result, but is *aware* that the conduct or result is *certain to follow*, this is *not* "purposely." [16]

   Example: D consciously desires to kill A, and does so by putting a bomb on board a plane that contains both A and B. Although D knew B's death was certain, a modern court would probably not hold that D "purposely" killed B, (although D might nonetheless be guilty of murder on the grounds that he acted with a "depraved heart").

   3. **Motive:** D's *motive* will usually be *irrelevant* in determining whether he acted "purposely" or "intentionally." [16]

Example: D, in an act of euthanasia, kills V, his wife, who has terminal cancer. D will be held to have "purposely" or "intentionally" killed V, even though he did it for ostensibly "good" motives.

    a. Relevant to defenses: Special motives may, however, be relevant to the existence of a *defense* (e.g., the defense of self-defense or necessity).

D. "Knowingly": Modern statutes, and the Model Penal Code, define some crimes to require that D *"knowingly"* take an act or produce a result. The biggest distinction between "purposely" and "knowingly" relates to D's awareness of the *consequences* of his act: if the crime is defined with respect to a certain result of D's conduct, D has acted knowingly (but not "purposely") if he was "aware that it is *practically certain* that his conduct will cause that result." [16-19]

    Example: On the facts of our earlier "bomb on the airplane" example, D will have "knowingly" killed B, but not "purposely" killed B, because he was aware that it was practically certain that his conduct would cause B's death.

    1. Presumption of knowledge: A statutory or judge-made *presumption* may be used to help prove that D acted "knowingly." (*Example:* In many statutes governing receipt of stolen property, D's unexplained possession of property which is in fact stolen gives rise to a presumption that D knew the property was stolen.) [18]

    2. Knowledge of attendant circumstances: Where a statute specifies that D must act "knowingly," and the statute then specifies various *attendant circumstances* which the definition of the crime makes important, usually the requirement of knowledge is held applicable to *all these attendant circumstances*. [18]

    Example: A statute provides that any dealer in used merchandise must file a report with the police if the dealer "knowingly purchases a used item from one who is not in the business of selling such items, at a price less than half of the fair market value of the item." The statute's purpose is to cut down on the "fencing" of stolen goods. D, a used merchandise dealer, buys a vase for $500 that is really worth $2,000. Most courts would require the prosecution to show that D knew not only that he was purchasing the vase, but that he knew he was paying less than half of the vase's fair market value. In other words, D must be shown to have acted knowingly with respect to all of the attendant circumstances, including the circumstance that the purchase price was much less than the value.

E. "Recklessly": A person acts *"recklessly"* if he *"consciously disregards a substantial and unjustifiable risk...."* MPC §2.02(2). The idea is that D has behaved in a way that represents a *gross deviation* from the conduct of a law-abiding person. [19-20]

    1. Must be aware of risk: Most courts, and the Model Penal Code, hold that D is reckless only if he was *aware* of the high risk of harm stemming from his conduct. This is a "subjective" standard for recklessness. But a substantial minority of courts and statutes hold that D can be reckless if he behaves extremely unreasonably even though he was unaware of the risk. [19]

Example: D runs a nightclub with inadequate fire exits. A fire breaks out, killing hundreds. Under the majority "subjective" standard for recklessness, D was reckless only if he *actually knew* of the high risk of harm posed by inadequate fire exits. Under the minority "objective" standard, it would be enough that D was extremely careless and that a reasonable person would have known of the great danger, even though D did not.

F. **"Negligently":** Some statutes make it a crime to behave *"negligently"* if certain results follow. For instance, the crime of "vehicular homicide" is sometimes defined to require a *mens rea* of "criminal negligence." [20-21]

   1. **Awareness not required:** Most modern statutes, and the Model Penal Code, allow a finding of criminal negligence even if D was *not aware* of the risk imposed by his conduct (as in the above night-club fire example). [20]

   2. **"Gross" negligence required:** Usually, criminal negligence is *"gross"* negligence. That is, the deviation from ordinary care must be greater than that which would be required for civil negligence. [21]

G. **Strict liability:** Some offenses are *"strict liability."* That is, no culpable mental state at all must be shown — it is enough that D performed the act in question, regardless of his mental state. [21-24]

   Examples of strict liability crimes: The following are often defined as strict liability offenses: Statutory rape (D is generally guilty if he has intercourse with a girl below the prescribed age, regardless of whether he knew or should have known her true age); mislabelling of drugs; polluting of water or air; concealment of a dangerous weapon while boarding an aircraft.

   1. **Constitutionality:** Generally there is no constitutional problem with punishing a defendant without regard to his mental state. [21]

   2. **Interpretation:** The mere fact that the statute does not specify a mental state does not mean that the crime is a strict liability one — judges must determine whether a particular mental state was intended by the legislature. In general, the older the statute (especially if it is a codification of a common-law crime), the less likely it is to be a strict-liability offense. Most strict liability offenses are modern, and are of relatively low heinousness. [22-23]

      a. **Complex statute that is easy to violate innocently:** If the statute is *complex*, or *easy to violate innocently,* or *imposes serious penalties,* the court is likely to read in a *mens rea* requirement, and thus to refuse to treat the statute as imposing strict liability. [*Staples v. U.S.*] [22]

      b. **MPC:** Under the MPC, the only offenses that are strict liability are ones called *"violations."* These are minor offenses that do not constitute a "crime" and that may be punished only by fine or forfeiture. [23]

H. **Vicarious liability:** Statutes sometimes impose upon one person liability for the *act of another*; this is commonly called *"vicarious liability."* In essence, the requirement of an act (*actus reus*) has been dispensed with, not the requirement of the wrongful intent. [24-26]

Example: Statutes frequently make an ***automobile owner*** liable for certain acts committed by those to whom he lends his car, even without a showing of culpable mental state on the part of the owner.

1. **Constitutionality:** Generally, the imposition of vicarious liability does ***not*** violate D's due process rights. However, there are exceptions: [24-25]

    a. **D has no control over offender:** If D did not have any ***ability to control*** the person who performed the actual *actus reus*, his conviction is probably unconstitutional. [24]

       Example: X steals D's car, and exceeds the speed limit. It is probably unconstitutional for the state to impose criminal sanctions upon D, since he had no ability to control X's conduct.

    b. **Imprisonment:** If D has been sentenced to ***imprisonment*** (or even if he is convicted of a crime for which imprisonment is authorized), some courts hold that his due process rights are violated unless he is shown to have at least ***known*** of the violation. [25]

       Example: D is a tavern owner whose employee served a minor. If D did not know of this act, or in any way acquiesce in its commission, some courts would hold that D may not constitutionally be imprisoned for it.

I. **Mistake:** Defendants raise the defense of ***mistake*** when they have been mistaken either about the facts or the law. Do not think of "mistake" as being a separate "doctrine." Instead, look at the effect of the particular mistake on D's ***mental state***, and examine whether he was thereby prevented from having the mental state required for the crime. [26-32]

   Example: Assume that the requisite mental intent for larceny is the intent to take property which one knows or believes to belong to another. D takes V's umbrella from a restaurant, thinking that it is his own. D's factual mistake — his belief about who owns the umbrella — is a defense to the theft charge, because it negates the requisite mental state (intent to take the property which one knows or believes belongs to another).

   1. **Crimes of "general intent":** D's mistake is ***least likely*** to assist him where the crime is a ***"general intent"*** crime (i.e., one for which the most general kind of culpable intent will suffice). [26]

      Example: Murder is often thought of as a "general intent" crime in the sense that it will be enough that D either intends to kill, intends to commit grievous bodily injury, is recklessly indifferent to the value of human life or intends to commit any of certain non-homicide felonies. Suppose D shoots a gun at V, intending to hit V in the arm and thus create a painful but not serious flesh wound. D mistakenly believes that V is in ordinary health, when in fact he is a hemopheliac. D's mistake will not help him, because even had the facts been as D supposed them to be, D would have had a requisite mental state, the intent to commit grievous bodily injury.

2. **"Lesser crime" theory:** D's mistake will almost never help him if, had the facts been as D mistakenly supposed them to be, his acts would still have been a crime, though a lesser one. This is the *"lesser crime"* theory. [29]

   Example: D steals a necklace from a costume jewelry store. The necklace is made of diamonds, and is worth $10,000, but D mistakenly believes it to be costume jewelry worth less than $500. In the jurisdiction, theft of something worth less than $500 is a misdemeanor, and theft of something worth more than that is a felony. D is guilty of a crime — a felony in most states — because even had the facts been as he supposed them to be, he still would have been guilty of some crime. (But some states, and the Model Penal Code, would scale his crime back to the crime that he would have committed had the facts been as he supposed, in this case, a misdemeanor.)

   a. **Moral wrong:** Older decisions extend this principle to deny D of the defense of mistake if, under the facts as D believed them to be, his conduct and intent would have been *"immoral."* But modern statutes reject this view. [26]

3. **Mistake must be "reasonable":** Older cases often impose the rule that a mistake cannot be a defense unless it was *"reasonable."* But the modern view, and the view of the MPC, is that *even an unreasonable mistake* will block conviction if the mistake prevented D from having the requisite intent or knowledge. [27]

   Example: D attempts (unsuccessfully) to have sex with a girl he meets on the street. He is charged with assault with intent to rape. D shows that he actually, but unreasonably, believed that V was a prostitute, because prostitutes frequented that area. A traditional court would probably hold that the mistake was no defense, since D's mistake was "unreasonable." But a modern court might allow the defense, since had the facts been as D supposed them to be, he would not have intended to commit a crime (unconsented-to sex).

   a. **Rejection by finder of fact:** Remember that even in a "modern" jurisdiction, the finder of fact is always free to *disbelieve* that the mistake really occurred. Thus on the facts of the above example, the more "unreasonable" D's story that he thought V was a prostitute, the quicker the jury (or the judge in a bench trial) can be to conclude simply that D was not in fact mistaken. [27]

4. **Mistake of law:** It is especially hard for D to prevail with a defense based on *"mistake of law."* [27]

   a. **Generally no defense:** As a general rule, *"mistake of law is no defense."* More precisely, this means that *the fact that D mistakenly believes that no statute makes his conduct a crime does not furnish a defense.* [27]

   Example: D, who is retarded, does not realize that unconsented-to intercourse is a crime. D has unconsented-to intercourse with V. D's ignorance that unconsented-to intercourse is a crime will not be a defense; so long as D intended the act of intercourse while knowing that V did not consent, he is guilty.

   i. Reasonable mistake: In this core "D mistakenly believes that no statute makes his conduct a crime" situation, even a ***reasonable mistake*** about the meaning of the statute will usually ***not*** protect D. In other words, so long as the crime is not itself defined in a way that makes D's guilty knowledge a prerequisite, there is usually no "reasonable mistake" exception to the core "mistake of law is no defense" rule.

b. Mistake of law as to collateral fact: It is important to remember that the oft-stated "rule," "ignorance of the law is no excuse," really only means *"ignorance that a statute makes one's conduct a crime is no excuse."* A mistake of law as to some ***collateral fact*** may negative the required mental state, just as a mistake of fact may do so. [29]

Example 1: D's car has been repossessed by Finance Co. D finds the car, breaks in, and takes it back. D's belief that the car is still legally his *will* absolve him, because it prevents him from having the requisite mental state for theft (intent to take property which one knows or believes to belong to another). (But if D had taken his neighbor's car, his ignorance that there is a statute making it a crime to take one's neighbor's property would not be a defense.)

Example 2: D reasonably believes that he has been divorced from W, his first wife, but in fact the "divorce" is an invalid foreign decree, which is not recognized under local law. D then marries V. D's "mistake of law" about the enforceability of the prior divorce *will* negative the intent needed for bigamy (intent to have two spouses at once).

c. Mistake of law defense built in: Of course, it's always possible for the legislature to write a statute in such a way that a mistake of law *will* constitute a defense (or so that awareness of the criminality of the conduct is an element of the offense). For instance, the legislature might do this by defining the crime to consist of a *"willful* violation" — the use of the word "willful" would probably be interpreted to require knowledge by the defendant that his act was prohibited by law. [32-33]

Example: A federal statute prohibits "structuring" bank transactions to evade the requirement that all transactions over $10,000 be reported to the government. Another statute makes it a crime to "willfully" violate the first statute. *Held,* D cannot be convicted of a willful violation of the statute unless the prosecution shows that he was aware of the ban on structuring. [*Ratzlaf v. U.S.*]

IV. CONCURRENCE

A. Two types of concurrence required: There are two ways in which there must be *"concurrence"* involving the *mens rea*: (1) there must be concurrence between D's *mental state* and the *act*; and (2) there must be concurrence between D's *mental state* and the *harmful result*, if the crime is one defined in terms of bad results. [35]

B. Concurrence between mind and act: There must be concurrence between the *mental state* and the *act*. [35-37]

    1. Same time: This requirement is not met if, *at the time of the act*, the required mental state does not exist. [35-37]

    Example: Common-law larceny is defined as the taking of another's property with intent to deprive him of it. D takes V's umbrella from a restaurant, thinking that it is his own. Five minutes later, he realizes that it belongs to V, and decides to keep it. D has not committed larceny, because at the time he committed the act (the taking), he did not have the requisite mental intent (the intent to deprive another of his property). The fact that D later acquired the requisite intent is irrelevant.

    2. Mental state must cause act: In fact, the mental state must *cause* the act. [36]

    Example: D intends to kill V. While driving to the store to buy a gun to carry out his intent, D accidentally runs over V and kills him. D is not guilty of murder, even though the intent to kill V existed at the time the act (driving the car over V) took place. This is because D's intent to kill did not "cause" the act (driving the car over V).

        a. Any action that is legal cause of harm: Most crimes are defined in terms of harmful results (e.g., homicide is the wrongful taking of a life). Where D takes *several acts* which together lead to the harmful result, the concurrence requirement is met if the mental state concurs with *any act that suffices as a legal cause* of the harm. [36-37]

            i. Destruction or concealment of a "body":   Because of this rule, D will be guilty if he attempts to kill his victim, believes the victim to be dead, and then destroys or conceals the "body," killing the victim for real. (*Example:* D strikes V over the head, and thinking V is dead, pushes him over a cliff to destroy the body. The autopsy shows that the blows did not kill V and probably would not have killed him. V really died from the fall off the cliff. Most courts would find D guilty, probably on the theory that the blows to the head were a cause of harm, and the guilty intent (to kill V) caused the blows. [*Thabo Meli v. Regina*, 1 All E.R. 373 (Eng. 1954)])

C. Concurrence between mind and result: There must also be concurrence between the mental state and the *harmful result*, if the crime is one defined in terms of bad results (such as homicide, rape, larceny, etc.) Basically this aspect of concurrence means that if what actually occurred is *too far removed* from what was intended, there will be no concurrence and thus no liability. [37-40]

    1. Different crime: Thus if the harm which actually occurs is of a completely different *type* from what D intended, D will generally not be guilty of the other crime. In other words, the intent for one crime may not usually be linked with a result associated with a different crime. [37]

    Example: D attempts to shoot V to death while V is leaving his house. The shot misses and ruptures V's stove, causing V's house to burn down. Assuming that arson is defined so as to require an intent to burn, D will not be guilty of arson, because the intent for one crime (murder) cannot be matched with the result for another crime (burning) to produce guilt for the latter crime.

2. **Recklessly- or negligently-caused result:** The same rule applies where D has *negligently* or *recklessly* acted with respect to the risk of a particular result, and a very different result occurs. [38]

    Example: D recklessly takes target practice with his rifle in a crowded area; what makes his conduct reckless is the high risk that D will injure or kill a person. One of D's shots hits a gas tank, and causes a large fire. Assuming that the danger of causing a fire was not large, D will not be convicted of arson (even if arson is defined to include reckless burning), since his conduct was reckless only with respect to the risk of bodily harm, not the risk of burning.

3. **Felony-murder and misdemeanor-manslaughter rules:** But this general principle that there is no liability for a resulting harm which is substantially different from that intended or risked by D is subject to two very important *exceptions*, both relating to *homicide*: [38]

    a. **Felony-murder:** First, if D is engaged in the commission of certain *dangerous felonies*, he will be liable for certain deaths which occur, even if he did not intend the deaths. This is the *"felony-murder" rule*. [38]

    b. **Misdemeanor-manslaughter:** Second, if D was engaged in a *malum in se* misdemeanor (a misdemeanor that is immoral, not just regulatory), and a death occurs, D may be liable for involuntary manslaughter, even though his conduct imposed very little risk of that death and the death was a freak accident. This is the *"misdemeanor-manslaughter" rule*. [38]

4. **Same harm but different degree:** If the harm which results is of the *same general type* as D intended, but of a *more or less serious degree*, D gets the benefit of the rules on concurrence. [39]

    a. **Actual result more serious than intended:** Thus if the actual harm is *greater*, and related to, the intended result, D is generally *not liable* for the greater harm. [39]

        Example: Assume simple battery is defined as the intentional causing of minor bodily harm, and aggravated battery is defined as the intentional causing of grievous bodily harm. D gets into a minor scuffle with V, intending merely to hit him lightly on the chin. But V turns out to have a "glass jaw," which is fractured by the blow. D will not be held guilty of aggravated battery, just simple battery, since his intent was only to produce that lesser degree of injury required for simple battery.

        i. **Exceptions in homicide cases:** But again, we have two exceptions to this rule when death results. First, under the misdemeanor-manslaughter rule, if D's minor attack on V unexpectedly causes V to die, D is guilty of manslaughter (as he would be on the facts of the above example if V unexpectedly bled to death). Second, if D intended to *seriously injure* V but not kill him, in most states he will be guilty of murder if V dies from the attack, because most states have a form of murder as to which the mental state is intent-to-grievously-injure.

Example: D intends to beat V to a pulp, but not to kill him; V dies unexpectedly. In a state defining murder to include a mental state of intent-to-grievously-injure, D is liable for murder.

CHAPTER 2

CAUSATION

I. INTRODUCTION

A. Two aspects of causation: "Causation" in criminal law relates to the link between the *act* and the *harmful result*. The prosecution must show that the defendant's *actus reus* "caused" the harmful result, in *two different senses*: (1) that the act was the *"cause in fact"* of the harm; and (2) that the act was the *"proximate"* cause (or the "legal" cause) of the harm. [44]

II. CAUSE IN FACT

A. Two ways: There are two ways in which an act can be the "cause in fact" of harm: (1) by being the *"but for"* cause of the harm; and (2) by being a *"substantial factor"* in creating the harm. These categories overlap, but not completely. [44]

B. The "but for" rule: Most often, the act will be the "cause in fact" of the harm by being the *"but for"* cause of that harm. To put the idea negatively, if the result *would have happened anyway*, even had the act not occurred, the act is *not a cause in fact* of that result. [44]

>   **Example:** D shoots at V, but only grazes him, leaving V with a slightly bleeding flesh wound. X, who has always wanted to kill V, finds V (in the same place V would have been in had D not shot at V), and shoots V through the heart, killing him instantly. D's act is not a "cause in fact" of V's death, under the "but for" test — since V would have died, in just the manner and at the same time he did, even if D had not shot him, D's act was not the "but for" cause of V's death. Unless D's act is found to have been a "substantial factor" in V's death (the other test for causation in fact), which it probably would not, D's act is not the "cause in fact" of V's death, and D therefore cannot be punished for that death.

C. "Substantial factor" test: D's act will be found to be the cause in fact of harm, even if the act is not the "but for" cause, if the act was a *"substantial factor"* in bringing about the result. [44]

>   **Example:** At a time of widespread riots, D sets fire to a house at 99 Main Street, and X simultaneously sets fire to one at 103 Main Street. A house at 101 Main Street is consumed by the blaze from the two fires. D is charged with arson. He shows that even had he not torched 99, the flames from 103 would have been enough to burn down 101 at the same time it actually did

burn. (Thus D's act was not the "but for" cause of the burning of 101.) However, since D's conduct was a (though not the sole) "substantial factor" in burning down 101, he was a "cause in fact" of the fire and will therefore be liable for arson.

1. **D's act shortened V's life:** In a homicide case, if D's act *shortened the victim's life*, this will strongly suggest that D's conduct was a "substantial factor" in producing the victim's death. [45]

   Example: X poisons D, in such a way that despite all medical efforts, V will definitely die within one day. One hour after V drinks the poison, D shoots V, killing him instantly. Since V would have died shortly anyway, it can be argued that D's shooting was not the "but for" cause of V's death. But since D shortened V's life, a court would certainly find that D was a "substantial factor" in causing V's death, and would find him guilty of murder.

   a. **Intervening act shortens V's life:** Where the *first* person to do harm is charged, and defends on the grounds that the second person's intervening act should relieve him of liability, it's a closer question, but many courts will find the first person to be guilty here as well. [45]

      Example: Same facts as above example, except now X, rather than D, is charged with murder. Assuming that V would inevitably have died from the poison had D not come along to shoot him, courts are split about whether D is relieved from liability by the intervening shooting.

2. **Conspiracy:** The above discussion of the "substantial factor" rule assumes that the two concurring acts occurred *independently* of each other. If the two occured as part of a *joint enterprise*, such as a *conspiracy*, the act of each person will be attributed to the other, and there will be no need to determine whether each act was a substantial factor in leading to the harm. [46]

   Example: X and D each shoot V, as part of a successful conspiracy to kill V. Even if D's shot only caused a small flesh wound and did not really contribute to V's death, D is guilty of murder, because his co-conspirator's fatal shot will be attributable to D under the law of conspiracy.

III. PROXIMATE CAUSE GENERALLY

A. **Definition of "proximate cause":** It is not enough that D's act was a "cause in fact" of the harm. The prosecution must also show that the act and harm are sufficiently closely related that the act is a *"proximate"* or "legal" cause of that harm. This is a *policy* question: *Is the connection between the act and the harm so stretched that it is unfair to hold D liable for that harm?* [46]

   1. **No precise definition:** There is no precise or mechanical definition of proximate cause — each case gets decided on its own facts. [46]

   2. **Model Penal Code formulation:** Under the MPC, in most cases D's act will be the proximate cause of the harmful result if the result is "not too remote or accidental in its occurrence to have a [just] bearing on the actor's liability or on the gravity of his offense." MPC 2.03(2)(b). [46]

B. Year-and-a-day rule in homicide: One common-law rule that expresses the proximate-cause idea is the *"year and a day"* rule in homicide cases: D cannot be convicted if the victim did not die until a year and a day following D's act. Many states continue to impose this rule. [47]

C. Types of problems raised: Look for two main types of proximate cause problems: (1) situations where the type of harm intended occurred, and occurred in roughly the manner intended, but the *victim was not the intended one*; and (2) cases where the general type of harm intended did occur and occurred to the intended victim, but occurred in an *unintended manner*. [47]

  1. Reckless and negligent crimes: Proximate cause issues are most common in cases where the *mens rea* for the crime is intent. But similar problems also arise where the mental state is recklessness or negligence. [47]

IV. PROXIMATE CAUSE — UNINTENDED VICTIMS

A. Transferred intent: It will not generally be a defense that the actual victim of D's act was *not the intended victim*. Instead, courts apply the doctrine of *"transferred intent,"* under which D's intent is "transferred" from the actual to the intended victim. [47-48]

  Example: D, intending to kill X, shoots at X. Because of D's bad aim, D hits and kills V instead. D is guilty of the murder of V, because his intent is said to be "transferred" from X to V.

  1. Danger to actual V unforeseeable: In most courts, the "unintended victim" rule probably applies even where the danger to the actual victim was *completely unforeseeable*. (*Example:* While D and X are out on the desert, D shoots at X, thinking the two are completely alone. V, sleeping behind some sagebrush, is hit by the errant bullet. Probably D may be convicted of murdering V.) [49]

B. Same defense: In general, D in an "unintended victim" case may raise the *same defenses* that he would have been able to raise had the intended victim been the one harmed. (*Example:* D shoots at X in legitimate self-defense. The bullet strikes V, a bystander. D may claim self-defense, just as he could if the bullet had struck the intended victim.) [49]

C. Mistaken ID: The fact that D is mistaken about the victim's *identity* will not be a defense. [49]

  Example: D shoots at V, mistakenly thinking that V is really X, D's enemy. D will be guilty of the murder of V, just as if he had been shooting at the person who was actually X, and had mistakenly hit V. The crime of murder requires an intent to kill, but does not require a correct belief as to the victim's identity.

D. Crimes of recklessness or negligence: The "unforeseen victim" problem also arises in crimes where the mental state is *recklessness* or *negligence*, rather than intent. But in these situations, a *tighter link* between D's act and V's injury is probably required than where the crime is intentional. [50]

V. PROXIMATE CAUSE — UNINTENDED MANNER OF HARM

A. **Generally:** If D's intended victim is harmed, but the harm occurs in an *unexpected manner* (though it is the same general type of harm intended), the unexpected manner of harm may or may not be enough to absolve D. In general, D will not be liable where the harm occurs through a *completely bizarre, unforeseeable chain of events*. [51]

> **Example:** D gets into a street fight with V, and tries to seriously injure him. As the result of the fight, V is knocked unconscious, recovers a few minutes later, drives away, and is hit by the 8:02 train at a crossing. D's act is certainly a "but for" cause of the harm to V, since had V not been knocked out, he would have continued on his way and crossed earlier than 8:02. And the general type of harm to V — severe bodily injury — is the same as that intended by D. Yet all courts would agree that the chain of events here was so unforeseeable from D's perspective that he should not be held liable for V's death.

  1. **"Direct" causation vs. "intervening" events:** Courts often distinguish cases in which D's act was a *"direct"* cause of the harm from those in which there was an *"intervening"* cause between D's act and the harm. But the direct/intervening distinction is only one factor — D has a somewhat better chance, on average, of escaping liability where there was intervening cause than where there was not. [51]

B. **Direct causation:** We say that D's act was a *"direct"* of V's harm if the harm followed D's act without the presence of any clearly-defined act or event by an outside person or thing. In direct causation situations, D is rarely able to convince the court that the chain of events was so bizarre that D should be absolved. [51-53]

  1. **Small differences in type of injury:** If the same general *type of injury* (e.g., serious bodily harm, death, burning) occurs as was intended by D, the fact that the harm deviates in some small manner from that intended is irrelevant. [51]

  2. **Slightly different mechanism:** Similarly, if the general type of harm intended actually occurs, D will not be absolved because the harm occurred in a slightly different *way* than intended. [52]

  > **Example:** D attempts to poison her husband, V, by putting strychnine in a glass of milk she serves him for breakfast. V drinks it, and becomes so dizzy from its effect that he falls while getting up from his chair, hitting his head on the table. He dies from the blow to the head, and the autopsy shows that the poison would not have been enough to kill him directly. Nearly all courts would hold that D is guilty of murder, because her act directly caused V's death, and there was nothing terribly bizarre about the chain of events leading to that death.

  3. **Pre-existing weakness:** If V has a *pre-existing condition*, unknown to D, that makes him much more *susceptible to injury or death* than a normal person would be, D *"takes his victim as he finds him."* Thus D may not argue

that his own act was not the proximate cause of the unusually severe result. [52]

Example: D beats V up, with intent to kill him. V runs away before many blows have fallen, and a person in ordinary health would not have been severely hurt by the blows that did fall. Unknown to D, however, V is a hemopheliac, who bleeds to death from one slight wound. D is guilty of murder, even though from D's viewpoint V's death from the slight wounds was unforeseeable.

Note: When you are looking at a proximate cause problem, don't forget to also apply the rules of concurrence and to insist on the *correct mental state*. For instance, suppose D in the above example had only been trying to commit a minor battery on V, instead of trying to kill him. If V died as a result of his hemophelia, D would not be liable for common-law intent-to-kill murder, because he did not have the requisite mental state, the intent to kill. (But he would probably be liable for *manslaughter* under the misdemeanor- manslaughter rule.)

4. **Fright or stress:** Where V's death results even *without physical impact*, as the result of a *fright* or *stress* caused by D, D's conduct can nonetheless be a proximate cause of the death. [52]

Example: During a holdup by D, V, a storekeeper, has a fatal heart attack from the stress. In most courts, V's death will be held to be the proximate result of D's act of robbery; coupled with the felony-murder doctrine, this will be enough for D to be guilty of murder, even if there was no way he could have known of V's heart condition. [*People v. Stamp*]

C. **Intervening acts:** D's odds of escaping liability are better where an *"intervening act"* or intervening *event* contributes to the result than where D has "directly" caused the harmful result. [53-60]

1. **Dependent vs. independent intervening acts:** Courts divide intervening acts into two categories: (1) *"dependent"* acts, which are ones which would not have occurred except for D's act (e.g., medical treatment for a wound caused by D); and (2) *"independent"* acts, which would have occurred even if D had not acted, but which combined with D's act produced the harmful result. [54]

Example of dependent act: D wounds V in a fight. X, a doctor, negligently treats V's wound, and V dies.

Example of independent act or event: D poisons V, weakening his immune system. D is then in a car accident which he would have been in even had the poisoning not taken place. V dies from the combined result of the accident and his pre-accident weakened condition.

a. **Significance:** D's odds of escaping responsibility are somewhat better where the intervening act is *"independent."* An independent intervention will break the chain of events if it was *"unforeseeable"* for one in D's position. A dependent intervening cause will break the chain only if it was both unforeseeable and *"abnormal."* An act is less likely to be considered "abnormal" than it is to be considered merely "unforeseeable," so D typically does better in the independent case. [54]

2. **Intervening acts by third persons:** [54-57]

    a. **Medical treatment:** The most common intervening act is *medical treatment* performed by a doctor or nurse upon V, where this treatment is necessitated by injuries inflicted by D. Here, the treatment is obviously in response to D's act, and therefore is a "dependent" intervening act, so it will only supersede if the treatment is *"abnormal."* [54-56]

        i. **Negligent treatment:** The fact that the treatment is *negligently performed* will *not*, by itself, usually be enough to make it so "abnormal" that it is a superceding event. But if the treatment is performed in a *reckless* or *grossly negligent* manner, the treatment *will* usually be found to be "abnormal" and thus superseding.

    b. **Failure to act never supersedes:** A third party's *failure to act* will almost *never* be a superseding cause. [57]

        Example: D shoots V. There is a doctor, X, standing by who could, with 100% certainty, prevent V from dying. X refuses to render assistance because he hates V and wants V to die. D will still be the proximate cause of death — a third party's failure to act will never supersede.

3. **Act by V:** Sometimes the *victim herself* will take an action that is possibly a superseding intervening cause. Acts by victims are generally taken in direct response to D's act, so they will not be superseding unless they are "abnormal" (not merely "unforeseeable"). [57-59]

    a. **Victim refuses medical aid:** If the victim refuses to receive *medical assistance* which might prevent the severe harm imposed by D, the victim's refusal usually will *not* be superseding. [58]

        Example: D stabs V repeatedly. V refuses a blood transfusion because she is a Jehovah's Witness. *Held*, V's refusal to allow the transfusion is not a superseding cause. [*Regina v. Blaue*]

    b. **Victim tries to avoid danger:** If the victim attempts to *avoid the danger* posed by D, and this attempted escape results in additional injury, the attempt will be a superseding cause only if it is an "abnormal" reaction. [58]

        Example: D kidnaps V by locking her in a room. V tries to escape by knotting bed sheets together, and falls to her death while climbing down. V's escape would probably be found not to be "abnormal" even if it is was "unforeseeable," so it will not be a superseding cause, and D will be the proximate cause of death. The felony-murder rule will then make D guilty of V's death, even though D did not have any of the mental states for ordinary murder.

    c. **V subjects self to danger:** Suppose D urges or encourages V to *expose himself to danger*. V's voluntary participation will *not* generally supersede, and D will be held to be a proximate cause of the result. [58-59]

Examples: D persuades V to play Russian Roulette, or to engage in a drag race — many courts will hold D to be the proximate cause of the injury when V shoots himself or crashes.

CHAPTER 3

RESPONSIBILITY

I.   THE INSANITY DEFENSE

  A. General purpose: If D can show he was *insane* at the time he committed a criminal act, he may be entitled to the verdict "not guilty by reason of insanity." [67]

    1. Mandatory commitment: If D succeeds with the insanity defense, he does not walk out of the courtroom free. In virtually every state, any D who succeeds with the insanity defense will be involuntarily *committed* to a mental institution. [67]

    2. Not constitutionally required: Virtually every state recognizes some form of the insanity defense. However, the federal constitution probably does *not require* the states to recognize insanity as a complete defense. [67]

    3. Limits use of mental disease: In many states, the insanity defense is coupled with a rule that *no evidence relating to mental disease or defect* may be introduced *except* as part of an insanity defense. (*Example:* D is charged with knifing his wife to death. In many states, D will not be permitted to show that his mental disease prevented him from forming an intent to kill her. In these states, D's sole method for showing the relevance of his mental disease is via the insanity defense.) [67]

  B. Tests for insanity: The principal tests for whether D was insane — each used in some jurisdictions — are as follows: [68-73]

    1. *M'Naghten* "right from wrong" rule: At least half the states apply the so-called *M'Naghten* rule: D must show: [68-69]

      a. Mental disease or defect: That he suffered a *mental disease* causing a *defect* in his reasoning powers [68]; and

      b. Result: That as a result, either: (1) he did not understand the *"nature and quality"* of his act; or (2) he did not know that his act was *wrong*. [69]

      Example 1: D strangles V, his wife, believing that he is squeezing a lemon. Even under the relatively strict *M'Naghten* test, D would probably be ruled insane, on the grounds that he did not understand the "nature and quality" of his act.

      Example 2: D is attracted to bright objects, and therefore shoplifts jewelry constantly, though intellectually he knows that this is morally wrong and also illegal. D is not insane under the *M'Naghten* test, because he understood the nature and quality of his act, and knew that his act was wrong. The fact that he may have acted under an "irresistible impulse" is irrelevant under the *M'Naghten* rule.

2. **"Irresistible impulse" test:** Many states, including about half of those states that follow *M'Naghten*, have added a *second standard* by which D can establish his insanity: that D was **unable to control his conduct**. This is sometimes loosely called the *"irresistible impulse"* defense. (*Example:* On the facts of Example 2 above, D would be acquitted, because although he understood that it was wrong to shoplift shiny things, he was unable to control his conduct.) [70]

3. **Model Penal Code standard:** The Model Penal Code (§4.01(1)) allows D to be acquitted if "as a result of mental disease or defect he lacks substantial capacity either to *appreciate the criminality* of his conduct or *to conform his conduct* to the requirements of the law." Thus D wins if he can show *either* that he didn't know his conduct was wrong, or that he couldn't control his conduct. Essentially, D wins if he satisfies either the *M'Naghten* test or the irresistible impulse test, under the MPC approach. [70-72]

4. **The federal standard:** The modern *federal* standard (in force since 1984) sets a very stringent standard for federal prosecutions. D wins only if "as a result of a severe mental disease or defect, [he] was unable to appreciate the *nature and quality* or the *wrongfulness* of his acts...." This is essentially the *M'Naghten* standard. The fact that D was unable to conform his conduct to the requirements of the law is *irrelevant* — in other words, in federal suits, there is no "irresistible impulse" defense. [72]

C. **Raising and establishing the defense:** [73-76]

1. **Who raises defense:** In nearly all states, the insanity defense is an *affirmative defense*. That is, D is required to *come forward with evidence* showing that he is insane — only then does D's sanity enter the case. [73]

2. **Burden of persuasion:** After D bears his burden of production by showing some evidence of insanity, courts are *split* about who bears the "burden of persuasion," i.e., the burden of convincing the fact-finder on the insanity issue. In half the states, the prosecution must prove beyond a reasonable doubt that D is not insane. In the remaining states, D bears the burden of proving his insanity, but only by a "preponderance of the evidence." In the federal system, the rule is even tougher on D: D must prove insanity by "clear and convincing evidence." [73]

3. **Psychiatric examination:** A defendant who demonstrates that sanity will be a significant factor at his trial has a *constitutional right* to have the *assistance of a psychiatrist* at state expense. [*Ake v. Oklahoma*] [74-75]

   a. **Court-appointed expert:** Whether or not a psychiatrist is appointed for D's benefit, in most states the court has the power to appoint a theoretically impartial psychiatrist to conduct an *independent examination* of D, the results of which will be admissible at the trial. Often, this appointment is done at the request of the prosecution. [74]

4. Judge/jury allocation: If the case is tried before a jury, it is the jury that will have the task of deciding the merits of D's insanity defense, based on instructions from the judge. [75-76]

    a. Decision left to jury: Courts try hard to ensure that the ultimate decision is in fact made by the jury, *not by the psychiatric expert witnesses*. The jury is always free to disregard or disbelieve the expert witness' evaluation of D's condition. In fact, in federal trials, the federal insanity statute *prevents* either side's expert from even *testifying* as to the ultimate issue of D's sanity. See FRE 704(b). [75]

D. XYY chromosome defense: Some states allow D to buttress his insanity defense by showing that he has a certain chromosomal abnormality, the so-called "XYY chromosome defense," since XYY men are much more likely to commit certain kinds of crimes than men with normal chromosomes. [77]

E. Commitment following insanity acquittal: In nearly every state, if D is acquitted by reason of insanity, he will end up being *committed* to a mental institution. In some states (and in the federal system) the judge is *required by law* to commit D to a mental institution, without even a hearing as to present sanity. [77] (Such a mandatory commitment procedure does not violate the constitution. [*Jones v. U.S.*, 463 U.S. 354 (1983)]) In other states, the judge or the jury conducts a *hearing* to decide whether D is still insane and in need of commitment. [77-78]

1. Release: Once D has been committed to an institution and petitions for release, the release decision typically depends on: (1) whether D continues to be *insane*; and (2) whether D continues to be *dangerous*. [77-78]

    a. Constitutional requirements: The Due Process Clause of the federal Constitution places limits on the conditions under which an insantiy acquitee may be kept in an institution. The state may automatically commit an insanity acquitee without a hearing, as noted above. But the state must then periodically offer D the opportunity to be released. The state must release D if he bears the burden of proving that he is *either no longer insane* or *no longer dangerous*. (Probably the state may not impose on D any burden more difficult than the "preponderance of the evidence" standard for establishing either that he is no longer insane or that he is no longer dangerous.) [*Foucha v. Louisiana*, 112 S.Ct. 1780 (1992)] [78]

F. Fitness to stand trial: The insanity defense can also be asserted as a grounds for *not trying D* on the grounds that he is *incompetent to stand trial*. In general, D will be held to be incompetent to stand trial if he is unable to do *both* of the following: (1) *understand* the proceedings against him; and (2) *assist counsel* in his defense. [78-79]

1. Burden of proof: Many jurisdictions place the *burden of proof* as to incompetence upon the *defendant*. The U.S. Supreme Court has held that it is *not unconstitutional* for the state to place upon D the burden of proving by a preponderance of the evidence that he is incompetent to stand trial. [*Medina v. California*, 505 U.S. 437 (1992)] [78]

G. Insanity at time set for execution: If the defendant is insane *at the time set for his execution*, he may *not* be executed. Execution of a prisoner who is currently insane violates the Eighth Amendment's ban on cruel and unusual punishment. [*Ford v. Wainwright*, 477 U.S. 399 (1986)] [79]

II. DIMINISHED RESPONSIBILITY

A. Where and how used: Under the defense of *"diminished responsibility,"* a non-insane D argues that he suffers such a mental impairment that he is *unable to formulate the requisite intent*. [80-83]

    1. Homicide cases: The defense is allowed most often in *homicide* cases, usually ones where D is charged with first-degree murder and attempts to reduce it to second-degree by showing that he was incapable of the requisite premeditation. [82]

B. Insanity supersedes: More than half of the states *reject* the doctrine of diminished responsibility. Usually, they do so by holding that *no evidence* that D suffers from a mental disease or defect may be introduced, except pursuant to a formal insanity defense. [81]

III. AUTOMATISM

A. Defense generally: Under the *"automatism"* defense, D tries to show that a mental or physical condition prevented his act from being *voluntary*. [83-84]

    Example: While D is in bed with his wife, V, he strangles her. D shows that the strangling occurred while he was in the throes of an epileptic seizure, and that he was not conscious of what he was doing. If the fact-finder believes this story, D will be acquitted, because the strangling was not a voluntary act.

B. Generally allowed: Most courts allow the automatism defense as a distinct defense from the insanity defense. [83]

    1. Model Penal Code allows: Thus the Model Penal Code effectively recognizes the defense: D is not liable if he does not commit a "voluntary act," and a "voluntary act" is defined so as to exclude a "reflex or convulsion" or movement during "unconsciousness." MPC §2.01(1) and (2). [83]

    2. Other variants: Apart from the common instance of epileptic seizures, the automatism defense might be used where: (1) D lapsed into unconsciousness because of low blood sugar; (2) D was unable to control her actions because of Premenstrual Syndrome; or (3) D was unable to control his conduct because of Post Traumatic Stress Disorder (PTSD) suffered as the result of wartime experiences. [83]

IV. INTOXICATION

A. Voluntary intoxication: *Voluntary self-induced intoxication* does *not* *"excuse"* criminal conduct, in general. [84-89]

Example: D decides to rob a bank. Normally, he would be too timid to do so. However, he takes several drinks to increase his courage, and goes out and does the robbery. The fact that D was legally intoxicated when he committed the robbery will be completely irrelevant.

1. **Effect on mental state:** Although voluntary intoxication is not an "excuse," it may *prevent D from having the required mental state*. If so, D will not be guilty. [85]

   a. **General/specific intent distinction:** Traditionally, courts have distinguished between crimes of "general intent" and "specific intent." In a crime of "general intent," intoxication would never be a defense. In a crime requiring "specific intent" (i.e., intent to do an act other than the *actus reus*, such as the intent to commit a felony as required for burglary), D would be allowed to show that intoxication prevented him from having the requisite specific intent. (*Example:* If D was charged with assault with intent to kill, he could show that he was too drunk to have an intent to kill.) [85]

2. **Modern trend:** But modern courts usually don't distinguish between general and specific intent. Instead, modern courts generally allow D to show that his intoxication, even involuntary, *prevented him from having the requisite mental state*. See MPC §2.08(1) (self-induced intoxication "is not a defense unless it negatives an element of the offense"). [85]

3. **Negatives intent:** Thus even self-induced intoxication may prevent D from having the requisite *intent*, if the crime is defined so as to require intent. [86]

   Example: Suppose that in a particular jurisdiction, first degree murder is defined so that D must be shown to have had the intent to kill, and it is not enough for him to recklessly disregard the risk of death. At a time when D has no intent to do anyone harm, he gets drunk in a bar. He then shoots his pistol towards V, intending only to frighten V as a joke. Had D been sober, he would have realized that V would be hit and possibly killed. D should be acquitted, because his drunken state prevented him from having the required intent, namely an intent to kill.

   a. **Pre-intoxication intent:** Remember that it is not necessary for D to have the required intent *at the time of the actus reus*. Therefore, the fact that D's drunkenness prevented him from having the requisite intent at the time of the *actus reus* will not necessarily get him off the hook if he had the intent earlier. [87]

   Example: D, sober, decides to place a bomb under V's car, in the hopes that V will be blown up. D prepares the bomb. D then gets drunk. In his drunken stupor, he places the bomb under X's car; he is so drunk that he forgets why he is doing this, and at the moment the bomb is placed (and the moment a little while later when it goes off), D has no intent to harm anyone. D's drunkenness will not get him off the hook, because he had the requisite intent to kill at the moment he first prepared the bomb.

   b. **State may opt out of allowing this type of evidence:** Also, states are free (constitutionally speaking) to legislate that D's intoxication shall not be admitted as evidence negating the required mental state. [*Montana v. Egelhoff*] [85]

4. **Doesn't negate recklessness:** The most important single fact to remember about intoxication is that in most courts, intoxication *will not negate the element of recklessness*. In other words, if a particular element of a crime can be satisfied by a mental state of recklessness, D's intoxication will be irrelevant. [86]

    a. **Rape:** For instance, in many *"date rape"* cases, D argues that V consented, or at least that D believed that V was consenting. But in most states (and under the MPC), D's *reckless* mistake about whether V consented will satisfy the *mens rea* requirements for that aspect of the crime. Consequently, if D's drunkenness prevents him from realizing that V is not consenting, D's defense of "I thought she was consenting" will *fail*, if a sober defendant would have realized V's lack of consent. [88]

    b. **Voluntary manslaughter:** Similarly, D will generally not be allowed to introduce evidence of his intoxication in an attempt to get a murder charge reduced to *voluntary manslaughter*. This reduction is available only where D, acting in the heat of passion, acts under provocation that would have been enough to cause an ordinary person to lose control. But the assumption is that the ordinary man is sober, so D's drunkenness does not help him. [87]

        Example: D, after getting drunk in a bar, believes that V is attacking him with a deadly weapon. An ordinary sober man would have realized that V was merely holding his car keys. D shoots V in an honest attempt to save his own life, and now seeks a reduction from murder to voluntary manslaughter. Because the defense of self-defense is not available when D's belief in the need for that defense is reckless, D's drunkenness will not help him — the act of voluntarily getting drunk itself constitutes recklessness.

B. **Involuntary intoxication:** In the rare case where D can show that his intoxication was *"involuntary,"* D is much more likely to have a valid defense. [89-91]

    1. **Mistake as to nature of substance:** For instance, if D intentionally ingests a substance, but *mistakenly believes that it is not intoxicating*, he may have two related defenses: (1) a sort of "temporary insanity" defense, due to his temporary lack of mental capacity; and (2) a defense that the intoxication negated an element of the offense, even if the element was one for which recklessness will suffice. [90]

        Example: Assume the facts of the above example, except that D's intoxication is involuntary because his friend gave him LSD-laced punch. Now, D will probably win with his self-defense claims, since he did not act recklessly in getting drunk, and a reasonable person in his "unintentionally impaired" situation might have made the same mistake.

C. **Alcoholism and narcotics addiction:** Defendants who are *chronic alcoholics* or *narcotics addicts* sometimes try to use their condition as a defense. [91-92]

1. **Rejected:** But courts almost always *reject* any defense based upon these diseases. For instance, D might argue that because he was an alcoholic, his intoxication was "involuntary," and he should therefore be subject to the more liberal standards for "involuntary" as opposed to "voluntary" self-intoxication described above. But almost all courts would reject the "involuntary" defense for alcoholics and addicts. [91]

2. **Crimes to gain funds:** Similarly, many Ds commit crimes to *gain funds* to support their addictions. Arguments by such Ds that they lack free will or self-control, and should thus be acquitted, are even more certain to be rejected by the courts. [91]

CHAPTER 4

JUSTIFICATION AND EXCUSE

I. GENERAL PRINCIPLES

A. **Justification and excuse generally:** The twin doctrines of *"justification"* and *"excuse"* allow D to escape conviction even if the prosecution proves all elements of the case. There is no important distinction between those defenses referred to as "justification" and those referred to as "excuses." Here is a list of the main justifications/excuses: [98]

   1. *Duress*;

   2. *Necessity*;

   3. *Self-defense*;

   4. *Defense of others*;

   5. *Defense of property*;

   6. *Law enforcement* (arrest, prevention of crime and of escape);

   7. *Consent*;

   8. *Maintenance of domestic authority*;

   9. *Entrapment*.

B. **Effect of mistake:** The effect of a *mistake of fact* by D on these defenses has changed over time: [98-99]

   1. **Traditional view:** The traditional rule has generally been that D's *reasonable* mistake will not negate the privilege, but that an *unreasonable* mistake by D will negate the defense. [98]

   2. **Modern view:** But the modern trend, as exemplified by the MPC, is to hold that so long as D genuinely believes (even if *unreasonably*) that the facts are such that the defense is merited, the defense will stand. (There is an exception if D is charged with an act that may be committed "recklessly" or "negligently" — here, he loses the defense if the mistake was "reckless" or "negligent.") [99]

II. DURESS

A. General nature: D is said to have committed a crime under *"duress"* if he performed the crime because of a *threat of*, or *use of*, *force* by a third person sufficiently strong that D's will was *overborne*. The term applies to force placed upon D's *mind*, not his body. [100]

> **Example:** X forces D to rob Y, by threatening D with immediate death if he does not. D will be able to raise the defense of duress.

B. Elements: D must establish the following elements for duress: [100]

    1. Threat: A *threat* by a third person, [100]

    2. Fear: Which produces a *reasonable fear* in D, [100]

    3. Imminent danger: That he will suffer *immediate* or *imminent*, [100]

    4. Bodily harm: *Death* or *serious bodily injury*. [100]

C. Model Penal Code test: Under the MPC, the defense is available where the threat to D was sufficiently great that "a person of *reasonable firmness* in [D's] situation would have been *unable to resist*." MPC §2.09(1). [100]

D. Not available for homicide: Traditionally, the defense of duress is not available if D is charged with *homicide*, i.e., the intentional killing of another. [100-101]

> **Example:** D is a member of a gang run by X. X and the other gang members tell D that if D does not kill V, an innocent witness to one of the group's crimes, they will kill D immediately. D reasonably and honestly believes this threat. D kills V. Few if any courts will allow D to assert the defense of duress on these facts, because he is charged with the intentional killing of another. (The result probably would not change even if D had originally been coerced into joining the gang.)

    1. Reduction of crime: A few states allow duress to *reduce the severity* of an intentional homicide (e.g., from first-degree premeditated murder to second-degree spur-of-the-moment murder).

    2. Felony-murder: Also, duress is accepted as a defense to a charge of *felony-murder*. (*Example:* D is coerced into driving X to a robbery site. During the robbery, X intentionally kills V, a witness, to stop V from calling the police. Although in most states D would ordinarily be liable for felony-murder, most states would allow him to raise the defense of duress here.) [101]

E. Imminence of threatened harm: D must be threatened with *imminent* or *immediate* harm, in most courts. Thus the threat of *future harm* is not sufficient. But modern courts are more willing to relax this requirement. [101]

> **Example:** D witnesses X kill V. X phones D to say that if D testifies against X at X's murder trial, X will kill D after the trial. D lies on the stand to avoid implicating X. D is then charged with perjury. Traditionally, most courts would not allow D to raise the defense of duress, since the threatened harm was not imminent. But a modern court, and the Model Penal Code, might not impose this requirement of immediacy.

F. Threat directed at person other than defendant: Traditionally, most courts have required that the threatened harm be directed *at the defendant*. [101]

1. **Modern view:**   But modern courts, and the MPC, are more liberal. Many courts now recognize the defense where the threat is made against a member of D's *family*. The MPC imposes no requirement at all about who must be threatened (but remember that under the MPC the test is whether a person of "reasonable firmness" would be coerced, and this may be hard to prove if D is coerced by the threat of harm to a complete stranger). [102]

G. Defendant subjects self to danger: Nearly all courts deny the defense to a D who has *voluntarily placed himself in a situation* where there is a substantial probability that he will be subjected to duress.

> **Example:** D voluntarily joins an organized crime group known to have the policy of *omerta*, or death to anyone who informs on the gang. D is called to the witness stand, and lies to protect other gang members. D will not be able to raise the defense of duress, since he voluntarily or at least recklessly placed himself in a position where he was likely to be subjected to duress. [102]

H. Guilt of coercer: Even though the person subjected to duress may have a valid defense on that ground, this will not absolve the person who did the coercing. [102]

> **Example:** A forces B to rob V, by threatening to kill B if he does not. Even though B probably has a duress defense to a robbery charge, A will be guilty of robbery, on an accomplice theory.

III. NECESSITY

A. Generally: The defense of *"necessity"* may be raised when D has been compelled to commit a criminal act, not by coercion from another human being, but by *non-human events*. The essence of the defense is that D has chosen the *lesser of two evils*. [103-106]

> **Example:** D needs to get his seriously ill wife to the hospital. He therefore violates the speed limit. Assuming that there is no available alternative, such as an ambulance, D may claim the defense of necessity, since the traffic violations were a lesser evil than letting his wife get sicker or die.

B. Requirements for defense: The principal requirements which D must meet for the necessity defense are: [104]

1. **Greater harm:**   The harm sought to be avoided is *greater* than the harm committed; [104]

2. **No alternative:**   There is no third *alternative* that would also avoid the harm, yet would be non-criminal or a less serious crime; [104]

3. **Imminence:**   The harm is *imminent*, not merely future; and [104]

4. **Situation not caused by D:**   The situation was not brought about by D's carelessly or recklessly *putting himself in a position* where the emergency would arise. [104]

Note: In contrast to the case of duress, the harm D is seeking to avoid need not be serious bodily harm, but may be non-serious bodily harm or even *property damage*.

C. **Homicide:** Courts have traditionally been very reluctant to permit the necessity defense where D is charged with an *intentional killing*. [105-106]

1. **Model Penal Code view:** The MPC does not rule out the necessity defense even in intentional homicide cases. But under the MPC, one may not sacrifice one life to save another, since the Code requires the choice of the lesser of two evils, not merely the equal of two evils, and all lives are presumed to be of equal value. But if a life can be sacrificed to save two or more lives, the Code would allow the defense. (*Example:* D, a mountain climber, is roped to V, who has fallen over a cliff. If the only alternative is that both climbers will die, D may cut the rope even if this will inevitably cause V's death.) [106]

D. **Economic necessity not sufficient:** The harm that confronts D may be of a non-bodily nature, such as damage to his property. But courts do not accept the defense of *"economic necessity."* (*Example:* D, an unemployed worker, may not steal food and then claim the defense of necessity. But if he is actually about to starve to death, then the defense may be allowed.) [106]

E. **Civil disobedience:** The necessity defense is almost always rejected in cases of *"civil disobedience."* [106]

Example: To protest U.S. military assistance to El Salvador, the Ds trespass in their local IRS office, splash blood on the walls, and do other criminal acts to draw attention to why U.S. policy is bad. *Held*, the Ds' necessity defense is invalid, because there were lawful ways of attempting to bring about changed government policies. [*U.S. v. Schoon*]

IV. SELF-DEFENSE

A. **Self-defense generally:** There is a general right to *defend oneself* against the use of *unlawful force*. When successfully asserted, the defense is a complete one, leading to acquittal. [107]

B. **Requirements:** The following requirements must generally be met: [107]

1. **Resist unlawful force:** D must have been resisting the *present or imminent use* of *unlawful force*; [107]

2. **Force must not be excessive:** The degree of force used by D must not have been *more than was reasonably necessary* to defend against the threatened harm; [107]

3. **Deadly force:** The force used by D may not have been *deadly* (i.e., intended or likely to cause death or serious bodily injury) unless the danger being resisted was also deadly force; [107]

4. **Aggressor:** D must not have been the *aggressor*, unless: (1) he was a *non-deadly aggressor* confronted with the unexpected use of deadly force; or (2) he *withdrew* after his initial aggression, and the other party continued to attack; and [107]

5. **Retreat:** (In some states) D must not have been in a position from which he could *retreat* with complete safety, unless: (1) the attack took place in D's dwelling; or (2) D used only non-deadly force. [107]

C. **Requirement of "unlawful force":** Self-defense applies only where D is resisting force that is *unlawful*. [107-108]

   1. **Other party commits tort or crime:** Generally, this means that the other party must be committing a *crime or tort*. [107]

      a. **Other party has privilege:** Thus if the other party, even though he is using force, is *entitled* to do so, the force is not unlawful, and D may not use force to defend against it. For instance, a property owner who is using non-deadly force to defend his property against attempted theft is not using "unlawful" force. [107]

         Example: D tries to pick V's pocket. V, not a trained or dangerous fist-fighter, hits D lightly with his fist. V has a privilege to use reasonable non-deadly force to defend his property, so V is not using "unlawful" force, and D therefore has no right to use any force in self-defense.

      b. **Other party uses excessive force:** However, if the other party is entitled to use some degree of force, but uses *more than is lawfully allowed*, the excess will probably be treated as unlawful, and D may resist it by using force himself. [107]

         Example: On the facts of the above example, suppose that V pulls out a gun and aims it at D and starts to pull the trigger, even though V realizes that D is unarmed and not dangerous. D may probably tackle V and knock away the gun, because V has gone beyond the scope of the privilege to use reasonable force to defend property.

      c. **Reasonable mistake by D:** If D makes a *reasonable mistake* about the unlawful status of the force being used against her, she will nonetheless be protected. (In general, the defense of self-defense is not voided by a reasonable mistake.) But in most states, D will lose the defense if her mistaken belief that the opposing force was unlawful was unreasonble. See the further discussion of mistake in self-defense below. [108-109]

D. **Degree of force:** D may not use more force than is *reasonably necessary* to protect himself. [108]

   1. **Use of non-deadly force:** D may use *non-deadly force* to resist virtually any kind of unlawful force (assuming that the level of non-deadly force D uses is not more than is necessary to meet the threat). [108]

      a. **No need to retreat:** D may use non-deadly force without *retreating* even if retreat could be safely done. [108]

      b. **Prevention of theft:** D may use non-deadly force to resist the other person's attempted theft of *property*. [108]

   2. **Deadly force:** D may defend himself with *deadly force* only if the attack threatens D with *serious bodily harm*. [108-109]

a. **Definition of "deadly force":** Remember that "deadly force" is usually defined as force that is *intended or likely* to cause *death or serious bodily harm*. [109]

    i. **Firing firearm:** Generally, if D purposely *fires a gun* in the direction of another person, this will be considered use of deadly force. See MPC §3.11(2).

    ii. **Result irrelevant:** The *actual result* of the deadly force is *irrelevant*, either way.

        Example 1: D shoots at V with a gun, and misses him entirely. D has used deadly force, and will be liable for assault and/or battery if deadly force was not permissible.

        Example 2: D, not a particularly capable fistfighter, swings his fist at V's stomach, intending to immobilize V. V unexpectedly suffers a ruptured spleen, and dies. D will not be deemed to have used deadly force, since the force was neither intended nor likely to cause death or serious bodily harm.

    iii. **Threats:** D's verbal *threat* to use deadly force does *not* itself constitute use of deadly force, provided that D *does not intend to carry out the threat*. (MPC §3.11(2))

b. **Nature of attack:** D may use deadly force to defend against the threat of *serious bodily harm*. Most courts also allow it to protect against *kidnapping* and forcible *rape*. [109]

c. **Effect of mistake:** As with other sorts of mistakes, if D is reasonably mistaken in the belief that he is threatened with serious bodily harm, he will not lose the right to reply with deadly force. [109]

E. **Imminence of harm:** The harm being defended against must be reasonably *imminent*. [109]

1. **MPC liberal view:** The MPC construes this requirement somewhat liberally — D may use force to protect himself against unlawful force that will be used *"on the present occasion."* [110]

    Example 1: V tells D on the telephone, "I will kill you tomorrow." D goes to V's house and shoots V. D may not claim self-defense, because V's threat was not for imminent force.

    Example 2: D is stranded in his broken-down car in the middle of a neighborhood he does not know well. V sees D defenseless, and says, "I'm gonna go get my friends and we're gonna come back and strip the tires off your car." Under the MPC, D may use non-violent force to prevent V from getting his friends, because the threat is that unlawful force will be used "on the present occasion," even though the force is not completely imminent.

2. **Withdrawal by aggressor:** One consequence of the requirement that the danger be imminent is that if the *aggressor withdraws* from the conflict, the victim *loses his right to use force,* at least where the withdrawal should reasonably be interpreted as indicating that the danger is over. (But if the assail-

ant seems to be getting *reinforcements*, that's not a "withdrawal," and the victim can keep using force.)

Example: V and D are friends. They get into a verbal dispute, and V takes a swing at D. D starts to swing back. V stops swinging and says, "Wait a minute, we've always been friends, let's stop fighting." D (who has no reason to believe that V's offer to stop the fight is phony) continues to beat V up. D will not be able to use the defense of self-defense if he is charged with battery occurring after V's offer to stop — once V withdrew from the conflict, the occasion requiring self-defense was over.

F. Aggressor may not claim self-defense: If D is the *initial aggressor* — that is, one who strikes the first blow or otherwise precipitates the conflict — he may ordinarily *not claim self-defense*. [110-111]

> **Example:** D starts a fight in a bar with V, by brandishing a knife at V. V, using his own knife, tries to cut D's knife-wielding hand. D hits V in the face with his other hand, injuring him. D cannot claim self-defense, because he precipitated the conflict by brandishing the knife.

1. Aggression without actual force: D can be treated as an aggressor, and thus lose the right of self-defense, even if D did not actually strike the first blow. It is enough if D did an *unlawful* (i.e., tortious or criminal) act which *"provoked"* the physical conflict. [110]

> **Example:** The above example illustrates this principle — D has merely brandished the knife, not used it, yet he is deemed the aggressor.

2. Exceptions: There are two *exceptions* to the rule that the one who is the aggressor may not claim self-defense: [111]

a. Non-deadly force met with deadly force: First, if D provokes the exchange but uses no actual force or only *non-deadly force*, and the other party *responds with deadly force*, D may then defend himself (even with deadly force, if necessary). [111]

> **Example:** D attacks V with his fists. V defends by knocking D down, then starting to smash D's head against the wall, so that D is in danger of being killed or badly hurt. D manages to pull a knife, and kills X. Probably D is entitled to a claim of self-defense. V, by meeting non-deadly force with deadly force, was acting unlawfully, and D will be permitted to save his life. (All of this assumes that D did not have the duty and opportunity to retreat, a duty which he might have in some states under some circumstances.)

b. Withdrawal: Second, if D *withdraws from the conflict*, and the other party (V) initiates a *second conflict*, D may use non-deadly force (and even deadly force if he is threatened with death or serious bodily harm). This is true even if D started the initial conflict with the use of deadly force. All of this is so because once D (the initial aggressor) withdraws, the conflict is over, so V's use of force becomes unlawful force that D can defend against. [111]

Example: In a bar, D attacks V with his fists, hits him several times, and knocks him down. D leaves the bar and gets into his car, intending to drive away. V, after getting up, follows D outside, and attacks D with his fists, just as D is getting to the car. D swings back, hitting and injuring V. D will be entitled to claim self-defense, because he withdrew from the conflict, and V was in effect starting a new conflict in which V was really the aggressor.

G. **Retreat:** Some states (but not yet a majority) require that if D could *safely retreat*, he must do so *rather than use deadly force*. [112-113]

1. **No retreat before non-deadly force:** No states require retreat before the use of *non-deadly force*. [112]

   Example: V attacks D with non-deadly force. D could withdraw from the encounter with complete safety, by getting into his car and driving away. D instead stands his ground and fights back with his fists, with which he is not especially proficient. In all states, even those with a general "duty to retreat," D is privileged, because no reatreat is ever required before the use of non-deadly force.

2. **Retreat only required where it can be safely done:** The retreat rule, in states requiring it, only applies where D could retreat with *complete safety* to himself and others. Also, if D reasonably but mistakenly believes that retreat cannot be safely done, he will be protected. [112]

3. **Retreat in D's dwelling:** Those states requiring retreat do not generally require it where the attack takes place in *D's dwelling*. [112-113]

   Example: D invites V to D's house, and the two parties get into a dispute. V attacks D with a knife. D could easily go into a bedroom which can be locked from the inside; while there, he could readily call the police. Instead, D grabs a knife — the only reasonably available means of combatting V, given D's inferior martial arts skills — and seriously wounds V. Even in states imposing a general duty of retreat, D is exempt from the duty here, since the attack is taking place in his own dwelling.

   a. **Not applicable if D was aggressor:** But this exception for a dwelling does not apply if D was the *aggressor*. [112]

   b. **Assailant also resident:** Also, some courts hold that the dwelling exception to the retreat requirement does not apply where the *assailant is also a resident* of the dwelling. But other courts, probably representing the more modern view, do not remove the exception in this situation. [113]

   Example: H and W are married. H attacks W at home. W could easily retreat to a lockable bedroom, but instead uses deadly force (though no more than reasonably necessary) to rebut the attack. Of the states requiring a duty to retreat, most would give W an exemption because she is in her dwelling, but a few would impose the duty of retreat even here because H is also a resident of the dwelling.

H. Effect of mistake: The effect of a *mistake* by D concerning the need for self-defense will depend largely on whether the mistake is *"reasonable."* Observe that there are various kinds of mistakes that D might make concerning the need for self-defense: (1) a mistaken belief that he is about to be attacked; (2) a mistake in belief that the force used against him is unlawful; (3) a mistaken belief that only deadly force will suffice to repel the threat; or (4) a mistaken belief that retreat could not be accomplished safely. [113-115]

1. **Reasonable:** As long as D's mistaken belief as to any of these points is *reasonable*, all courts will allow him to claim self-defense. [113]

    Example: While D is walking down the street one evening, V says, "Your money or your life," and points what appears to be a gun at D. In fact, the "gun" is merely V's finger poking through V's jacket. A reasonable person in D's position would be likely to believe that there was a real gun. D also reasonably believes that V may shoot D even if D gives up the property, because this has happened in the neighborhood on several recent occasions. D pulls his own gun and shoots V to death. Later evidence shows that V, a career mugger, would never have dreamt of actually doing physical harm to a victim. Because D's mistakes (about the existence of a gun, and about whether it would be used against him) were "reasonable," D is entitled to claim self-defense despite the mistakes.

2. **Unreasonable mistake:** But if D's mistake is *unreasonable*, most states hold that he *loses* the right to claim self-defense. [113-115]

    Example: D travels on a New York City subway while carrying an unlicensed loaded pistol. Four youths approach him, and one states, "Give me $5." D pulls out the gun and shoots at each of the four, one of whom is sitting on a bench and apparently posing no imminent threat to D at the time. D later admits that he did not think the youths had a gun, but that he had a fear, based on prior times when he was mugged, that he might be maimed as a result of this encounter.

    Held, D's claim of self-defense is valid only if he "reasonably believed" that one of the victims was about to use deadly physical force or about to commit one of certain violent crimes upon him. This imposes an objective standard, by which D's conduct must be that of a reasonable person in D's situation. [*People v. Goetz,* 497 N.E.2d 41 (N.Y. 1986)]

    a. **MPC/minority view:** A minority of courts, and the Model Penal Code, hold that even an *unreasonable* (but genuine) mistake as to the need for self-defense will protect D. This is, in a sense, the more "modern" view. (But if the crime is one that can be committed by a "reckless" or "negligent" state of mind, even under the MPC D's reckless or negligent mistake as to the need for self-defense will not absolve him.) [115]

    b. **Not totally subjective:** Even in courts following the majority "objective" standard for reasonableness of mistake, the standard is not completely objective.

      i. D's physical disadvantages: Courts generally take D's *physical disadvantages* into account in determining the reasonableness of his mistake. [114]

      Example: If D is a small woman, and V is a large man, obviously it is reasonable for D to fear harm more readily than if the roles were reversed.

      ii. D's past experiences and knowledge: Similarly, courts generally hold that D's *past experiences* and knowledge are to be taken into account in determining whether D's mistake was a "reasonable" one. [114]

      Example: In *People v. Goetz, supra,* D was allowed to put on evidence that he was previously mugged, thus contributing to his belief that danger to him was likely in the present encounter.

  c. Intoxication: If the cause of D's unreasonable mistake as to the need for self-defense is his *intoxication*, all courts agree that the intoxication does not excuse the mistake, and D will not be entitled to a claim of self-defense. [115]

  Example: D gets drunk in a bar. He mistakenly believes that V is about to shoot him. He instead draws first, and shoots V to death. Had D been sober, he would have realized that V was not about to attack him. All courts agree that because D's mistake was caused by his intoxication, he loses the claim of self-defense.

I. Battered women and self-defense: Where a woman *kills her spouse* because she believes this is the only way she can protect herself against ongoing *battering* by him, courts normally do not change the generally-applicable rules of self-defense. [115-118]

  1. Standard for "reasonableness": In a battered-woman case, the courts try not to allow too much subjectivity into the determination of whether the woman has acted reasonably. Most courts make the test, What would a reasonable woman do in the defendant's situation, taking into account the prior history of abuse, but not taking into account the particular psychology of the woman herself (e.g., that she is unusually depressed, or aggressive, or otherwise different)? [117]

  2. Imminence of danger: Nearly all courts continue to require in battered-woman cases, as in other cases, that self-defense be used only where the danger is *imminent*. For instance, courts have not modified the traditional requirement of imminent danger to cover situations where the woman's counter-strike *does not come during a physical confrontation*. Thus D would probably be convicted of murder for killing her abusing husband, V, in any of the following situations:

    ❏ V, after abusing D, has *gone to sleep*, and D shoots him in the head while he sleeps;

    ❏ D *waits* for V to return home, and kills him immediately, before any kind of argument has arisen; and

❑ D *arranges with someone else* (at the most extreme, a hired killer) to kill V.

(But if the absense of confrontation is merely a *momentary lull* in the attack — e.g., V's back is temporarily turned, but D reasonably believes that the attack will resume any moment — then the requirement of imminence is typically found to be satisfied.) [117-118]

3. **Battered child:** Essentially the same rules apply where a *battered child* kills the abusive parent or step-parent, typically the father. Thus many courts allow psychologists to testify about a "battered child's syndrome." But courts apply the imminence requirement in the case of killings by children, just as in the case of killings by the wife. [118]

J. Resisting arrest: A person's right to use force to *resist an unlawful arrest* is much more limited than his right to use force to resist other kinds of unlawful attack. [118]

1. **Deadly force:** Virtually no state allows a suspect to use *deadly force* to resist an unlawful arrest. [118]

2. **Non-deadly force:** A substantial minority of states now bar even the use of *non-deadly force* against an unlawful arrest. The MPC, for instance, refuses to allow the use of force to resist an unlawful arrest, if D knows that the person doing the arresting is a police officer. MPC §3.04(2)(a)(i). [119]

Example: Officer comes to D's house to arrest D for a felony committed a long time ago, as to which the police have long suspected D. Officer does not have a warrant. D knows that Officer is a police officer, but D also knows that constitutionally, a warrant is required for entering a suspect's house to arrest him unless there are exigent circumstances. Although D thus knows that the arrest is unlawful, D may not use even non-deadly force — such as punching or kicking the officer — to resist arrest, under minority/MPC view.

a. **Traditional view:** But the traditional view, probably still followed by a bare majority of states, is that a suspect *may* use *non-deadly* force to resist an unlawful arrest. [119]

3. **Excessive force:** Nearly all states allow the use of non-deadly force to resist an arrest made with *excessive force*, or in any situation where D reasonably believes that he will be *injured*. (But even here, deadly force may not be used.) [119]

Example: In a Rodney King-like scenario, D is arrested properly, then kicked and beaten with truncheons for several minutes, while he does not resist. Nearly all states would allow D to punch or kick the arresting officer and to run away, in order to escape the blows. But D could not pull out a knife and stab the arresting officer, even in this extreme situation.

K. Injury to third persons: If while D is using force to protect himself, he *injures a bystander*, his criminal liability with respect to this injury will be measured by the same standards as if it was the assailant who was injured. [119]

1. **D not reckless or negligent:** Thus if D's conduct was not reckless or negligent with respect to the bystander, he will not be liable, assuming that self-defense as to the assailant was proper. [119]

2. **Recklessness or negligence:** Conversely, if D *is* reckless or negligent with respect to the risk of injuring a bystander, D may not claim self-defense if the charge is one that requires only recklessness or negligence (as the case may be). [120]

   Example: X, wielding a knife, attacks D in a crowded bar. D pulls out what he knows to be a very powerful gun, and shoots at X. The bullet misses X and kills Y, a bystander. Even if, as seems likely, D had a general right to use deadly force in his own defense in this situation, a jury could find that D was reckless as to the risk of killing a bystander. If the jury so concluded, D would then be guilty of voluntary manslaughter, because his mental state with respect to Y — recklessness — suffices for manslaughter.

L. **"Imperfect" self-defense:** D may be entitled to a claim of *"imperfect"* self-defense, sufficient to reduce his crime from murder to *voluntary manslaughter*, if D killed in self-defense but failed to satisfy one of the requirements for acquittal by reason of self-defense. [120]

   1. **Unreasonable mistake:** Thus if D makes an *unreasonable mistake* as to the need for force, or as to the unlawfulness of the other party's force, most states give him the claim of imperfect self-defense. [120]

   2. **Initial aggressor:** Similarly, if D was the *initial aggressor*, and thus lost the right to claim true self-defense, he can still use imperfect self-defense to get his crime reduced to manslaughter. [120]

      Example: X insults D. D pulls a knife and advances towards X. X pulls a gun and is about to shoot D. With his spare hand, D pulls a gun and shoots X to death. Because D was the aggressor — and he was the first to use physical violence rather than mere words — he does not have a "full" claim of self-defense. However, he met all the requirements for use of deadly force except that he not have been the aggressor, so he'll probably be entitled to have the charge reduced from murder to voluntary manslaughter.

   3. **Model Penal Code view:** The MPC similarly says that an unreasonable belief in the need for deadly force will give rise to manslaughter if D was reckless in his mistake. (If D's unreasonable belief was merely negligent, under the MPC he cannot be charged with anything higher than criminally negligent homicide.) [120]

M. **Burden of proof:** Nearly all states make a claim of self-defense an *affirmative defense*, i.e., one which must be raised, in the first instance, by D. Many states also place the *burden of persuasion* on D, requiring him to prove by a *preponderance of the evidence* that all the requirements for the defense are met. It is constitutional for a state to put this burden of persuasion upon the defendant. [*Martin v. Ohio*, 480 U.S. 228 (1987)] [120]

V. DEFENSE OF OTHERS

A. Right to defend others in general: A person may use force to *defend another* in roughly the same circumstances in which he would be justified in using force in his own defense. [121]

B. Relation between defendant and aided person: At common law, a person was permitted to defend only his *relatives*. [121]

1. Modern rule: Today, however, most courts and statutes permit one to use force to defend anyone, even a *total stranger*, from threat of harm from another. [121]

C. Requirements: D must generally meet the following requirements in order to have a claim of defense of others: [121]

1. Danger to other: He reasonably believes that the other person is in *imminent danger* of *unlawful bodily harm*; [121]

2. Degree of force: The *degree of force* used by D is no greater than that which seems reasonably *necessary* to prevent the harm; and [121]

3. Belief in the other person's right to use force: D reasonably believes that the party being assisted would have the right to use in his *own defense* the force that D proposes to use in assistance. [121]

D. Retreat: Most courts hold that D may not use deadly force if he has reason to believe that the person being aided could *retreat with safety*. Thus the MPC requires that D at least "try to cause" the person being aided to retreat if retreat with safety is possible (although D may then use deadly force if his attempt at causing retreat fails). [121]

1. Home of either party: Probably retreat is not necessary if the place where the encounter takes place is the *dwelling* or *place of business* of either the defendant or the party assisted. [121]

E. Mistake as to who is aggressor: Courts are split about the effect of D's mistake concerning *who was really the aggressor*. [122]

1. Traditional view: The traditional view, called the *"alter ego"* rule, is that D "stands in the shoes" of the person he aids. Under this view, if the person aided would not have had the right to use that degree of force in his own defense, D's claim fails. [122]

Example: D observes two middle-aged men beating and struggling with an 18-year-old youth; D reasonably concludes that these two are unlawfully attacking the youth. D hits X, one of the older men, in an attempt to get him off the youth; he breaks X's jaw. It turns out that X and the other older man were plainclothes police officers trying to make a lawful arrest of the youth for an attempted mugging. Under the traditional "alter ego" view, since the youth did not have the privilege to hit back to prevent a lawful arrest, D did not have that privilege to do so for the youth's benefit.

2. Modern view: But the modern view is that so long as D's belief that unlawful force is being used against the aidee is *reasonable*, D may assert a claim of defense of others even if his evaluation turns out to have been wrong. Thus the MPC gives the right based on "the circumstances as the actor believes them to be...." (*Example:* On the facts of the above example, the modern/MPC view would permit D to use the claim of defense of others.) [122]

VI. DEFENSE OF PROPERTY

A. **Generally:** A person has a limited right to use force to *defend his or her property* against a wrongful taking. [123]

1. **Non-deadly force:** *Non-deadly force* may be used to prevent a *wrongful entry on one's real property*, and the *wrongful taking of one's personal property*. [123]

2. **Reasonable degree:** The degree of force used must not be *more than appears reasonably necessary* to prevent the taking. For instance, if one in D's position should believe that a *request to desist* would be sufficient, force may not be used. [123]

   Example of proper use of non-deadly force: D sees X attempting to break into D's car, parked on the street. At least if D has no reason to believe that words alone will dissuade X, D may punch X, spray mace at him, or otherwise use non-deadly force to stop the break-in.

3. **Subsequent use of deadly force:** If D begins by using a reasonable degree of non-deadly force, and the wrongdoer responds with a personal attack, then the rules governing self-defense come into play. It may then become permissible for D to use deadly force to protect himself. [123]

B. **Deadly force:** In general, one may *not use deadly force* to defend personal property or real estate. [123-124]

1. **Dwelling:** However, in limited circumstances, one may be able to use deadly force to defend *one's dwelling*. [123-124]

   a. **Modern view requires violent felony:** Under the modern view, deadly force may be used *only where the intrusion appears to pose a danger of a violent felony*. Under this view, a homeowner may *not* shoot a *suspected burglar*, unless the the owner believes the burglar to be *armed* or *dangerous to the safety of the inhabitants*. [123]

C. **Mechanical devices:** A property owner may ordinarily use *mechanical devices* to protect his property. [124-125]

1. **Non-deadly devices:** A device that is *non-deadly* (i.e., one that is not likely or intended to cause death or serious bodily harm) may be used whenever it is *reasonable* to do so. Thus a property owner may put *barbed wire* or a *spiked fence* (but not an electrical fence) around his property. (Under the MPC, the owner must give a *warning* to intruders about the device unless it is one that is "customarily used for such a purpose.") [124]

2. **Deadly force:** Courts are much less likely to allow a mechanical device that constitutes *deadly force*. [124]

a. **Traditional view:**   Traditionally, D could use a mechanical deadly device if the situation were one in which D himself could use deadly force. [124]

Example: D, a homeowner, sets up a spring gun attached to the door. The gun shoots X, who turns out to be an armed and dangerous burglar. Under the traditional view, D would not be guilty of anything, since he would have had the right to use deadly force against the burglar personally.

b. **Modern view prohibits:**   But the *modern* view *prohibits* the use of such devices altogether, even if they happen to go off in a situation where the owner himself would have been justified in using deadly force. [124]

Example: Under the modern/MPC view, on the facts of the above example, D would be guilty of murder if the gun went off and shot to death even an armed and dangerous burglar.

D. **Recapture of chattel and re-entry on land:**   A person has a privilege to use reasonable force to *re-take* his personal or real property. [125]

1. **Personal property:**   Where personal property has been taken, all courts agree that D may use reasonable non-deadly force to *recapture* it, provided that he does so *immediately* following the taking. [125]

    a. **Interval:**   But if a substantial period of time has *elapsed* since the taking, courts are split. The modern/MPC view is that D may use force to retake his property at any time, provided that the owner believes that the other has no "claim of right" to possess the object. (*Example:* D's bicycle is stolen, and he sees X riding down the street on it several days later. If D reasonably believes he recognizes X as being the thief, he can use reasonable force to take back the bicycle. But if he sees that X is not the thief, and believes that X may have bought it from the thief, D cannot use reasonable force because X would be acting under a "claim of right to possession" of the bike, even though X does not have title.) [125]

2. **Re-entry on real estate:**   Similarly, under the modern view, D may use force to *re-enter* his real estate, even if there has been a lapse of time, if the non-owner has no claim of right to possession and it would be a hardship for the owner to wait to get a court order. [125]

VII. LAW ENFORCEMENT (ARREST; PREVENTION OF ESCAPE AND CRIME)

A. **General privilege:**   A person engaged in *law enforcement* has a general privilege to violate the law when it is reasonable to do so. [125]

Example: D, a police officer, is chasing a fleeing convict. D may drive his car through a stop light, or 20 m.p.h. above the speed limit, provided that a reasonable officer in D's position would believe that this was necessary to recapture the escapee.

1. **Use of force:** The main question that arises is whether an officer's *use of force* was lawful. See below. [126]

B. **Arrest:** A law enforcement officer is privileged to use reasonable force in *effecting an arrest*. However, this privilege exists only where the arrest being made is a *lawful one*. [126-129]

1. **Summary of arrest rules:** The rules for determining whether an arrest is lawful depend in part on whether the arrest is for a felony or a misdemeanor: [126]

   a. **Felony:** At common law, a police officer may make an arrest for a *felony* if: (1) it was commited in the officer's presence; or (2) it was committed outside the officer's presence, but the officer has reasonable cause to believe that it was committed, and by the person to be arrested. [126]

      i. **Warrant not required:** In these situations, the arresting officer is *not required* to have a *warrant*.

   b. **Misdemeanor:** An officer may also arrest for a *misdemeanor*. [126]

      i. **Warrant:** If the misdemeanor occurred in the officer's presence, no warrant is required. But at common law, if the misdemeanor occurred outside of the officer's presence, then a warrant *is* required (though this rule has often been changed by statute).

2. **Arrest resisted:** If an officer who is attempting to make a lawful arrest meets resistance, he may use reasonable force to protect himself. In general, the rules applicable to self-defense apply here. [126]

   a. **No retreat:** There is one important difference: even in those states requiring one to retreat before using deadly force where it is safe to do so, an officer is *not required to retreat* rather than make the arrest. [126]

3. **Fleeing suspect:** An officer may use *non-deadly force* wherever it is reasonably necessary to arrest a *fleeing* suspect. But there are important limits on the use of *deadly* force where the suspect is fleeing: [127-128]

   a. **Misdemeanor:** If the suspect is fleeing from an arrest for a *misdemeanor*, deadly force may *not* be used against him. [127]

      Example: If the police are chasing a garden-variety speeder, they may not shoot at him or at his car. If they shoot at the tires and cause a fatal crash, they will be liable for manslaughter, since shooting a gun in the direction of a person, even without intent to hit him, is generally considered to be the use of deadly force.

   b. **Non-dangerous felony:** Where the suspect is fleeing an arrest for a *non-dangerous* felony, the modern, and Supreme Court, view is that the police may *not* use deadly force to catch the suspect. [127-128]

      Example: Where an officer is chasing an escaping burglar whom the officer has no reason to believe is armed, the officer may not shoot the burglar in the back. This is true even if the burglar ignores a command to stop and raise his hands. [*Tennessee v. Garner*, 471 U.S. 1 (1985)]

c. **Dangerous felony:** If the felony or the felon is a *"dangerous"* one, the arresting officer may use deadly force if that is the only way that the arrest can be made. The issue is whether the suspect poses a threat of *serious physical harm*, either to the officer or to others. [128]

Example: The typical car thief or burglar is not "dangerous," and thus cannot be stopped with deadly force. But the typical armed bank robbery suspect, and perhaps the typical rapist, is probably "dangerous" and thus may be stopped with deadly force.

4. **Arrest by private citizen:** A *private citizen* who is attempting to make a "citizen's arrest" may use reasonable non-deadly force. The private citizen may also use deadly force, but only in extremely limited circumstances: the citizen takes the *full risk of a mistake*. [129]

Example: If it turns out that no dangerous felony was actually committed, or that the suspect was not the one who committed it, the citizen will be criminally liable for death or injury to the suspect.

a. **More extreme view:** Some states, and the MPC, go further: they do not allow private citizens to use deadly force *at all* to make a citizen's arrest, even if the suspect really *has* committed a dangerous felony.

b. **Escape of non-deadly felon:** Virtually all courts agree that a private citizen, like a police officer, may not use deadly force to stop a fleeing felon if the felon poses *no immediate threat* to the citizen or to others. That is, the rationale of *Tennessee v. Garner* (see *supra*) presumably applies to attempted arrests by private citizens just as to attempted arrests by police officers. (Of course, this rule would be invoked only where the court rejects — as most courts do — the MPC's blanket rule that the arresting citizen may *never* use deadly force, even to arrest a felon who *is* dangerous.) [129]

C. **Prevention of escape:** An officer may use reasonable force to *prevent the escape* of a suspect who has already been arrested. The above rules apply in this situation as well. [129]

D. **Crime prevention:** Similarly, officers may use force to *prevent a crime* from taking place, or from being completed. [129]

1. **Reasonable non-deadly force:** Both law enforcement officers and private citizens may use reasonable *non-deadly force* to prevent the commission of a felony, or of a misdemeanor amounting to a breach of the peace. [129]

2. **Deadly force:** Deadly force may be used to prevent only *dangerous felonies*. [130]

VIII. MAINTAINING AUTHORITY

A. **Right to maintain authority generally:** *Parents* of minor children, *school teachers*, and other persons who have a duty of supervision, have a limited right to use force to discharge their duties. [130]

B. Parents of minor: Parents of a minor child may use a ***reasonable degree of force*** to guard the child's welfare. [130]

> **Example:** A parent who hits or spanks his child will not be guilty of battery, provided that the purpose is to promote the welfare of the child, including preventing or punishing misconduct. However, the parent loses the privilege if the degree of force is unreasonable under the circumstances.

IX. CONSENT

A. Effect of consent by victim: Generally, the fact that the victim of a crime has *consented* does not bar criminal liability. [131]

> **Example:** Suppose V, who is terminally ill, consents to have D perform a mercy killing on V. This consent does not protect D from murder charges.

However, there are two major exceptions to this rule that consent does not bar criminal liability:

1. Consent as element of crime: First, some crimes are defined in such a way that lack of consent is an ***element of the crime***. [131]

> **Example:** Common-law rape is defined to include the element of lack of consent. Therefore, if V consents, there is automatically no crime, no matter how culpable D's mental state.

2. Consent as negating of harm: Second, for some crimes, in some courts, the fact that V has consented prevents D's conduct from constituting the ***harm*** from arising that the law is trying to prevent. [131]

> **a. Athletic contest:** Thus if the crime involves threatened or actual ***bodily harm***, consent is a defense if the bodily harm is ***not serious*** or is part of a lawful ***athletic contest*** or ***competitive sport***. [131]
>
> > **Example:** D and V agree to a lawfully-sanctioned boxing match. D strikes V repeatedly, trying to injure V, knowing that V is already hurt. D will not be liable for battery, attempted murder, murder, or any other crime. See MPC §2.11(1).

B. Incapacity to consent: Even where the crime is one as to which consent can be a defense, consent will not be found where V is too ***young***, mentally defective, intoxicated, or for other reasons unable to give a meaningful assent. [132]

1. Fraud: Similarly, if the consent was obtained by ***fraud***, it will generally not be valid. However, the fraud will negate the consent only where it goes to the ***essence*** of the harmful activity. [132]

C. Contributory negligence of V: The fact that V may have been ***contributorily negligent*** will not, by itself, be a defense to any crime. [132]

> **Example:** D and V agree to drag race. D's car slams into V's, killing him. If D is prosecuted for criminally negligent homicide or voluntary manslaughter, V's consent will not be a defense, though it might give D a chance to show that V's negligence, not his own, was the sole proximate cause of the accident.

D. Guilt of V: The fact that V is himself engaged in the same or a different illegal activity will not generally prevent the person who takes advantage of him from being criminally liable. (*Example:* D and V agree to an illegal boxing match, during which V is killed. V's equal culpability will not be a defense for D.) [132]

E. Forgiveness or settlement: The fact that V forgives the injury, is unwilling to prosecute, or *settles a civil suit* against D, will *not* absolve D from liability. The crime is considered to be against the people, not against V as an individual. [132]

X. ENTRAPMENT

A. Entrapment generally: The defense of *entrapment* exists where a *law enforcement official*, or someone cooperating with him, has *induced* D to commit the crime. [133-134]

B. Two tests for entrapment: There are two distinct tests used by courts for whether there has been entrapment: [133-134]

   1. "Predisposition" test: The majority test, and the one used in the federal system, is that entrapment exists where: (1) the government *originates* the crime and *induces* its commission; and (2) D is an *innocent person*, i.e., one who is *not predisposed* to committing this sort of crime. This is the so-called *"predisposition"* test. [133-134]

   Example: X, an undercover narcotics operative, offers to sell V heroin for V's own use. If the offer originated entirely with X, and V had never used or sought heroin, V would have a good chance at an entrapment defense, on the theory that he was an "innocent" person who was not predisposed to committing this sort of crime. But if the evidence showed that V had frequently purchased heroin from other sources, then V would not be entrapped under the "predisposition" test, even if the transaction between X and V was entirely at X's instigation.

   2. "Police conduct" rule: A minority of courts apply the *"police conduct"* rule. Under this rule, entrapment exists where the government agents originate the crime, and their participation is such as is likely to induce *unpredisposed* persons to commit the crime, regardless of whether D himself is predisposed. This test is usually easier for the defendant to meet. [134]

C. Other aspects of entrapment: [134]

   1. False representations regarding legality: A separate kind of entrapment exists where the government agent knowingly makes a *false representation* that the act in question is *legal*. [134]

   2. Violent crimes: Some courts refuse to allow the entrapment defense where the crime is one involving *violence*. [134]

   3. Distinguished from "missing element" cases: Distinguish entrapment situations from cases where, because of the participation of government agents, an *element* of the crime is *missing*. [134]

   Example: X, a government agent, suspects that D is a confidence man who swindles people out of their property. X pretends to go along with D's scheme, and gives D money which D appropriates. D is not guilty of obtaining money by false pretenses, because one of the elements of that crime is reliance on the part of the victim, and X was not really fooled.

CHAPTER 5

ATTEMPT

I. INTRODUCTION

A. Attempt generally: All states, in general, punish certain unsuccessful *attempts* to commit crimes. [146-147]

    1. General attempt statutes: Nearly all prosecutions for attempt occur under *general attempt statutes*. That is, the typical criminal code does not specifically make it a crime to attempt murder, to attempt robbery, etc. Instead, a separate statutory section makes it a crime to attempt to commit any of the substantive crimes enumerated elsewhere in the code. [147]

B. Two requirements: For most attempt statutes, there are two principal requirements, corresponding to the *mens rea* and the *actus reus*: [148]

    1. Mental state: First, D must have had a *mental state* which would have been enough to satisfy the *mens rea* requirement of the substantive crime itself. Typically, D will *intend* to commit the crime. But if a mental state less than intent (e.g., recklessness) suffices for the substantive crime, there may be instances where this same less-than-intent mental state will suffice for attempted commission of that crime. This is discussed further below (p. C92). [147]

    2. Act requirement: Second, D must be shown to have committed some *overt act* in furtherance of his plan of criminality. A leading modern view, that of the MPC, is that the act must constitute "a *substantial step*" in a course of conduct planned to culminate in the commission of the crime, but only if the substantial step is *"strongly corroborative"* of D's criminal purpose. MPC §5.01(1)(c). [147]

C. Broader liability: Modern courts impose attempt liability more *broadly* than older cases did. Two major illustrations of this broader trend are: [147]

    1. Looser act requirement: The overt act that D needs to commit can be further away from actual completion of the crime than used to be the case. [147]

    2. Impossibility: The defense of "legal impossibility" has been dramatically restricted. [147]

II. MENTAL STATE

A. Intent usually required: Generally, D will be liable for an attempt only if he *intended* to do acts which, if they had been carried out, would have resulted in the commission of that crime. [148-149]

Example: D hits V in the jaw, intending only to slightly injure V. Instead, V suffers serious injuries due to hemophelia, but recovers. D will not be liable for attempted murder, even though he came close to killing V; this is because D is liable for attempted murder only if he had the mental state needed for actual murder (in this case, either an intent to kill or an intent to do serious bodily injury).

1. **Specific crime:** Furthermore, D must have had an attempt to commit an act which would constitute the *same crime* as he is charged with attempting. [148]

   Example: On the facts of the above example, it is not enough that D attempted a crime, namely battery against V. What must be shown by the prosecution is that D had the mental state needed for the very crime D is charged with attempting — murder.

2. **Knowledge of likely consequences:** Nor is it enough that D knew that certain consequences were *highly likely* to result from his act. [148]

   a. **"Substantially certain" results:** But if it is shown that D knew that a certain result was *"substantially certain"* to occur, then this may be enough to meet the intent requirement, even though D did not desire that result to occur. [148]

3. **Crimes defined by recklessness, negligence or strict liability:** Ordinarily, there can be no attempt to commit a crime defined in terms of *recklessness* or *negligence* or *strict liability*. [149]

   a. **Bringing about certain result:** This is clearly true as to crimes defined in terms of recklessly or negligently bringing about a *certain result* — there can be no attempt liability for these crimes. [149]

   Example: D gets into his car knowing that it has bad brakes, but recklessly decides to take a chance. D almost runs into V because he can't stop in time, but V dives out of the way. D will not be guilty of attempted involuntary manslaughter, because crimes defined in terms of recklessly or negligently bringing about a certain result cannot give rise to attempt liability.

   b. **Strict-liability crimes:** Generally, courts will not convict D of attempting a *strict-liability crime* unless D had a culpable state of mind. [149]

4. **Intent as to surrounding circumstances:** It is probably *not* necessary that D's intent encompass all of the *surrounding circumstances* that are elements of the crime. [149]

   Example: A federal statute makes it a federal crime to kill an FBI agent. Case law demonstrates that for the completed crime, it is enough that the defendant was reckless or even negligent with respect to the victim's identity. D tries to shoot V (an FBI agent) to death, but his shot misses; D recklessly disregarded the chance that V might be an FBI agent. Probably D may be found guilty of attempted killing of an FBI agent.

III. THE ACT — ATTEMPT VS. "MERE PREPARATION"

A. The problem: All courts agree that D cannot be convicted of attempt merely for thinking evil thoughts, or plotting in his mind to commit a crime. Thus all courts agree that D must have committed some *"overt act"* in furtherance of his plan of ciminality. But courts disagree about what sort of act will suffice. In general, modern courts hold that D must come much *less close to success* than older courts required. [150]

B. Various approaches: There are two main approaches which courts use to decide whether D's act was sufficient, the "proximity" approach and the "equivocality" approach. [150-156]

    1. The "proximity" approach: Most courts have based their decision on *how close D came to completing the offense*. This is the *"proximity"* approach. In general, older decisions required D to come very close to success — thus older decisions frequently require D to achieve a *"dangerous proximity to success."* But modern courts tend to require merely that D take a *"substantial step"* towards carrying out his criminal plan. [150-153]

    2. The "equivocality" approach: Other courts follow a completely different approach, concentrating not on how close D came to success, but on whether D's conduct *unequivocally manifested his criminal intent*. Under this *"equivocality"* approach, if D's conduct could indicate either a non-criminal intent or a criminal one, it is not sufficient — but if it does unequivocally manifest criminal intent, it suffices even though completion of the plan is many steps away. [153]

        a. Confession excluded: Under the "equivocality" test, any *confession* by D, made either to police or to other persons, is usually *not to be considered* in determining whether D's acts were unequivocally criminal in intent. [153]

    3. MPC's "substantial step" test: The MPC incorporates aspects of both the "proximity" test and the "equivocality" test. But the incorporated aspects of each test are relatively unstringent in the MPC approach, so that almost any conduct meeting any of the variations of *either* of these tests would be sufficient under the Code. Under the MPC, conduct meets the act requirement if, under the circumstances as D believes them to be: (1) there occurs "an act or omission constituting a *substantial step* in a course of conduct planned to culminate in [D's] commission of the crime"; and (2) the act is *"strongly corroborative"* of the actor's criminal purpose. [154-156]

        a. Illustrations: Here are some illustrations of conduct that would suffice as overt acts under the MPC's "substantial step" approach: [155-156]

            i. *Lying in wait, searching* for or *following* the contemplated victim of the crime. [155]

            ii. *Enticing* or seeking to entice the contemplated victim to *go to the* place contemplated for its commission. [155]

            iii. *Reconnoitering* the place contemplated for commission of the crime. (*Example:* D is caught while hiding in the bushes observing V's residence, while V is away from home. This "casing the joint" will probably suffice.) [156]

    iv. Unlawful *entry* of a structure, vehicle or enclosure where the crime is to be committed. [156]

    v. *Possession of materials* to be employed in the commission of the crime, if the materials are *specially designed* for such unlawful use or can serve no lawful purpose of D under the circumstances. (*Example:* D is stopped on the street at night and is found to be in possession of lock-picking tools. Probably he can be convicted of attempted burglary.) [156]

  b. **Followed in many states:** The MPC's "substantial step" test is a popular one. About half the states, and two-thirds of the federal circuits, now use something like this test. [156]

IV. IMPOSSIBILITY

  A. **Nature of "impossibility" defense:** The *"impossibility"* defense is raised where D has done everything in his power to accomplish the result he desires, but, due to external circumstances, no substantive crime has been committed. Most variants of the defense are *unsuccessful* today, but it is still important to be able to recognize situations where the defense might plausibly be raised. Here are some examples: [157]

    Example 1: D, a would-be pickpocket, reaches into V's pocket, but discovers that it is empty.

    Example 2: D, a would-be rapist, achieves penetration of V, but discovers that V is a corpse, not a living woman.

    Example 3: D buys a substance from V, thinking that it is heroin. In fact, the substance is sugar, because V is an undercover narcotics operative.

    Note: In these three examples, a modern court would almost certainly hold that D is *liable* for attempt (to commit the substantive crime of larceny, rape and narcotics possession, respectively).

  B. **Factual impossibility:** A claim of *factual* impossibility arises out of D's mistake concerning an issue of fact. D in effect says, "I made a mistake of fact. Had the facts been as I believed them to be, there would have been a crime. But under the true facts, my attempt to commit a crime could not possibly have succeeded." [157-158]

  1. **Not accepted:** The defense of factual impossibility is *rejected* by all modern courts. Impossibility is *no defense* in those cases where, *had the facts been as D believed them to be, there would have been a crime*. Thus D is guilty of an attempt (and his "factual impossibility" defense will fail) in all of the following examples: [157]

    Example 1: D points his gun at A, and pulls the trigger. The gun does not fire because, unbeknownst to D, it is not loaded.

Example 2: D intends to rape X, but is unable to do so because he is impotent.

Example 3: D is a "con man" who tries to get X to entrust money to him, which D intends to steal. Unbeknownst to D, X is a plainclothes police officer who is not fooled.

Example 4: D attempts to poison X with a substance D believes is arsenic, but which is in fact harmless.

C. **"True legal" impossibility:** A different sort of defense arises where D is mistaken about *how an offense is defined*. That is, D engages in conduct which he believes is forbidden by a statute, but D has misunderstood the meaning of the statute. Here, D will be *acquitted* — the defense of "true legal" impossibility is a successful one. You can recognize the situation giving rise to the "true legal" impossibility defense by looking for situations where, *even had the facts been as D supposed them to be*, no crime would have been committed. [158]

Example 1: D obtains a check for $2.50. He alters the numerals in the upper right hand corner, changing them to "12.50." But D does not change the written-out portion of the check, which remains "two and 50/100 dollars." Because the crime of forgery is defined as the material alteration of an instrument, and the numerals are considered an immaterial part of a check (the amount written out in words controls), D will be acquitted of attempted forgery. [*Wilson v. State*]

Example 2: D is questioned by X, a police officer, during a criminal investigation. D lies, while believing that lying to the police constitutes perjury. D cannot be convicted of attempted perjury, because the act he was performing (and in fact the act he thought he was performing) is simply not a violation of the perjury statute.

Note: The defense of "true legal impossibility" is the flip side of the rule that "mistake of law is no excuse." Just as D cannot defend on the grounds that he did not know that his acts were prohibited, so D will be acquitted where he commits an act that he thinks is forbidden but that is not forbidden.

D. **Mistake of fact governing legal relationship:** There is a third category, involving a *mistake of fact* that *bears upon legal relationships*. In this situation, D understands what the statute prohibits, but mistakenly believes that the facts bring his situation within the statute. Here, D will be *convicted* of attempt. This is because *had the facts been as D supposed them to be, his conduct would have been a crime.* [158-161]

Example: D buys goods which he believes are stolen. In fact, the goods are police "bait," and D has been tricked by the seller, an undercover police officer, into thinking that they are stolen. D is guilty of attempted possession of stolen property.

Example: D has intercourse with X, who he believes is in an unconscious drunken stupor. In fact, X is already dead at the time of intercourse. D is guilty of attempted rape, since had the facts been as he supposed them to be, his conduct would have been a crime. [*U.S. v. Thomas*, 13 U.S.C.M.A. 278 (1962)]

Note: All three categories — "factual" impossibility, "true legal impossibility" and "factual mistake bearing on legal relationship" — can be explained with one principle. Ask, "Would D's conduct have been criminal had the facts been as D supposed them to be?" For the "true legal impossibility" situation, the answer is "no." For the other two situations, the answer is "yes," so D is guilty of attempt in just the latter two situations.

E. "Inherent" impossibility (ineptness and superstition): If D's act is, to a reasonable observer, so *farfetched* that it had *no probability of success*, D may be able to successfully assert the defense of *"inherent impossibility."* [161]

    1. Courts split: Courts are *split* about whether to recognize a defense of "inherent impossibility." The MPC authorizes a *conviction* in such cases, but also allows conviction of a lesser grade or degree, or in extreme circumstances even a dismissal, if the conduct charged "is so inherently unlikely to result or culminate in a commission of a crime that neither such conduct nor the actor presents a public danger…." [162]

    Example: D, a Haitian witch doctor, immigrates to the U.S. and continues practicing voodoo. A police officer sees D sticking pins in a doll representing V, in an attempt to kill V. D is charged with attempted murder of V. A court might conclude that D's conduct was so inherently unlikely to kill V (and that D himself was so unlikely to commit the substantive crime of murder or to make a more "serious" attempt to kill V) that D should be acquitted, or convicted of a lesser crime such as attempted battery.

V. RENUNCIATION

A. Defense generally accepted: Where D is charged with an attempted crime, most courts accept the defense of *renunciation*. To establish this defense, D must show that he *voluntarily abandoned* his attempt before completion of the substantive crime. [162-163]

    Example: D decides to shoot V when V comes out of V's house. D carries a loaded gun, and waits in the bushes outside V's house. Five minutes before he expects V to come out, D decides that he doesn't really want to kill V at all. D returns home, and is arrested and charged with attempted murder. All courts would acquit D in this circumstance, because he voluntarily abandoned his plan before completing it (even though the abandonment came after D took sufficient overt acts that he could have been arrested for an attempt right before the renunciation).

B. Voluntariness: All courts accepting the defense of abandonment require that the abandonment be *"voluntary."* [164-165]

    1. Threat of imminent apprehension: Thus if D, at the last moment, learns facts causing him to believe that he will be *caught* if he goes through with his plan, the abandonment will generally not be deemed voluntary. [164]

Example: On the facts of the above example, just before V is scheduled to come out of his house, D spots a police officer on the sidewalk near D. D's abandonment has been motivated by the fear of imminent apprehension, so his abandonment will not be deemed voluntary, and D can be convicted of attempted murder.

2. **Generalized fear:** On the other hand, if D abandons because of a *generalized* fear of apprehension, not linked to any *particular* threat or event, his abandonment will probably be deemed voluntary. [164]

   Example: On the facts of the above two examples, suppose that D's decision to abandon is motivated not by the appearance of a police officer, but by D's sudden thought, "If I get caught, I'll go to prison for life." D's abandonment will probably be treated as voluntary, and will be a bar to his prosecution for attempt.

3. **Other special circumstances:** [164-165]

   a. **Postponement:** If D merely *postpones* his plan, because the scheduled time proves less advantageous than he thought it would be, this does *not* constitute a voluntary abandonment. [164]

   b. **Dissuasion by victim:** Similarly, if D's renunciation is the result of *dissuasion by the victim*, it will probably be deemed involuntary. [165]

   Example: D decides to rob V, a pedestrian, on a secluded street at night. D says, "Your money or your life," and brandishes a knife at V. V pulls out his own switchblade and says, "If you come any closer, I'll carve you up." D turns around and walks away. D's abandonment will almost certainly be found to be involuntary, because it was motivated by the victim's conduct. Therefore, D can be convicted of attempted robbery.

VI. ATTEMPT-LIKE CRIMES

A. **Problem generally:** Some *substantive* crimes punish incompleted or "inchoate" behavior. If D intends to commit acts which, if completed, would constitute one of these inchoate crimes, D may raise the defense that he cannot be convicted of "an attempt to commit a crime which is itself an attempt." [165-166]

1. **Occasionally successful:** Very occasionally, defendants have succeeded with this defense. [165]

   Example: D, who is very weak, throws a rock at V, a police officer, but his arm is not strong enough to get the rock even close to V. One type of "assault" defined by statute in the jurisdiction is "an attempt to commit battery by one having present ability to do so." D is charged with "attempted assault." A court might hold that D should not be convicted, because the crime of assault (of the attempted-battery type) is intended to cover near-battery, and the crime here is effectively near-near-battery. But most courts would probably reject this defense and would convict D on these facts.

VII. MECHANICS OF TRIAL; PUNISHMENT

A. Relation between charge and conviction: Complications arise where D is: (1) charged with a completed substantive crime, but shown at trial to be guilty of at most an attempt; or (2) charged with attempt, but shown at trial to have committed the underlying substantive crime. [166]

1. **Substantive crime charged, attempt proved:** If D is charged with a completed crime but shown to have committed only an attempt, the courts agree that D *may be convicted of attempt*. The attempt is said to be a "lesser included offense." [167]

2. **Attempt charged, completed crime proved:** Conversely, if D is charged with an attempt and is shown at trial to have committed the underlying complete crime, D may normally be *convicted of attempt*. (But the attempt statute may be drafted so as to make failure an element of attempt; if so, D will escape liability.) [167]

CHAPTER 6

CONSPIRACY

I. INTRODUCTION

A. Definition of "conspiracy": The common-law crime of *conspiracy* is defined as *an agreement between two or more persons to do either an unlawful act or a lawful act by unlawful means*. At common law, the prosecution must show the following: [174]

1. **Agreement:** An *agreement* between two or more persons; [174]

2. **Objective:** To carry out an act which is either *unlawful* or which is lawful but to be accomplished by *unlawful means*; and [174]

3. *Mens rea:* A *culpable intent* on the part of the defendant. [174]

B. Procedural advantages: The prosecution gets a number of *procedural* advantages in a conspiracy case. [175] The two most important are:

1. **Joint trial:** Joinder laws generally let the prosecution try in a *single proceeding* all persons indicted on a single conspiracy charge. [175]

2. **Admission of hearsay:** Statements made by any member of the conspiracy can generally be admitted against all, without constraint from the *hearsay* rule. *Any previous incriminating statement by any member of the conspiracy, if made in furtherance of the conspiracy, may be introduced into evidence against all of the conspirators.* See FRE 801(d)(2)(E). [175]

Example: D1, D2 and D3 are charged with conspiracy to rob a bank. D1, the mastermind, tries to recruit X, an arms supplier, into the conspiracy, by telling X that D3 is also part of the conspiracy. X refuses to join the conspiracy. At the Ds' trial for conspiracy, X testifies as to D1's statements about D3's participation. This testimony will be admitted against D3 for the substantive purpose of showing that D3 was part of the conspiracy. This will be true even though the statement by D1 is hearsay as to D3.

    a. Hearsay considered in determining admissibility: In the federal system, and in many states, the judge may determine the admissibility of hearsay *without respect to the rules of evidence*. This means that the incriminating statement by a member of the alleged conspiracy *may itself be considered* in determining whether the conspiracy has been sufficiently documented that the hearsay should be admissible against the defendant. [175]

II. THE AGREEMENT

  A. "Meeting of the minds" not required: The essence of a conspiracy is an *agreement* for the joint pursuit of unlawful ends. However, no true "meeting of the minds" is necessary — all that is needed is that the parties communicate to each other in some way their intention to pursue a joint objective. [175-176]

    1. Implied agreement: Thus words are not necessary — each party may, by his *actions alone*, make it clear to the other that they will pursue a common objective. [176]

    Example: A is in the process of mugging V on the street, when B comes along. B pins V to the ground, while A takes his wallet. A conspiracy to commit robbery could be found on these facts, even though there was no spoken communication between A and B.

    2. Proof by circumstantial evidence: The prosecution may prove agreement by mere *circumstantial evidence*. That is, the prosecution can show that the parties committed acts in circumstances strongly suggesting that there *must* have been a *common plan*. [176]

    Example: V, a politician, is riding in a motorcade down a crowded city street. A and B both simultaneously shoot at V. The fact that both people shot simultaneously would be strong, and admissible, evidence that A and B had agreed to jointly attempt to kill V, and would thus support prosecution of the two for conspiracy to commit murder.

  B. Aiding and abetting: Suppose that A and B conspire to commit a crime (let's call the crime "X"). C then "aids and abets" A and B in the commission of crime X, but never reaches explicit agreement with A and B that he is helping them. It is clear that C will be liable for X if A and B actually commit X. But if A and B never commit X, courts are *split* about whether C, as a mere aider and abetter, is also liable for conspiracy to commit X. The MPC holds that a person does *not* become a co-conspirator merely by aiding and abetting the conspirators, if he himself does not reach agreement with them. [176]

    Example: D knows that A and B plan to kill X. D, without making any agreement with A and B, prevents a telegram of warning from reaching X. If X is thus unable to flee, and A and B kill X, it is clear that D is liable for the substantive crime of murder, since he aided and abetted A and B in carrying out the murder. But if X escapes, so there is no substantive crime of murder to be charged, can D be convicted of conspiracy to commit murder? Courts are split. The MPC would acquit D on these facts, since under the MPC an aider and abetter is not liable for the conspiracy if he did not reach any agreement with the conspirators.

C. Parties don't agree to commit object crime: Although there must be an agreement, it is not necessary that each conspirator agree to commit the *substantive object crime(s)*. A particular D can be a conspirator even though he agreed to help only in the *planning stages*. (*Example:* D1, D2 and D3 work together to commit a bank robbery. D3's only participation is to agree to obtain the getaway car, not to participate in the bank robbery itself. D3 is still guilty of conspiracy to commit bank robbery.) [177]

D. Feigned agreement: Courts disagree about the proper result where one of the parties to a "conspiracy" is merely *feigning* his agreement. The problem typically arises where one of the parties is secretly an *undercover agent*. [177]

> **Example:** A and B agree that they will rob a bank. B is secretly an undercover agent, and never has any intention of committing the robbery. In fact, B makes sure that the FBI is present at the bank, and A is arrested when he and B show up. Courts disagree about whether the requisite "agreement" between A and B took place, and thus about whether A can be prosecuted for conspiracy to commit bank robbery.

> **1. Traditional view that there is no conspiracy:** The traditional, common-law view is that there is *no agreement*, and therefore *no conspiracy*. Thus on the facts of the above example, A could not be charged with conspiracy to commit bank robbery. This traditional view is sometimes called the *"bilateral"* view, in the sense that the agreement must be a bilateral one if either party is to be bound. [177]

> **2. Modern view allows conspiracy finding:** But the modern view is that regardless of one party's lack of subjective intent to carry out the object crime, *the other party may nonetheless be convicted of conspiracy.* [177]

>> **a. Model Penal Code agrees:** The Model Penal Code agrees with the modern view. The Code follows a *"unilateral"* approach to conspiracy — a given individual is liable for conspiracy if he "agrees with another person or persons," whether or not the other person is really part of the plan. Thus under the MPC, A in the above example has clearly agreed to rob the bank (even though B has not truly agreed), and A can therefore be prosecuted for conspiracy. [178]

III. *MENS REA*

A. Intent to commit object crime: Normally, the conspirators must be shown to have agreed to commit a crime. It is then universally held that each of the conspirators must be shown to have had *at least the mental state required for the object crime.* [178-182]

> **Example:** A and B are caught trying to break into a dwelling at night. The prosecution shows only that A and B agreed to attempt to break and enter the

dwelling, and does not show anything about what A and B intended to do once they were inside. A and B cannot be convicted of conspiracy to commit burglary, because there has been no showing that they had the intent necessary for the substantive crime of burglary, i.e., it has not been shown that they had the intent to commit any felony once they got inside.

1. **Must have intent to achieve objective:** Also, where the substantive crime is defined in terms of causing a *harmful result*, for conspiracy to commit that crime the conspirators must be shown to have *intended to bring about that result*. This is true even though the intent is not necessary for conviction of the substantive crime. [179]

   Example: A and B plan to blow up a building by exploding a bomb. They know there are people in the building who are highly likely to be killed. If the bomb goes off and kills X, A and B are guilty of murder even though they did not intend to kill X (because one form of murder is the "depraved heart" or "reckless indifference to the value of human life" kind). But A and B are *not* guilty of conspiracy to murder X, because they did not have an affirmative intent to bring about X's death.

2. **Crime of recklessness or negligence:** It's probably also the case that there can be no conspiracy to commit a crime that is defined in terms of recklessly or negligently causing a particular result. [179]

3. **Attendant circumstances:** But where the substantive crime contains some elements relating to the *attendant circumstances* surrounding the crime, and strict liability applies to those attendant circumstances, then two people *can* be convicted of conspiracy even though they had no knowledge or intent regarding the surrounding circumstances. [179-180]

   a. **Federal jurisdiction:** Elements relating to *federal jurisdiction* illustrate this problem. Even if the Ds are shown not to have been aware that the elements of federal jurisdiction were present, they can still be held liable for conspiracy to commit the underlying federal crime. [179]

      Example: It is a federal crime to assault a federal officer engaged in the performance of his duties. Cases on this crime hold that the defendant need not be shown to have been aware that his victim was a federal officer. D1 and D2 orally agree to attack V, thinking he is a rival drug dealer. In fact, V is a federal officer. D1 and D2 can be convicted of conspiracy to assault a federal officer, because V's status as such was merely an attendant circumstance, as to which intent need not be shown. [*U.S. v. Feola*, 420 U.S. 671 (1975)]

B. **Supplying of goods and services:** The Ds must be shown to have *intended* to further a criminal objective. It is not generally enough that a particular D merely *knew* that his acts might tend to enable others to pursue criminal ends. The issue arises most often where D is charged with conspiracy because he *supplied goods or services* to others who committed or planned to commit a substantive crime. [180-181]

   1. **Mere knowledge not sufficient:** It is *not* enough for the prosecution to show that D supplied goods or services with *knowledge* that his supplies

might enable others to pursue a criminal objective. Instead, the supplier must be shown to have **desired** to further the criminal objective. On the other hand, this desire or intent can be shown by **circumstantial** evidence. [180-181]

a. **"Stake in venture":** For instance, the requisite desire to further the criminal objective can be shown circumstantially by the fact that the supplier in some sense acquired a *"stake in the venture."* [180]

Example: D and S agree that if S supplies D with equipment to make an illegal still, D will pay S 10% of the profits S makes from his illegal liquor operations. S will be held to have had such a stake in the venture that the jury may infer that he desired to bring about the illegal act of operating his still.

b. **Controlled commodities:** The supplier is more likely to be found to be a participant in a conspiracy if the substance he sold was a *governmentally controlled* one that could only have been used for illegal purposes. (*Example:* S supplies the Ds with horse-racing information of benefit only to bookmakers, in a state where bookmaking is illegal.) [181]

c. **Inflated charges:** The fact that the supplier is charging his criminal purchasers an *inflated price* compared with the cost of the items if sold for legal purposes, is evidence of intent. [181]

d. **Large proportion of sales:** If sales to criminal purchasers represent a *large portion* of the supplier's overall sales of the item, the supplier is more likely to be held to have had the requisite intent. [181]

e. **Serious crime:** The more *serious* the crime, the more likely it is that the supplier's participation will be found to be part of the conspiracy. [181]

IV. THE CONSPIRATORIAL OBJECTIVE

A. **Non-criminal objective:** Traditionally, and in England, the Ds could be convicted of conspiracy upon proof that they intended to commit acts that were *"immoral"* or "contrary to the public interest." In other words, the fact that the act or ultimate object was not explicitly criminal was not an automatic defense. [182-183]

1. **Modern American view rejects:** But the modern American tendency is to allow a conspiracy conviction *only* if the Ds intended to perform an act that is *explicitly criminal*. Thus the MPC allows a conspiracy only where the defendants intend to commit a crime. [183]

Example: D1 collaborates with various prostitutes, with the intention of publishing a directory of prostitutes. Under the traditional/English view, D1 and the prostitutes can be convicted of conspiracy to "corrupt public morals," even though actual publication of the directory would not itself have been a crime. But under the modern American view, there could be no conspiracy here, since no act was intended which would have been criminal. [*Shaw v. Dir. Pub. Prosec.*, 2 W.L.R. 897 (Eng. 1961)]

B. The "overt act" requirement: At common law, the crime of conspiracy is *complete as soon as the agreement has been made*. But about half the states have statutes requiring, in addition, that some *overt act* in furtherance of the conspiracy must also be committed. [183]

    1. MPC limits requirement: The MPC limits the overt act requirement to *non-serious crimes*. Under the MPC, a conspiracy to commit a felony of the first or second degree may be proved even without an overt act. [183]

    2. Kind of act required: The overt act, where required, may be *any act* which is taken in furtherance of the conspiracy. It does *not* have to be an act that is *criminal in itself*. Thus acts of *mere preparation* will be sufficient. (*Example:* If the conspiracy is to make moonshine liquor, purchase of sugar from a grocery store would meet the overt act requirement.) [183]

    3. Act of one attributable to all: Even in states requiring an overt act, it is not necessary that each D charged with the conspiracy be shown to have committed an overt act. Instead, if the overt act requirement applies, the overt act of a *single person* will be *attributable to all*. [183]

C. Impossibility: The same rules concerning *"impossibility"* apply in conspiracy as in attempt. [184] For instance, the defense of *"factual impossibility"* is always rejected. (*Example:* D1 and D2 agree to pick the pocket of a certain victim. The pocket turns out to be empty. The Ds are liable for conspiracy to commit larceny.) [184]

D. Substantive liability for crimes of other conspirators: The most frequently-tested aspect of conspiracy law relates to a member's liability for the *substantive crimes* committed by other members of the conspiracy. This subject is complicated, and requires close analysis. [184-185]

    1. Aiding and abetting: Normally, each conspirator *"aids and abets"* the others in furtherance of the aims of the conspiracy. Where this is the case, a D who has aided and abetted one of the others in accomplishing a particular substantive crime will be liable for that substantive crime — this is not a result having anything to do with conspiracy law, but is instead merely a product of the general rules about accomplice liability (discussed *infra*, pp. 109-115). [184-185]

    Example: A and B agree to a scheme whereby A will steal a car, pick B up in it, and wait outside the First National Bank while B goes in and robs the teller. A steals the car, picks up B, and delivers B to the bank. Before B can even rob the teller, A is arrested out on the street. B robs the teller anyway. A is clearly liable for the substantive crime of bank robbery, because he has "aided and abetted" B in carrying out this crime. It is also true that A and B are guilty of conspiracy to commit bank robbery, but this fact is not necessary to a finding that A is liable for B's substantive crime — aiding and abetting is all that is required for A to be liable for bank robbery.

    2. Substantive liability without "aiding and abetting": The more difficult question arises where A and B conspire to commit crime X, and B commits *additional crimes* "in furtherance" of the conspiracy, but without the direct assistance of A. Does A, by his *mere membership* in the conspiracy, become liable for these additional crimes by B in furtherance of the conspiracy? [184-185]

    a. Traditional view: The traditional "common law" view is that each member of a conspiracy, by virtue of his *membership alone*, is likely for reasonably foreseeable crimes committed by the others in *"furtherance"* of the conspiracy. [184]

    Example: Same basic fact pattern as prior example. Now, however, assume that A knows that B is carrying a gun into the bank, and A also knows that B would rather shoot anyone attempting to stop him than go to prison. However, A has done nothing to help B get the gun, and has not encouraged B to use the gun. B goes into the bank, and shoots V, a guard, while V is trying to capture B. V is seriously wounded. Under the traditional view, if B is liable for assault with a deadly weapon, A will be liable also, merely because he was a member of a conspiracy, and the crime was committed by another member in furtherance of the aims of the conspiracy (robbery with successful escape).

    b. Modern/MPC view: But modern courts, and the MPC, are *less likely to hold that mere membership in the conspiracy*, without anything more, automatically makes each member liable for substantive crimes committed by any other member in furtherance of the conspiracy. [185]

    Example: Same facts as above example. Assuming that A in no way encouraged or helped B to use his gun, a modern court might not hold A substantively liable for the assault on V, despite the fact that it was done in furtherance of the conspiracy.

V. SCOPE: MULTIPLE PARTIES

A. Not all parties know each other: When not all parties *know* each other, you may have to decide whether there was one large conspiracy or a series of smaller ones. [185]

B. "Wheel" conspiracies: In a *"wheel"* or *"circle"* conspiracy, a "ring leader" participates with each of the conspirators, but these conspirators deal only with the ring leader, not with each other. [186]

    1. "Community of interest" test: In the "wheel" situation, there can either be a single large conspiracy covering the entire wheel, or a series of smaller conspiracies, each involving the "hub" (the ring leader) and a single spoke (an individual who works with the ring leader). There will be a single conspiracy only if two requirements are met: (1) each spoke *knows that the other spokes exist* (though not necessarily the identity of each other spoke); and (2) the various spokes have, and realize that they have, a *"community of interest."* [186]

C. "Chain" conspiracies: In a *"chain"* conspiracy, there is a distribution chain of a commodity (usually *drugs*). As with "wheel" conspiracies, the main determinant of whether there is a single or multiple conspiracies is whether all the participants have a "community of interest." [187]

Example: A group of smugglers import illegal drugs; they sell the drugs to middlemen, who distribute them to retailers, who sell them to addicts. If all members of the conspiracy knew of each other's existence, and regarded themselves as being engaged in a single distribution venture, then a court might hold that there was a single conspiracy. Otherwise, there might be merely individual conspiracies, one involving smugglers and middlemen, another involving middlemen and retailers, etc.

D. **Party who comes late or leaves early:** Special problems arise as to a conspirator who *enters* the conspiracy *after* it has begun, or *leaves it before* it is finished. [188]

1. **Party comes late:** One who enters a conspiracy that has *already committed substantive acts* will be a conspirator as to those acts only if he is not only told about them, but *accepts them* as part of the general scheme in which he is participating. [188]

   Example: D is a fence who buys from A and B, two jewelry thieves. D is clearly conspiring to receive stolen property. But he will normally *not* be a conspirator to the original crime of theft, unless he somehow involved himself in that venture, as by making the request for particular items in advance.

2. **Party who leaves early:** One who *leaves* a conspiracy before it is finished is liable for acts that occur later only if those acts are *fairly within the confines of the conspiracy as it existed* at the time D was still present. [188]

   Example: D agrees to help A and B rob a bank; D is to procure the transportation, and to deliver it to A. D steals a car and delivers it to A, then leaves the conspiracy. D is guilty of conspiring to rob the bank even though he does nothing further, since the bank robbery is part of the original agreement. But if A and B, totally unbeknownst to D, decided after D left the conspiracy that they wished to use the car to rob a grocery store, D would not be guilty of conspiracy to rob the grocery store.

VI. DURATION OF THE CONSPIRACY

A. **Why it matters:** You may have to determine the *ending point* of a conspiracy. Here are some issues on which the ending point may make a difference: [188]

1. **Who has joined:** A person can be held to have *joined* the conspiracy only if it still existed at the time he got involved in it; [188]

2. **Statute of limitations:** The *statute of limitations* on conspiracy does not start to run until the conspiracy has ended; and [188]

3. **Statements by co-defendants:** Declarations of co-conspirators may be admissible against each other, despite the hearsay rule, but only if those declarations were made in furtherance of the conspiracy while it was still in progress. [188]

B. **Abandonment:** A conspiracy will come to an end if it is *abandoned* by the participants. [189-191]

1. **Abandoned by all:** If *all* the parties abandon the plan, this will be enough to end the conspiracy (and thus, for instance, to start the statute of limitations running). [189]

    a. **No defense to conspiracy charge:** But abandonment does *not* serve as a defense to the *conspiracy charge itself*. Under the common-law approach, the conspiracy is *complete as soon as the agreement is made*. Therefore, abandonment is irrelevant. [189]

        Example: A and B, while in their prison cell, decide to rob the first national bank the Tuesday after they are released. Before they are even released, they decide not to go through with the plan. However, X, to whom they previously confided their plans, turns them into the authorities. A and B are liable for conspiracy to commit bank robbery, even though they abandoned the plan — their crime of conspiracy was complete as soon as they made their agreement, and their subsequent abandonment did not, at common law, change the result.

2. **Withdrawal by individual conspirator:** A similar rule applies to the *withdrawal* by an *individual conspirator*. [189-190]

    a. **Procedural issues:** Thus for *procedural* purposes, D's withdrawal ends the conspiracy as to him. So long as D has made an *affirmative act* bringing home the fact of his withdrawal to his confederates, the conspiracy is over as to him, for purposes of: (1) running of the statute of limitations; (2) inadmissibility of declarations by other conspirators after he left; or (3) non-liability for the substantive crimes committed by the others after his departure. (Instead of notifying each of the other conspirators, the person withdrawing can instead notify the police.) [189]

    b. **As defense to conspiracy charge:** But if D tries to show withdrawal as a *substantive defense* against the conspiracy charge itself, he will fail: the common-law rule is that *no act of withdrawal*, even thwarting the conspiracy by turning others into the police, will be a defense. This comes from the principle that the crime is *complete* once the agreement has been made. [189]

        i. **More liberal Model Penal Code view:** But the MPC relaxes the common-law rule a bit. The MPC allows a limited defense of *"renunciation of criminal purpose."* D can avoid liability for the conspiracy itself if: (1) his renunciation was *voluntary*; and (2) he *thwarted* the conspiracy, typically by *informing the police*. (Good faith efforts by D to thwart the conspiracy, which fail for reasons beyond D's control, such as police inefficiency, are *not* enough, even under the liberal MPC view.) [190]

VII. PLURALITY

A. **Significance of the plurality requirement:** A conspiracy necessarily involves *two or more* persons. This is called the *"plurality"* requirement. [191]

B. Wharton's Rule: Under the common-law *Wharton's Rule*, where a substantive offense is defined so as to necessarily require more than one person, a prosecution for the substantive offense must be brought, rather than a conspiracy prosecution. The classic examples are *adultery*, *incest*, *bigamy* and *dueling* crimes. [191-193]

Example: Howard and Wanda are husband and wife. Marsha is a single woman. Howard and Marsha agree to meet later one night at a specified motel, to have sex. They are arrested before the rendezvous can take place. Since the crime of adultery is defined so as to require at least two people, Howard and Marsha cannot be convicted of conspiracy to commit adultery, under the common law Wharton's Rule.

1. More persons than necessary: A key *exception* to Wharton's Rule is that there is no bar to a conspiracy conviction where there were *more participants* than were logically necessary to complete the crime. [191]

Example: Same facts as above example. Now, however, assume that Steve, Howard's friend, has urged him to have sex with Marsha, and has reserved the hotel room for them. Despite Wharton's Rule, Howard, Marsha and Steve can all be prosecuted for conspiracy, because there were more persons involved than merely the two necessary direct parties to the substantive crime of adultery.

2. Sometimes only a presumption: Modern courts, including the federal system, frequently hold that Wharton's Rule is not an inflexible rule but merely a *presumption* about what the legislature intended. Under courts following this approach, if the legislative history behind the substantive crime is silent about whether the legislature intended to bar conspiracy convictions, a conspiracy charge is allowed. [192]

Example: A federal act makes it a federal crime for five or more persons to conduct a gambling business prohibited by state law. The five Ds are charged with conspiracy to violate this federal act. *Held*, the legislative history behind the federal act shows no congressional intent to merge conspiracy charges into the substantive crime, so a conspiracy charge is valid here. [*Iannelli v. U.S.*, 420 U.S. 770 (1975)]

3. Model Penal Code rejects Rule: The Model Penal Code almost completely *rejects* Wharton's Rule. [193]

   a. No conviction for conspiracy and substantive offense: However, the Code does provide that one may not be convicted of *both* a substantive crime and a conspiracy to commit that crime. (By contrast, most states *allow* this sort of *"cumulative"* punishment scheme, as long as the situation is not the classic Wharton's Rule scenario where only the parties logically necessary for the completed crime have been charged.) [193]

C. Statutory purpose not to punish one party: The court will not convict a party of conspiracy where it finds that the legislature intended not to punish such a party for the *substantive* crime. Typically, this situation arises where the legislature that defined the substantive crime recognized that two parties were necessarily involved, but chose to punish only one of those parties as being the "more guilty" one. [193]

> **Example:** Stewart and Barbara, who are not married to each other, agree that Stewart will transport Barbara across state lines, so that they can have sex. The federal Mann Act prohibits the transportation of a woman across state lines for purposes of sexual intercourse. Cases interpreting the Mann Act itself hold that the woman is an innocent "victim" and thus does not violate the act merely by allowing herself to be transported interstate. Stewart and Barbara are arrested before they cross the state line, and are prosecuted for conspiracy to violate the Mann Act.
>
> *Held*, Barbara may not be convicted of conspiracy, because the legislature did not intend to punish her for the substantive crime that she is accused of conspiring to commit. (A modern court would probably allow *Stewart* to be convicted, however.) [*Gebardi v. U.S.*, 287 U.S. 112 (1932)]

D. Spouses and corporations: [194]

    1. Spouses: At common law, a *husband and wife* cannot by themselves make up a *conspiracy*. But virtually all modern courts have *rejected* this common law rule, so a conspiracy composed solely of husband and wife is punishable. [194]

    2. Corporations: There must at least be two *human* members of any conspiracy. Thus although a corporation can be punished as a conspirator, there can be no conspiracy when only one corporation and one human being (e.g., an officer or stockholder of the corporation) are implicated. [194]

E. Inconsistent disposition: Look out for situations where one or more members of the alleged conspiracy are not convicted — does this prevent the conviction of the others? For now, let's assume that there are only two purported members, A and B. [194-195]

    1. Acquittal: Where A and B are tried in the *same proceeding*, and A is acquitted, all courts agree that B must also be acquitted. But if the two are tried in *separate* proceedings, courts are split. Most courts today hold that A's acquittal does *not* require B's release. [194]

        a. Model Penal Code rejects consistency requirement: The MPC, as the result of its "unilateral" approach, follows the majority rule of not requiring consistency where separate trials occur. [195]

        Example: A and B are the only two alleged conspirators. A is acquitted in his trial. B is then tried. B may be convicted, because under the "unilateral" approach, we look only at whether B conspired with anyone else, not whether "A and B conspired together."

    2. One conspirator not tried: If A is *not brought to justice* at all, this will *not* prevent conviction of B (assuming that the prosecution shows, in B's trial, that both A and B participated in the agreement). [195]

VIII. PUNISHMENT

A. Cumulative sentencing: May a member of the conspiracy be convicted of **both** conspiracy to commit the crime and the substantive crime itself? [195]

    1. Cumulative sentencing usually allowed: Most states allow a **cumulative sentence**, i.e., conviction for both conspiracy and the underlying crime. [195]

    2. MPC limits: But the Model Penal Code does not follow this majority approach — D may not be convicted simultaneously of crime X, and conspiracy to commit crime X. [195]

        a. Some objectives not realized: If, however, the conspiracy has a number of objectives, and less than all are carried out, even under the MPC there can be a conviction of both conspiracy and the carried-out crimes. [195]

CHAPTER 7

ACCOMPLICE LIABILITY AND SOLICITATION

I. PARTIES TO CRIME

A. Modern nomenclature: Modern courts and statutes dispense with common-law designations like "principal in the first degree," "accessory before the fact," "accessory after the fact," etc. Instead, modern courts and statutes usually refer only to two different types of criminal actors: "accomplices" and "principals." [205-206]

    1. Accomplice: An *"accomplice"* is one who **assists** or **encourages** the carrying out of a crime, but does not commit the *actus reus*. [206]

    2. Principal: A *"principal,"* by contrast, is one who **commits** the *actus reus* (with or without the assistance of an accomplice). [206]

    Example: As part of a bank robbery plan, A steals a car, and drives B to the First National Bank. A remains in the car acting as lookout. B goes inside and demands money, which he receives and leaves the bank with. A drives the getaway car. Since B carried out the physical act of robbery, he is a "principal" to bank robbery. Since A merely assisted B, but did not carry out the physical act of bank robbery, he is an "accomplice" to bank robbery.

    3. Significance of distinction: Relatively little turns today on the distinction between "accomplice" and "principal." The main significance of the distinction is that generally, the accomplice may not be convicted unless the prosecution also proves that the principal is guilty of the substantive crime in question. The most important rule to remember in dealing with accomplices is that generally, the accomplice is **guilty of the substantive crimes** he assisted or encouraged. [206]

II. ACCOMPLICES — THE ACT REQUIREMENT

A. Liability for aiding and abetting: The key principle of accomplice liability is that one who *aids*, *abets*, *encourages* or *assists* another to perform a crime, will himself be *liable for that crime*. [206-207]

> **Example 1:** Same facts as the above bank-robbery example. A is guilty of bank robbery, even though he did not himself use any violence, or even set foot inside the bank or touch the money.

> **Example 2:** A and B have a common enemy, V. A and B, in conversation, realize that they would both like V dead. A encourages B to kill V, and supplies B with a rifle with which to do the deed. B kills V with the rifle. A is guilty of murder — he assisted and encouraged another to commit murder, so he is himself guilty of murder.

1. Words alone may be enough: *Words*, by themselves, may be enough to constitute the requisite link between accomplice and principal — if the words constituted *encouragement* and *approval* of the crime, and thereby assisted commission of the crime, then the speaker is liable even if he did not take any physical acts. [206]

2. Presence at crime scene not required: One can be an accomplice even without ever being *present* at the *crime scene*. That is, the requisite encouragement, assistance, etc., may all take place before the actual occasion on which the crime takes place. [206]

> **Example:** On the facts of Example 2 above, A is not shielded from guilt of murder merely because he was a 1,000 miles away when B fired the rifle at V.

3. Presence not sufficient: Conversely, *mere presence* at the scene of the crime is *not*, by itself, sufficient to render one an accomplice. The prosecution must also show that D was at the crime scene for the *purpose of approving and encouraging* commission of the offense. [206]

a. Presence as evidence: But D's presence at the crime scene can, of course, be convincing circumstantial *evidence* that D encouraged or assisted the crime. [207]

> **Example:** If the prosecution shows that A's presence at the crime was so that he could serve as a "look out" while B carried out the physical acts, A is obviously an accomplice and is thus guilty of the substantive crime.

4. Failure to intervene: Normally, the mere fact that D *failed to intervene* to prevent the crime will *not* make him an accomplice, even if the intervention could have been accomplished easily. [207]

> **Example:** A and B, who are good friends, walk down a city street together. B decides to shoplift a ring from a sidewalk vendor. A remains silent, when he could easily have dissuaded B. A is not an accomplice to theft of the ring.

a. Duty to intervene: There are a few situations, however, where D has an *affirmative legal duty* to intervene. If he fails to exercise this duty, he may be an accomplice. [207]

Example: Under general legal principles, both parents have an affirmative duty to safeguard the welfare of their child. Mother severely beats Child while Father remains silently by. Father is probably an accomplice to battery or child abuse, because he had an affirmative duty to protect Child and failed to carry out that duty.

B. Aid not crucial: Suppose that D gives assistance in furtherance of a crime, but the assistance turns out *not to have been necessary*. In this situation, D is generally *guilty* — as long as D intended to aid the crime, and took acts or spoke words in furtherance of this goal, the fact that the crime would probably have been carried out anyway will be irrelevant. [207-208]

1. **Attempts to aid where no crime occurs:** If D attempts to give aid, but the substantive crime never takes place because the principal is *unsuccessful*, D may be liable for an *attempt*. [208]

   Example: A gives B a gun with which to kill V, and encourages B to do so. B shoots at V, but misses. A is guilty of attempted murder, just as B is.

   a. **Crime not attempted by the principal:** If, on the other hand, the principal does not even *attempt* the crime, most courts will *not* hold D guilty of even the crime of attempt on an accomplice theory. However, D is probably guilty of the crime of "solicitation," and a minority of courts might hold him guilty of attempt. [208]

      Example: A tries to persuade B to murder V, and gives B a rifle with which to do so. B turns A into the police, rather than trying to kill V. In most states, A is not liable for attempted murder on an accomplice theory, but may be liable for criminal solicitation. A few states, and the MPC, would hold D liable for attempted murder on these facts.

C. Conspiracy as meeting the act requirement: Some cases, especially older ones, hold that if D is found to have been in a *conspiracy* with another, he is automatically liable for any crimes committed by the other in furtherance of the conspiracy. (See *supra*, p. C-110.) [208]

1. **Insufficient under modern view:** However, the modern view, and the view of the MPC, is that the act of joining a conspiracy is *not, by itself, enough* to make one an accomplice to all crimes carried out by any conspirator in furtherance of the conspiracy. But even in courts following this modern view, membership in the conspiracy will be strong *evidence* that D gave the other conspirators the required assistance or encouragement in the commission of the crimes that were the object of the conspiracy. [209]

III. ACCOMPLICES — MENTAL STATE

A. General rule: For D to have accomplice liability for a crime, the prosecution must generally show the following about D's mental state: (1) that D *intentionally aided or encouraged* the other to commit the criminal act; and (2) that D had the mental state *necessary for the crime* actually committed by the other. [209-212]

1. **Must have purpose to further crime:**   The first requirement listed above means that it is not enough that D intends acts which have the *effect* of inducing another person to commit a crime — D must have the *purpose* of helping bring that crime about. [209]

    Example: D writes to X, "Your wife is sleeping with V." X, enraged, shoots V to death. D does not have the requisite mental state for accomplice liability for murder or manslaughter merely by virtue of intending to write the letter — the prosecution must also show that D intended to encourage X to kill V.

2. **Must have *mens rea* for crime actually committed:**   D must be shown to have the *mens rea* for the *underlying crime*. Thus if the person assisted commits a *different crime* from that intended by D, D may escape liability. [209-210]

    Example: D believes that X will commit a burglary, and wants to help X do so. D procures a weapon for X, and drives X to the crime scene. Unbeknownst to D, X really intends all along to use the weapon to frighten V so that X can rape V; X carries out this scheme. D is not an accomplice to rape, because he did not have the *mens rea* — that is, he did not intend to cause unconsented-to sexual intercourse. The fact that D may have had the *mens rea* for burglary or robbery is irrelevant to the rape charge, though D might be held liable for attempted burglary or attempted robbery on these facts.

3. **Police undercover agents:**   Where a *police undercover agent* helps bring about a crime by a suspect, the agent will usually have a valid defense based on his lack of the appropriate mental state.

B. **Knowledge, but not intent, as to criminal result:**   The most important thing to watch out for regarding the mental state for accomplice is the situation where D *knows* that his conduct will encourage or assist another person in committing a crime, but D does not *intend* or *desire* to bring about that criminal result. [210-211]

    1. **Not usually sufficient:**   Most courts hold that D is *not* an accomplice in this "knowledge but not intent" situation. [210]

        Example: X asks his friend D for a ride to a particular address. X is dressed all in black, and D knows that X has previously committed burglary. D does not desire that X commit a burglary, but figures, "If I don't give X a ride, someone else will, so I might as well stay on his good side." D drives X to the site, and X burgles the site. D is not guilty of burglary on an accomplice theory, because mere knowledge of X's purpose is not enough — D must be shown to have intended or desired to help X commit the crime.)

C. **Assistance with crime of recklessness or negligence:**   If the underlying crime is not one that requires intent, but merely *recklessness or negligence*, *some* courts hold D liable as an accomplice upon a mere showing that D was reckless or negligent concerning the risk that the principal would commit the crime. [211-212]

    1. **Lending car to drunk driver:**   Thus if D *lends his car to one that he knows to be drunk*, and the driver kills or wounds a pedestrian or other

driver, some courts find D liable as an accomplice to manslaughter or battery. On these facts, D has had the mental state of recklessness (sufficient for involuntary manslaughter or battery), so a court may — but will not necessarily — hold that D's lack of intent to bring about the death or injury to another is irrelevant. [211]

  a. **Negligence-manslaughter:** Observe that in the above "lend car to drunk driver" scenario, D may be liable for manslaughter even if accomplice theory is not used — the crime of manslaughter is generally committed when one recklessly brings about the death of another, so D may, by entrusting his car to a known drunk, be guilty of manslaughter as a principal. [212]

IV. ACCOMPLICES — ADDITIONAL CRIMES BY PRINCIPAL

A. **"Natural and probable" results that are not intended:** A frequently-tested scenario involves a principal who commits not only the offense that the accomplice has assisted or encouraged, but *other offenses* as well. The accomplice will be liable for these additional crimes if: (1) the additional offenses are the *"natural and probable" consequences* of the conduct that D did intend to assist (even though D did not intend these additional offenses); *and* (2) the principal committed the additional crimes *in furtherance of the original criminal objective* that D was trying to assist. [212-215]

  Example: D1 and D2 agree to commit an armed robbery of a convenience store owned by V. D1 personally abhors violence. However, he knows that D2 is armed, and that D2 has been known to shoot in the course of prior robberies. D1 urges D2 not to shoot no matter what, but D2 refuses to make this promise. During the robbery, V attempts to trip an alarm, and D2 shoots her to death. A court would probably hold that D1 is liable for murder on an accomplice theory, since the shooting was a "natural and probable" consequence of armed robbery, and the shooting was carried out to further the original criminal objective of getting away with robbery.

  On the other hand, if D2 forcibly raped V instead of shooting her, and D1 had no reason to expect D2 to do this, D1 would not be liable for rape on an accomplice theory. This is because the rape was not the "natural and probable" consequence of the conduct encouraged by D1, nor was it committed in furtherance of the original objective of robbery.

  1. **Unforeseeable:** Thus if D can show that the additional offenses were *unlikely* or *unforeseeable*, D will not be liable for them. (*Example:* This is why D1 would not be liable for rape on the above hypothetical.)

  2. **MPC rejects extended liability:** The Model Penal Code rejects even the basic principle allowing an accomplice to be held liable for "natural and probable" crimes beyond those which he intended to aid or encourage. Under the MPC, only those crimes that D *intended* to aid or encourage will be laid at his door. [214]

3. **Felony-murder and misdemeanor-manslaughter rules:** Wherever the additional offense is a *death*, the accomplice may end up being guilty not because of the "natural and probable consequences" rule, but because of the specialized *felony-murder* or *misdemeanor-manslaughter* rules. For instance, under the felony-murder rule (discussed *infra*, pp. C122-C125), if in the course of certain dangerous felonies the felon kills another, even *accidentally*, he is liable for murder. This can be combined with the general principles of accomplice liability to make the accessory liable for an unintended death. [214-215]

Example: D1 and D2 agree to commit an armed robbery together, with D2 carrying the only gun. D1 does not desire that anybody be shot. D2 points his gun at V and asks for money; the gun accidentally goes off, killing V. D1 is probably guilty of murder on these facts. However, this is not because V's death was a "natural and probable consequence" of armed robbery.

Instead, it is because under the felony-murder doctrine, even an accidental death that directly stems from the commission of a dangerous felony such as armed robbery will constitute murder. By felony-murder alone, D2 is thus guilty of murder even though he did not intend to shoot, let alone kill, V. Then, since D1 was D2's accomplice in the armed robbery, D1 is liable for armed robbery. Since the killing occurred in the furtherance of the robbery *by D1* (even though he was not the shooter), and since D1 had the mental state required for felony-murder (intent to commit a dangerous felony), D1 is liable for murder without any use of the "natural and probable consequences" rule.

V. GUILT OF THE PRINCIPAL

A. Principal must be guilty: Generally, the accomplice cannot be convicted unless the prosecution shows that the person being aided or encouraged — the principal — is *in fact guilty* of the underlying crime. [216-217]

1. **Principal's conviction not necessary:** But it is not necessary that the principal be *convicted*. (*Example:* A is charged with assisting B to commit a robbery. B is never arrested or brought to trial. Instead, B gets immunity and turns state's evidence against A. A can be convicted of being an accomplice to the robbery upon proof that B committed the robbery, and that A helped B carry it out — the fact that B is never charged or convicted is irrelevant.) [216]

2. **Inconsistent verdicts:** But if the principal is actually *acquitted*, the accomplice must normally be acquitted as well. This is clearly true if the principal is acquitted in the *same trial*, and probably true even if the principal is acquitted in an *earlier* trial. [*People v. Taylor*, 527 P.2d 622 (Cal. 1974)] [216]

VI. WITHDRAWAL BY THE ACCOMPLICE

A. Withdrawal as defense: One who has given aid or encouragement prior to a crime may *withdraw* and thus avoid accomplice liability. In other words, withdrawal is generally a ***defense*** to accomplice liability (in contrast to the conspiracy situation, where it is usually not a defense to the conspiracy charge itself, merely to substantive crimes later commited in furtherance of the conspiracy). The withdrawal will only be effective if D has ***undone*** the effects of his assistance or encouragement. [218]

> **Example:** X tells D that X wants to rob a gas station at gun point, and that he needs a gun to do so. D supplies X with a gun for this purpose. D then has second thoughts, and takes the gun back from X, while also telling X, "I don't think this robbery is a good idea." X gets a different gun from someone else, and carries out the same robbery of the same store. D is not guilty of being an accomplice to the robbery, because he withdrew, in a way that undid the effect of his earlier assistance and encouragement.

1. **Effect of aid must be undone:** It is not enough that D has a subjective change of heart, and gives no further assistance prior to the crime. He must, at the very least, make it ***clear to the other party*** that he is repudiating his past aid or encouragement. [219]

2. **Verbal withdrawal not always enough:** If D's aid has been only ***verbal***, he may be able to withdraw merely by stating to the "principal" that he now withdraws and disapproves of the project. But if D's assistance has been more ***tangible***, he probably has to take ***affirmative action*** to undo his affects. [219]

> **Example:** On the facts of the prior example, where D supplies a gun to X, it probably would not be enough for D to say, "I think the robbery is a bad idea," while letting X keep the gun — D probably has to get the gun back.

   a. **Warning to authorities:** Alternatively, D can almost always make an effective withdrawal by ***warning the authorities*** prior to commission of the crime. [219]

3. **Not required that crime be thwarted:** Regardless of the means used to withdraw, it is ***not necessary*** that D actually ***thwart*** the crime. [219]

> **Example:** D encourages X to commit a particular burglary at a specified time and place. X thinks better of it, and leaves a message at the local police station alerting the police to the place and time for the crime. He does not make any effort to talk X out of the crime, however. Due to police inefficiency, the message gets lost, and X carries out the crime. D's notice to the authorities will probably be held to be enough to constitute an effective withdrawal, even though D was not successful in actually thwarting the crime.

VII. VICTIMS AND OTHER EXCEPTIONS TO ACCOMPLICE LIABILITY

A. **Exceptions for certain classes:** There are certain ***classes*** of persons as to whom no accomplice liablilty will be imposed: [220]

1. **Victims:** Most obviously, where the legislature regards a certain type of person as being the *victim* of the crime, that victim will not be subject to accomplice liability. [220]

   a. **Statutory rape:** Thus a *female below the age of consent* will not be liable as an accessory to *statutory rape* of herself, even if she gives assistance and encouragement to the male. [220]

   b. **Kidnapping and extortion:** Similarly, a person who meets the demands of an *extortionist*, or a person who pays a ransom to *kidnappers* to secure the release of a loved one, will not be an accomplice to the extortion or kidnapping. [220]

2. **Crime logically requiring second person:** Where a crime is defined so as to logically require participation by a second person, as to whom *no direct punishment* has been authorized by the legislature, that second person will not be liable as an accomplice. [220]

   Examples: Since an abortion cannot be performed without a pregnant woman, the pregnant woman will not be liable as an accomplice to her own abortion, assuming that the legislature has not specifically authorized punishment for the woman in this situation. The same would be true of a customer who patronizes a prostitute, or one who purchases illegal drugs — if the legislature has not specifically punished customers of prostitutes or purchasers of drugs, these will not be liable as accomplices to prostitution/drug sales.

VIII. POST-CRIME ASSISTANCE

A. **Accessory after the fact:** One who knowingly gives assistance to felon, for the purpose of helping him *avoid apprehension* following his crime, is an *accessory after the fact*. Under modern law, the accessory after the fact is *not liable* for the *felony itself*, as an accomplice would be. Instead, he has committed a distinct crime based upon obstruction of justice, and his punishment does not depend on the punishment for the underlying felony. [221]

B. **Elements:** Here are the elements for accessory after the fact: [221]

1. **Commission of a felony:** A *completed felony* must have been committed. (It is not enough that D *mistakenly believed* that the person he was assisting committed a felony — but the person aided need not have been formally charged, or even caught.) [221]

2. **Knowledge of felony:** D must be shown to have *known*, not merely *suspected*, that the felony was committed. [221]

3. **Assistance to felon personally:** The assistance must have been given to the *felon personally*. (Thus it is not enough that D knows that a crime has been committed by some unknown person, and D destroys evidence or otherwise obstructs prosecution.) [221]

4. **Affirmative acts:** D must be shown to have taken *affirmative acts* to hinder the felon's arrest. It is not enough that D *fails to report the felon*, or fails to turn in *evidence* that he possesses. [221]

C. **Misprision of felony:** At common law, one who simply fails to report a crime or known felon — without committing any affirmative acts to hinder the felon's arrest — is guilty of the separate crime of *"misprision of felony."* However, almost no states recognize this crime today. [221]

IX. SOLICITATION

A. **Solicitation defined:** The common-law crime of *solicitation* occurs when one *requests or encourages another* to perform a criminal act, regardless of whether the latter agrees. [222]

1. **Utility:** The main utility of the crime is that it allows punishment of the solicitor if the person who is requested to commit the crime *refuses*. [222]

   Example: Wendy is unhappily married to Herbert, and has been having an affair with Bart. Wendy says to Bart, "Won't you please kill Herbert? If you do, we can live happily ever after." Bart does not respond either way, but tells the police what has happened. The police arrest Wendy before Bart takes any action regarding Herbert. On these facts, Wendy is guilty of solicitation — she has requested or encouraged another to perform a criminal act, and it does not matter that the other has refused.

B. **No overt act required:** The crime of solicitation is never construed so as to require an *overt act* — as soon as D makes his request or proposal, the crime is complete (as in the above example). [222]

C. **Communication not received:** Courts disagree about whether D can be convicted of solicitation where he attempts to communicate his criminal proposal, but the proposal is never *received*. [223]

1. **Model Penal Code:** The Model Penal Code imposes liability in this "failed communication" situation. [223]

   Example: On the facts of the above example, Wendy sends a letter to Bart asking Bart to kill Herbert. The letter is intercepted by police before Bart can get it. Courts are split as to whether Wendy can be convicted of solicitation; the MPC would impose liability here. (Even courts not following the MPC approach would probably allow a conviction for "attempted solicitation" on these facts.) [223]

D. **Renunciation:** Some courts allow the defense that the solicitor *voluntarily renounced* his crime. Thus the MPC allows the defense of renunciation if D *prevents* the commission of the crime, and does so voluntarily. [223]

E. **Solicitation as an attempted crime:** If all D has done is to request or encourage another to commit a crime ("bare" solicitation), this is *not* enough to make D guilty of an *attempt* to commit the object crime. However, if D has gone further, by making extensive preparations with or on behalf of the solicitee, or otherwise making overt acts, this may be enough to cause him to be guilty of not only solicitation but an attempt [223] at the crime (even if the solicitee himself refuses to participate).

CHAPTER 8

HOMICIDE AND OTHER CRIMES AGAINST THE PERSON

I. HOMICIDE — INTRODUCTION

A. Different grades of homicide: Any unlawful taking of the life of another falls within the generic class *"homicide."* The two principal kinds of homicide are *murder* and *manslaughter*. [230]

  1. Degrees of murder: In many jurisdictions, murder is divided into first-degree and second-degree murder. Generally, first-degree murder consists of murders committed "with premeditation and deliberation," and killings committed during the course of certain felonies. [230]

  2. Two kinds of manslaughter: Similarly, manslaughter is usually divided into: (1) *voluntary* manslaughter (in most cases, a killing occurring the "heat of passion"); and (2) *involuntary* manslaughter (an unintentional killing committed recklessly, grossly negligently, or during commission of an unlawful act.) [230]

  3. Other statutory forms of homicide: Additional forms of homicide exist by statute in some states. Many states have created the crime of *vehicular homicide* (an unintentional death caused by the driver of a moter vehicle). Similarly, some states, and the MPC, have created the crime of "negligent homicide." [230]

II. MURDER — GENERALLY

A. Definition of "murder": There is no simple definition of "murder" that is sufficient to distinguish killings that are murder from killings that are not. At the most general level, murder is defined as the *unlawful killing* of *another person*. [230]

  1. Four types: In most states, there are four types of murder, distinguished principally by the defendant's mental state:

   [1] *intent-to-kill* murder;

   [2] *intent-to-commit-grievous-bodily-injury* murder;

   [3] *"depraved heart"* (a/k/a "reckless indifference to the value of human life") murder; and

   [4] *felony-murder*, i.e., a killing occurring during the course of a dangerous felony.

  Each of these types is discussed in detail below.

B. Taking of life: Murder exists only where a life has been taken. Therefore, be ready to spot situations where there is no murder because either: (1) the victim had not yet been born alive when D acted, and was never born alive; or (2) the victim's life had ended before D's act. [230-232]

1. **Fetus:** A *fetus* is not a human being for homicide purposes, in most states. Thus if D commits an act which kills the fetus, this does not fall within the general murder statute in most states. [231]

    Example: D shoots X, a pregnant woman. The bullet goes into X's uterus and instantly kills V, a fetus which has not yet started the birth process. In most states, D has not committed garden-variety murder of V, though he may have committed the separate statutory crime of feticide, defined in many states.

    a. **Fetus born alive:** But if the infant is *born alive* and then dies, D is guilty of murdering it even though his acts took place before the birth. (*Example:* Same facts as in the above example. Now, however, assume that the shooting causes X to go into premature labor, V is born alive, and immediately thereafter V dies of the bullet wound. D has murdered V.) [231]

2. **End of life:** Traditionally, *death* has been deemed to occur only when the victim's heart has stopped beating. The modern tendancy, however, is to recognize *"brain death"* as also being a type of death. [232]

    Example: D, a physician, concludes that V is "brain dead," and thus removes V's heart to use it in an organ transplant. Most courts today would probably hold that D has not murdered V, because V was already dead even though her heart was still beating.

C. **Elements of murder:** Here are the elements which the prosecution must prove to obtain a murder conviction: [232-233]

    1. *Actus reus:* There must be *conduct by the defendant* (an *"actus reus"*) either an affirmative act by D an omission by D where he had a duty to act. [232]

    2. *Corpus delecti:* There must be shown to have been a *death* of the victim. Death is the *"corpus delecti"* ("body of the crime") of murder. But the prosecution does *not* have to produce a *corpse*. Like any element of any crime, existence of death may be proved by *circumstantial evidence*. [232]

        Example: D and V are known to be getting along badly, and D has a motive — financial gain — for wanting V dead. V is last seen alive while about to visit D's remote mountain cabin. V is never seen again, and no body is ever found. V's wallet is found in the cabin. Seven years have gone by without a trace of V. A jury could probably reasonably conclude that V is now dead, and that D caused the death by methods unknown.

    3. *Mens rea:* D must be shown to have had an appropriate *mental state* for murder. The required mental state is sometimes called *"malice aforethought,"* but this is merely a term of art, which can be satisfied by any of several mental states. In most jurisdictions, any of the four following intents will suffice: [233]

        a. An intent to *kill*; [233-234]

      b. An intent to *commit grievous bodily injury*; [234-235]

      c. *Reckless indifference* to the *value of human life* (or a *"depraved heart,"* as the concept is sometimes put); [235-236] and

      d. An intent to commit any of certain non-homicide *dangerous felonies*. [237-246]

4. Proximate cause: There must be a *causal relationship* between D's act and V's death. D's conduct must be both the "cause in fact" of the death and also its "proximate cause." [233]

      a. Year-and-a-day rule: Most states continue a common-law proximate cause rule that applies only in murder cases: V must die within a *year and a day* of D's conduct. [233]

      Note on four types of murder: Anytime D can be said to have killed V, you should go through all four types of murder before concluding that no murder has occurred. In other words, examine the possibility that D: (1) intended to kill V; (2) intended to inflict serious bodily harm upon V; (3) knew V or someone else had a substantial chance of dying, but with "reckless indifference" or "depraved heart" ignored this risk; or (4) intended to commit some dangerous felony, not itself a form of homicide (e.g., robbery, rape, kidnapping, etc.) Only if D's intent did not fall within any of these cases can you be confident that V's death does not constitute murder.

D. Intent-to-kill murder: The most common state of mind that suffices for murder is the *intent to kill*. [233-234]

1. Desire to kill: This intent exists, of course, when D has the *desire* to bring about the death of another. [233]

2. Substantial certainty of death: The requisite intent also exists where D knows that death is *substantially certain* to occur, but does not actively desire to bring about V's death. (*Example:* D, a terrorist, puts a bomb onto an airliner. He does not desire the death of any passengers, but knows that at least one death is almost certain to occur. D has the state of mind needed for "intent to kill" murder.) [233]

3. Ill-will unnecessary: The requisite intent to kill may exist even where D does not bear any *ill will* towards the victim. (*Example:* D's wife, V, is suffering from terminal cancer, but still has at least several weeks to live. D feeds her poison without telling her what this is, in order to spare her suffering. As a strictly legal matter, D has the mental state required for "intent to kill" murder, though a jury might well decide to convict only of manslaughter.) [234]

4. Circumstantial evidence: Intent to kill may be proved by *circumstantial evidence*. (*Example:* If death occurs as the result of a deadly weapon used by D, the jury is usually permitted to infer that D intended to bring about the death.) [234]

5. Compare with voluntary manslaughter: It does not automatically follow that because D intended to kill and did kill, that D is guilty of murder. (For instance, most cases of ***voluntary manslaughter*** — generally, a killing occurring in a "heat of passion" — are ones where D intended to kill.) In a prosecution for intent-to-kill murder, the mental state is an intent to kill ***not accompanied by other redeeming or mitigating factors***. [234]

E. **Intent-to-do-serious-bodily-injury murder:** In most states, the *mens rea* requirement for murder is satisfied if D intended not to kill, but to do ***serious bodily injury*** to V. [234-235]

> **Example:** D is angry at V for welching on a debt. D beats V with brass knuckles, intending only to break V's nose and jaw, and to knock out most of his teeth. In most states, D has the mental state required for murder of the "intent to do serious bodily injury" sort. Therefore, if V unexpectedly dies, D is guilty of murder in these states.

1. **Subjective standard:** Most states apply a ***subjective*** standard as to the risk of serious bodily harm — D has the requisite mental state only if he ***actually realized*** that there was a high probability of serious harm (not necessarily death) to V, and the fact that a "reasonable person" would have realized the danger is not sufficient. [235]

2. **"Serious bodily injury" defined:** Some courts hold that only conduct which is likely to be ***"life threatening"*** suffices for "intent to commit serious bodily injury." Other courts take a broader view of what constitutes serious bodily harm. However, all courts recognizing this form of murder hold that a mere intent to commit some sort of bodily injury does not suffice. [235]

> **Example:** D punches V in the face, intending merely to knock V down. V strikes his head while falling, and dies. Probably no court would hold that D is liable for "intent to do serious bodily harm" murder on these facts, though he would be liable for manslaughter under the misdemeanor-manslaughter rule.

3. **Model Penal Code rejects:** The Model Penal Code does ***not*** recognize "intent to do serious bodily harm" murder. The MPC regards the "reckless indifference to value of human life" or "depraved heart" standard, discussed below, as being enough to take care of cases where D wilfully endangers the life or safety of others and death results. [235]

F. **"Reckless indifference to value of human life" or "depraved heart" murder:** Nearly all states hold D liable if he causes a death, while acting with such great ***recklessness*** that he can be said to have a ***"depraved heart"*** or an ***"extreme indifference to the value of human life."*** [235-236]

1. **Illustrations:** Here are some illustrations of "depraved heart" or "extreme indifference" murder: [236]

> **Example 1:** D sets fire to a building where he knows people are sleeping; he does not desire their death, but knows that there is a high risk of death. One inhabitant dies in the fire.

> **Example 2:** D fires a bullet into a passing passenger train, without any intent to kill any particular person. The bullet happens to strike and kill V, a passenger.

Example 3: D, trying to escape from pursuing police, drives his car at 75 mph the wrong way down a one-way residential street that has a 30 mph speed limit. D hits V, a pedestrian.

2. **Awareness of risk:** Courts are split as to whether D shows the requisite "depravity" where he is *not aware* of the risk involved in his conduct. [236]

   a. **MPC view:** The Model Penal Code follows the "subjective" approach to this problem: D shows the required extreme recklessness only if he *"consciously disregards* a substantial and unjustifiable risk." [236]

   b. **Intoxication:** If D fails to appreciate the risk of his conduct because he is *intoxicated*, even courts (and the MPC) that would ordinarily follow a "subjective" standard *allow a conviction*. [236]

III. FELONY-MURDER

A. **Generally:** Under the *felony-murder rule, if D, while he is in the process of committing certain felonies, kills another (even accidentally), the killing is murder*. In other words, the intent to commit any of certain felonies (unrelated to homicide) is sufficient to meet the *mens rea* requirement for murder. [237]

   1. **Common law and today:** The felony-murder rule was applied at common law, and continues to be applied by most states today. [237]

   Example: D, while carrying a loaded gun, decides to rob V, a pedestrian. While D is pointing his gun at V and demanding money, the gun accidentally goes off, and kills V. Even though D never intended to kill V or even shoot at him, D is guilty of murder, because the killing occurred while D was in the course of carrying out a dangerous felony.

B. **Dangerous felonies:** Nearly all courts and legislatures today restrict application of the felony-murder doctrine to *certain felonies*. [237-238]

   1. **"Inherently dangerous" felonies:** Most courts today use the *"inherently dangerous"* test — only those felonies which are inherently dangerous to life and health count, for purposes of the felony-murder rule. [238]

      a. **Two standards:** Courts are *split* about how to determine whether a felony is "inherently dangerous." Some courts judge dangerousness in the *abstract* (e.g., by asking whether larceny is in general a dangerous crime), whereas others evaluate the felony based on the *facts of that particular case* (so that if, say, the particular larceny in question is committed in a very dangerous manner, the felony is "inherently dangerous" even though most other larcenies are not physically dangerous). [238]

      b. **Listing:** In courts that judge "inherent dangerousness" in the abstract, here are felonies that are typically considered inherently dangerous: *robbery*, *burglary*, *rape*, *arson*, *assault* and *kidnapping*. By contrast, the various theft-related felonies are generally not considered inherently dangerous: larceny, embezzlement and false pretenses. [238]

C. Causal relationship: There must be a *causal relationship* between the felony and the killing. First, the felony must in some sense be the "but for" cause of the killing. Second, the felony must be the *proximate cause* of the killing. [238-241]

1. **"Natural and probable" consequences:** The requirement of proximate cause here is usually expressed by saying that D is only liable where the death is the *"natural and probable consequence"* of D's conduct. [239]

2. **Robberies and gunfights:** Most commonly, proximate cause questions arise in the case of *robberies*. [239-241]

   a. **Robber fires shot:** If the fatal shot is fired by the *robber* (even if accidentally), virtually all courts agree that D is the proximate cause of death, and that the felony-murder doctrine should apply. This is true whether the shot kills the robbery victim, or a *bystander*. [239]

   Example 1: On a city street, D points a gun at V, and says, "Your money or your life." While V is reaching into his pocket for his wallet, D drops his gun. The gun strikes the pavement and goes off accidentally, killing V. D's acts of robbery are clearly the proximate cause of V's death, and D is guilty of murder under the felony-murder rule.

   Example 2: Same facts as above example. Now, assume that when the gun strikes the pavement and goes off, it kills B, a bystander 20 feet away. D's acts are the proximate cause of B's death, so D is guilty of murdering B under the felony-murder doctrine.

   b. **Victim or police officer kills bystander:** Where the fatal shot is fired by the *robbery victim* or by a *police officer*, and a *bystander* is accidentally killed, courts are split as to whether the robber is the proximate cause of the death. California, for instance, does not apply the felony-murder doctrine in any situation where the fatal shot comes from the gun of a person other than the robber. In other states, the result might depend on whether the robber fired the first shot, so that if the first shot was fired by the victim and struck a bystander, the robber would not be guilty. [239]

   c. **Robber dies, shot by victim, police officer or other felon:** Where the person who dies is *one of the robbers*, and the fatal shot is fired by another robber, the robbery victim or by police officers, courts are even more reluctant to apply the felony-murder doctrine. Some courts hold that the felony-murder doctrine is intended to protect only innocent persons, so it should not apply where a robber is killed. Where a robber is killed not by one of his cohorts but by the robbery victim or the police, the case for applying the felony murder rule is the weakest of all. [240]

   Example: D and X are co-robbers. X is killed by a police officer who is trying to apprehend the pair. *Held*, D is not guilty of felony murder. [*Comm. v. Redline*, 137 A.2d 472 (Pa. 1958)]

   Note on "depraved heart" as alternative: In any robbery situation, in addition to the possibility of "felony murder" as a theory, examine the possibility of using "depraved heart" as an alternate theory. For instance, if D, while committing a robbery, initiates a gun fight, and a police officer shoots back, killing a bystander, it may be easier to argue that D behaved with reckless indifference to the value of human life (thus making him guilty of "depraved heart" murder) than to find that the felony murder doctrine should apply (since many courts hold that the felony-murder doctrine applies only where the killing is by the defendant's own hand or the hand of his accomplice). [241]

D. Accomplice liability of co-felons: Frequently, the doctrine of felony-murder combines with the rules on *accomplice* liability. The net result is that if two or more people work together to commit a felony, and one of them commits a killing during the felony, the others may also be guilty of felony-murder. [241-242]

   1. "In furtherance" test: In most courts, all of the co-felons are liable for a killing committed by one of them, if the killing was: (1) committed *in furtherance of the felony*; and (2) a *"natural and probable" result* of the felony. [242]

      a. Accidental killing: Thus one felon will commonly be guilty of murder based on another felon's *accidental* killing. [241]

      Example: A and B decide to rob a convenience store together. A carries no gun. A knows that B is carrying a loaded gun, but also knows that B has never used a gun in similar robberies in the past, and that B does not believe in doing so. During the robbery, B accidentally drops the gun, and the gun goes off when it hits the floor, killing V, the convenience store operator. Because B was holding the gun "in furtherance" of the robbery when he dropped it, and because an accident involving a loaded gun is a somewhat "natural and probable" consequence of carrying the loaded gun during the felony, there is a good chance that the court will hold not only that B is guilty of felony-murder, but that A is also guilty of felony murder as an accomplice to B's act of felony murder.

      b. Intentional killing: Similarly, if the killing by one co-felon is *intentional* rather than accidental, the other co-felons will probably still be liable under accomplice principles as long as the killing was committed "in furtherance" of the felony. This will normally be true even though the other co-felons can show that they did not desire or foresee the killing. But if the other co-felons can show that the killing was *not committed for the purpose of furthering the felony*, they may be able to escape accomplice liability. [242]

      Example: A and B rob a convenience store together; as A knows, B is carrying a loaded gun, but B has never used the gun on any previous robberies and is generally opposed to violence. Unknown to either, the new owner of the store is V, an old enemy of B's. B decides to shoot V to death during the course of the robbery, even though V is not threatening to call the police or resisting the robbery in any way. A will have a good chance of persuading the court that the killing was not "in furtherance of" the robbery, and thus of escaping accomplice liability for felony-murder.

E. "In commission of" a felony: The felony-murder doctrine applies only to killings which occur *"in the commission of"* a felony. [242-243]

    1. Causal: There must be a *causal relationship* between felony and killing. [242]

    2. Escape as part of felony: If the killing occurs while the felons are attempting to *escape*, it will probably be held to have occurred "in the commission of" the felony, at least if it occurred reasonably close, both in *time and place*, to the felony itself. [242]

    3. Killing before felony: Even if the killing occurs *before* the accompanying felony, the felony-murder doctrine will apply if the killing was in some way in furtherance of the felony. [243]

    Example: D intends to rape V. In order to quiet her, he puts his hand over her mouth, thereby asphyxiating her. D is almost certainly liable for felony-murder, even though he killed V before he tried to rape her, and even though the final felony was only an attempted rape (since one cannot rape a corpse).

F. Felony must be independent of the killing: For applicaton of the felony-murder doctrine, the felony must be *independent* of the killing. This prevents the felony-murder rule from turning virtually any attack that culminates in death into automatic murder. [243-244]

    Example 1: D kills V in a heat of passion, under circumstances that would justify a conviction of voluntary manslaughter but not murder. Even though manslaughter is obviously a "dangerous felony," the felony-murder rule will not apply to upgrade the manslaughter to felony-murder. The reason is that the underlying felony must be independent of the killing, a requirement not satisfied here.

    Example 2: D intends to punch V in the jaw, but not to seriously injure him or kill him. V, while falling from the blow, hits his head on the curb and dies. Even though D was committing the dangerous felony of assault or battery, this will not be upgraded to felony-murder, because the felony was not independent of the killing.

G. Model Penal Code approach: The Model Penal Code does *not* adopt the felony-murder rule *per se*. Instead, the MPC establishes a *rebuttable presumption* of "recklessness...manifesting extreme indifference to the value of life" where D is engaged in or an accomplice to robbery, rape, arson, burglary, kidnapping or felonious escape. Thus if an unintentional killing occurs during one of these crimes, the prosecution gets to the jury on the issue of "depraved heart" murder. But D is free to *rebut* the presumption that he acted with reckless indifference to the value of human life. The MPC provision is thus quite different from the usual felony-murder provision, by which D is *automatically* guilty of murder even if he can show that he was not reckless with respect to the risk of death. [245]

IV. DEGREES OF MURDER

A. Death penalty: At least 35 states now authorize the *death penalty* for some kinds of murder. [246-248]

1. **Not necessarily "cruel and unusual":**   The death penalty is not necessarily a "cruel and unusual" punishment, and thus does not necessarily violate the Eighth Amendment. [*Gregg v. Georgia*, 428 U.S. 153 (1976)] [246]

2. **Must not be "arbitrary or capricious":**   However, a state's death-penalty scheme must not be *"arbitrary or capricious."* That is, the state may not give too much discretion to juries in deciding whether or not to recommend the death penalty in a particular case. Typically, the state avoids undue discretion by listing in the death penalty statute certain **aggravating circumstances** (e.g., the presence of torture) — then, if the jury finds one or more of the aggravating circumstances to exist beyond a reasonable doubt, the jury may recommend the death penalty. In general, this "aggravating circumstance" approach has been upheld by the Supreme Court as constitutional. [246]

3. **Mandatory sentences not constitutional:**   By contrast, it is usually **unconstitutional** for a state to try to avoid undue jury discretion by making a death sentence **mandatory** for certain crimes (e.g., killing of a police officer, or killing by one already under life sentence). The Supreme Court has held that the states must basically allow the jury to consider the **individual circumstances** of a particular case (e.g., the presence of extenuating circumstances), and a mandatory-sentence scheme by definition does not allow this. [*Woodson v. North Carolina*, 428 U.S. 280 (1976)] [247]

4. **Racial prejudice:**   A defendant can avoid a death sentence by showing that the jury was motivated by **racial** considerations, in violation of his Eighth Amendment or equal protection rights. However, the Supreme Court has held that any proof of impermissible racial bias must be directed to the *facts of the particular case*, and may not be proved by large-scale **statistical studies**. [*McCleskey v. Kemp*, 481 U.S. 279 (1987).] [247]

5. **Non-intentional killings:**   The Eighth Amendment appears to prevent use of the death penalty against a defendant who does not himself kill, attempt to kill or intend that a killing take place, or that lethal force be employed. [*Enmund v. Florida*, 458 U.S. 782 (1982).] [247]

    Example: D drives a getaway car while his two accomplices go into a farm house and murder the inhabitants. *Held*, since D did not commit the killing or desire it, he may not be executed, even though he is guilty of murder by virtue of the felony-murder doctrine and the rules on accomplice liability. [*Enmund, supra*]

6. **Non-murder cases:**   The Supreme Court probably will not allow the death penalty for crimes *other than murder*. Thus capital punishment may not constitutionally be imposed on one who commits **rape**. [*Coker v. Georgia*, 433 U.S. 584 (1977)] [248]

B. **First-degree murder:**   Most states recognize at least two degrees of murder. *First-degree murder* in most states is a killing that is *"premeditated and deliberate."* [248-250]

1. **Only short time required for premeditation:**   Courts do not require a long period of premeditation. Traditionally, no substantial amount of time has needed to elapse between formation of the intent to kill and execution of the

killing. Most modern courts require a reasonable period of time during which deliberation exists, but even this is not a very stringent requirement — five minutes, for example, would suffice in most courts even today. [248]

    a. **Planning, motive or careful manner of killing:** Like any other form of intent, premeditation and deliberation can be shown by circumstantial evidence. Typical ways of showing that D premeditated are: (1) *planning activity* occurring prior to the killing (e.g., purchase of a weapon just before the crime); (2) evidence of a *"motive"* in contrast to a sudden impulse; and (3) a *manner* of killing so precise that it suggests D must have a preconceived design. [249]

  2. **Intoxication as negating deliberation:** If D is so *intoxicated* that he lost the ability to deliberate or premeditate, this may be a defense to first-degree murder (though not a defense to murder generally, such as second-degree murder). [249]

  3. **Certain felony murders:** Statutes in some states make some or all *felony-murders* (typically, those involving rape, robbery, arson and burglary) first-degree. [250]

  4. **Model Penal Code:** The Model Penal Code does *not* divide murder into first- and second-degree, and attaches no significance to the fact that D did or did not premeditate/deliberate. [249]

C. **Second-degree murder:** Murders that are not first-degree are second-degree. These typically include the following classes: [250]

  1. **No premeditation:** Cases in which there is *no premeditation*. [250]

  2. **Intent to seriously injure:** Cases where D may have premeditated, but his intent was not to kill, but to do *serious bodily injury* (a *mens rea* sufficient for murder). [250]

  3. **Reckless indifference:** Cases in which D did not intend to kill, but was *recklessly indifferent* to the value of human life. [250]

  4. **Felony-murders:** Killings committed during the course of felonies other than those specified in the first-degree murder statute (i.e., typically felonies other than rape, robbery, arson and burglary). [250]

V. MANSLAUGHTER — VOLUNTARY

A. **Two types of manslaughter:** In most states, there are two types of manslaughter: (1) *voluntary manslaughter*, in which there is generally an *intent to kill*; and (2) *involuntary manslaughter*, in which the death is *accidental*. [250]

B. **"Heat of passion" manslaughter:** The most common kind of voluntary manslaughter is that in which D kills while in a *"heat of passion,"* i.e., an extremely *angry* or disturbed state. [250]

  1. **Four elements:** Assuming that the facts would otherwise constitute murder, D is entitled to a conviction on the lesser charge of voluntary manslaughter if he meets four requirements: [250]

     a. Reasonable provocation: He acted in response to a *provocation* that would have been sufficient to cause a *reasonable person* to *lose his self-control.* [250]

     b. Actually act in "heat of passion": D was *in fact* in a "heat of passion" at the time he acted; [250]

     c. No time for reasonable person to cool off: The lapse of time between the provocation and the killing was not great enough that a *reasonable person* would have *"cooled off,"* i.e., regained his self-control; [250] and

     d. D not in fact cooled off: D did not *in fact* "cool off" by the time he killed. [250]

  2. Consequence of missing hurdle: If D fails to clear hurdles (a) or (c) above (i.e., he is actually provoked, and has not cooled off, but a reasonable person would have either not lost his self-control or would have cooled off), D will normally be liable only for *second-degree* murder, not first-degree, since he will probably be found to have lacked the necessary premeditation. But if D trips up on hurdles (b) or (d) (i.e., he is not in fact driven into a heat of passion, or has in fact already cooled off), he is likely to be convicted of *first-degree* murder, since his act of killing is in "cold blood." [251]

C. Provocation: As noted, D's act must be in response to a *provocation* that is: (1) sufficiently strong that a *"reasonable person"* would have been *caused to lose his self control*; and (2) strong enough that *D himself* lost his self-control. [251-254]

  1. Lost temper: The provocation need not be enough to cause a reasonable person to kill. The provocation merely needs to be enough that it would make a reasonable person *lose his temper.* [251]

  2. Objective standard for emotional characteristics: Courts generally do *not* recognize the peculiar *emotional* characteristics of D in determining how a reasonable person would act. (*Example:* All courts agree that the fact that D is unusually bad-tempered, or unusually quick to anger, is not to be taken into account.) [251]

  3. Particular categories: Courts have established certain rules, as a matter of law, about what kind of provocation will suffice: [252]

     a. Battery: More-than-trivial *battery* committed on D is usually considered to be sufficient provocation. [252]

     Example: V, a man, slaps D, a man, because D has failed to pay back a debt. This will probably constitute adequate provocation, so if D then flies into a rage and kills V, this will be manslaughter rather than murder.

       i. D initiates: However, if D brought on the battery by his own initial aggressive conduct, he will *not* be entitled to a manslaughter verdict.

       ii. Assault: If V *attempts* to commit a battery on D, but fails (thereby committing a criminal assault), most courts regard this as sufficient provocation.

b. Mutual combat: If D and V get into a ***mutual combat***, in which neither one can be said to have been the aggressor, most courts will treat this as sufficient provocation to D. [252]

c. Adultery: The classic voluntary manslaughter situation is that in which Husband surprises Wife in the act of ***adultery*** with her paramour, and kills either Wife or Lover. This will almost always be sufficient provocation. (But courts do not necessarily recognize provocation where the couple is ***unmarried***.) [252]

d. Words alone: Traditionally, ***words alone*** cannot constitute the requisite provocation — no matter how abusive, insulting or harassing, D will be guilty of murder, not manslaughter, if he kills in retaliation. [253]

   i. Words carrying information: But if the words ***convey information***, most courts today hold that the words will suffice if a reasonable person would have lost his self-control upon hearing them.

   Example: V says to D, formerly his best friend, "You know, I've been having an affair with your wife for the last six months. She's a heck of a girl, and we'd like you to give her a divorce so that we can get married." This is probably sufficient provocation, so that if D kills V, he is probably entitled to a manslaughter verdict.

4. Effect of mistake: If D ***reasonably*** but ***mistakenly*** reaches a conclusion which, if accurate, would constitute sufficient provocation, courts will generally allow manslaughter. (*Example:* Based on circumstantial evidence, D reasonably but erroneously suspects that his wife has been sleeping with his best-friend. Probably this will suffice as provocation.) [254]

5. Actual provocation: Remember that the provocation must be not only sufficient to cause a reasonable person to lose his self-control, but also sufficient to have ***in fact*** enraged D. [254]

   Example: D finds his wife together with V, his best friend. D has in fact suspected the affair for some time, and thus cooly says to himself, "Now's my chance to kill V and get off with just voluntary manslaughter." He cold-bloodedly shoots V in the heart. Even though the provocation would have been sufficient to cause a reasonable person to lose control, D does not qualify for manslaughter here because he was not in fact enraged at the moment of the shooting.

D. "Cooling off" period: The ***time*** between D's discovery of the upsetting facts and his act of killing must be sufficiently short that: (1) a ***reasonable person*** would not have had time to "cool off"; and (2) D himself did not ***in fact*** cool off. [254]

   1. Rekindling: But even if there is a substantial cooling-off period between the initial provocation and the killing, if a ***new provocation*** occurs which would ***rekindle*** the passion of a reasonable person, the cooling-off rule is not violated. This is true even if the new provocation would not ***by itself*** be sufficient to inflame a reasonable person. [254]

E. Other kinds of voluntary manslaughter: In addition to manslaughter based upon a "heat of passion" killing, there are a number of other situations in which voluntary manslaughter may be found. [255-256]

1. "Imperfect" defenses: Mostly, these other kinds of voluntary manslaughter are situations in which what would otherwise be a *complete defense or justification* does not exist due to D's unreasonable mistake or for some other reason: [255]

a. Imperfect self-defense: Thus some states give D a manslaughter verdict for *"imperfect self-defense,"* where D killed to defend himself but is not entitled to an acquittal because: (1) he was unreasonably mistaken about the existence of danger; or (2) he was unreasonably mistaken about the need for deadly force; or (3) he was the aggressor. [255]

b. Imperfect defense of others: Similarly, if D uses deadly force in *defense of another*, but does not meet all of the requirements for exculpation, some courts give him the lesser charge of voluntary manslaughter. (*Example:* If D witnesses a fight between V and X, and honestly but unreasonably concludes that X was the aggressor, D may be entitled to manslaughter for killing V.) [255]

c. Other situations: If D comes close to qualifying for the defense of *prevention of crime*, or *necessity* or *coercion*, he may be similarly entitled to reduction to manslaughter. [255]

2. Mercy killings: Some courts — and many juries — frequently give D a lesser verdict of voluntary manslaughter when he commits a *mercy killing*, i.e., a killing to terminate the life of one suffering from a painful or incurable disease. [256]

3. Intoxication rarely suffices: Most states do *not* permit D's voluntary *intoxication* to reduce murder to manslaughter. [256]

VI. MANSLAUGHTER — INVOLUNTARY

A. Involuntary manslaughter based on criminal negligence: A person whose behavior is *grossly negligent* may be liable for *involuntary manslaughter* if his conduct results in the accidental death of another person. [257-259]

1. Gross negligence required: Nearly all states hold that *something more than ordinary tort negligence* must be shown before D is liable for involuntary manslaughter. Most states require *"gross negligence"*. Usually, D must be shown to have disregarded a very substantial danger not just of bodily harm, but of *serious* bodily harm or death. [257]

a. Model Penal Code: The MPC requires that D act *"recklessly."* (The MPC also requires that D be aware of the risk, as discussed below.) [257]

2. All circumstances considered: The existence of gross negligence is to be measured in light of *all the "circumstances."* The *social utility* of any objective D is trying to fulfill is part of the equation. [257]

Example: D kills V, a pedestrian, by driving at 50 mph in a 30 mph residential zone. D's conduct may be grossly negligent if D was out for a pleasure spin, but not if D was rushing his critically ill wife to the hospital.

3. **"Inherently dangerous" objects:** Where D uses an object that is *"inherently dangerous,"* the courts are quicker to find him guilty of involuntary manslaughter. This is especially true where the accident involves a *firearm*. [258]

4. **Defendant's awareness of risk:** Courts are split as to whether D may be liable for manslaughter if he was *unaware* of the risk posed by his conduct. [258]

   a. **Awareness usually required:** As noted, most states require D to have acted with "gross negligence" or "recklessness." In these states, courts usually require that D have been *actually aware* of the danger. [258]

   i. **Model Penal Code agrees:** The MPC, which requires "recklessness" for involuntary manslaughter, similarly requires actual awareness. Under the MPC, a person acts recklessly only when he *consciously disregards* a substantial and unjustifiable risk. [258]

5. **Victim's contributory negligence:** The fact that the *victim* was *contributorily negligent* is *not* a defense to manslaughter. (However, the victim's negligence may tend to show that the accident was proximately caused by this action on the victim's part, rather than by any gross negligence on D's part.) [259]

6. **Vehicular homicide:** Many states have defined the lesser crime of *vehicular homicide*, for cases in which death has occurred as the result of the defendant's poor driving, but where the driving was not reckless or grossly negligent. (Most successful involuntary manslaughter cases also involve death by automobile.) [259]

   a. **Intoxication statutes:** Also, some states have special statutes which make it a crime to cause death by *driving while intoxicated*. [259]

   b. **Criminally negligent homicide:** Additionally, some states define the crime of *"criminally negligent homicide,"* whose penalties are typically less than the penalties for involuntary manslaughter. These statutes are not limited to vehicular deaths. (*Example:* The MPC defines the crime of "negligent homicide," which covers cases where D behaves with gross negligence, but is *not aware* of the risk posed by his conduct.) [259]

B. **The misdemeanor-manslaughter rule:** Just as the felony-murder rule permits a *murder* conviction when a death occurs during the course of certain felonies, so the *"misdemeanor-manslaughter"* rule permits a conviction for *involuntary manslaughter* when a death occurs accidentally during the commission of a misdemeanor or other *unlawful act*. [259-261]

1. **Most states apply:** Most states continue to apply the misdemeanor-manslaughter rule. [259]

2. **Substitute for criminal negligence:**   The theory behind the rule is that the unlawful act is treated as a ***substitute for criminal negligence*** (by analogy to the "negligence *per se*" doctrine in tort law). [259]

3. **"Unlawful act" defined:**   *Any misdemeanor* may serve as the basis for application of the misdemeanor-manslaughter doctrine. Also, some states permit the prosecution to show that D violated a ***local ordinance*** or ***administrative regulation***. And if a particular *felony* does not suffice for the felony-murder rule (e.g., because it is not "inherently dangerous to life"), it may be used. [259]

   a. **Battery:**   The most common misdemeanor in misdemeanor-manslaughter cases is ***battery***. [260]

      Example: D gets into an argument with V, and gives him a light tap on the chin with his fist. D intends only to stun V. Unbeknownst to D, V is a hemopheliac and bleeds to death. Since D has committed the misdemeanor of simple battery, and a death has resulted, he is guilty of manslaughter under the misdemeanor-manslaughter rule. The same result would occur if as the result of the light tap, V fell and fatally hit his head on the sidewalk.

   b. **Traffic violations:**   The violation of ***traffic laws*** is another frequent source of misdemeanor-manslaughter liability. [260]

      Example: D fails to stop at a stop sign, and hits V, a pedestrian crossing at a crosswalk. V dies. Even if D does not have the "gross negligence" typically required for ordinary voluntary manslaughter, D's violation of the traffic rule requiring that one stop at stop signs will be enough to make him guilty of manslaughter under the misdemeanor-manslaughter rule.

4. **Causation:**   There must be a ***causal relation*** between the violation and the death. [260]

   a. ***Malum in se:***   In the case of a violation that is ***"malum in se"*** (dangerous in itself, such as driving at an excessive speed), the requisite causal relationship is often found so long as the violation is the "cause in fact" of the death, even though it was not "natural and probable" or even "foreseeable" that the death would occur. That is, in *malum in se* cases, the usual requirement of "proximate cause" is often suspended. [260]

   b. ***Malum prohibitum:***   But if D's offense is ***"malum prohibitum,"*** (i.e., not dangerous in itself, but simply in violation of a ***public-welfare*** regulation), most states do require a showing that the violation was the proximate cause of the death. [260-261]

      i. **"Natural" or "foreseeable" result:**   Some courts impose a requirement of proximate cause by holding that the death must be the ***"natural"*** or ***"foreseeable"*** consequence of the unlawful conduct. (*Example:* D fails to renew his driver's license, and then runs over V, a pedestrian. A court might well hold that since failure to renew a driver's license is *malum prohibitum*, and since V's death was not a "natural" or "probable" consequence of D's failure, D is not guilty under the misdemeanor-manslaughter rule.)

ii. **Violation irrelevant:** Other courts simply do not apply the misdemeanor-manslaughter rule at all to conduct that is *malum prohibitum* — D's conduct must be shown to amount to actual criminal negligence, just as if there had been no violation.

5. **Model Penal Code abolishes:** The Model Penal Code *rejects* the misdemeanor-manslaughter rule in its entirety. However, under the MPC, the fact that an act is unlawful may be *evidence* that the act was reckless (the Code's *mens rea* for manslaughter). [261]

VII. ASSAULT, BATTERY AND MAYHEM

A. **Battery:** The crime of *battery* exists where D causes either: (1) *bodily injury*; or (2) *offensive touching*. [266-267]

1. **Injury or offensive touching:** Any kind of physical injury, even a bruise from a blow, will meet the physical harm requirement. Also, in most states an *offensive touching* will suffice. (*Example:* D, without V's consent, kisses V. Since this is an offensive touching, it will constitute battery in most states even though V was not physically injured.) [266]

2. **Mental state:** D's *intent* to inflict the offensive touching or the injury will suffice, of course. But also, in most states, if the contact is committed *recklessly*, or with gross negligence, this will also suffice. [266]

   Example: D throws a baseball with a friend, in a crowded city street. The ball strikes V, a passerby. If a court finds that D behaved recklessly, he will probably be guilty of battery, even though he did not intend to touch or injure V.

3. **Degrees of battery:** Simple battery is generally a misdemeanor. However, most states have one or more additional, aggravated, forms of battery, some of which are felonies. (*Examples:* Some states make it aggravated battery if D uses a deadly weapon, or acts with "intent to kill" or with "intent to rape.") [266]

B. **Assault:** The crime of *assault* exists where either: (1) D *attempts to commit a battery*, and fails; or (2) D places another in *fear of imminent injury*. [267-268]

1. **Attempted-battery assault:** D is guilty of assault if he *unsuccessfully attempts* to commit a battery. (*Example:* D shoots at V, attempting to hit him in the leg. The bullet misses. D is guilty of the attempted-battery form of assault.) [267]

2. **Intentional-frightening assault:** Some states also recognize a second form of assault, that in which D intentionally *frightens his victim* into fearing *immediate bodily harm*. [267]

   Example: During an attempted bank robbery, D points his gun at V, a customer at the bank, and says, "One false step and I'll fill you full of lead." This is assault of the intentional-frightening variety; the fact that D's threat is conditional does not prevent the crime from existing.

    a. Words alone: *Words alone* will *not* suffice for assault. The words must be accompanied by some overt gesture (e.g., the pointing of a gun) or other physical act. [267]

  3. Aggravated assault: Simple assault is a misdemeanor. However, most states recognize various kinds of felonious *aggravated assault* (e.g., "assault with intent to kill" or "assault with intent to rape"). [268]

C. Mayhem: The common-law crime of *mayhem* is committed whenever D intentionally *maims* or permanently *disables* his victim. Thus mayhem is a battery causing *great bodily harm*. [268]

  1. Injury must be permanent: The injury must not only be serious, but *permanent*. (*Example:* It is not mayhem to break V's jaw, or to cut him with a knife in a way that causes a small scar. On the other hand, it is mayhem to cut out V's eye, or to make him a cripple by shooting off his kneecap.) [268]

VIII. RAPE

A. Rape defined: Rape is generally defined as *unlawful sexual intercourse with a female without her consent*. [268-271]

  1. Intercourse: It is not necessary that D achieve an emission. All that is required is that there be a sexual *penetration*, however slight. [268]

  2. The spousal exception: Common-law rape requires that the victim be one *other than the defendant's wife*. However, this complete spousal exemption at common law has been weakened by statutory reform. [269]

    a. Forcible rape even while living together: A substantial minority of states now permit prosecution for *forcible rape* even if H and W are living together. In other words, in these states, the spousal exemption is virtually eliminated. [269]

    b. Separated or living apart: An additional substantial minority eliminate the spousal exemption based on the parties' current living arrangements or marital status. Some of these eliminate the exemption where the parties are *not living together*. Others eliminate it only if the parties are separated by court order, or one has filed for divorce or separation. [269]

  3. Without consent: The intercourse must occur without the woman's *consent*. [269]

    a. Victim drunk or drugged: If D causes V to become *drunk*, *drugged* or *unconscious*, the requisite lack of consent is present. In some but not all states, consent is lacking if the woman is drunk, drugged or unconscious even if this condition was not induced by D. [269]

    b. Fraud: If consent is obtained by *fraud*, the status depends on the nature of the fraud. Where D tells a lie in order to induce V to agree to have what V knows is intercourse with him, the fraud is "in the inducement" and does *not* vitiate the consent. (*Example:* D says to V, "Have sex with me, and I promise we'll get married tomorrow." Even if D is knowingly misleading V about the probability of marriage, D has not committed rape.) [269]

    i. Fraud in the essence: But if the fraud is such that V does not even realize that she is having intercourse at all ("fraud in the essence"), this will suffice for rape. (*Example:* D, a doctor, has sex with V by telling her that he is treating her with a surgical instrument. This is rape.) [269]

  c. Mistake as to consent: If D makes a ***reasonable mistake*** as to whether V consented, he does ***not*** have the *mens rea* for rape. If D's mistake, however, is a negligent or reckless one, courts are split about whether it furnishes a defense. [269]

4. Force: The vast majority of rape statutes apply only where the intercourse is committed by *"force"* or "forcible compulsion." In other words, it is not enough that the woman fails to consent; she must also be "forced" to have the intercourse. (If the woman is unconscious or drugged, or is under-age, force is not an element of the crime; but in other instances of rape, force is required.) [269-271]

  a. Threat of force: D's ***threat*** to commit ***imminent serious bodily harm*** on the woman will be a substitute for the use of actual physical force, in virtually all states. Some states also recognize the threat to do other kinds of acts not involving serious bodily harm (e.g., a threat of "extreme pain or kidnapping" may suffice under the Model Penal Code). [270]

    i. Implied threats or threats of non-imminent harm: On the other hand, ***implied threats***, or threats to commit harm on some *future occasion*, or *duress* stemming from the victim's circumstances, are all things that will ***not suffice***, because they are not threats to use force on the particular occasion. [270]

  b. Resistance: Traditionally, rape did not exist unless the woman ***physically resisted***. This requirement is gradually being weakened. [270]

    i. Reasonable resistance: No state requires that the woman resist "to the utmost" anymore, as some states used to. Typically, the woman must now make merely *"reasonable"* resistance, as measured by the circumstances. (*Example:* Where D is threatening V with a gun or knife, presumably it is "reasonable" for V not to resist at all.) [270]

5. Homosexual rape: Because common-law rape is defined so as to require both penetration and a female victim, there can be no common-law ***homosexual rape***. (However, a majority of states have amended their rape statutes to be gender-neutral, so that homosexual rape is now the same crime as heterosexual rape in most states.) [271]

B. Statutory rape: All states establish an ***age of consent***, below which the law regards a female's consent as ***impossible***. One who has intercourse with a female below this age is punished for what is usually called "statutory rape." [271]

1. **Reasonable mistake:**   In most states, even a *reasonable belief* by D that the girl was over the age of consent is not a defense. [271]

   a. **MPC allows:**   But the Model Penal Code allows the "reasonable mistake as to age" defense, at least where the offense is garden-variety statutory rape (intercourse with a girl under the age of 16). [272]

2. **Encouragement by girl:**   The fact that the under-age girl has *encouraged* the sex is irrelevant. Also, the fact that the girl has lied about her age is no defense (unless it contributes to D's reasonable mistake as to age, in a state recognizing reasonable mistake as a defense). [271]

IX. KIDNAPPING

A. **Definition of kidnapping:**   Kidnapping is the *unlawful confinement* of another, accompanied by either a *moving* of the victim or a *secreting* of him. [272]

   1. **Asportation:**   Assuming that the crime does not involve secret imprisonment, the prosecution must show that the victim was *moved* ("asportation"). [272]

      a. **Large distance not required:**   The asportation need not be over a large distance. (*Example:* D accosts V on the street, and makes her walk a few feet to his car, where he detains her. The requisite asportation will probably be found.) [272]

      b. **Must not be incidental to some other offense:**   However, the asportation must not be merely *incidental to some other offense*. [272]

      Example: D, in order to rob V, forces him to stand up and put his hands against the wall, while D empties V's pockets. There is probably no asportation since there was no independent purpose to the confinement and movement; therefore, there is probably no kidnapping. But if B had been bound and gagged and left in a strange place to allow D to escape, this probably *would* be kidnapping.

CHAPTER 9

THEFT CRIMES

I.   INTRODUCTION

A. **List of theft crimes:**   There are seven crimes that can loosely be called "theft" crimes: [283]

   1. *Larceny*

   2. *Embezzlement*

   3. *False pretenses*

   4. *Receipt of stolen property*

   5. *Burglary*

6. *Robbery*

7. *Extortion* (blackmail) [283]

B. **Distinguishing the basic three:** The three "basic" theft crimes are *larceny*, *embezzlement* and *false pretenses*. Most exam questions relating to theft focus on the distinctions among these three categories. Therefore, you must focus on two particular dividing lines: [283]

1. **Larceny vs. embezzlement:** First, focus on the dividing line between *larceny* and *embezzlement*. This comes down to the question, "Was possession originally obtained unlawfully [larceny] or lawfully [embezzlement]?" [283-284]

2. **Larceny vs. false pretenses:** Second, focus on the dividing line between *larceny* and *false pretenses*. This comes down to the question, "What was obtained unlawfully, mere possession [larceny] or title [false pretenses]?" [284]

Note on consolidation: Some American states have now consolidated the three main theft crimes into one basic crime of "theft." But for the most part, you will generally be called upon to make these distinctions among the three common-law crimes. [284]

II. LARCENY

A. **Definition:** Common-law larceny is defined as follows: [284]

1. The *trespassory*

2. *taking* and

3. *carrying away* of

4. *personal property*

5. of *another* with

6. *intent to steal*.

Example: D, a pickpocket, removes V's wallet from V's pocket, and runs away with it, without V discovering for some time what has happened. D has committed common-law larceny. That is, he has taken property that belonged to another and that was in the other's possession, and has carried it away, with an intent to steal it.

B. **Trespassory taking:** The requirement of a "trespassory taking" means that if D is *already in rightful possession* of the property at the time he appropriates it to his own use, he cannot be guilty of larceny. [284-288]

Example: D rents a car from V, a car-rental agency. At the time D consummates the rental transaction, he intends to use the car for one week (and so notifies V), then return it. After the week has passed, D decides to keep the car permanently, without paying any further rental fee. At common law, D is not guilty of larceny. This is because at the time he made the decision to appropriate the car, he was already in rightful possession, under the rental contract. But if at the moment D rented the car he intended to steal it, this would be a "trespassory taking" and thus larceny.

1. **Taking by employee:**   Where an *employee* steals property belonging to the employer, and the employee had at least some physical control over the property at the time he made the decision to steal it, the existence of the requisite "trespassory taking" can be unclear. [286]

   a. **Minor employee:**   If the employee is a relatively low-level one, the court is likely to hold that she had only *custody*, so that the employer retained possession. In this event, the employee would commit the necessary trespass, and would be guilty of common-law larceny. [286]

      Example: D is an entry-level bank clerk at V, a bank. D takes a stack of $100 bills out of her cash drawer, and walks out of the bank with them. A court would probably hold that D had only temporary "custody" of the bills in her cash register, not true "possession." Therefore, when D left the bank with the bills, she trespassorily took the bills from V's possession, and is guilty of common-law larceny.

      i. **Property received from third person:**   But if the low-level employee receives property for the employer's benefit from a *third person*, the employee will generally be deemed to have possession, not mere custody — if he then later appropriates it, he is not guilty of larceny.

         Example: D, a messenger, works for V, a business. D goes to the bank and picks up money from the bank, which is V's property needed for payroll. Here, D has possession, not mere custody, so if he then absconds with the money he is not guilty of larceny. Instead, he would be guilty of embezzlement.

   b. **High employee:**   If the employee is one who has a *high position*, with broad authority, he will usually be deemed to have possession, not just custody, of property that he holds for the employer's benefit. Therefore, if he subsequently appropriates the property for his own purposes, he is not guilty of larceny, but rather, embezzlement. [286]

      Example: D, the president of V, a publicly-held corporation, has the right to sign checks on V's bank accounts. He writes a check for $1,000, which he uses for his own purposes, and in a way that is not authorized by his employment contract with V. D has possession of the contents of the bank account, not mere custody, so his use of the money for his own purposes is embezzlement rather than larceny.

2. **Transactions in owner's presence:**   If the owner of property delivers it to D as part of an exchange transaction which the owner *intends to be completed in his presence*, D receives only custody, and the owner retains "constructive possession." Therefore, if D appropriates the property, the requisite trespass exists, and the crime is larceny. [286]

   Example: D drives into V's gas station. He asks for his tank to be filled up, and drives off without paying. Since the transaction was to be completed in

V's presence, V retained "constructive possession" of the gas, and D's driving away was a trespassory taking and thus larceny. Some courts might call this "larceny by trick," but this is merely a particular way in which larceny can be committed, not a separate crime.

3. **Lost or mislaid property:** Where D finds *lost or mislaid property*, he may or may not commit the requisite trespass, depending on his state of mind at the time of the finding. [287-288]

   a. **Initial intent to keep it:** If D *intends to keep the property* at the time he finds it, he has committed the requisite trespass, and can be liable for larceny. (But he will not be guilty of larceny unless he also either knows who the owner is, or has reason to believe that he may be *able to find out* who and where the owner is. If D does not have such knowledge or reasonable belief at the time of finding, he does not become guilty of common-law larceny even if, subsequently, he discovers the owner's identity.) [287]

   b. **No initial intent to keep:** Conversely, if D does *not* intend to keep the property at the time he finds it (that is, he intends to try to return it to the owner), his possession is rightful and there is no trespass. Then, if D later changes his mind and does keep the property, he is *not guilty of larceny* at common law, since he is already in lawful possession. [287]

   c. **Property delivered by mistake:** The same rules apply where the owner of the property delivers it to D *by mistake* — D is not guilty of larceny, unless *at the time he receives the property*, he both realizes the mistake and intends to keep the property. [287]

   d. **MPC changes rule:** The Model Penal Code changes the common-law trespass rules in cases of lost, mislaid or misdelivered property. Under the MPC, D's intent at the time he obtains the property is *irrelevant* — instead, D becomes liable for theft if "with purpose to deprive the owner thereof, he *fails to take reasonable measures* to *restore the property* to a person entitled to have it." [288]

   Example: D finds a wallet on the street, with money in it. At the time he picks it up, he intends to return it to V, its owner, who is identified on a driver's license inside the wallet. After D keeps the wallet on his dresser for two days, he decides, "I think I'll just keep it — no one will ever know." At common law, D is not guilty of larceny, because at the time he found the wallet, he intended to return it V. But under the MPC, D becomes guilty of larceny at the moment he decides to keep the property and fails to take reasonable steps to get it back to V.

4. **Larceny by trick:** If D gains possession of property by *fraud or deceit*, the requisite trespassory taking takes place. The larceny in this situation is said to be *"by trick"* — larceny by trick is simply one way in which larceny may be committed, not a separate crime. [288]

   Example: D rents a car from V, a car rental agency. At the moment of the rental transaction, D has already decided that he will not return the car, and will not pay for it. D has committed larceny of the "by trick" variety, because his initial taking of possession was obtained by fraud or deceit.

    a. Distinguished from false pretenses: Distinguish the taking of possession by fraud or deceit (leading to larceny by trick) from the taking of *title* by fraud or deceit (which is not larceny at all). If title passes, the crime is theft by false pretenses. [288]

C. Carrying away ("asportation"): D, to commit larceny, must not only commit a trespassory taking, but must also *carry the property away*. This is called *"asportation."* [289]

    1. Slight distance sufficient: However, as long as every portion of the property is moved, even a *slight distance* will suffice. [289]

    Example: D enters V's car, turns on the lights and starts the engine. At that point he is arrested. At common law, this would probably not be enough movement to satisfy the asportation requirement. But many courts today would hold that since D brought the car under his dominion and control, he did enough to satisfy the requirement. If D drove the car even a few feet, *all* courts would agree that he had met the asportation requirement.

D. Personal property of another: Common-law larceny exists only where the property that is taken is *tangible personal property*. [289]

    1. Intangibles: Thus at common law, one could not commit larceny of *intangible* personal property, such as stocks, bonds, checks, notes, etc. But today, all states have expanded larceny to cover many intangible items such as stocks and bonds; some states also cover such items as gas and electricity and services. [289]

    2. Trade secrets: Some courts have held that the taking of *trade secrets* can constitute larceny. [289]

E. Property of another: The property taken, to constitute larceny, must be property *belonging to another*. Where D and another person are *co-owners*, the common-law view is that there can be no larceny. [290]

    1. Recapture of chattel: If D is attempting to *retake* a *specific chattel* that belongs to him, D will not be guilty of larceny, because he is not taking property "of another." In most states, this is also true if D is genuinely *mistaken* (even if unreasonably) in thinking that the thing he is taking belongs to himself rather than the other person. But this rule does not apply where D is taking *cash* or some other property in satisfaction of a *debt* (though the "claim of right" defense may exist here; see *infra*, p. C-147). [290]

    Example 1: D's bicycle is stolen. Two days later he sees what is apparently the same bike, chained to a lamp post. D genuinely believes that this is his own stolen bike. He cuts the chain and removes the bike. If the bike was in fact his own, D is clearly not guilty of larceny, because he has not taken the property "of another." If D genuinely believes that the bike was his — even if this belief is unreasonable — most courts will similarly hold that he has not committed larceny.

Example 2: D is owed $100 by V. D sees V's bicycle (worth $75) parked on the street. If D takes the bike as a substitute form of payment, he probably cannot defend on the grounds that the bike is not "property of another." On the other hand, most states would allow him to raise the "claim of right" defense, discussed in Par. F(2) below.

F. Intent to steal: Larceny is a crime that can only be committed ***intentionally***, not negligently or recklessly. [291-293]

1. **Intent to permanently deprive owner:** D must thus generally be shown to have an intent to ***permanently deprive*** the owner of his property. An intent to take property ***temporarily*** is not sufficient. [291]

   Example: D enters V's car, intending to take it on a three-mile "joy ride." After one mile, D crashes the car, destroying it totally. At common law, D is not guilty of larceny, because he did not intend to permanently deprive V of his property.

   a. **Substantial deprivation:** But if D intends to use the property for such a long time, or in such a way, that the owner will be deprived of a ***significant portion of the property's economic value***, the requisite intent to steal exists. [291]

      Example: D takes a lawnmower belonging to V, with an intent to keep it all summer and fall. This probably constitutes larceny, because D intends to deprive V of a substantial part of the useful life of the mower.

   b. **Issue is intent, not result:** The issue regarding permanent-or-substantial-deprivation is D's ***intent***, not what actually happens. [291]

      Example: In the above example concerning the joy ride, D did not meet the intent-to steal requirement because he did not intend to permanently deprive V of the car, even though this was the result of D's acts. Conversely, if D takes a car with intent to resell it or strip it for parts, D will not avoid a larceny conviction because the police stop him one block away with the car in perfect condition.

2. **Claim of right:** If D takes another's property under a ***claim of right***, D will not be found to have had the requisite guilty intent. [292-293]

   a. **Money taken to satisfy claim:** Thus if D takes V's property with an intent to ***collect a debt*** which V owes D, or to satisfy some other kind of ***claim*** which D has against V, D will not be guilty of larceny. D is especially likely to have a good defense where D's claim against V is a "liquidated" one, that is, one is with a fixed monetary value. [292]

      Example: D works for V. V fires D, and illegally refuses to pay D D's last week of wages, equaling $100. D reaches into V's cash register and removes $100 and walks out with it. D is not guilty of larceny, because his intent was to collect a debt which V owed him.

      i. **Mistake:** Most significantly, D lacks the requisite intent for larceny even if he is ***mistaken*** about the validity of his claim against V. And this is true even if D's mistake is ***unreasonable***, so long as it is sincere. [292]

Example: D works for V. V fires D, and refuses to pay him for three weeks of vacation pay, which D genuinely believes is owed to him. Assume that under applicable legal principles, and as any reasonably knowledgeable employee would understand, D was not entitled to any vacation pay, because D had taken all the vacation to which he was entitled up to the moment he was fired. D nonetheless reaches into V's cash register and removes three weeks' pay. D is not guilty of larceny, because he took pursuant to an honest, though unreasonable and mistaken, belief that he had a legally-enforceable claim against V for the money.

   b. Usually not a defense to robbery: Most states hold that the "claim of right" defense is *not available* where D is charged with a crime of *violence*, including *robbery*. [292]

   Example: V owes D $25. D and V meet on the street, and V refuses to pay any of the money back, even though it is overdue. D sees that V has the entire sum owed, $25, on V's person. D takes the $25 back by force. Most courts would hold that this is robbery, because the "claim of right" defense is not available for crimes of violence such as robbery. [*People v. Reid*, 508 N.E.2d 661 (N.Y.1987)]

III. EMBEZZLEMENT

A. Definition: Embezzlement usually is defined as follows: [294-298]

   1. A *fraudulent*

   2. *conversion* of

   3. the *property*

   4. of *another*

   5. by one who is *already in lawful possession* of it. [294]

B. No overlap with larceny: Embezzlement statutes are generally construed so as *not to overlap* with larceny — a given fact pattern must be either larceny or embezzlement, and cannot be both. [295]

C. Conversion: For most larceny, D needs only to take and carry away the property. But for embezzlement, D must *convert it*, i.e., deprive the owner of a significant part of its usefulness. If D merely uses the property for a short time, or moves it slightly, he is not guilty of embezzlement (regardless of whether he *intended* to convert it.) [295]

   Example: D's boss lends D the company car to do a company errand, and D decides to abscond with it or sell it. The police stop D after he has driven the car for one mile. D is not technically guilty of embezzlement, since he has not yet deprived the company of a significant part of the car's usefulness, and thus has not converted it.

D. Property of another: The property must be *"property of another."* [295-297]

   1. Meaning of "property": Embezzlement statutes typically are somewhat broader than larceny statutes, in terms of the *property* covered. Anything that can be taken by larceny may be embezzled (i.e., not just tangible personal property but, for instance, stocks and bonds). Also, some embezzlement statutes cover real property (e.g., D uses a power of attorney received from O to deed O's property to D.) [295]

2. **Property "of another":** The property must be property belonging to *another* rather than to D. [295-297]

   a. **D to pay from own funds:** Thus if D has an obligation to *make payment from his own funds*, he *cannot embezzle* even if he fraudulently fails to make the payment. [295-296]

   Example: D, a coal mine operator, has his employees sign orders directing D to deduct from their wages the amount that each owes to a grocery store. D deducts the amount, but then fails to pay the store owner. D is not guilty of common-law embezzlement, because he did not misappropriate the employees' money, but rather, failed to make payment from his own funds. He is civilly liable but not criminally liable. [*Commonwealth v. Mitchneck*, 198 A. 463 (Pa. 1938)]

   i. **Model Penal Code changes:** The Model Penal Code changes the common law rule described above, by creating a new crime of "theft by failure to make the required disposition of funds received." The provision applies wherever D not only agrees to make a payment but *reserves funds* for this obligation. D in *Mitchneck*, *supra*, would be liable under the MPC rule.

   b. **Co-owners:** One who is *co-owner* of the property together with another cannot, at common law, embezzle the joint property, because it is deemed to be his "own." Thus one *partner* in a business cannot commit common-law embezzlement against the other. (But some modern embezzlement statutes explicitly apply to co-owned property.)

   c. **Security interest:** Suppose D *buys goods on credit*, and gives the seller a *"security interest,"* entitling the seller to *repossess* the goods if D does not pay the price. If D then fails to repay the money and sells the goods in violation of the security agreement, this will usually *not* be treated as embezzlement. [296]

E. **"By one in lawful possession":** The main distinction between larceny and embezzlement is that embezzlement is committed by one who is *already in lawful possession* of the property before he appropriates it to his own use. [297-298]

   Example: D, a lawyer, is appointed trustee of a trust for the benefit of V. The trust principal consists of $10,000, held by D in a bank account named "D in trust for V." D takes the money and buys a new car for himself. D is guilty of embezzlement, because he took property of which he was already in lawful possession.

1. **Employees:** Most commonly, embezzlers are *employees* who misappropriate property with which there employer has entrusted them. [297-298]

   a. **Minor employee:** But remember that a *low-level employee* may be held to have received only *custody* of the item, not true "possession." If such a minor employee takes the property for his own purposes, he would be committing larceny rather than embezzlement. (Many states have changed this rule by statute, however — they make it embezzlement rather than larceny for any employee to take property in his possession or "under his care," thus covering even low-level employees who have only custody.) [298]

2. **Finders:** Recall that one who finds *lost or mislaid property*, or to whom property is *mistakenly delivered*, is not guilty of common law larceny if he gains possession without intent to steal (see *supra*, pp. C139-C139). But most embezzlement statutes don't cover this situation either. However, some states have special *"larceny by bailee"* statutes covering this situation, and other states have embezzlement statutes that explicitly cover finders and other bailees. [298]

F. **Fraudulent taking:** The taking must be *"fraudulent."* [298-299]

1. **Claim of right:** Thus if D honestly believes that he has a *right* to take the property, this will usually negate the existence of fraud. Thus if D mistakenly believes that the property is *his*, or that he is authorized to use it in a certain way, this will be a defense (probably even if the mistake is unreasonable). [298]

2. **Debt collection:** Similarly, if D takes the property in order to *collect a debt* owed to him by the owner (or even a debt which D believes the owner owes him), D is not an embezzler. [298]

Example: D, president of V Corp., is dismissed by the board of directors. The board refuses to pay D a $20,000 bonus, which D genuinely believes the company was contractually committed to pay D for D's work in the prior year. D writes himself out a check for $20,000. D's taking here is probably not "fraudulent" and D is not an embezzler, even if D's claim of right was a mistaken one.

3. **Intent to repay:** If D takes *money*, it is *no defense* to an embezzlement charge that D *intended to repay* the money. This is true even if D has a complete *ability* to repay the money. [299]

Example: D, president of V Corp., "borrows" $10,000 from the corporate treasury with which to play the stock market. At the time of this borrowing, D has a net worth of several million dollars, and honestly intends to repay the money within one week. D is arrested before he can repay the money. It is clear that D is guilty of embezzlement, despite his intent and ability to repay.

Note: But if the property is something other than money, and D shows that he has an intent to return the *very property taken* (and has a substantial ability to do so at the time of taking), this *will* be a defense to embezzlement. (*Example:* D uses the company car for a two-hour personal trip, intending to return it. He is not an embezzler even if he accidentally destroys the car.)

IV. FALSE PRETENSES

A. **Definition:** The crime of obtaining property by false pretenses — usually called simply *"false pretenses"* — has these elements: [299]

1. A *false representation* of a

2. *material present or past fact*

3. which *causes* the person to whom it is made

4. to *pass title to*

5. his *property* to the misrepresenter, who

6. *knows* that his representation is false, and *intends to defraud*. [299]

B. **Nature of crime:** Thus false pretenses occurs where D uses fraud or deceit to obtain not only possession but also *ownership* (title). The crime differs from larceny with respect to what is obtained: in larceny, D obtains possession only, not title. [300]

C. **False representation of present or past fact:** There must be a *false representation* of a *material present or past fact*. [300-301]

1. **Non-disclosure and concealment:** The false representation is usually an explicit verbal one. But there are other types of misrepresentation that will qualify: [300]

   a. **Reinforcing false impressions:** It is a misrepresentation to knowingly *reinforce a false impression* held by another. [300]

      Example: Buyer wants to buy Seller's ring, which as Seller knows Buyer thinks is diamond. Seller knows that the ring is really glass. Seller quotes a price that would be a low price for diamonds, but hundreds of times too high for glass. Seller has probably committed a false representation as to the nature of the ring by reinforcing what he knows to be Buyer's misconception.

   b. **Concealment:** Similarly, the requisite misrepresentation can exist if D takes affirmative acts to *conceal* a material fact. [300]

      Example: D, owner of a car whose engine block is broken, paints the engine block in such a way as to conceal the defect, then sells the car to V at a price that would be a fair price for a car with a good engine. D would probably be held to have made a misrepresentation by his act of concealment and would therefore be guilty of false pretenses.

   c. **Fiduciary relationship:** If D is in a *fiduciary relationship* with the other party, he will generally have an affirmative duty to speak the truth, and is thus not free to remain silent. [300]

      Example: D has long been the family jeweler for V and his family. D knows that V trusts D in matters relating to jewelry. V sees a ring in D's window and says, "Oh, what a lovely diamond ring; I'll pay you $1,000." D knows that the ring is cubic zirconium, but remains silent and accepts the $1,000. Because D probably had a fiduciary relationship with V based on their past dealing and V's extra trust in D, D has probably made a misrepresentation and can be guilty of false pretenses.

    d. Silence normally not enough: But these are all *exceptions* to the *general rule*: a party to a bargaining situation may generally *remain silent* even though he knows that the other party is under a false impression (provided that D did not cause that false impression in the first place). [300]

2. False promises not sufficient: Most courts hold that the representation must relate to a *past or present fact*. *False promises*, even when made with an intent not to keep them, are *not* sufficient in most courts. (But an increasing *minority* of courts do treat knowingly false promises as sufficient.) [301]

Example: D borrows money from V Bank, promising to repay it on a particular date. D in reality has no intention of ever repaying the money, and plans to abscond with it to South America. In most courts, this is not taking money by false pretenses, but in an increasing minority of courts it is.

D. Reliance: The victim must *rely* upon the representation. [301]

1. Belief required: Thus if the victim does *not believe* the representation, there is no crime of false pretenses. [301]

2. Materiality: Also, the false representation must be a *"material"* one. That is, it must be a representation which would play an important role in a *reasonable person's decision* whether to enter into the transaction. [301]

E. Passing of title: Remember that *title*, not merely possession, must pass for false pretenses. Generally, this turns on what the *victim intends* to do. [302]

1. Sale as opposed to loan or lease: If the victim parts with property in return for other property or money, there is a transfer of title if a *sale* occurs, of course. But if the victim merely *lends* or *leases* his property, only possession has been transferred, so that the offense is larceny by trick rather than false pretenses. [302]

2. Handing over money: Where V *hands over money* to D, this will usually be a passing of title, and the crime will thus be false pretenses. (*Example:* D borrows money from V, a bank, by lying on the credit application. The bank is deemed to have passed over title to the money in return for D's promise to repay with interest, so D has committed false pretenses.) [302]

    a. Money for specific purposes: But if V gives D money with the understanding that D will apply it towards a *particular purpose*, this is likely to be a passage of possession rather than title, and thus larceny rather than false pretenses. This is especially the case where it can be argued that D has taken the money in "constructive trust" for V.

    Example: V, a client, gives $1,000 to D, a lawyer who is assisting V in the sale of some property. V tells D that D should use the money to pay off a tax lien against the property. Instead, D gambles away the money. Assuming that from the very moment of the transfer of funds D intended to misuse the money — thus preventing the case from being embezzlement — D would be guilty of larceny rather than false pretenses, because the property was given to him earmarked for a specific purpose.

F. **Property "of another":** The property received by D must have belonged to *"another."* [303]

1. **Joint ownership:** Thus as in embezzlement and larceny, most courts still hold that property D *co-owns* with V is not property of another. [303]

a. **Modern view finds liability:** But modern courts are increasingly likely to hold that where D takes property belonging to himself and a co-owner, this *is* property of "another" and thus false pretenses. [303]

G. **D's mental state:** False pretenses is essentially a crime requiring intent. However, the intent requirement is deemed met if either: (1) D *knows* that the representation is untrue; (2) D *believes*, but does not know, that the representation is untrue; or (3) D *knows that he does not know* whether the representation is true or false. [303]

> **Example:** D has a painting found in his attic, signed "van Gogh." D knows nothing about art or the circumstances in which the painting came to be in his attic. D nonetheless tells V, a prospective amateur buyer who also knows nothing about art, "This painting is a genuine van Gogh." Because D knows that he does not in fact know the provenance of the painting, D has committed the requisite false representation. He is therefore guilty of false pretenses when he makes the sale to V at a price that would be appropriate for a genuine van Gogh.

1. **Unreasonable belief in truth:** But if D *believes* the representation to be true, he is not liable for false pretenses even if his belief is *unreasonable*. [303]

2. **Claim of right:** If D goes through the transaction under a *claim of right*, this will be a defense to false pretenses just as to embezzlement or larceny. This is true, for instance, where D uses subterfuge to collect a debt. [304]

> **Example:** V owes D $1,000, which V has refused to repay in a timely way. D then offers to sell V a ring which D says is a true diamond worth $2,000. The ring is in fact cubic zirconium worth $20. V agrees to buy the ring for $1,000. Assuming that D's purpose in entering into the "fraudulent" transaction was merely to recoup the $1,000 that V owed him, D's misrepresentation is not truly fraudulent, and D is not guilty of false pretenses.

a. **Mistake:** The same is probably true even if D is *mistaken* as to the validity of his claim of right.

H. **Defenses:** [304]

1. **Gullibility of victim:** D may *not* defend a false pretenses case by showing that the misrepresentation was one which would not have deceived an ordinarily intelligent person. In other words, the *victim's gullibility* is no defense. [304]

2. **No pecuniary loss:** Similarly, the fact that V has suffered no actual *pecuniary loss* is usually not a defense. So long as D has knowingly made the requi-

site material false representation of fact that causes V to transfer property, the fact that the trade may be approximately "even" is irrelevant. [304]

Example: D sells office supplies to V, a large company, by bribing V's purchasing agent. The prices charged by D are "ordinary" prices in the trade, neither as low as some charge nor as high as others charge. D cannot defend a false pretenses prosecution on the grounds that V has suffered no financial loss. This is because D has acquired property (V's money) by fraud, and V would not have paid the money had it known that the sales were procured by bribery of an employee.

I. **Related crimes:** Here are some statutory crimes, found in many jurisdictions, that are related to false pretenses but deal with slightly different situations: [304]

1. **Bad checks:** Most jurisdictions make it a crime to obtain property by writing a ***bad check***. This crime is committed even if the check never clears and the title never transfers (which would not be the case for false pretenses). [304]

2. **Federal mail fraud:** The ***federal mail fraud*** statute makes it a crime to use the mails as part of a scheme to defraud a victim of his property. Here, too, the scheme ***does not have to be successful*** for liability to exist. [304]

3. **Forgery:** The crime of ***forgery*** exists where a document (usually a check or other negotiable instrument) is ***falsified***. The falsification must relate to the ***genuineness*** of the instrument itself. Again, it is not necessary that the forged document actually be used to obtain property from another. (*Example:* D steals checks from V, then signs V's name to them. If D is found with the checks in his possession, he is already liable for forgery even if he has not used the checks to gain property.) [305]

V. CONSOLIDATION OF THEFT CRIMES

A. **Consolidation generally:** Some states, though still a minority, have joined two or more of the group of larceny, embezzlement and false pretenses into a ***unified*** crime called "theft." [305-306]

1. **MPC consolidation:** The MPC achieves a similar, though not identical, consolidation. Larceny and embezzlement are consolidated as "theft by unlawful taking or disposition." "Larceny by trick" (classically a form of larceny) and false pretenses are combined into "theft by deception." Also, several new crimes are created, including "theft of property lost, mislaid, or delivered by mistake" (which previously could have been either larceny or embezzlement, depending on the facts). [305]

VI. RECEIVING STOLEN PROPERTY

A. **Targetted at fences:** The crime of ***"receipt of stolen property"*** is directed primarily at ***"fences,"*** middlemen who buy goods at a very low price from thieves and resell them to end-users. [306]

B. **Elements of offense:** Most stolen property statutes make it a crime to: [307]

1.   *receive*

2.   *stolen property*

3.   with *knowledge* that it has been stolen and

4.   with *intent to deprive* the owner. [306]

C. **Discussion:**

1.   **"Stolen":**   Most statutes cover not only property taken by larceny, but also property that was taken by *embezzlement* or *false pretenses*. [306]

2.   **Trap laid by police:**   If property is sold by a thief who is cooperating with the police, or by the police themselves, the fence who buys it is *not guilty* of receiving stolen property, even if he believes the property is stolen. This is because the property is no longer in fact stolen. However, the fence will typically be guilty of *attempted* receipt of stolen goods. [306]

3.   **Knowledge that property is stolen:**   Statutes typically say that D must have *"known"* that the property was stolen. However, knowledge in the sense of certainty is typically *not* required. [306]

   a.   **Belief:**   Thus in all states, it is enough that D *believes that the goods are stolen*.

   b.   **Suspicion:**   On the other hand, if D merely *suspected* that the goods might be stolen (in the sense that he recognized a possibility that they were stolen), this will not meet the knowledge requirement. And needless to say, the mere fact that a *reasonable person* in D's position would have suspected that the goods were stolen, or would have believed them to be stolen, is not enough (though this will of course be circumstantial evidence as to what D actually believed). [307]

   c.   **Model Penal Code applies presumption:**   The MPC institutes a *presumption* that a dealer possesses the required knowledge or belief in some circumstances (e.g., he is found in possession of property stolen from two or more persons on separate occasions, or buys for far below the goods' reasonable value). But under the MPC, the dealer can rebut this presumption. [307]

VII. BURGLARY

A. **Common-law definition:**   The common-law crime of burglary is defined as follows: [307]

1.   The *breaking* and

2.   *entering* of

3.   the *dwelling of another*

4.   at *night*

5.   with *intent to commit a felony* therein. [307]

    a. Modern statutes: Modern statutes eliminate most of these requirements (as discussed below) for at least the lowest degree of the crime. [307]

B. Breaking: At common law, there must be a *"breaking."* This means that an *opening* must be *created* by the burglar. [307]

    Example: If Owner simply leaves his door or window *open*, the requisite breaking does not exist. However, no force or violence is needed; the mere opening of a closed but unlocked door, followed by entry, suffices.

    1. No consent: Also, breaking does not exist at common law if D is *invited* into the house (assuming that he does not stray into a portion of the house where he was not invited).

    2. Statutes modify: Most states no longer require breaking for all degrees of burglary. [307]

C. Entry: There must also be, at common law, an *entry* following a breaking. However, it is sufficient that *any part* of D's anatomy enters the structure, even for a moment. [307]

    Example: D reaches his hand through a window to grab an item just on the inside of the window; this suffices for breaking and entering, so if D carries the property away, he has committed common-law burglary.

    1. Maintained: Nearly all states continue to impose the requirement of an entry. [308]

D. Dwelling of another: The common law required that the structure be the *dwelling of another*. Thus a place of business did not suffice. [308]

    1. Modified by statute: All states now have at least one form of statutory burglary that does not require that the structure be a dwelling (though nearly all require that there be either a building or a vehicle). [308]

E. Nighttime: At common law, the breaking and entering had to occur *at night*. [308]

    1. Not now required: No state now requires, for all degrees of burglary, that entry be at night. [308]

F. Intent to commit felony therein: At common law, the burglar must, at the time he entered, have *intended to commit a felony* once he got inside. [308]

    1. Crime intended: Today, an intent to commit a *felony* is not required. However, all states require that D have an intent to commit *some crime* (at least a misdemeanor) within the structure. [308]

VIII. ROBBERY

A. Definition: Robbery is defined as *larceny* committed with two additional elements: [308]

    1. The property is taken from the *person or presence* of the owner [309]; and

    2. The taking is accomplished by using *force* or putting the owner in *fear*. [309]

Example: D accosts V on the street at night, and says to V, "Give me your wallet or I'll punch you in the face." V complies, and D carries the property away. D has committed robbery, because D has committed larceny (the taking and carrying away of the property of another with intent to permanently deprive him of it), and has done so by taking the property from V's person, and putting V in fear of what would happen if he did not comply with D's demand.

B. Presence or person of V: The property must be taken from the *presence or person* of its owner. [309]

    1. "Presence" of victim: Most robberies take place directly from the victim's "person." But it is enough that the taking is from V's *"presence."* The test for "presence" is whether V, if he had not been intimidated or forcibly restrained, could have prevented the taking. [309]

    Example: D enters V's house and bedroom. While pointing a gun at V, who is on the bed, D takes V's purse from her dresser, and carries it away. Since the property was taken from V's "presence" — V could have prevented the taking if not intimidated — robbery has taken place even though the taking was not from V's "person."

C. Use of violence or intimidation: The taking must be by use of *violence* or *intimidation*. [309]

    Example 1: V is walking down the street, and is momentarily distracted by a near collision. D stealthily plucks V's wallet out of V's half-open purse. V does not realize what has happened until some time later. D has committed larceny but not robbery, because D did not use violence or intimidation.

    Example 2: Same basic fact pattern as prior example, except that D simply snatches V's purse from her grasp. V has no chance to resist, though she is aware for a fleeting second of what is happening. This is not robbery, because there has been no violence or intimidation. (But if V had been able to put up even a brief struggle, the requisite violence would exist for robbery.)

    1. Intimidation: A *threat of harm* may suffice in lieu of violence. V must be placed in *apprehension* of harm. (*Example:* D pulls a gun on V, and says, "Your money or your life." This is robbery even though no actual force is used.) [309]

        a. "Reasonable person" standard not applied: It is irrelevant that a *"reasonable person"* would not have been apprehensive of bodily harm. Thus if V is frightened of bodily harm due to his unusual timidity, robbery will exist even though most people would not have been afraid. [309]

D. No simultaneous larceny and robbery: The same transaction *cannot* give rise to *simultaneous convictions* for larceny and robbery. This is because robbery is a form of larceny, with the additional element of force present. [309]

E. "Armed" robbery: One aggravated form of robbery, defined in most states, is *"armed* robbery." This exists where D uses a *deadly weapon*. [309]

1. **Gun need not be loaded:** Armed robbery is usually found even though D's gun is *unloaded*. Some cases hold that even a *toy pistol* suffices, though probably this would happen only if V is shown to have believed that the pistol was real. [309]

IX. BLACKMAIL AND EXTORTION

A. **Definition:** If D obtains property by a threat of *future harm*, he is guilty of *extortion*. The crime is called "blackmail" in some states (but there is no significant difference between what some states call blackmail and other call extortion). [310]

   1. **Distinction:** Distinguish extortion from robbery: robbery exists where the property is taken by use of violence or threat of *immediate* harm, whereas extortion exists where the threat is of future harm. [310]

B. **Nature of threat:** The threat can be of various types: to cause physical harm to V or his family or relatives; to *cause economic injury*; or (most commonly) to *accuse V* of a crime, or to divulge disgracing information about V. [310]

   Example: D secretly photographs V, a married man, in the arms of V's lover. D shows V copies of the photos, and threatens to send the photos to V's wife if V does not pay D $2,000. This is extortion, because D has threatened to cause V future harm (exposure) if V does not give D property.

C. **Attempt by D to recover property:** Suppose D uses threats of future harm to *recover property* that V has taken from D. Courts are split as to whether D may defend against an extortion charge by showing that he was operating under a *"claim of right."* Most courts today would probably allow this defense, provided that D is merely recovering the same property or value that V previously, and wrongfully, took from him. [310]

   Example: D, a storekeeper, watches V shoplift $50 worth of merchandise. D is unable to stop V as V leaves the store. The next day, V comes back to the store. D, after writing down V's license plate number, tells V, "If you don't sign a confession to shoplifting and pay me $50, I will turn you in to the police." Most courts today would probably hold that this is not extortion by D, because D is merely making an effort to reclaim property which V has taken from him.

   1. **Reasonable mistake:** Some of the courts allowing D a defense on facts like those in the above example would probably also grant a defense where D has made a *reasonable mistake* about whether V owed the property or money to D. (*Example:* On the facts of the above example, some courts would grant D a defense to extortion if he showed that he mistakenly, but reasonably, believed that V had stolen $50 of merchandise.) [310]

      a. **MPC allows:** The Model Penal Code seems to take this approach, by granting a defense if D "honestly claimed [the property] as restitution...or as compensation for property or lawful services." [310]

EXAM TIPS

SUMMARY OF CONTENTS
of EXAM TIPS

ACTUS REAS AND MENS REA 157

Duty to act 157
Statutory Language (as to both
   Actus Reus and Mens Rea) 158

CAUSATION 160

Cause In Fact 160
Proximate Cause 161

RESPONSIBILITY 163

Insanity 163
Intoxication 165

JUSTIFICATION AND EXCUSE 167

Self-defense 167
Defense of property 169
Fleeing Felons and Law Enforcement 169
Entrapment 171
Duress 171

ATTEMPT 172

Mental State 172
Requirement of Act 173
Impossibility 173
Merger, and Convictions of Both Attempt
   and the Underlying Crime 175

CONSPIRACY 176

Agreement and Intent 176
Overt act 178
Vicarious liability for substantive crimes by
   other conspirators 178
Abandonment 179
Wharton's rule 180
Conspiracy vs. the Substantive Crime 180

ACCOMPLICE LIABILITY AND SOLICITATION..... 181

    Accomplice Liability, Generally 181
    Solicitation 183

HOMICIDE & OTHER CRIMES
AGAINST THE PERSON 183

    Homicides Generally 183
    Intent in Homicide Cases 184
    Felony-murder 186
    Voluntary manslaughter ("v.m.") 188
    Involuntary manslaughter ("i.m.") 189
    Battery 191
    Assault 192
    Rape / Sexual Assault 192
    Kidnapping 193

THEFT CRIMES................................. 193

    Larceny 193
    Robbery 197
    Embezzlement 197
    False pretenses 198
    Burglary 199
    Receiving stolen property 201

EXAM TIPS

Exam Tips on
ACTUS REAS AND MENS REA

☛ The most common issues that arise on exams regarding the requirements of an "actus reus" and a "mens rea" are the following:

Duty to act

☛ Duty-to-act is tested with some frequency on exams, because it calls for the close analysis of a fact pattern. Look for a party who *fails to help another party in distress.* Remember that a party is criminally liable for an omission *only if there exists a duty for her to act.*

☞ **Trap:** Profs will try to distract you by presenting a very callous witness to an accident — one who fails to render aid. Don't be swayed by unsympathetic feelings toward the bystander. Instead, concentrate on whether she had a duty to act. *The ordinary bystander, who has no previous involvement with the peril, has no duty to act.*

Example: A lifeguard at a public swimming pool leaves work early with the permission of her employer. While the pool is unattended a child falls in, striking her head against the edge of the pool. A bystander, B, witnesses the child's fall, but fails to act, despite her knowledge that there is no lifeguard on duty and the fact that she is a strong swimmer. B had no duty to act and cannot be found guilty of any common-law crime.

☞ **Exceptions:** There are two kinds of situations to watch for, exceptions in which there will be a duty to assist:

[1] A *contractual obligation* to act.

Example: D, an apartment-house landlord, receives repeated complaints about a malfunctioning heating system, and fails to respond. The lease says that the landlord will maintain the furnace. The furnace explodes and causes a fire, which leads to the death of V, the complaining tenant. D had a contractual obligation to fix the furnace, and therefore his failure to fix it met the actus reus requirement.

[2] A party *undertakes to give assistance* and fails to follow

through.

Example: D, a prominent heart surgeon, is called by the U.S. Government and asked to perform an unusual heart operation for free on V, an public official. D agrees, but then without warning fails to show up at the appointed time. It's too late to find another surgeon, and V dies without the surgery. (Timely surgery would almost surely have saved him.) When D undertook to do the operation — in circumstances where he knew the search for a surgeon would stop — he incurred an obligation to do what he said he'd do, or at least to notify the government of a change of mind. His failure to perform that duty supplies the actus reus needed for criminal liability in V's death.

Statutory Language (as to both Actus Reus and Mens Rea)

☛ Whenever a question asks you to contemplate a party's violation of a jurisdiction's statute, pay close attention to the statute's wording. This is true whether you're focusing on the actus reus or the mens rea. *Trap:* Profs will try to fool you by drafting a statute differently than the rule prevalent in most jurisdictions or different than the common law. Remember to distinguish between *strict liability* statutes and those requiring *intent*.

These "statutory interpretation" question are pretty much freebies — you don't really need to know any substantive law to answer them, you just need to read and think carefully. So *don't waste these freebies by carelessness*.

☛ **Tips on statutory interpretation:**

☞ **Knowledge:** Look for the words "knowledge" or "knowing." This will often be a clue that a required element (knowledge as to some aspect) is missing.

Example: A statute provides: "Any person who sells an intoxicating substance to a person with knowledge that the person is under the age of 18 years shall be guilty of a misdemeanor." Observe that although most statutes that forbid the sale of alcohol to minors impose strict liability, this one does not. And, under this statute, if a bartender believes (reasonably or unreasonably) that a patron is over 18, then that required element is lacking and there is no violation.

☞ **Ambiguous elements:** If it's unclear from the wording whether knowledge is a requirement, *argue both ways*.

Example: A statute provides: "Whoever assaults with a deadly weapon any federal officer engaged in the performance of his duties is guilty of a felony." It's plausible that this statute might be interpreted to require that the defendant have known or believed that the victim was a federal officer. So you should make arguments both ways on this point.

☞ Identify the specific conduct prohibited, and make sure that the conduct in question qualifies.

Example: A statute provides that "Any person who knowingly sells an intoxicating substance to a person under the age of 18 years shall be guilty of a misdemeanor." This statute prohibits a *sale* of an intoxicating substance, without any further conduct by the customer. So the fact that the customer never *drank* the liquor (or didn't get drunk) is irrelevant.

☛ **Ignorance of law:** Watch for an indication that a defendant was unaware of or did not understand a statute. Because all people are ***conclusively presumed to know the law***, this is not a general defense.

☞ **Exceptions:** However, there are some (modern) crimes that are expressly defined so as to require that the defendant know of the statutory prohibition. But if that's the case, your prof will have to signal this fact to you. So if you don't see any such signal, you can presume that the general rule of "ignorance of the law is no excuse" applies.

☛ **Arson:** Pay special attention to ***arson*** problems, because element-of-the-crime issues abound when arson is involved.

Example: At common law, arson could be committed only on another's *dwelling*. But many modern statutes extend the definition to buildings other than dwellings, and profs often test this point. If your prof wants to test you on a modern statutory variation on the common-law arson requirements, he/she will *have* to specify the text of the statute, so when you see the statutory text be on the lookout for coverage of buildings other than dwellings.

☛ **Civil statutory violation as evidence of mens rea**: Fact patterns often involve violations of *civil* (as opposed to criminal) statutes. Note that, although violation of a civil statute may be *evidence* of negligence or recklessness, a civil statutory violation alone does not automatically *satisfy* the mens rea requirement for negligence or recklessness.

☞ **Example:** A state statute requires that any person engaging in the use of fireworks have a license which is issued upon the completion of a safety course. D, who does not have a license, believes he is competent to use fireworks and brings some to X's party. D sets off some of the fireworks in X's backyard. Although D acts "reasonably," one of the fireworks explodes prematurely, causing a fire which completely destroys X's home. The criminal arson statute requires recklessness or intent to start a fire. D cannot be found guilty of arson solely because of his violation of the statute requiring a license for the use of fireworks — the prosecutor will have to show that D's overall behavior constituted recklessness.

Exam Tips on
CAUSATION

☛ Be on the lookout for causation issues, especially in fact patterns that involve homicide — the fact that V (victim) ended up dead doesn't mean that D caused the death, as a legal matter.

Cause In Fact

☛ First determine whether the defendant's act was the cause-in-fact of the harm. Usually, this will be because D's act was the but-for cause of the harm.

☞ Analyze the situation to determine *whether the result would have happened anyway (in exactly the same way) even had D's act not occurred.* If it would have, then D's act won't be the but-for cause, or cause-in-fact, of the harm, and D can't be guilty.

Example: D, A prominent heart surgeon, agrees at the request of the U.S. Government to perform a heart operation on V, an important official. Relying on his agreement, the government ceases its search for another physician. D then fails to show up to do the operation, and it's too late for the government to find another. V dies. D could plausibly contend that, even if he had performed the operation, it is uncertain that it would have been successful. If he can show this, then his wrongful act (his promising to do the operation and then not doing it) has not been proved beyond a reasonable doubt to have been the cause-in-fact of V's death.

☞ Remember that for D's act to be the cause in fact of a homicide, the victim must be *alive at the time of the act.*

Example: D shoots to kill V, whom he believes is asleep, but who actually died of a heart attack moments before. D's act of shooting is not the cause in fact of V's death. Therefore, regardless of D's culpable state of mind and wrongful act, D can't be guilty of homicide.

☞ Remember that a death may have *several causes-in-fact.* That is, there may be several acts or events each of which is a cause in fact, because the death wouldn't have happened without all of those acts/events. When this happens, the person who does a single one of the acts can be guilty (because he's *a* cause-in-fact even though not *the sole* cause in fact).

Proximate Cause

☛ **Generally:** Proximate cause is very frequently tested. Several things to watch out for:

☞ **Year-and-a-Day-Rule:** Remember that at common law (and still in most states), if a death occurs *at least a year-and-a-day after D's act*, D can't be the proximate cause of the death.

☞ **Unintended victim:** Profs will try to sidetrack you by presenting a fact pattern where there is an inadvertent killing of a person who was not the original target. Remember that, as long as the defendant shows the requisite mental state, *it is inconsequential that the victim is different than the one D was focusing on* (assuming the victim suffers a harm similar to what was intended). Distinguish between the two similar situations of transferred intent and mistaken identity (D will be on the hook in both):

☞ **Transferred intent:** In a fact pattern involving *transferred intent*, the defendant aims at his targeted party (X) but because of bad aim, a ricocheting bullet, or something of that sort, another person (V) is hit. If D had the requisite mental state vis a vis X, D is guilty of the same crime against V as D would have been had the harm that befell V really befallen X.

Example: D returns home and catches B climbing out the window of his home. He pursues B down the street. D fires a shot at B with a hunting rifle, attempting to shoot him in the leg. The bullet misses B, but hits V, who is driving a car down the street. V later dies. D's intent to cause serious bodily harm to B (a mental state sufficient for murder) would be transferred to V. Therefore, D is the proximate cause of V's death, and can be found guilty of murder, assuming that no defense applies.

☞ **Mistaken identity:** In a fact pattern involving *mistaken identity*, the defendant injures or kills the party at which he aimed; but the victim is not who the defendant thought he was. Here, too, the mistake doesn't prevent D from being guilty.

Example: V, who has just robbed a casino, encounters D on the steps of the casino. D is not aware of V's criminal activity. In fact,

D is waiting on the steps of the casino so that he can shoot its owner because D has just lost all his savings there. When D sees V, he mistakenly believes that V is the casino owner. He shouts, "Death to gamblers," and shoots at V, killing him. Knowledge of the victim's identity is not an essential element of the crime. Because D yelled, "Death to gamblers," and fired at V, he showed the necessary intent to kill or cause serious bodily harm. Therefore, D is guilty of murdering X notwithstanding his mistake about X's identity.

☞ **Intervening causes:** Determine whether the intervening act is *"independent"* or *"dependent."* Remember that an independent act will break the causation chain if it's *"unforeseeable"* but a dependent act will only break the chain if it's *"abnormal"* (*plus* unforeseeable). "Abnormal" is rarer, so an independent act is more likely to break the chain than a dependent one.

☞ **Medical aid:** Most common scenario for dependent intervening cause: the victim is given *medical aid*, and something goes wrong during the aid-giving process.

Example: D attacks V, a basketball player, with a baseball bat, inflicting serious injuries. V is admitted to the hospital and is injected with a pain reliever to which he has a fatal allergic reaction. Because the drug was given to relieve pain which resulted from the beating, the administration of the pain reliever and the reaction to it are dependent acts. Therefore, as long as these events are not abnormal (and mere negligence, as opposed to gross negligence, is probably not an "abnormal" response to a need for medical assistance), the chain of causation has not been broken.

☞ **Victim's intervening act:** Look for a situation where. after the initial harm caused by D, the victim *exposes himself to additional danger.* If the exposure is brought about by D's act, the exposure is a dependent event, and won't be superseding unless abnormal.

Example: D sets fire to X's home. X flees the burning home, then reenters to rescue his baby trapped inside. He later dies of burns. Since it is not uncommon for someone to risk his life to save his child, the act would be foreseeable (and certainly not "abnormal"), so even if it was in some sense a bad move for X from a risk-reward perspective, it won't be deemed superseding.

☞ **Defendant's intervening act:** Look for a situation where D has the intent to kill, erroneously believes his victim is dead, and attempts to destroy or conceal the "corpse." Usually, this second act by D won't be superseding.

Example: D beats V to the point of unconsciousness. Then, thinking that V is dead, D takes the "corpse" to a secluded spot. V ultimately dies of exposure. D's intervening act of moving V's body (and not checking to see that V was dead) was a dependent act. The act was not unforeseeable or abnormal, and was therefore not superseding. Therefore, the death will be deemed to have been proximately caused by the original beating, so D can be prosecuted for some version of homicide. (*Which* type would depend on his mental state during the beating.)

☛

Exam Tips on
RESPONSIBILITY

☛ Many exam questions involve issues of insanity or intoxication. So always be attuned to the possibility of a defendant raising these defenses.

Insanity

☛ Don't come to a quick conclusion that a defendant is legally insane just because the fact pattern depicts outlandish behavior by her. Always check the jurisdiction's definition of insanity and analyze carefully the behavior against the required elements.

☞ ***M'Naghten* test:** *M'Naghten* is the test most frequently used on exams. Remember, D meets the test if *either* he (1) didn't **know the nature and quality of the act** he was doing; or (2) he didn't know that what he was doing was ***wrong***.

Key things to look for:

☞ **When the insanity occurs:** Make sure the elements of the test were present ***at the time of the offense*** in question. *Trap:* Don't be fooled by a fact pattern that tells you that D has already been declared insane in another case or at another time — this doesn't matter. Nor is it enough that D has been diagnosed with "mental illness."

☞ **"Understood that act was wrong" prong:** Look in the fact pattern for information indicating that this prong was satisfied, such as that D knew his conduct to be "unlawful" or knew that he could be imprisoned for it.

Conversely, look for objective signs that D was **unaware** of the wrongfulness of the act.

Example: D, who has been previously diagnosed with schizophrenia, strangles his fiancee, Marie. Just before he does that, he says to his psychiatrist, "I'm being stalked by a robot who's hidden Marie and impersonated her. I've got to disable the robot by strangling it, and then I'll work on finding Marie." You should say that if D was telling the truth to his psychiatrist, this is a strong indication that he didn't understand that he was killing Marie, and that he thought instead that he was disabling a robot. In that case, he'd qualify under the "didn't know that what he was doing was wrong" prong (and also the "didn't know the nature and quality of the act" prong) of *M'Naghten*.

☞ **"Understood the nature and quality of the act" prong:** This prong is usually held to be satisfied if D merely understood the physical consequences of his act — the fact that D had some crazy motive for doing the act won't help him.

☞ **Delusions:** This principle is often shown by fact patterns involving **delusions**. If the delusion just relates to D's motive for the act, and doesn't prevent D from understanding both that his act is illegal and that it will have certain physical consequences, then D can't take advantage of *M'Naghten*, in most states.

Example: D is mentally ill, and, as a result, believes that his wife W is building a bomb in the basement of their house and that she plans to blow up the world. Although he knows that he could be punished for murder, he pushes W down a flight of stairs in order to save the world by killing her. D's delusion probably won't help him under *M'Naghten*, because D understood that pushing W down the stairs was illegal and would probably kill her. The fact that D had what he thought was a good motive (save the world) won't make a difference.

☞ **"Irresistible impulse" test:** If the fact pattern doesn't specify what insanity test applies in the jurisdiction, consider whether **irresistible impulse** might produce a different result on your facts than *M'Naghten*. Generally, for irresistible-impulse to apply, the fact pattern will have to signal to you that D feels powerless to stop even though he realizes what he's doing is wrong. (*Example:* D, who's very religious, hears God telling him to kill his wife — if the trier believes this, irresistible-impulse probably applies.)

☞ **Diminished capacity:** If an insanity defense is likely to fail, consider the defense of *diminished capacity.* A defendant in a specific intent crime may negate the specific intent element by claiming that he had a mental defect that prevented him from forming the required mens rea. This defense is usually used to reduce a charge from murder to voluntary manslaughter.

Intoxication

☛ Often a fact pattern will indicate that a defendant has been drinking or taking drugs. In the usual case, the intoxication will be *"voluntary,"* and the basic discussion below assumes that this is so.

☞ **Specific mental state:** Most important, figure out whether the intoxication *blocked the defendant from forming the requisite mental state.* If it did, the intoxication will require a finding of not guilty. In deciding this issue, the classic general-intent/specific-intent distinction isn't dispositive, but it still has some value.

☞ **General intent:** Where the crime is a so-called *"general intent"* crime — i.e., the only intent needed is the intent is to do the actus reus — voluntary intoxication usually *won't* prevent the requisite intent from being formed. (But this is just a generalization, and isn't always accurate.)

Example 1 — Sexual assault: D rapes V — the only intent needed is the intent to have intercourse, and intoxication probably won't negate that intent. (Intoxication that prevents D from *noticing that V isn't consenting* won't negate the requisite intent).

Example 2 — Battery: D physically attacks V — the only intent needed for battery is intent to make harmful contact, and intoxication that makes D belligerent (or that causes him to be insulted where a sober person wouldn't be) isn't inconsistent with that intent.

☞ **Specific intent:** Where the crime is a so-called *"specific intent"* crime (i.e., the intent needed is something beyond the mere intent to do the actus reus), voluntary intoxication is *more likely to block* the requisite intent. So analyze D's state of mind closely against *all* mental elements.

Example 1 — Pre-meditated murder: If D is very drunk, his intoxication may have prevented him from doing the requisite pre-meditation. (But check to make sure he didn't do the pre-meditating before he got drunk, in which case he meets the requirement even if he was incapable of still pre-meditating just before the killing.)

Example 2 — Larceny: If D is so drunk that he didn't know the property he was taking belonged to another, the requisite intent (to wrongfully take property of another) will be missing.

☞ **Involuntary intoxication:** Look out for facts suggesting *"involuntary"* intoxication. This occurs most often where either: (1) D is mistaken about the nature of what he's taking (e.g., he doesn't realize there's LSD in the fruit punch); or (2) D knowingly takes a small quantity of a psychoactive substance, but has a grossly excessive, unpredictable reaction to it (e.g., D gets totally drunk and enraged the first time he has a single drink). Here, if D was not reckless in ingesting the substance, he may be able to avoid meeting the mental state for any crime requiring recklessness or intent.

☞ **Wanton or Reckless:** But in any involuntary-intoxication case, analyze the facts to determine whether the defendant's actions in ingesting the substance may be considered reckless or wanton. If they are, the wanton or reckless state of mind may be enough for the crime.

Example: D suffers from paranoid schizophrenia that becomes acute whenever he drinks an excessive quantity of alcohol. D drinks five glasses of beer while having lunch with his friend, F, at a bar/restaurant. F insults D and D shouts that he will kill him. D leaves the bar, comes back with a gun, and shoots F. D may well be deemed to have been intoxicated and unable to form the requisite mens rea for pre-meditation-style murder. But if he knows that his paranoia spikes whenever he drinks and often causes him to attack others, you could argue that by the mere act of drinking heavily, D acted with wanton indifference to the safety of others. Therefore, he might be guilty of wanton-indifference-to-the-value-of-human-life murder.

On the other hand, if D had no history of violent behavior as a consequence of his condition, his conduct would probably rise at most to the level of recklessness, in which case he couldn't be convicted of any crime more serious than involuntary manslaughter (for which recklessness meets the mental-state requirement).

Exam Tips *on* JUSTIFICATION AND EXCUSE

☛ Consider all possible justifications and excuses discussed in this chapter when analyzing a fact pattern, because it is possible to assert several of them at the same time. Be aware that the defenses of self-defense, defense of property, and the "fleeing felon" defense present themselves most frequently.

Self-defense

☛ Key issues to consider when a party uses deadly force to defend herself from an attack or threat of an attack from another person:

☞ **Serious bodily harm:** When D has been attacked, concentrate on analyzing whether the attack threatened him with what D reasonably believed was *serious bodily harm.* This matters because you can only use *deadly force* (force likely to kill or do serious bodily harm) to repel an attack that you reasonably believe threatens serious bodily harm.

☞ **Mistaken perception of threat:** When deadly force has not yet been used, you must analyze the *reasonableness* of D's belief that there was an imminent threat of deadly force. Even if D is wrong in this belief, he can plead self-defense so long as his belief was reasonable.

> **Example (reasonable belief):** D is selling cocaine outside a high school. T sticks his hand in his pocket, thrusts a finger forward, jabs D with it, and says, "I've got a gun. Give me the dope or I'll blow you away." D shoots T. It doesn't matter that T didn't really have a gun — so long as D's belief that there was a gun (and that T might use that gun) was reasonable, D was entitled to use deadly force in return.

> **Example (unreasonable belief):** D brings her watch in to be repaired and the jewelry store owner sells it to V. At a bowling alley, D notices her watch on V's wrist. D angrily demands the watch. Concerned because of a previous argument with D, V fumbles in her pockets for the receipt to show she had purchased the watch. Thinking that V is reaching for a weapon, D strikes V on the head with a heavy metal ashtray, seriously injuring her. D would probably not be able to assert the privilege of self-defense, because her belief that V was reaching for a gun when she put her hands in her pockets was probably unreasonable in the circumstances.

☞   *Trap:* Don't be fooled by a fact pattern in which D shoots a *police officer* — if D had a reasonable belief that the police officer was a dangerous intruder, this may still be self-defense.

Example: D, the owner of a tavern, has been burglarized several times. As a result, he sleeps at the tavern with a pistol. V, a police officer, sees the tavern window open at night and climbs in to investigate. D cocks his pistol at V. V doesn't say he's a police officer, but shouts, "Drop that gun or I'll shoot." D, believing that V is an armed burglar, shoots V. D's belief that V was an armed burglar may well have been reasonable; if so (and if he reasonably feared that V would use deadly force), this was valid self-defense.

☞   **Belief must be bona fide:** Remember that even if a reasonable person might have believed that a threat exists, if the defendant did not *actually* believe that there was one, then the defense may not be asserted.

☛ **Retreat or otherwise incapable of inflicting harm:** Remember that if the *initial threat no longer exists*, the defense of self-defense no longer applies.

Example: Following a rape, the rapist falls asleep. The victim ties his hands and feet to the posts of the bed, and beats him severely. The victim may not assert the privilege of self-defense as to the serious injury because once the rapist was tied up, the threat was over.

☞   **Aggressor may not assert privilege:** Also, look for a fact pattern where the initial aggressor's actual threat of or use of deadly force is responded to with force (perhaps deadly force) and the initial aggressor then defends himself. Remember that *a wrongful aggressor has no right of self-defense against a reasonable response to her initial aggression.*

☞   **Example:** After an exchange of insults, D pulls a gun and points it at V. V pulls out a knife and moves towards D. D shoots V. Since D was the wrongful aggressor and used deadly force, V's response was permissible (deadly force proportional to the threat). Therefore, D was not permitted to use deadly force to counter it.

☞ **Exception for withdrawal:** But remember that even this rule has an exception: if the initial (wrongful) aggressor retreats, attempting to end the encounter, the aggressor is entitled to use force — even, where necessary, deadly force — to protect himself if the target persists in his defense. (And, the target's use of deadly force following the retreat is itself not reasonable). So be on the lookout for the retreat of the initial aggressor.

Example: D attends weekly sessions with a psychotherapist.

While in the waiting room of the psychotherapist's office, D draws a knife, waving it at N, the nurse, and screaming, "Vader must die. The Empire will be restored." N takes a heavy, replica of a medieval sword and holds it in front of him. D hands the knife to N, kneels before him and says, "Forgive me, Lord of the Galaxy." N, who should (but doesn't) realize that he is no longer in danger of being injured by D, swings at D with the sword, narrowly missing him. D then grabs back his knife and stabs N. Despite the fact that D was the initial aggressor, his initial aggression had ended by the time N swung the sword. Therefore, N's response was not reasonable. This unreasonableness entitled D to use self-defense just as if N had never been a wrongful aggressor in the first place. So if D's use of the knife was proportional to the threat he reasonably perceived from N, D can successfully plead self-defense.

Defense of property

☛ **Deadly force not privileged:** When a party uses ***deadly force*** to protect his property, you should write in your answer that, generally, the use of deadly force is not privileged. However, note that in some jurisdictions, a party may use deadly force to prevent another from invading that party's ***home***. In that case you must analyze the following:

☞ **Definition of dwelling:** The privilege applies only to intrusion of a *dwelling*, i.e., an occupied residence. So, for instance, a tool shed on the property would probably not be covered. But any room within the residence would be covered even if the room is used only for business (e.g., a doctor's office inside the doctor's house).

☛ **Degree of force:** Under the modern view, deadly force may be used only when the home occupier reasonably believes that an intruder is about to ***commit a violent felony*** within the premises and poses a danger to the inhabitants. So there's ***no automatic right to shoot at a burglar.***

Fleeing Felons and Law Enforcement

☛ **Private citizens:** The most common fact pattern in this area concerns a ***private citizen*** using force to ***stop a fleeing felon.*** If a party has just committed a dangerous felony and is fleeing, a private citizen is justified in using deadly force only if the felon poses an ***immediate threat*** to the citizen or others. Check for the following:

☞ Make sure the party asserting the defense ***actually believes*** that the victim has just committed a felony.

Example: X, Y and Z commit a robbery in a casino. As they are leaving, on the steps of a gambling casino, D approaches them, believing them to be the operators of the casino. He shouts, "Death to gamblers," and shoots at them. D was unaware of the robbery — his motive for shooting was to close down the casino because he had lost all his savings there and his life had been ruined. Therefore, although X, Y and Z were in fact fleeing felons, D may not assert apprehension-of-felons as a defense.

☞ Make sure the party asserting the defense was **correct** in his belief that the victim had just committed a felony. If he is mistaken, he bears the risk of his mistake, even if the mistake is "reasonable".

Example: U, an undercover police agent, participates in the robbery of a drugstore with members of a group of thieves that U has infiltrated. U approaches the store owner, O, draws her gun, and hands to O a note that reads: "I am a police undercover agent. Pretend to be frightened. Give me the money in the cash register." O is illiterate, and therefore doesn't read the note. When U turns to leave, O shoots at her. Since U was not in fact a fleeing felon, O is not entitled to the fleeing-felon defense.

☛ **Police arrest:** Remember that a **police officer** who has probable cause to believe that a person has committed a **felony** (and is **dangerous** to others) may use **deadly force** to make an arrest. But where the officer believes that the person has merely committed a **misdemeanor**, or has committed a felony but poses **no threat** to others, the officer may **not** use deadly force to make the arrest.

☞ Don't be fooled by a fact pattern in which the arrestee has committed a dangerous felony, but the officer is making the arrest for a different crime, which is a mere misdemeanor or non-dangerous felony. What matters is what the officer reasonably believes, not the underlying facts.

> **Example:** After fatally stabbing somebody in a bar brawl, X drives away in her car. A few blocks away, a police officer, D, observes X going through a stop sign and begins to chase her. X speeds away because she thinks she is being chased regarding the stabbing. D fires at X's tires, but the shot accidentally kills a pedestrian, V. If D is charged with homicide in the death of V, he probably won't succeed, because he was trying to arrest X for a misdemeanor (running a stop sign), and D wasn't privileged to use deadly force in doing so. The fact that X may have been guilty of a dangerous felony and could have been arrested with use of deadly force for that won't bail D out, since he didn't know these facts

and his state of mind is the issue.

Entrapment

☛ **Requirements:** Remember that D usually must prove that (1) the government agent **originated** the crime and **induced** D to commit it; *and* (2) D was **not predisposed** to committing the crime.

☛ **Induce commission:** You will usually find that the police officer (or agent) did not **induce or instigate** the commission of the crime.

   ☞ **Absence of inducement:** Watch for a police officer who involves himself heavily in the planning or commission of the crime, but is not the actual one to suggest that it be committed. This won't be entrapment, because of the lack of inducement.

      Example: X and Y are suspected of having committed a series of recent robberies. P, an undercover police agent, invites X and Y to her home for drinks and mentions to them that she is impressed with the perpetrators of the recent robberies in the neighborhood. X then suggests that a neighborhood drugstore would be an easy target for a robbery. P agrees to join in the robbery, in order to obtain evidence of X's and Y's past crimes. X and Y are arrested as they enter the drugstore accompanied by P. Since P never suggested the commission of the crime, or otherwise induced X and Y to commit it, there's no entrapment despite her participation in the planning.

   ☞ **Predisposition:** You will also usually find that the party asserting the defense was predisposed to commit the crime, again blocking a finding of entrapment.

      Example: P agrees to assist the police in return for reduced charges on a drug-related crime. The police set him up in a used-car business and spread the rumor that he deals in stolen vehicles. With police permission, P purchases a stolen vehicle from X. Then D comes to P's place of business requesting to purchase a stolen vehicle. With police permission, P sells the stolen vehicle to D. This is not entrapment, because by seeking out the dealership and asking for a stolen vehicle, D showed a predisposition to commit the crime.

Duress

☛ **Duress generally:** When considering the defense of duress, the most important things to remember are:

   ☞ The defense **may not be used** in a **murder** charge.

   ☞ D's fear of harm must have been both **reasonable** and **actual**.

Exam Tips *on*
ATTEMPT

☞ When a defendant is unsuccessful in committing a substantive crime, consider a charge of criminal attempt.

☞ **Definition of "attempt":** You should have a general definition of "attempt" in mind. A good definition (but not necessarily precisely the law in any particular jurisdiction) would be: A person is guilty of a criminal attempt when: (1) with an ***intent to commit acts*** that are the ***actus reus*** for a particular ***substantive crime***, she (2) takes a ***substantial step*** towards the commission of that crime.

Mental State

☞ **Specific intent required:** Remember that ***specific intent*** is required, regardless of the level of intent necessary to be convicted of the completed offense. That is, D must ***intend to take an act*** (or bring about a result) that, if committed, would constitute the underlying crime.

☞ **Strict liability, negligence or recklessness:** Thus if an underlying crime is defined to require only negligence, recklessness or even no mental state at all (i.e., a strict liability crime), that state of mind won't be enough for an attempt to commit that underlying crime.

Example: The state Liquor Sales Act prohibits the sale of liquor between the hours of midnight and 8 A.M., regardless of the mental state of the seller. V, an undercover police officer pretending to be a customer, enters a liquor store and asks to buy a bottle of vodka. D, an employee, looks at the clock and it reads five minutes after eleven in the evening. D does not realize that there was a change to daylight savings time the night before and that the store's clock has not been changed. Just as D is about to hand over the bottle and receive V's money, V arrests him, and charges him with an attempt to violate the Liquor Sales Act. D can't be convicted, under the majority view, because he didn't intend to commit an act (*after-hours* sale of liquor) that was prohibited by the underlying statute. This is so even though D would have been guilty of violating the underlying statute had he finished the transaction.

☞ **Attempted murder:** If the crime is defined in terms of a particular result, the required mental state is the desire to bring about that result. Thus, since murder is defined in terms of a result (death of another), in order to successfully prosecute for *attempted murder* the defendant must have had the specific intent to cause that result (*death of another*).

Example: D, while trying to study for an exam, hears a loud argument coming from V's house across the street. She fires a rifle out her own window and into the front window of the living room of V's house, which D thinks is vacant. D's motive is merely to frighten V and the other arguer into silence. Unbeknownst to D, V is in fact in the living room, and is hit in the leg. V survives. D can't be convicted of attempted murder, because she didn't intend to bring about V's death. That's true even though, had V died from the shot, D would probably have been guilty of actual murder (of the depraved-indifference variety).

Requirement of Act

☛ **"Substantial step" test):** Remember that under the modern/Model-Penal-Code approach, the requirement of an act is met by any act that is a *"substantial step"* towards completion of the underlying crime.

Example: X wants to test the faithfulness of his girlfriend, G, and if she proves to be unfaithful, to kill her. X plans with Y to give Y a box of chocolates laced with poison. Y is to pretend to like G, and to offer her the chocolates. If she accepts the chocolates, then X will believe her to be unfaithful and deserving to die (from the poison). X brings the box of poisoned chocolates to the pool hall he and Y frequent and places the chocolates near his coat on the bench. Somebody else takes the chocolates (and throws them away without eating them), so X can't give them to Y. X's act of poisoning the chocolates and bringing them to the pool hall would probably be found to constitute a substantial step toward completion of the crime of murdering G, despite the fact that the chocolates were never given to G.

Impossibility

☞ **Factual impossibility:** Look for a fact pattern where: (1) *had the facts been as D believed them to be, his act would have constituted a crime*; but (2) under the facts as they really were, his act did not constitute a completed crime. This is *"factual impossibility,"* and it is *not a valid defense*.

Examples:

[1] D shoots to kill V, whom he believes is asleep, but V actually died of a heart attack moments before. (This is still attempted murder.)

[2] D shoots to kill V with an unloaded gun, although D thinks it's loaded. (This is still attempted murder.)

[3] D puts LSD into chocolate intending to kill the person consuming it, but does not know that the amount of LSD put into the food cannot cause death. (This is still attempted murder).

☞ **Factual mistake bearing on legal relations:** Where D's mistake is a factual mistake about the *legal status* of some person or thing, the mistake is still not a defense, any more than any other kind of factual mistake is a defense. So if D is mistaken about whether V is still alive (Example 1 above) or mistaken about whether a car is stolen (see example below), this won't be a defense to an attempt charge.

Example: X and Y, undercover police officers, pretend to be criminals in order to catch D, a criminal known to buy and sell stolen cars. X meets D and tells him that Y is looking for a buyer for stolen cars. After D says that he might be interested in buying one for resale, X offers to buy it with him as a partner. X sets up a meeting between D and Y. Y offers to sell D what he says is a stolen car. (The car has actually been requisitioned from the police department.) D pays Y for the car. Although the car was not actually "stolen property" (so D cannot be convicted of receiving stolen property), he's guilty of attempt to receive stolen property. That's because D's factual mistake about legal status (whether the car was stolen) is irrelevant, since had the facts been as D thought they were, he would have completed the crime of receiving stolen property.

☞ **True legal impossibility (mistake about how a crime is defined):** On the other hand, if D's mistake is about *how a particular crime is defined* — that is, D thinks his act matches the definition but it really doesn't — then this *is* a defense. This is the defense of *"true legal impossibility."* (But be sure to distinguish between this true legal-impossibility situation, and the "factual mistake bearing on legal relations" situation, described above, that *isn't* a defense).

Example 1: Due to the advice of an attorney, D believes that the crime of arson in her jurisdiction covers the intentional burning of any dwelling, although it actually applies only to the dwelling of "another." With a belief that she is committing arson, D burns down her house in order to collect insurance proceeds. D thought she was committing arson, but she may not be charged with attempted arson. The defense of "legal impossibility" applies: D's mistake was a mistake about how the crime of arson is defined.

Example 2: Until recently, the hunting season for the flivver, a rare migratory bird, was restricted to March and April. The law fixing the hunting season was recently amended to permit hunting during May and June. D, unaware of the change in the law, decides to go flivver hunting in May, because he does not like to compete with other hunters. D shoots and kills a flivver. Despite the fact that D thought he was in violation of the hunting law, he may not be charged with an attempt to violate it. Again, the defense of legal impossibility applies: D's mistake was a mistake about how the crime of flivver-hunting is defined.

Merger, and Convictions of Both Attempt and Underlying Crime

☛ **Merger:** Remember that a lesser included offense, such as attempt, *merges* with the more serious one if the crime was completed — merger means that D can't be convicted of both.

   ☞   **No merger of attempt and conspiracy:** However, remember that the crime of attempt *does not merge with conspiracy*, so a person can be convicted of both, arising out of a single fact pattern and a single underlying crime.

      Example: X and Y agree to kill V. Y loads the gun, and X pulls the trigger. The bullet misses. X and Y can each be convicted of *both* attempted murder *and* conspiracy to commit murder.

☛ **Standalone prosecution for attempt:** Also, remember that the prosecutor can choose to charge the defendant *only* with attempt, even if a conviction for the substantive crime could have been attained.

      Example: D shoots at V, intending to kill him. V is wounded, and dies in the hospital. D can't be convicted of both murder and attempted murder. But the prosecutor may choose to bring just an attempted-murder charge; D may be convicted of that charge, even though the facts might also support a murder conviction.

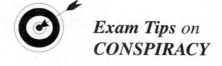

Exam Tips on
CONSPIRACY

☞ This topic is heavily tested. Some key aspects to keep in mind:

Agreement and Intent

🖝 **Agreement required:** Remember that the co-conspirators must somehow *agree* to pursue a joint objective.

☞ **Agreement without active participation:** But a party may make the necessary agreement without doing so explicitly, and without formally committing to do any specific thing. It's usually enough if the party somehow (by word, by silence, by deed, or whatever) *encourages* the project to move forward. *"Aiding and abetting,"* for instance, is usually enough.

Example: Z operates a store across the street from, and competitive to, Y's store. Because of Z's unfair business practices, Y worries that Z may force him out of business. Y tells X in a half-jesting manner that if X were a real friend he would "take care" of Z. As a result of Y's remark, X plans for another party to break into Z's store and destroy Z's merchandise. When X tells Y of his plan, Y says, "Sounds great, but don't ask me to do anything to help." X replies, "All you have to do is sit back and let it happen." Because Y made it clear to X that he and X shared a common goal, his actions indicate an agreement and he is guilty of conspiracy to vandalize the store.

☞ **Surrounding circumstances:** Words of agreement are not needed — actions and even silence may be sufficient in the circumstances to indicate agreement. Look for defendants who conduct themselves in such a manner as to manifest jointness of action.

Example: X and Y are suspected of having committed a series of recent robberies. P, an undercover police agent, invites X and Y to her home for drinks and mentions to them that she is impressed with the perpetrators of the recent robberies in the neighborhood. X then suggests that a neighborhood drugstore would be an easy target for a robbery. Y says nothing. P decides to pretend to join in the robbery, in order to obtain evidence of X's and Y's past crimes. All three immediately drive to the store. X is about to enter the store to rob it (with Y waiting in the car) when P arrests both X and Y. Y can be found to have agreed on the robbery plan with X — although Y never verbally agreed to participate in the robbery, his silence plus his driving to the site and waiting is enough to show that he agreed with X to pursue the robbery plan. Therefore Y (as well as X) can be found guilty of conspiracy to rob.

☛ **Only one person holds intent ("unilateral" conspiracy):** If *only one party* has the requisite intent to pursue the criminal objective, then you must address in your essay the issue of whether that party alone may be prosecuted for conspiracy. Remember that: (1) Under the traditional view, unless there were at least two parties holding the requisite intent, there could be *no* prosecution for conspiracy; but (2) Most modern courts (and the MPC) *allow* prosecution for such a "unilateral" conspiracy.

  ☞ **Feigned agreement:** Many fact patterns will present a party who *pretends to agree* to commission of the crime.

     Example (undercover agent): U, an undercover agent, pretends to agree with D, a professional thief, that the two will rob a drugstore. D really intends to cooperate with U in the crime. They drive together to the crime scene, at which point D is arrested before either enter the store. Under the modern view, D is guilty of conspiracy — he had the requisite mental state (agreement to commit a crime with a third person's help), and the fact that U's apparent agreement was fake doesn't change this result.

☛ **D furnishes assistance without agreement:** Don't be fooled by a D who shares the objective of the conspirator(s), but secretly helps without anybody knowing. Although D may be guilty of aiding and abetting, he probably can't be prosecuted for conspiracy.

     Example: X and Y, summer campers, decide to kill V, a camp counselor who has punished them. To accomplish their plan, they agree to steal V's asthma medicine. Z, another camper, overhears their conversation and decides to help them without letting them know. He goes to V's room, searches for the medicine, and puts it on V's night table so that X and Y will find it. Several minutes later, X and Y find the medicine on the night table and throw it away. Because he is unable to find the medicine later, V dies. Z would not be liable for conspiracy, because he never made an actual agreement with any other conspirator. (But Z *could* be found guilty of murder as an accomplice.)

      ☞ **Stake in venture:** On the other hand, the requisite agreement probably *will* exist if D1 furnishes preliminary help (goods or services) to D2 with an intent to help D2 commit the crime, and D2 knows that D1 intends to help. Here, the supplying shows the requisite agreement. The issue is whether D1 can be said to have a *"stake in the venture,"* i.e., whether D1 has an active desire for the venture to succeed and is trying to bring about that success.

Example: X asks Y to join him in robbing a bank. When Y refuses, X says that he will rob the bank himself if Y will provide a hiding place for him to use after the robbery. Y agrees, if X will pay him $200 from the robbery proceeds. Since Y has a stake in the criminal enterprise, his advance agreement to furnish services may constitute a conspiracy. (The same would be true if Y agreed, in return for similar profit-sharing, just to drive X to the crime scene, or just to act as lookout, or just to drive the getaway car).

Overt act

☛ **States split:** Remember that states are split about whether the conspiracy can be complete even though no conspirator has committed an overt act in furtherance of the conspiracy. So on any fact pattern where there doesn't seem to be an overt act, mention that states may or may not recognize a conspiracy as already existing.

　　☞　**Act of one attributable to all:** Also, remember that even in states requiring an overt act, the overt act of *any* individual conspirator will be deemed an act by *all* conspirators.

Vicarious liability for substantive crimes by other conspirators

☛ In almost any fact pattern involving a conspiracy, you'll have to deal with whether each conspirator is guilty of the substantive crimes carried out by other conspirators. This is especially likely where D1 doesn't expect that D2 will carry out some particular crime as part of the conspiracy, but D2 does so anyway, in order to help the conspiracy succeed.

☛ Remember that in this situation, courts are *split* between two positions, with the second being the modern, and probably majority, view:

　　❏　**View 1 (traditional):** Under this traditional *"Pinkerton"* view, the *mere fact* that D is part of a conspiracy *automatically* makes him *liable for any substantive crime committed by other conspirators in furtherance of the conspiracy*, at least if the crime was a foreseeable outcome of the conspiracy.

　　❏　**View 2 (modern):** Under the modern / MPC view, D1 is only liable for substantive crimes by a co-conspirator (call him D2) if D1 meets the standards for *aiding-and-abetting* that crime (i.e., D1 was an "accomplice" to that substantive crime). Usually, if a substantive crime was in furtherance of the conspiracy, D1 will be found to have aided-and-abetted (encouraged or helped) the substantive crime, but this won't always be true.

☞ **Physically absent:** Especially be on the lookout for situations where one of the co-conspirators is *not physically present* when his fellow co-conspirator perpetrates the crime — this is the situation most likely to present the automatic-liability-for-substantive-crimes problem. So look for co-conspirators who *get cold feet*, and also those that are absent for other reasons, such as they're in prison or they're asleep.

> **Example:** D1 and D2 agree to commit a burglary by entering V's house to steal her diamonds. They break in, but D1 rapidly gets discouraged when they can't find the diamonds, and leaves. Shortly thereafter, D2 finds the diamonds, and is putting them in his pocket when he is confronted by V. D2, in an attempt to escape with the diamonds, pushes V down stairs, seriously injuring her. (Assume that D2's conduct constitutes battery.) In a "traditional" state, D1 will be liable for the battery committed by D2, since the battery was in furtherance of the objectives of the conspiracy (getting the diamonds), and the traditional rule is that a conspirator is automatically guilty of any substantive crime foreseeably committed by another conspirator in furtherance of the conspiracy's aims. But in a modern / MPC state, D1 will not be liable for battery unless he's found to have "aided and abetted" the battery, which he probably didn't.

Abandonment

☛ When a party *withdraws* his participation before the substantive crime is completed, keep in mind these rules:

☞ **Liability for substantive crimes:** To avoid guilt for the *substantive crimes* committed by the co-conspirators (in a state where being part of the conspiracy is automatically enough to make one guilty of the crimes committed in furtherance of it) it's *not necessary* that the withdrawing D try to *thwart* the success of the conspiracy. All D has to do is to *give notice* of withdrawal (prior to the substantive crime) to each of the co-conspirators, or, alternatively, notify the police that the conspiracy is going on.

☞ **Liability for conspiracy itself:** But the withdrawal does *not* avoid guilt for the *conspiracy itself,* according to the traditional view (since as soon as the agreement is made, the crime of conspiracy is complete).

> ☞ **MPC gives renunciation defense:** But the MPC *does* recognize a defense of *renunciation* in this case, if the conspiracy was

thwarted *and* the renunciation was *voluntary*.

Wharton's rule

☛ **Wharton's rule summarized:** Keep Wharton's Rule in mind at all times: When a substantive offense is defined so as to require two or persons, the Rule says that there can't be conspiracy to commit that crime unless at least one extra person (i.e., one more than the logically required minimum for the substantive crime) is involved. Watch for this especially on fact patterns involving *bribery*. (But remember that many jurisdictions, and the MPC, *reject* the Rule, or treat it as merely a rebuttable presumption).

> **Example:** A statute provides: "Any person who shall give or accept a fee not authorized by law as consideration for the act of any public employee is guilty of bribery," a felony. Contractor needs a building permit that normally takes 30 days to issue. Clerk, a clerk in the buildings department, offers to create a false entry in the department's records indicating that the required permit was already issued, if Contractor will pay Clerk $500. They agree to meet the next morning to consummate the transaction. When Contractor arrives with the money, he finds that Clerk has been fired. In a jurisdiction following Wharton's Rule (and treating it as a substantive rule rather than just a presumption about what the legislature intended), neither Contractor nor Clerk can be convicted of conspiracy to bribe, because bribery requires two parties and here, only the minimum two parties were involved.

Conspiracy vs. the Substantive Crime

☛ Distinguish a prosecution for conspiracy from a prosecution for the substantive crime.

   ☞ **Success not needed:** Don't be fooled by a fact pattern where the conspirators *never actually accomplish* what they conspired to do — this *doesn't matter*, because a conspiracy is committed *as soon as the agreement is made* (except in jurisdictions requiring an overt act).

   ☞ **No merger:** Remember that a defendant can be convicted of *both* conspiracy *and* the substantive crime the conspirators agreed to commit — these *don't merge* together. Even the crime of *attempt* does not merge with conspiracy. So make sure to analyze each possible charge separately.

Exam Tips *on* ACCOMPLICE LIABILITY AND SOLICITATION

Accomplice Liability, Generally

☛ **Summary:** Remember that D is liable as an accomplice if he intentionally acts or encourages another (call her X) to commit a "target" crime. Accomplice liability means that D will be liable for the target (substantive) crime committed by X. So D must satisfy two requirements — act and mental state — before he'll have accomplice liability:

☐ **Act:** D must commit an *act* that *aids or encourages X* to commit the "target" crime; and

☐ **Mental state:** He must have the *mental state* required for the target crime. Typically, this means that D must *intend* to assist X in committing the target crime.

☛ **Act requirement:** The most testable area is whether the act element has been fulfilled. Therefore, look for:

☞ **Silent observer:** Just *knowing* that a crime is being committed and *silently observing* is *not* considered to be aiding and abetting. (But if X *knows* that D stands ready to assist if needed, and this fact encourages X, then D *does* meet the act requirement.)

   ☞ **Trap:** Don't be fooled by a fact pattern that indicates merely that D was present and had criminal intent. Mere presence and intent are not sufficient.

   Example: Y and Z agree to set fire to their neighbor's home because they suspect that drugs are being trafficked there. They start pouring gasoline around the house. A crowd of onlookers begins to gather. X, an onlooker, hopes that Y and Z will burn the house down (and decides to help them if they can't get the fire burning by themselves), but says and does nothing. Y and Z aren't aware that this is how X feels. Z lights a match and the house is burned. X cannot be prosecuted as an accessory, because although he had the requisite intent (desire to have the house be burned) he did not commit the requisite act (aiding or encouraging Y and Z).

☞ **Verbal encouragement:** Generally, *verbal encouragement satisfies* the act requirement.

   Example: Suppose that on the facts of the above example, as Y and Z are trying to get the fire started, X shouts to them, "Burn that baby down." At least if Y and Z hear and are encouraged to continue, X has committed the required act, and can be held liable for arson as an accomplice.

☞ **Actions:** Other kinds of actions that are likely to suffice:

☐ By pre-arrangement, D operates a *getaway car* for X after X commits the substantive crime;

☐ D agrees in advance to *provide a safe harbor* for X after he commits the crime, and then does so. (Actually, the advance agreement *alone*, if it encourages X to go ahead and commit the crime, will suffice, even if D then changes his mind after the crime is over.)

☞ **Trap:** Be on the lookout for a party who does not have a stake in the commission of the crime and becomes involved *only after the basic crime has been committed.* This is likely *not* to be enough for accomplice liability, just for the lesser crime of *"accessory after the fact."*

Example: X, Y, and Z drive to a liquor store to purchase liquor. X stays in the car while Y and Z enter the store. Just before entering, Y and Z realize they have no money. Subsequently they commit a robbery in the store. They run from the store with Z waving a bottle of whiskey and Y holding a gun. As they jump into the car, Y says to X, "Step on it before the cops get here." X drives off. X probably does not have accomplice liability for the robbery (and is therefore not guilty of robbery), because he did not encourage or assist the commission of the crime, which was complete as soon as Y and Z left the store with the money. X has at most accessory-after-the-fact liability.

☛ **Other crimes:** Courts disagree about whether D is substantively liable for additional crimes that are *"natural and probable"* consequences of the target crime, but that D did not intend to bring about.

Example: D agrees to drive X to a store so X can rob it with X's gun. They say nothing about whether X will use the gun. In the store, the owner, V, resists giving the cash, and X shoots him, injuring him. Even assuming that it was a "natural and probable" consequence of the robbery that X would use the gun if the owner resisted, not all states would hold D guilty of being an accomplice to battery. If the shooting was *not* a natural and probable consequence of the robbery, no court would hold D guilty of being an accomplice to battery.

☞ **Distinction:** But don't confuse the natural-and-probable doctrine with the specialized doctrines of felony-murder and misdemeanor-manslaughter — although these doctrines have an effect that's similar to natural-and-probable, they apply *only* in homicide cases.)

Solicitation

☛ **Generally:** Watch for a party *requesting or encouraging another to perform a criminal act*, where the *other party refuses*. This is likely to be the crime of solicitation, defined as:

the requesting or encouraging of another to commit a crime, done with an intent to persuade the other to do the completed crime.

(It can still be solicitation if the other party *agrees*, but then it's also conspiracy, which is the more serious crime. So only worry about solicitation if the other party refuses, or there's some other obstacle to its being conspiracy.)

☞ **Surrounding circumstances:** Analyze the surrounding circumstances in order to determine whether the requisite intent (intent to induce the other to commit the underlying crime) can be proven. So evidence that the speaker was *joking*, or intended *some other result* than completion of the target crime, will tend to show that the required intent was not present.

Example: Z has opened a competing store across the street from X's store and, because of unfair business practices, will likely force X out of business. X, in a half-jesting manner, tells Y that if Y were a real friend he would "take care" of Z. As a result, Y breaks into Z's store and destroys Z's merchandise. Given that X's statement was made in a half-jesting and casual manner (and that X had no reason to believe that Y was likely to engage in criminal behavior), it is unlikely that a court would find that X intended to encourage or persuade Y to commit any crime, in which case X can't be guilty of solicitation.

Exam Tips on
HOMICIDE & OTHER CRIMES AGAINST THE PERSON

Homicides Generally

☛ Homicides occur regularly on exams. So it's well worth your time mastering the details covered in this chapter.

Intent in Homicide Cases

☛ **Intent, generally:** The issue of whether the defendant had the *requisite intent* for a particular form of homicide is commonly tested. Look for a defendant who is *unconscious* or *intoxicated*.

   ☞ **Intoxication:** In intoxication scenarios, analyze the situation carefully to determine whether D was sufficiently drunk to *prevent him from forming the requisite intent.* For instance, in a murder case drunkenness might have prevented D from forming an intent to kill or an intent to seriously injure (the two most common mental states for murder).

   ☞ **Motive vs. intent:** Also, don't confuse *motive* with intent. A defendant needs some sort of qualifying intent, but need not be shown to have any "motive," i.e., any "reason" to kill. So for instance D need not show ill will towards a victim.

☛ **Intent in murder cases:** Remember that there are several different mental states that can suffice for murder. Here's an overview:

   ☞ **Intent-to-kill murder:** First, of course, there's intent-to-kill murder. Here are some of the twists on this version:

      ☞ **Acting with the desire to kill:** If D *desires* to kill, that's enough, even though it was *very improbable* that D's conduct actually would result in the death.

      Example: D knows that his neighbor, N, has a weak heart and has suffered several heart attacks. D is angry at N and wants to kills him. He decides to scare him into having another heart attack. When N leaves his house, D runs to him shouting, "Look out! Look out! The sky is falling." Although D thinks this probably will not kill N, he hopes it will. When N sees D running towards him shouting he gets frightened and dies of a heart attack. D has an appropriate mental state for murder (desire to kill), and he's in fact guilty of murder, notwithstanding the unlikelihood of his plan's working.

      ☞ **Substantial certainty of death:** Where D knows that death is *substantially certain* to occur, then the requisite intent will be found, even if D *does not actively desire* the death.

      Example: D puts a bomb in a plane owned by X Airlines. He desires that the bomb go off, but only so the plane will explode in the air and hurt X's reputation. However, D knows that people will almost certainly be on board, and will be killed. If the plane explodes in the sky and the passengers die, D will have the mental state required for intent-to-kill murder, because he knew the deaths were substantially certain to occur if his plan succeeded, and the fact that D didn't actively desire the deaths is irrelevant.

☞ **Intent-to-cause-serious-bodily-harm murder:** Next, remember that an intent to *cause serious bodily harm* will suffice, even if D does *not* desire to kill.

☞ **Serious injury highly likely:** In fact, if D knows that serious bodily injury is substantially certain to occur from his act, then this is tantamount to an intent to cause serious harm, and will suffice.

Example: D wants to get revenge on her coworker, V, by exposing her to a poisonous pesticide gas D uses for her work. D does not desire to kill V, but does desire to make her sick enough that she'll have temporary blindness, and have to be hospitalized for several days. (D sees from the manual for the poison gas that such results are common if humans ingest very much of the gas.) D releases the poison in V's car. V unexpectedly dies of the exposure to the poison. Because D desired to cause what a court would consider to be serious bodily harm, D can be prosecuted for murder.

☞ **Inference of intent:** Furthermore, a jury can infer a desire to cause serious bodily harm from the fact that D uses a weapon in a way that will generally inflict such harm.

Example: D is a good marksman. D shoots a rifle at V's legs, in an attempt to coerce V into paying a debt. Unexpectedly, V dies of shock. Since firing a rifle at someone's legs will often cause serious bodily injury, a jury can infer that D desired to cause serious (not just minor) injury. Therefore, D has the intent required for intent-to-inflict-serious-injury murder.

☞ **Reckless-indifference-to-the-value-of-human-life murder:** Profs. love to test this one, because it makes for nice fact patterns. This form exists where D disregards a *high risk* that his act will cause death (or serious bodily harm) to others. The classic illustration is firing a rifle into a building known to be occupied.

☞ **Illustrations:** Generally, you should discuss reckless-indifference in these kinds of situations:

❏ D *drives a car at extremely high speeds*;

❏ D *fires a shot in a public place* with lots of people around;

❏ D *gets drunk* while knowing that he often behaves very violently if drunk;

- ❏ **D *wants to scare*** (but not kill or injure) someone badly, and uses what he knows is a very dangerous method to do so, which then goes awry. (*Example:* D tries to fire a gun near V's head to scare him, but miscalculates and hits V.)

☞ **Consciousness of risk:** Remember that courts *disagree* about whether reckless-indifference murder can exist if D is reckless, but is *unaware* that the risk of death or serious injury is very high. So if the facts indicate that D has behaved in a very reckless and dangerous way without being aware of the danger, discuss whether the lack of unaware of the danger would prevent reckless-disregard from existing. (*Example:* D gets so drunk that he doesn't realize that what he's about to do is extremely dangerous — most courts would probably find reckless-disregard here.)

☞ **Distinguish from negligence:** Remember that the unthinking creation of an "unreasonable" (but not extremely high) risk is merely negligent behavior, and does not rise to the level of reckless indifference. Reckless-indifference requires a disregard of a *very high* probability of *death or serious harm*.

Felony-murder

Profs love to test felony-murder, because it can involve so many sub-issues. So any time anyone is committing a felony during the course of which someone dies, you've got to think felony-murder (we'll call it f.m. here).

☛ **Definition:** Look for a fact pattern where *during or as a consequence* of D's perpetration of an *inherently-dangerous felony* (other than the homicide itself), D *causes a death*, even accidentally.

☛ **Situations:** Here are the most common felonies that can give rise to f.m.:

- ❏ ***Robbery*** (most common of all). (*Example:* D robs V's store while pointing a gun at V. V has a fatal heart attack, or D's gun goes off by accident and kills V. In both scenarios, D has committed f.m.)

- ❏ ***Burglary.*** (*Example:* D is breaking into V's house, thinking it's empty. V surprises D, they struggle, V falls and hits her head, then dies from the wound. Even if D wasn't trying to injure V, just escape, D is guilty of f.m.)

- ❏ ***Arson.*** (*Example:* D sets fire to X's house. V, a firefighter, dies fighting the blaze. D is guilty of f.m. in V's death.)

☛ **D's guilt of underlying crime:** Make sure that D would probably be found guilty of the underlying felony — if not, the death can't be f.m.

☛ **Death of co-felon:** Often the death will be that of a *co-felon* (either killed by a victim or by a police officer, or killed by himself in an accident). Here, note that courts are split about whether f.m. can apply where one of the participants in the felony is killed.

☛ **Causal relationship, and intervening acts:** *Causation* is the most testable issue in this area. If the death is brought about by an *intervening act* (and is not the direct consequence of D's own act), D will be guilty only if his participation in the felony was the *"proximate cause"* of the death. Generally, this means that you must find that the death was the *"natural and probable consequence"* of the felony — if the intervening act was too abnormal or bizarre, D will get off the hook.

☞ **Examples of foreseeable consequences & thus causal connection:**

❑ The normal reactions of *victims, bystanders, and police* make violence a foreseeable result of any *robbery*. Therefore, if a death results from these reactions, it's at least arguable that the death was a natural and probable consequence of the robbery.

Example: D robs S's store at gun point. If S tries to stop the robbery by shooting at D, and hits-and-kills a bystander V accidentally, that's probably f.m. Ditto if a police officer responding to S's call for help accidentally hits V or S. Not so clear if D's accomplice is accidentally killed — some states say the killing of a co-felon during the felony can't be f.m.

❑ It is reasonably foreseeable that the occupants of a *burglarized* dwelling might return before an intruder has left and confront the burglar. Therefore, a killing that flows naturally from such a confrontation is probably a natural-and-probable result of the burglary, triggering f.m.

Example: While D is burglarizing O's house, O pulls a gun and, while trying to stop D, accidentally shoots O's wife V. D's arguably guilty of f.m. for V's death.

Example of no causal connection: X, Y and Z commit a robbery in a casino. As they are leaving, on the steps of a gambling casino, D approaches them, believing them to be the operators of the casino. D shouts, "Death to gamblers," shoots at them, and kills Y. D was unaware of the robbery. His motive for shooting was to close down the casino because he had lost all his savings there and his life had been ruined. There is no causal relationship between perpetration of the felony and Y's death — the death resulted from a truly independent, intervening event. Therefore, even in a state allowing one felon to be guilty of f.m. for the death of a co-felon, X and Z won't be guilty of f.m.

☛ **"During commission of" the felony:** Make sure the death occurs *during the perpetration of the felony.*

> **Example:** V, a store owner, returns from vacation to find out that her store was held up the previous day. V becomes so upset that she suffers a cerebral hemorrhage and dies. F.M. doesn't apply to her death, because the death wasn't "during the perpetration" of the felony.

> ☞ **Immediate flight:** But the "during the perpetration" element is *satisfied* if the death occurs while the defendant is *attempting to escape,* as long as the attempt occurs reasonably close, in time and place, to the felony. (*Example:* D accidentally runs over V while driving the getaway car from the scene of a bank robbery.)

☛ **Lack of desire to hurt is no defense:** Beware a common trap: the fact pattern indicates that D did not want to harm (or at least physically injure) anyone. This doesn't matter — it's still f.m. if the death proximately results from the felony.

> **Example:** D holds up V's store with a toy pistol. V has a heart attack and dies. The fact that D never intended to cause physical injury or any harm other than economic is irrelevant — it's still f.m.

☛ **Accomplice liability:** Be on the lookout for *accomplice liability* in f.m. scenarios. If D2 is guilty of f.m., and D1 is D2's accomplice in the underlying felony, then D1 is guilty of f.m. as well, as long as the killing was the *"natural and probable result"* of the felony.

> **Example:** R tells D that he wants to rob a candy store, and asks D if D wants to join in. D says no, but agrees that he will drive R to the store, and drive the getaway car thereafter. (D does not expect any violence to occur.) D's gun goes off during the robbery, killing V. R is clearly an accomplice to the bank robbery, so he's guilty of the substantive crime of robbery. Then, D (not just R) is guilty of f.m. as well, because he's committed a dangerous felony (robbery, under accomplice rules) which has "caused" a death during its perpetration. The fact that it wasn't D's gun that went off is irrelevant, because a mistaken or accidental shooting is certainly a "natural" result of an armed robbery.

Voluntary manslaughter ("v.m.")

☛ **Provocation:** The most frequently tested issue in this area is whether there was *reasonable provocation* for D's actions. Remember that this is an *objective* test, measured by the characteristics of a person of ordinary temperament.

Examples that <u>are</u> probably reasonable provocation (in all cases, V is the dead victim):

- ❏ V physically attacks, rapes, or murders D's friend or relative.

- ❏ V is D's wife or girlfriend, and has consensual sex with X, which D has just learned of.

- ❏ X is D's wife or girlfriend, and X has consensual sex with V, which D has just learned of.

Examples that are probably <u>not</u> reasonable provocation:

- ❏ V verbally insults D.

- ❏ V steals some relatively inexpensive items from D.

☞ **Cooling off period:** Also, look for a lapse of time within which a reasonable person would have *cooled off.* If there was such a lapse, then D can't use v.m.

   ☞ **Time frame in fact pattern:** Often the fact pattern will give you a time frame, and help you answer the question, Was there adequate time to cool off?

   Example 1: Where the facts says that D avenged his wife's rape "the morning after learning about it," there is a question whether enough time went by that a reasonable person would have cooled off.

   Example 2: Where the facts say that D is too stunned to act "for a moment," the momentary pause would certainly not be sufficient to constitute a cooling-off period, if D had suffered a severe shock.

   ☞ **Retrieval of weapon:** Also, look for a situation where D *goes elsewhere to retrieve a weapon*, then kills the provoker. This is probably your prof's signal that she wants you to at least consider the issue of whether D had time to cool off.

☛ **Imperfect self-defense:** Remember that in some states, liability may be reduced from murder to manslaughter, if the defendant was *unreasonably mistaken* in believing that his actions were justified by the need for, say, self-defense. This is the "imperfect self-defense" form of v.m. (*Example:* D unreasonably, but genuinely, believes that V is about to attack him, so he shoots V first.)

Involuntary manslaughter ("i.m.")

☛ **Definition in fact pattern:** If the fact pattern tells you the jurisdiction's definition of i.m., read it carefully to see just how extreme D's negligence must be to trigger i.m.

☞ **Gross negligence (or "recklessness") usually required:** If the fact pattern does not contain a statute, remember that typically, D must behave with "gross negligence" or "recklessness." Typically, this means that D must disregard a substantial danger of serious bodily harm or death — garden-variety negligence is not enough.

> **Example:** D, the operator of an automobile service station, advises a customer, V, that removing an air pollution device (a state law requires that all cars be equipped with such a device) would increase her car's fuel efficiency. At V's direction, D works carefully to remove the device, but accidentally loosens a connection in the exhaust system. This causes exhaust gases to leak into the car, poisoning and killing V. Probably D would not be convicted of i.m., because there's no indication that he knew (or should have known) that there was a substantial risk of death or serious injury from what he was doing.

☛ **Alternative to reckless-indifference murder:** Generally, if you argue in your answer that the defendant could be prosecuted for reckless-indifference murder, you should argue in the alternative (in case D's behavior does not rise to that level) that his reckless behavior would make him guilty of i.m.

> **Example:** V contacts D, his landlord, for the sixth time in two days to report that the heating system in his apartment building is malfunctioning. D does nothing. The furnace explodes and causes a fire, and V is killed while trying to rescue his baby. You should first discuss the possibility that L is guilty of reckless-indifference murder, on the theory that he disregarded a very high risk that the malfunction might cause a fire or explosion. But then, you should say that at the least, D is probably guilty of i.m., since his disregard of the risk was reckless.

> **Reckless drivers:** Drivers who *exceed the speed limit* by a lot, or otherwise drive recklessly (e.g., wrong-way down a 1-way street), should always suggest i.m. to you if a death results. Ditto for people who drive while intoxicated.

☛ **Attempted i.m. not possible:** When D is reckless but V doesn't die, don't be tempted to charge D with *attempted* i.m. Attempt crimes require an intent to bring about a result — i.m., since it's based on recklessness rather than intent, can't be "attempted."

☛ **Misdemeanor-manslaughter rule:** If the defendant is guilty of a *misdemeanor* the commission of which is causally linked to a death, consider the *"misdemeanor manslaughter" rule*: this rule permits a conviction for i.m. if a death occurs accidentally during the commission of a misdemeanor or other unlawful act. (Remember that not all states recognize it; and the MPC doesn't).

☞ **Assault or battery as misdemeanor:** The classic fact patterns for misdemeanor-manslaughter are assaults and batteries.

> **Example 1 (assault):** D tries to frighten V by pointing a gun at him and pretending to fire. D is just playing a joke, but V has a fatal heart attack. Since this was assault, the misdemeanor-manslaughter rule will be triggered if the jurisdiction recognizes it.

> **Example 2 (battery):** V insults D. D hits V with his fist, just intending to injure him slightly (not enough to constitute even "serious bodily harm.") V falls, hits his head on the edge of the sidewalk, and dies of brain trauma from the fall. Since D committed battery, this qualifies for misdemeanor-manslaughter.

☞ **Malum prohibitum:** If the offense is *"malum prohibitum"* — i.e., not dangerous in itself, but just a violation of a regulatory-type rule — in most states this *can't* be used for misdemeanor-manslaughter unless there is a close relationship between the violation and the death (which there usually won't be).

> **Example:** D's license is suspended for non-payment (not for prior accidents). While driving without a license, but otherwise driving properly, he accidentally hits and kills V. This won't be misdemeanor manslaughter, because there was no close causal relationship between D's failure to pay a license fee and his causing V's death.

Battery

☛ **Definition:** Remember that a battery is an intentional, reckless, or criminally negligent application of force that results in either *bodily injury* or an *offensive touching*.

> *Examples:*

> [1] D strikes V with a heavy ashtray;

> [2] D pushes V

> [3] D sticks a pipe against V's back so it feels like a gun

☞ Remember that there must be a physical contact between D (or some instrumental that he controls) and V's body. Some physical effect that V suffers in response to events — but that occurs without any physical contact between D and V — won't suffice.

> **Example:** D shoots X, V's wife, in front of V. V has a stroke when

he sees this. D has not committed battery on V, because there was no physical contact between D (or an instrumentality controlled or launched by D) and V's body.

Assault

☛ There are two situations in which you should discuss assault:

    ☞ **Attempted battery:** Assault can occur where D is unsuccessful in his *attempt to commit a battery.* Remember that: (1) the act must be done with *intent* to commit a harmful or offensive touching (recklessness or negligence aren't enough); and (2) the would-be-victim *need not be aware* of the danger.

       Example: The President of the United States is driving in a car with bullet-proof glass. Intending to shoot the President, D shoots three times at the car with a rifle, striking the glass, but not penetrating it. Because of the noise of the crowd, the President is unaware of the shots. A police officer who witnesses the shots being fired arrests D. Because D perpetrated an attempted battery, he is guilty of assault.

    ☞ **Intentional frightening:** Alternatively, assault occurs if D intentionally *frightens the victim* into fearing immediate bodily harm.

     Examples:

       ❑ Chasing and shooting at somebody with a hunting rifle;

       ❑ Sticking a pipe against somebody's back and saying, "Don't move or I'll shoot."

     ☞ **Doesn't see attacker:** Analyze the situation carefully where the victim *does not see his attacker* — it's not "intentional-frightening" assault unless there's a moment where V fears an imminent harmful or offensive contact.

       Example: D shoots at V, attempting to frighten him. Because of crowd noise, V doesn't learn of the attempt until several seconds later, by which time police have already tackled D. This isn't intentional-frightening assault, because there was no moment when V actually feared an imminent contact.

Rape / Sexual Assault

☛ Rape is not tested too often. When it is, two issues are most likely:

    ☞ **Statutory rape:** This is a strict liability crime, The defendant needs just to have the intent to have intercourse. *Important:* D's knowledge of V's age is not an element of the crime, so he's guilty even if he (reasonably) thinks V is an adult.

☞ **Intoxication of defendant:** Because rape / sexual assault is a so-called "general intent" crime, D's *voluntary intoxication* is *not* a defense as long as D *intended to have intercourse.* So, for instance, if D's drunkenness prevented him from realizing that V wasn't consenting, D's out of luck. However, if D is so intoxicated that he does not even know that he is engaging in intercourse, then he cannot be guilty of rape (even statutory rape).

Kidnapping

☛ This crime is not heavily tested. Basically look for:

☞ **Intent to confine:** D must intend to confine another.

Example: D steals a car and is unaware that a sleeping child is in the back seat. D does not possess the intent to commit kidnapping, since he has not intended to confine or transport anyone.

☞ **Asportation:** V must either be hidden or moved (*"asportation"*). Many jurisdictions hold that there is no asportation if the movement of the victim was incidental to and a necessary part of the commission of some other substantive crime.

Example: During the course of a bank robbery, R points a gun at and orders the bank tellers and manager to go from the bank lobby to the back room while R's partner attempts to open the safe. There has probably been no asportation, in which case there has been no kidnapping.

Exam Tips on
THEFT CRIMES

☛ *Larceny* and *burglary* are the theft crimes most frequently tested.

Larceny

☛ If you think you have larceny in your facts, confirm that all the required elements of common-law larceny have been met: The (1) trespassory (2) taking and carrying away of (3) personal property of (4) another (5) with the intent to steal.

☛ **Trespassory taking:** Look for a defendant who is *already in rightful pos-*

session of the property at the time he decides to appropriate it for his own purposes — if so, he is **not** guilty of larceny because the "trespassory" taking element is missing.

> **Example:** D is walking in the street at night and finds a watch (with the owner's name engraved on it) lying on the ground near a pawnshop. He decides to take it home and to try to locate the owner. However, once he gets home, he decides to keep it. Since D was already in lawful possession of the watch at the moment he decided to keep it, he will not be guilty of common-law larceny.

☛ **Carrying away:** Determine whether the defendant assumed *dominion and control* over the object. Generally, but not always, this means that there must be a physical *movement* of the object.

> ☞ **Slight distance sufficient:** But if D causes even a *slight movement* of the object (after forming the intent to misappropriate), this will suffice for the dominion-and-control element.

> > **Example:** D is having dinner in a restaurant with V. V leaves the table to go to the restroom and D notices V's expensive watch on the table. She decides to steal it and puts it into her pocket. D begins to feel guilty, so when V returns to the table, D hands her the watch and says, "Here, you dropped this, and I put it into my pocket for safekeeping." Since D moved the watch from the table to her pocket with the intention of keeping it, she carried it away. She was actually guilty of larceny at that moment. (The fact that D changed her mind shortly thereafter and tried to "undo" the crime doesn't change this result.)

☛ **Intangible property:** Be on the lookout for property that is intangible. Remember that at common law, only tangible property could be the subject of larceny. But if your fact pattern has intangible property (e.g., a check, or services), say that under modern statutes, larceny has usually been expanded to cover intangibles.

> **Example:** D, a student, breaks into the offices of X, her professor, and photographs the original text of the exam that X will be giving the next day. (D never physically moves the original.) Although the original text is intangible property in a sense, a modern larceny statute would probably still cover it, making this larceny.

☛ **Property of "another":** Be on the lookout for property that appears to be property of one other than D, but really belongs to D. When this happens, D can't be guilty of larceny for taking the property, because it's not property of *"another."*

Example: D pawns his watch to X, a pawnbroker. The pawn agreement says that D may reclaim the watch by paying $100 at any time during the next month. Two weeks later, D breaks in to X's store and takes the watch. D has at least a good argument that he hasn't committed common-law larceny, because he hasn't taken property of "another" (he himself still has title to the watch, subject to X's right to possess it as security for repayment).

☞ **Collecting a debt:** As a twist on "property of another," watch for a situation in which *V owes D money* or an item, and D takes a different item (or money) with an equal or lesser value, as a form of *self-help*. Here, V probably *won't be guilty* of larceny — his honest claim of "right" will negate the intent to take property "of another". And that's probably true even if D is *wrong* (though honest) in his belief that V owes him the debt.

Example: V has borrowed $50 from D, and has also borrowed D's watch (worth $50). V has repeatedly refused either to give back the watch or repay the $50 debt. While D is visiting V, he finds V's wallet on a table. D takes $100 from the wallet, intending this to constitute repayment for both the $50 and the watch. D is not guilty of c/l larceny, because he took under a claim of right. (Probably the same result would apply if D honestly but mistakenly believed that V had never repaid the $50 loan.)

☛ **Intent to permanently deprive:** This issue frequently arises on exams. The two rules to keep in mind are: (1) The only intent that matters is the intent *at the time of the taking* (not at some point after); and (2) There must be an intent to *permanently* deprive the owner of the property (or at least of a significant portion of the property's economic value).

☞ **Intent to borrow item:** Often, the defendant has a viable argument that he merely wanted to *borrow* the item. If so, there's no c/l larceny, because there's no intent-to-permanently-deprive.

Example: D breaks into her the office of V, her professor, to photocopy his notes. While in the office, she notices a gold-plated pen on V's desk and takes it with the intent of returning it in a week or two, hoping in the meantime that V will be so distressed about losing his pen that he will not notice that his notes have been disturbed. The next day, the pen is stolen from D's briefcase. D is not guilty of c/l larceny, because at the time she took the pen she did not intend to permanently deprive V of it (and the fact that the pen was later stolen by someone else, so as to prevent her from returning it, is irrelevant).

☞ **Actual ability to return:** But in intent-to-borrow situations, keep in mind that D will lack the requisite intent only if, viewed as of the time of D's taking, there is a substantial likelihood that D will in fact be able to return the property to V in pretty much its original form. If the facts show that the property probably won't be returned to V (or will likely be returned in damaged form), then D will be found to have the requisite intent-to-steal despite the intent to "return" it.

> **Example:** Outside and during the night, D robs V of his billfold in order to retrieve a memorandum from it. After removing only the memorandum from the billfold, D throws V's billfold into the gutter, where he "expects" V to find it. In your answer, you should analyze the probability of the billfold being found and returned to V. If a jury finds that D should have realized that leaving the billfold there made it unlikely that D would get it back, then D probably has the requisite intent-to-steal the billfold even though D may have hoped or expected that D would get it back.

☞ **Property returned:** Conversely, don't be fooled by a fact pattern which indicates that the item was *actually returned*. That fact is inconsequential if D's decision to return it was formed subsequent to the taking. (*Example:* In the fact pattern above where D puts V's watch in her pocket at the restaurant and then changes her mind and returns it, this is still larceny.)

☞ **Contingent borrowing:** Lastly, be on the lookout for what could be termed a "contingent intent" to return "borrowed" property. For an intent-to-return to negate intent, D's intent must clearly be to return the item and not be contingent on any circumstances.

> **Example:** D, V's employee, "borrows" money from V's cash register, intending to gamble with it and to return it if she wins. She does in fact win, and returns the full amount. Regardless, D had the requisite intent to steal, because her intent-to-return was subject to a contingency.

☛ **Larceny by trick:** It can still be c/l larceny when D obtains possession of the property by fraud or deceit, instead of by force. But in this situation, make sure V was induced only to transfer temporary possession (not ownership or title) — if title is transferred, it's false pretenses, not larceny-by-trick.

> **Example:** V rents a car to D, who pays with what turns out to be a worthless check. D keeps the car (as he intended all along). This is c/l

larceny (of the larceny-by-trick variety), because D has fraudulently induced V to part with mere possession, not title. But if V had *sold* (transferred title) to the car to V in return for the worthless check, this would be false pretenses rather than c/l larceny, since in that situation title (rather than mere possession) would have been procured by D's deceit.

☞ **Where V doesn't have lawful possession:** Don't be tricked by a fact pattern which indicates that the *victim* of the theft *does not have lawful possession of the property.* As long as V's claim to the property is better than D's, that's enough for larceny. So, for instance, the fact that V himself previously stole the property, or possessed it illegally, is irrelevant. (*Example:* D may commit a larceny by stealing V's illegal-to-possess marijuana plant.)

Robbery

☞ **Definition:** Remember that robbery is defined as larceny with two additional elements: (1) the property is *taken from the person or presence* of the owner, and (2) the taking is accomplished by *force or putting the owner in fear.* Remember to note in your answer that the crime of larceny merges into that of robbery.

☞ **Intent:** Since robbery is built on larceny, D must have the specific intent to permanently deprive another of the other's personal property. Refer to the discussion regarding larceny above. So watch for situations where D believes that the property actually belongs to him, or where his intent at the time of the taking is not to permanently deprive — there can't be robbery in these situations, since there's no underlying larceny.

☞ **Force:** This element is occasionally tested. Generally, it's obvious when a taking is accomplished by using force or a threat of force, but there can be close questions, where your job is to notice that there's an issue about whether force-or-threat-of-force is present.

> **Example:** V is shot while driving his car. The car rolls into a tree and comes to a stop. D, a bystander, opens the driver's door with the intention of helping V. However, when he sees that V has been shot, he decides there's nothing he can do. D notices that V is wearing an expensive watch and begins to remove it. V opens one eye and faintly motions D away. D takes the watch and says, "You won't need this where you're going." V dies moments later. Given the circumstances, V's faint protestations were adequate to demonstrate he was not relinquishing the watch freely. Therefore, D probably would be deemed to have obtained the watch by force or threat of force.

Embezzlement

☞ **Definition:** In many fact patterns, embezzlement should be argued as an alternative to larceny. Remember the definition of c/l embezzlement: A fraudulent conversion of the property of another, by one who is *already in lawful possession* of that property.

☞ **Employees:** Think of embezzlement anytime an employee misappropriates the employer's money. Remember that c/l embezzlement exists only where the employee is originally in lawful *possession* of the employer's property (not merely *custody*). This means that if an employee has custody of the employer's property, but not true "possession," the misappropriation would be larceny, not embezzlement. Point this out whenever the employee is a minor, clerical-type person.

> **Example:** D is a cashier at the V supermarket. D periodically pocket $5 or $10 from the cash register. D's minor-employee status indicates that she probably has only temporary custody of the cash in the drawer, and that "constructive possession" remains with V. If so, D's conduct is probably larceny, not embezzlement. (But if D was V's controller, entrusted with investing the company's cash, his misappropriation would probably be embezzlement, since his seniority indicates he was given "possession," not just temporary custody, of the funds.)

☞ **Bailees:** Also think of embezzlement where the property is in the lawful possession of a *bailee* (repair-person, pawnbroker, etc.), who then appropriates it.

> **Example:** V's watch is broken, so he gives it to D, a jeweller, to be repaired. D takes it, fixes it, and then (because he's deeply in debt to bookies) puts it for sale in his store. X buys it. D has committed embezzlement, since he was in lawful possession of the watch at the time he sold it.

☞ **Possession must be lawful:** Remember that the defendant's possession must be *lawful*, not produced by fraud or other crime.

> **Example:** D offers for "sale" various cars that he doesn't in fact own. He collects a $100 cash down payment from V, then vanishes without producing the car. D cannot be guilty of embezzling money because his possession of the $100 is the result of fraud and was never lawful. (In other words, his crime is larceny, not embezzlement.)

☞ **Intent to repay:** Remember that if what's embezzled is money, D's *intent to repay* the money is never a defense to embezzlement charges. And that's true even if the repayment actually occurs.

False pretenses

☞ The crime of obtaining property by false pretenses is not heavily tested.

☞   **Definition:** This crime is committed when, with the intent to cause V to transfer title to personal property, D makes a fraudulent misrepresentation which causes V to make the transfer.

☞   **Title passes:** Distinguish false pretenses from larceny by trick. In false pretenses, title passes. In larceny by trick, only possession passes.

☞   **Purchase with bad check:** Think false-pretenses if D purchases V's property with what D knows is a ***bad check.***

☞   **Swindle:** Also, think false pretenses if D *swindles* V, by charging V money for something that doesn't have the qualities D says it has.

> **Example:** D sells V a potion that D says will cure impotence. D knows it's actually a completely inert substances. This is obtaining money by false pretenses.

Burglary

☛ When a question requires you to analyze whether a defendant can be convicted of burglary, first attempt to ascertain the particular jurisdiction's required elements of the crime. If the fact pattern does not mention them, discuss the common-law requirements: (1) the ***breaking & entering*** of (2) the ***dwelling*** of ***another*** (3) in the ***night***; (4) with ***intent to commit a felony*** therein. Some things to keep in mind about this definition:

☞   **Breaking:** Remember that ***no force*** is required.

> ☞   **Unlocked door:** So for instance, a defendant who ***opens a closed door or window*** (even an unlocked one) has fulfilled the "breaking" requirement, if this is done without the owner's authorization.

> ☞   **Use of key:** But if D uses a ***key*** to gain ***authorized*** entry, this is not "breaking." (*Example:* V gives D her key so she can water her plants while V is on vacation. D then enters and steals. This is not "breaking," and therefore not burglary.)

> ☞   **Closed area:** Watch for a fact pattern that describes an initial entry that clearly does not involve a "breaking," but the defendant subsequently breaks into a ***large enclosed structure*** located within the larger structure. In some states, breaking and entering such a closed area within which a person is capable of standing is sufficient.

> > **Example:** X, Y, and Z enter a casino shortly before closing and hide in the bathroom until it closes. After closing, they hold the employees at gun point. A heavy safe, large enough to walk into, is blown open by X; Y and Z enter it and grab sacks of money

from it. Although their initial entry into the casino did not constitute a breaking, blowing open the safe probably does, in which
case X has committed burglary (and Y and Z are his accomplices
to that burglary).

☞ **Entry:** Remember that an *entry* must follow the breaking. But it
doesn't take much to satisfy this element — even putting a hand or
foot into the previously-enclosed space will suffice.

> **Example:** X kicks in the door to someone's room and fires a shot
> at somebody inside. The bullet certainly entered the room and X's
> foot probably did when he kicked in the door. So either probably
> qualifies as an entry, making the whole transaction a burglary.

☞ **Dwelling of another:** Although the c/l definition requires that the
entry be into the "dwelling" of another, you may want to note in your
answer that some jurisdictions have *broadened* the definition. So it
may be sufficient that the structure is *attached* to a dwelling, such as a
garage, or a pawnshop that has living quarters upstairs. Additionally,
note that many jurisdictions have extended the definition to *any* structure, even one with no connection to a residence (e.g., an office; a
warehouse; or a store.)

☞ **Nighttime:** Pay attention to the *time of day*. If there's no mention of
this in the fact pattern, write that you're assuming that the burglary
occurred at night or that the jurisdiction has abandoned the nighttime
requirement for all degrees of burglary.

☞ **Intent to commit crime inside structure:** Under the common law, the
defendant must have intended to commit a *felony* inside the structure.
But where appropriate, note in your answer that in some states today,
all that's required is the intent to commit some crime, whether felony
or non-felony theft crime. Two key points:

> ☞ **Not just theft:** Don't mistakenly assumes that burglary requires
> an intent to commit a *theft* crime within. Intent to commit *any* fel-
> ony will do, even at common law.
>
> **Example:** D breaks into a house with the intent to shoot and kill V,
> the house's owner. At the moment D breaks and enters at night,
> he's committed burglary, because he had an intent to commit a fel-
> ony (murder) inside.
>
> ☞ **Intent at time of entering:** Make sure that D intended, at the time
> of the breaking and entering, to later commit a felony. Don't be
> tricked by a defendant's *subsequent* decision to take something or
> to commit some other crime within the structure.

☞ **Recovering own property:** Even though D has the intent to take something at the time of entering the structure, if he *believes (even incorrectly) that it belongs to him*, there is *no intent* to commit a crime.

Example: Although D knows that V is out of town, he goes to V's apartment to retrieve his own camera so that he can take pictures at his sister's wedding. V's apartment door is locked, but D shakes the doorknob and the door opens. D searches for the camera, but can't find it. On his way out he takes a silver candy dish from a shelf to give as a wedding present. Although V committed a breaking and entering and a larceny, the fact that he entered only with the intent to recover his own camera prevented him from having the requisite intent to be convicted of burglary. (And the later decision to take the candy dish doesn't count, because it wasn't an act that D intended at the moment of the breaking-and-entering.)

Receiving stolen property

☛ Two key issues:

☞ **Stolen property:** Remember that for D to be guilty of receiving stolen property, the property must *in fact be stolen,* under the jurisdiction's theft statute. So you'll have to carefully analyze the property in terms of larceny, embezzlement, etc.

Example: X is walking in the street and finds a watch lying on the ground. He decides to take it home and to try to locate the owner. However, once he gets home, he decides to keep it. He then becomes nervous and gives the watch to his friend D saying, "Here, you can have this watch, but be careful, it's hot." D keeps the watch. Since X was not guilty of c/l larceny (he did not have the intent to permanently deprive the owner of possession at the time of the taking), the watch was not the subject of larceny. Therefore, D was not guilty of receiving stolen property.

☞ **Decoy:** Look for a fact pattern where the police are attempting to trap a thief or receiver of stolen goods. The decoy property used in such a scheme has probably been recovered by the police and has therefore *lost its character as stolen.* Therefore, D can't be guilty of receiving stolen property.

☞ **Knowledge that it's stolen:** Make sure D *knew* the property was stolen *at the moment he acquired possession* of it.

Example: D's friend T gives him a new television as a birthday gift. The next day D asks T for the warranty document. T informs D that there isn't any because the television was stolen. D keeps the television. D is not guilty of receiving stolen property, because he did not know it was stolen when he received it.

SHORT-ANSWER QUESTIONS AND ANSWERS

SHORT-ANSWER QUESTIONS

Note: These questions are selected from among the "Quiz Yourself" questions in the full-length *Emanuel on Criminal Law (EOCL)*, which were in turn adapted from *Law in a Flash* on Criminal Law. We've kept the same question numbering here as in *EOCL*.

CHAPTER 1
ACTUS REUS AND MENS REA

1. Cain hates Abel and wants to kill him. Cain, Abel and their third brother, Seth, visit the Grand Canyon. Abel is peering over the edge.

   (A) Cain pushes Seth into Abel, causing Abel to fall to his death. Has *Seth* committed an act that could result in criminal liability? _____

   (B) Instead of the facts in Part A, assume that Cain tells Seth: "If you don't kill Abel, I'll tell Mom you've been eating forbidden fruit." If Seth pushes Abel off a cliff under this threat, has he committed an act that could result in criminal liability? _____

2. King George III, an epileptic, has a seizure in a crowded bus. During his seizure, he hits another passenger, breaking his jaw. In hitting the passenger, has George committed the actus reus required for a crime (in this case, battery)? _____

3. Sigmund Freud is addicted to cocaine.

   (A) First, assume Freud is arrested under a state statute making it a crime to be addicted to a controlled substance. (The arrest comes about because Freud's doctor realizes that Freud is addicted, and informs the police of this fact.) Is the statute constitutionally valid, as applied to Freud? _____

   (B) Now, assume that Freud is arrested for possession of cocaine when a police officer spots a baggy of the stuff on the passenger seat of Freud's car during a routine traffic stop. The statute makes it a crime to possess cocaine, even if the possession is exclusively for the defendant's own use on account of the defendant's drug addiction. Is the possession statute constitutionally valid, as applied to Freud? _____

4. India Hauser, champion swimmer, is lounging on a riverbank reading John Stuart Mill's autobiography. Ima Gonner, India's sworn enemy, strolls up in her bathing suit and goes for a dip in the river. In fact the water is deeper than Ima expected, and she begins to drown. India looks up from her book and watches, laughing, as

Ima drowns. When Ima goes down for the last time, India sighs and says: "Oh well. Back to the Mill."

(A) Is India criminally liable for Ima's death? _____

(B) Assume the same facts as above, except that Ima went into the river because India told her, "Go on in and swim. The water's only three feet deep." (India actually believed this, because a friend whom India had reason to trust told her that the water was only three feet deep.) Is India criminally liable for Ima's death? _____

5. John Wilkes Booth decides to kill Lincoln, because he thinks Lincoln is a tyrant. Booth notes in his diary, "I have decided to kill Lincoln the day after tomorrow." Before anything further happens, Booth is arrested by the FBI. Is Booth subject to criminal liability?_____

6. Kramer and George are motorists in the State of Seinfeld. The two approach an empty parking spot at the same time. After each yells at the other about who is entitled to the spot, Kramer leaves his car and walks over to George's car. Kramer pulls a screwdriver from his pocket and touches it to George's throat, hoping that the touch will scare George away. In fact, however, George reacts by twisting his head, and in so doing, cuts himself severely against the blade of the screwdriver. Kramer did not intend to physically injure George, merely to frighten him. The State of Seinfeld defines the crime of assault as occurring where one "purposely causes bodily injury to another...." A decision of the Seinfeld Supreme Court states that assault is a crime which requires "general intent." May Kramer properly be found guilty of assault? _____

7. The State of Maine enacts a criminal statute stating that "Any person who sells misbranded hair care products shall be guilty of a misdemeanor, punishable by up to 7 days in jail." Delilah is charged with selling to Samson a can of hair spray labelled "Makes your hair grow longer," when in fact the can makes your hair all fall out.

(A) Assume for this part that the statute's legislative history makes it clear that the Mane legislature intended that the statute shall apply even though the seller does not know (and has no reason to know) of the mislabelling. Assume further that Delilah demonstrates that she neither knew nor had any particular reason to know that the can she sold Samson was mislabelled. May Delilah constitutionally be convicted of a statutory violation and sentenced to 6 days in jail? _____

(B) Assume for this part that everything specified in Part (A) remains true, except that: (1) There is no legislative history shedding any light on whether the Mane legislature intended to require any particular mental state for a violation of the statute; and (2) The statute mandates a jail sentence of between 30 days and one year upon any conviction. Should a court convict Delilah of the violation?_____

8. Abbott and Costello, who do not know each other, meet on the street one day and begin to talk. Abbott tells Costello that he is late for an appointment in the building they are standing near, and that he will pay Costello $250 to do him a favor. Abbott explains that he has borrowed his friend's red Porsche and parked it down the street, but has lost the keys. Having learned that Costello is an auto mechanic, Abbott asks Costello to break into the Porsche, hot-wire it, and deliver it to an address that Abbott scribbles on a piece of paper.

Costello accepts the offer and carries it out. The story later turns out to be false — in fact, the Porsche belongs to a stranger, and Abbott is really a thief who has duped Costello into delivering the car to Abbott's fence. Costello is charged with auto theft, defined in the jurisdiction as "knowingly or purposefully taking a vehicle belonging to another." The case is tried before a judge, who finds that Costello actually believed Abbott's story, but that a "reasonable person" would not have believed the story. If the state follows the Model Penal Code approach to mistake, can Costello be convicted? _____

9. Guy Fawkes goes to the corner bar and says to himself, "I'm going to drink until I'm completely smashed, and then I'm going to stagger drunkenly around town until they lock me up." He drinks until, as he knows, he's completely smashed. He then leaves the bar and wanders around drunkenly. At one point, he he stops to light a cigarette, drops the match, and burns down his neighbor's garage. The jurisdiction's public intoxication statute applies to "a person who intentionally appears in public in a state of intoxication." The jurisdiction's arson statute applies to one who "intentionally sets fire to real property not his own." Can Guy be convicted of arson on the grounds that his general criminal intent to commit the crime of public intoxication is transferred to his commission of the crime of arson? _____

10. On July 4, Dr. Evil firmly decides to do away with Austin Powers by killing him with a super-sonic freeze gun. He plans to commit the crime on July 5.

(A) For this part only, assume that during the night of July 4-5, Dr. Evil has a dream in which he is damned to hell. On the morning of July 5, he wakes up with a change of heart, and no longer plans to kill Powers. Later that day, while he is walking down the street with his supersonic freeze gun, he happens to pass Powers. He is so startled that he reflexively and unintentionally squeezes the trigger of the gun, and it goes off, freezing Powers to death. Is Dr. Evil guilty of murder? _____

(B) Same facts as above, except that Dr. Evil does not have the dream or the change of heart. He plans to kill Powers at Powers' home at 8:00 pm using the freeze gun. At 5:30 p.m., while Dr. Evil is en route to his favorite restaurant with the gun in hand, Powers passes by. Dr. Evil is so startled that he reflexively squeezes the trigger and the gun goes off, freezing Powers to death. Is Dr. Evil guilty of murder? _____

CHAPTER 2

CAUSATION

11. Jesse James is trapped at the I'm O.K. Corral. Doc Holiday fires a bullet at James, and hits him. 1/2 second later, Wyatt Earp fires a shot at James, and also hits him (while he's still standing). (Holliday and Earp are not acting in concern, they each independently have it in for James.) James dies immediately. Either bullet would have been enough to kill James. Who is the cause-in-fact of James' death, Holiday, Earp, both or neither? _____

12. Yosemite Sam has his heart set on rabbit stew for dinner. He sees Bugs Bunny off in the distance, aims his gun right at him, and fires. (Assume that if Sam had hit Bugs, this would have been murder, i.e., there's no defense of rabbit-hunting.) Unfortunately, Sam's aim is

very bad and he instead hits and kills Daffy Duck, whom he never even saw.

(A) Is Yosemite Sam guilty of murdering Daffy Duck? _____

(B) Same facts as (A), except that instead of killing Daffy Duck, he merely wounds him. What crimes is Sam guilty of now? _____

13. Cheshire Cat is tired of being chased by Tweedle Dee all day long and decides to "off" him. He buys an AK-47 at the local convenience store and hides in the bushes, waiting for his victim to pass by. Tweedle Dum, Tweedle Dee's twin brother, happens to walk by. Thinking that he's looking at Tweedle Dee, Cheshire Cat aims right at him and fires. Tweedle Dum is killed instantly. Since Cheshire Cat only had the intention to kill Tweedle Dee, is he guilty of the murder of Tweedle Dum? _____

14. Antony gives Cleopatra a glass of wine tainted with arsenic, intending to kill her. However, the poison does not instantly kill Cleo.

(A) For this part only, assume that the arsenic was (unbeknownst to Antony) so weak that it would almost certainly not have killed Cleo, even if she had had no medical treatment. Cleo was rushed to the hospital. A nurse there gave her a potion that was intended to be an antidote. What the nurse didn't know was that the potion was in fact a rat poison intended to exterminate the hospital's growing rat population, which had been mislabelled due to another nurse's gross negligence. Cleo died principally from the effects of the rat poison, but had she not been weakened from the earlier arsenic poisoning, she probably would have survived. Will Antony's act be deemed a proximate cause of Cleo's death? _____

(B) For this part, assume that Cleo refused to go to the hospital – even though she knew she would not otherwise likely recover from the poison. She died several hours later. Will Antony's act be deemed the proximate cause of Cleo's death? _____

15. Bob Ford intends to kill Jesse James. He shoots at James, but misses. In an attempt to escape Ford's shots, James turns his horse and gallops off in the opposite direction. Shortly after he starts the escape gallop, he is struck and killed by a boulder from an unexpected rockfall. Is Ford's conduct a proximate cause of James' death? _____

CHAPTER 3

RESPONSIBILITY

16. Jack T. Ripper knows that killing a person is legally wrong. Nevertheless, he slashes the throats of several prostitutes for the purpose of killing them. He does this because he believes that has been instructed by God to "kill all prostitutes — they are evil." Jack tries to resist God's instructions (because he really doesn't enjoy the killing), but is powerless to prevent himself from obeying what he believes are God's orders.

(A) Is Jack insane under the *M'Naghten* Rule? _____

(B) Is Jack insane under the federal insanity statute? _____

(C) Is Jack insane under the Model Penal Code? _____

(D) Under the federal insanity statute, which party (Jack or the prosecution) will bear the burden of (1) raising the issue of sanity; and (2) proving sanity/insanity? _____

17. Hansel goes to the local tavern one night and ties one on. He stumbles out, and drives away. Hansel then forcibly opens the door to Witch Hazel's house, believing it's his own (which is really one block over in their development of nearly-identical tract homes). When Witch Hazel walks into the room Hansel thinks she's a burglar and beats her up. Hansel is criminally charged with both burglary and battery. Burglary is defined in the jurisdiction as an intentional entry into the dwelling of another at night, with an intent to commit a felony therein. Battery is defined as intentionally or recklessly causing a harmful or offensive contact with the body of another. To which (if either) of these two charges — burglary and battery — will Hansel's intoxication be a defense? _____

18. Popeye spends the afternoon drinking in a bar and gets plastered. As he is leaving to go home, he encounters Brutus, who approaches him while waving his arms wildly to swat away a fly. Popeye, believing that Brutus is going to attack him, picks up a bar stool and hits Brutus over the head with it. (A sober man in Popeye's position would not have believed that Brutus was attacking him.) Can Popeye successfully plead self-defense? _____

19. Othello has for some time suspected that his beloved wife Desdemona may have been unfaithful to him. One evening he gets quite drunk at a neighboring tavern, and then comes home to discover that his wife's favorite handkerchief is missing. As the result of Othello's drunken logic (plus a little help from his evil friend Iago, who has planted the idea of Desdemona's infidelity in Othello's head), Othello incorrectly believes that the missing handkerchief is proof that Desdemona has cheated on him. He kills Desdemona in a jealous rage. Assume that a sober man in Othello's position would not have believed that the missing handkerchief suggested anything about Dedemona's fidelity. Assume further that where a man reasonably believes that his spouse has been unfaithful, his killing of the spouse in a fit of jealous rage may be reduced from murder to manslaughter. May Othello successfully plead manslaughter on these facts? _____

CHAPTER 4

JUSTIFICATION AND EXCUSE

20. Lewis threatens to kill Clark if Clark does not steal certain valuable camping equipment from their employer, Sacagewea, before they leave for the next leg of their trip the following week. Clark reasonably believes that Lewis will do what he says, given Lewis' past violent behavior. Clark steals the equipment and is charged with larceny.

   (A) What defense offers Clark his best chance at an acquittal? _____

   (B) In most states, will the defense you listed in (A) be accepted on these facts? _____

   (C) Will the defense you listed in (A) be accepted on these facts under the Model Penal Code? _____

21. Norton holds a knife to the throat of Alice, Ralph's wife, and threatens to kill her unless

Ralph robs the local convenience store.

(A) If Ralph robs the store, is he guilty of larceny? _____

(B) Same facts as above, except that Norton's threat is that he will kill Alice unless Ralph kills Trixie, Norton's wife. Ralph does so, and Norton releases Alice, thanking Ralph for making him a free man. Is Ralph guilty of criminal homicide? _____

22. Etta is kidnapped by Sundance and forced at gunpoint to participate in a bank robbery. (Before she participates in the robbery, Etta realizes that Sundance may well use deadly force to complete the robbery.) During the robbery, Sundance shoots and kills a bank teller, who is trying to summon the police. Etta is charged with felony-murder. Guilty or not guilty? _____

23. Phineas Phogg is piloting a hot air balloon around the world, accompanied by five paying passengers. The balloon starts to lose altitude, and Phineas must take immediate action.

(A) For this part only, assume that Phineas throws all the passengers' belongings overboard, hoping to lighten the basket's load and regain altitude. If Phineas is charged with larceny,   what   defense   should   he   assert,   and   will   that   defense prevail? _____

(B) Say instead that after Phineas throws overboard all the belongings (including his own), and anything else that's not human, the balloon is still plunging at an alarming rate. Phineas makes the reasonable determination that unless he throws one passenger overboard, the balloon will crash land at a speed that is likely to kill anyone aboard. He therefore throws overboard the heaviest passenger. If Phineas is charged with murder, will the defense you asserted in part (A) prevail? _____

24. Dorothy sees a tornado heading toward her while she is walking home from school with her dog Toto. In order to escape the danger, she breaks a window to get into the only nearby structure, a house, and runs into the basement. Is Dorothy guilty of trespass? _____

25. Rocky and Rambo meet on a sidewalk one day. Without any apparent provocation, Rocky begins to physically attack Rambo. Rambo reasonably fears that Rocky is about to kill him or do him serious bodily harm.

(A) For this part only, assume the following additional facts: Rambo knows that Rocky is a skilled and brutal fighter, and reasonably believes that if he, Rambo, fights back with non-deadly force (such as his own fists), Rocky is likely to overpower him and hurt him badly. Rambo also realizes that he could simply run away, because he's a faster runner than Rocky. But Rambo does not want to do anything so cowardly as that. Therefore, without any warning, Rambo whips out a hidden gun and shoots Rocky to death. Under the   approach   of   most   states,   is   Rambo   guilty   of   homicide   in   Rocky's death? _____

(B) Assume the same facts as in part (A), except that: shortly after the Rocky's attack starts — before Rambo has made any real decision about how to defend himself — Rocky calms down, and starts to walk away. As Rocky is walking away, Rambo whips out his gun and shoots Rocky in the back. Rambo does this not because he fears that Rocky will change his mind and re-attack, but because he's enraged that Rocky had the gall to assault him in the first place. Can Rambo successfully plead self-defense against a charge of murder? _____

26. Alfalfa insults Butch's mother. Butch responds by slapping Alfalfa once on the cheek. Alfalfa (who thinks that the slap is just a prelude to a bigger attack) fights back by swinging with a closed fist. Butch, who reasonably fears that Alfalfa may slightly hurt him with his swings, swings back, breaking Alfalfa's jaw.

(A) If Butch is charged with battery for the swing that broke Alfalfa's jaw, will he be found guilty? _____

(B) Assume the same facts, except as follows: Alfalfa, instead of merely swinging at Butch after Butch's slap, wraps his hands around Butch's throat, and starts to squeeze hard. Butch responds by punching Alfalfa in the face (in order to break the choke-hold), and as in part (A) breaks Alfalfa's jaw. If Butch is charged with battery for the jaw-breaking, will he be found guilty? _____

27. Juliet is in her fifth month of pregnancy. Romeo walks up to her with a knife, and tells her, "Once you have the baby, I'm going to kill you." Juliet pulls out a gun and shoots him. Can Juliet defend on self-defense grounds? _____

28. Fletcher Christian shoots and kills Captain Bligh because he thinks Bligh is about to shoot and kill him. Actually, Bligh pulled out his gun to shoot deckhand Dick Hand, who was standing behind Christian and looking like he was about to strangle Christian with a clothesline. Can Christian successfully assert the defense of self-defense? _____

29. Papa Bear and his family are asleep in their home when he is awakened by mysterious noises coming from downstairs. He gets up and picks up a baseball bat from his son's room, and goes downstairs. There he confronts an apparently-unarmed Goldilocks, who is stealing silverware.

(A) For this part only, assume that Goldilocks is startled, but makes no move to leave. Nor does she put down the silverware. Papa Bear tells her to leave, and she starts walking out, taking the silverware with her. Papa Bear (who knows he's very strong) swings a baseball bat at Goldilocks' head, intending to knock her unconscious so he can retrieve the silverware. Goldilocks dies from the blow. Papa Bear is charged with manslaughter. Under the Model Penal Code, should he be convicted? _____

(B) For this part, assume the same facts, except that after Papa Bear tells Goldilocks to leave, she runs towards the carving knives at the side of the kitchen. Before she can pick up a knife, Papa Bear swings at her with the baseball bat, fearing that if he doesn't, Goldilocks may attack him with the knife. (In fact, Goldilocks just wants to grab a few knives so she can steal them for their silver value.) Goldilocks dies from the blow. Again, Papa Bear is charged with manslaughter. Under the Model Penal Code, should he be convicted? _____

30. Paul Bunyon owns a hunting cabin in Northwoods that has been broken into several times during his absences. He devises a trap door just inside the entryway which, when triggered, drops an intruder into a rattlesnake pit. Several weeks later, Daniel Goon, unarmed,

breaks into the cabin, intending to take away with him whatever he can carry. However, he falls through the trap door and into the pit, where he is bitten to death by the snakes. Can Paul Bunyon defend a murder charge on the grounds of privilege to defend his property?

_____

31. Police officer Dudley Do-Righteous, walking the beat in the financial district, gets a call on his police radio that there has been an embezzlement at the Awesome Bank, and that the suspect is about to leave the scene with a large satchel in which to carry cash. (The report does not indicate that the suspect is armed.) Dudley happens to be right in front of the bank. He sees Snively Whiplash run out of the building carrying a large satchel, jump in a car, and start to drive away. Dudley yells "Stop, Embezzler!" Snively keeps going. The only way Dudley will be able to detain and arrest Snively is by shooting at him. Can Dudley do so? _____

32. John Gotti is a law-abiding citizen. One afternoon, while walking down a street in Little Italy, John observes a teenager running out of a store, holding a box. An old man chases the teenager, screaming in Italian (a language that John recognizes but doesn't under- stand). Some of the other people in the street around him begin speaking Italian and point- ing towards the teenager. John reasonably believes that the boy has just committed shoplifting (a felony in the jurisdiction) from the man. Therefore, John gives chase. As he gets close to the boy, John makes a flying tackle, hoping just to bring the teenager down. Instead, the teenager, while falling, cracks his head and suffers serious injuries. It later turns out that the teenager was the grandson of the old man, and that there had not been any crime, merely a family argument. Assume that John acted reasonably (at least given his lack of ability to understand Italian) in concluding that the teenager was a fleeing thief. If John is charged with the crime of assault, will he be able to raise the defense of private arrest? _____

33. Bunko, a police officer, convinces Ratso that Bunko is a junkie and that he'll pay anything to get a fix. Ratso refuses to sell him anything, saying he has nothing to do with drugs. Bunko pleads, "Come on, Pal. Have a heart. I'll give you $100 for yourself, plus whatever the stuff itself costs, if you'll help me out." Ratso finally agrees. When Ratso hands over the drugs, Bunko arrests him on narcotics charges.

(A) Assume for this part only that at the time of the transaction Ratso had in fact never dealt in narcotics. Will Ratso have a valid entrapment defense under the majority approach to entrapment? _____

(B) For this part, assume that Ratso had, in the previous two years, been arrested twice on drug-selling charges, and convicted once. Will Ratso have a valid entrapment defense under the majority approach to entrapment? _____

34. Annie Oakley, age 17, repeatedly asks Jessie James, a rifle dealer, to sell her a firearm. She finally succeeds, by telling James (who has long been attracted to Annie) that she'll have sex with him if he makes the sale. It's not a crime in the jurisdiction for an adult to have sex with a 17-year-old minor. It is, however, a crime to sell a firearm to a person under 18. James has never sold a firearm to a minor before. As soon as the sale is complete, Annie (who is secretly motivated by a desire to get unregistered firearms off the streets) turns Jessie in to the police. Can Jessie defend on grounds of entrapment, according to the majority definition of entrapment? _____

CHAPTER 5

ATTEMPT

35. Boris Badanov wants to make a political statement by blowing up the United Nations Building. He does not particularly want to kill any people – he just wants to destroy the building. He sets a very powerful charge, one that if detonated will almost certainly cause the entire multi-story building to collapse. Just as he is about to press the detonator on a Friday afternoon at 3 p.m., he is arrested by the police, and the explosion does not occur. Obviously Boris can be convicted of attempted bombing; but may he be convicted of attempted *murder*? _____

36. Hatshepsut likes to drive fast. She gets behind the wheel one day and races through a school zone at 90 m.p.h., not caring about the possibility she may hit a child. She hits Tut King, who is crossing at a crosswalk, and serious injures him.

(A) Suppose Hatshepsut is brought up on attempted murder charges. Can she be convicted? _____

(B) Suppose instead that Hatshepsut is charged with attempted involuntary manslaughter. Can she be convicted? _____

37. Nero, who makes a habit of torching buildings belonging to his employers, gathers a bunch of rags, papers and other combustibles in the basement of a warehouse with the intention of returning later to ignite them. He also buys 2 gallons of lighter fluid, which he stores on site. The combustibles are discovered, and Nero is tracked down and arrested. Under the Model Penal Code, can Nero be convicted of attempted arson?

_____

38. In mid-October, Don Juan and Sancho Panza plan to burglarize Zorro's home (which they have never seen) sometime during the following week. Their plans are overheard by Zorro, who calls the police. The police arrest Don Juan and Sancho Panza on their way out of a costume shop where they have rented black masks, which they consider essential to a successful burglary. The two have not yet taken any other acts in furtherance of their burglary plan. Can Juan and Panza be convicted of attempted burglary? _____

39. Lucrezia Borgia slips a small amount of poison into her husband's morning coffee, intending to slowly poison him. Lucrezia knows her poisons, and knows it will take at least seven doses to kill him. After the first cup of coffee, hubby suspects something's wrong, and has the coffee analyzed in a lab. Lucrezia is immediately arrested and charged with attempted murder. Can she properly be convicted? _____

40. Mickey Spillane intends to kill Mike Hammer. He pulls out his gun (which he believes to be a .357 Magnum) and aims it at Hammer, saying, "Prepare to die." Unbeknownst to him, his gun has been switched with a toy, and a paper banner reading "bang" pops out when he pulls the trigger. Is Mickey guilty of attempted murder? _____

41. Irving Brilliant fancies himself as a legal scholar. While lacking formal training, he watches "People's Court" faithfully, and buys every alcoholic beverage endorsed by famous trial lawyers. Irving's back yard is a popular watering hole for crows. One day, Irv takes out his shotgun and shoots at one of the crows, even though he believes this violates the Migratory Birds Act of 1918. Unbeknownst to Irving, the Migratory Birds Act does not apply to crows, because they don't migrate in the way the act covers. Can Irving be convicted for attempted violation of the Migratory Birds Act? _____

42. Phil Goode is a small-time drug dealer. After his previous supplier is arrested, Phil changes to a new supplier, Yuwanna Bye. In their first transaction, Yuwanna sells Phil 10 packets that he says are cocaine. Phil goes out on the street, and begins "advertising" the bags as cocaine, and selling them. He sells one bag to Narco, who unbeknownst to Phil is an undercover narcotics officer. Narco immediately arrests Phil. Upon testing, the packet proves to contain only talcum powder, a substance that is not banned. Phil is charged with attempting to distribute cocaine, and evidence at his trial shows that Phil in fact believed that the substance was cocaine. May Phil properly be convicted? _____

CHAPTER 6

CONSPIRACY

43. Che, an internationally-famous left-wing guerilla from South America, migrates to the U.S. He decides to try to overthrow the government of Miami Beach, Florida. To that end, he approaches Sam Surplus, a dealer in excess Army supplies. He tells Sam, "I'll be planning a little insurrection over at City Hall sometime soon, and I'll need some supplies." Sam is himself a pretty right-wing kind of a guy, but he figures that Che's bucks are as green as anyone else's. Therefore, Sam sells Che, at his standard prices, some military uniforms, knapsacks, and surplus Uzis. (All items are ones that appropriately-licensed government-surplus dealers are legally permitted to sell in the ordinary course of business.) Che uses the supplies to outfit his army, and he successfully — though very temporarily — ousts the elected government of Miami Beach. A federal statute makes it a crime to overthrow a municipal government. Is Sam guilty of conspiracy to overthrow the government? _____

44. Sitting Bull wants to get revenge on Custer by burning down Custer's barn. Therefore, Sitting Bull tells Crazy Horse that the barn is on Bull's property, and asks Crazy Horse to help him raze it to "clear the land."

(A) For this part only, assume that Crazy Horse believes Bull's bull, and agrees to help Bull light a fire to burn down the property. Before they can light the fire, both are arrested and charged with conspiracy to commit arson. Assume that the crime of arson is defined as intentionally burning the property of another without the owner's consent. Is Crazy Horse guilty of conspiracy to commit arson? _____

(B) Assume the same facts, except this time, Sitting Bull tells Crazy Horse that he wants to use a particular substance, dextromethorpan, or DXM, as the igniter in the fire. As Crazy Horse knows, it is illegal to possess DXM without a license. Crazy Horse nonetheless agrees to purchase some DXM from a crooked dealer. After he buys the DXM, but before he can light the fire with Bull, they are both arrested and charged with conspiracy to commit arson (defined as in part (A)). Is Crazy Horse guilty of conspiracy to commit arson? _____

45. Penguin intends to rob the Gotham City Bank. He asks Joker to help him out. Joker agrees to go through with the plan — although secretly Joker intends to inform the police of Penguin's plan. No one else is involved in the planning. Shortly before the scheduled robbery, Joker informs the police of the plan, and Penguin (but not Joker) is charged with conspiracy to commit bank robbery. May Penguin properly be convicted, under the modern/ M.P.C. approach? _____

46. Boris Badenov, Snidely Whiplash, and Natasha Fatale conspire to kill Dudley Doright. They draw elaborate diagrams of the proposed murder, and plan the act to the last detail. To insure that all the parties remain silent, they execute a blood oath not to reveal their plans. In the end, their plans are never acted upon because Doright gets a job on a daytime soap opera and moves to another state. Are Boris, Snidely and Natasha guilty of conspiracy to commit murder …

(A) under the common-law approach? _____

(B) under the Model Penal Code? _____

47. The Flying Albatrosses are a team of six circus aerialists. Five of the members hate the sixth, Alva. The five therefore decide that one of them should loosen the fastener on Alva's trapeze so that it will break when Alva grabs it. Accordingly, Ariel Albatross, the most mechanically-minded of the five, is given this task, and loosens the fastener. No other member of the team takes any physical action to help the plan. When Alva does the routine, due to his recent weight loss the trapeze does not break, and the routine goes flawlessly. The police learn of the plot, and arrest the five immediately afterwards, before they can try again. Are the four members of the Albatrosses other than Ariel guilty of conspiracy to commit murder? (Assume this all takes place in a jurisdiction that requires an overt act in furtherance of the conspiracy.) _____

48. Tarzan is planning to rob the Jungle and Vine Bank, and make off with a load of bananas. Jane offers to act as a lookout and driver of the getaway car. Jane knows that Tarzan will be armed, and that he's determined not to get caught no matter what (because he's terrified of being returned to the jungle.) When they get to the bank, Jane waits outside with the motor running. Tarzan goes in and meets Sheena, who (unbeknownst to Jane) has previously agreed to help him out. During the robbery, a bank guard, trying to stop the robbery and arrest the suspects, tackles Tarzan. Sheena, who knows how Tarzan feels about getting caught, takes Tarzan's gun and shoots the guard to death, so they can all escape. Alas, all three are apprehended outside the bank. Is *Jane* guilty of murder in the guard's death?

_____

49. Blacque Jacques Shellacque, a criminal sort, makes $1 million in counterfeit money, and by pre-arrangement sells it all to Boodles at a steep discount. Boodles sells $50,000 of that money to Ken Gelt, who sells it all to Minnie Moolah. (Boodles sells the other $950,000 to a variety of buyers.) Minnie does not know anything about any of the activities further upstream; she only knows that Gelt is a source of counterfeit currency. Minnie passes her $50,000 off as real money to stores and banks. A statute makes it a Class A felony to distribute, or conspire to distribute, in excess of $100,000 in counterfeit currency. Distribution or conspiracy to distribute less than $100,000 is a Class B felony. What is the highest felony of which Minnie can be convicted? _____

50. Winken, Blinken and Nod agree to work together to kill the Calico Cat. A few days later, about a week before the killing is to take place, Winken gets cold feet — he quits the conspiracy, telling the others he wants nothing further to do with the plan and asking them to abandon it. Blinken and Nod carry out the murder of Calico Cat anyway. Is Winken guilty of:

(A) conspiracy to commit murder? _____

(B) murder? _____

51. Bob is married to Carol. Alice is married to Ted. Bob and Alice have been attracted to each other for several years, but have not done anything about it. Finally, one day, Bob telephones Alice and asks her to meet him at the Ames Acres Motel, where they will conduct an assignation. Alice agrees. Unbeknownst to them, Carol is listening on an extension. She arranges to have the police meet her at the Motel at the appointed time. The police arrest Bob and Alice in their room, while they are in a state of partial undress but have not yet committed adultery. In the state of which Ames is a part, adultery is a substantive crime. The prosecutor charges Bob and Alice with conspiracy to commit adultery.

(A) If you are defending Bob or Alice, (i) what defense should you assert? and (ii) will it be successful? _____

(B) Same basic fact pattern as Part (A). Now, however, assume that the way Bob and Alice come to be together in the motel room is that Bob's friend Peter says to both Bob and Alice, "You know, you'd make a great couple, you should really try to get something going together." In a jurisdiction which would recognize the defense you asserted in your answer to Part (A), may Peter, Bob and Alice all be charged with and convicted of conspiracy to commit adultery? _____

52. Abbot and Costello are charged with conspiracy to defraud retirees in a scheme to sell retirement homes in the Florida Everglades. Abbot is acquitted at trial, but Costello is found guilty.

(A) Assume for this part that Abbot and Costello are tried in a single, joint trial. On Costello's appeal on the grounds that the inconsistent verdicts should entitle him to acquittal, will the appellate court find for Costello? _____

(B) Assume for this part that Abbot and Costello are tried in separate trials. In Costello's appeal on the grounds of the inconsistent verdicts, will the appellate court find for Costello under: (i) the prevailing approach; and (ii) the Model Penal Code approach? _____

CHAPTER 7

ACCOMPLICE LIABILITY AND SOLICITATION

53. Dan Hicks sees that the famous outlaw, Ned Kelly, is about to enter the Provincial Bank. Since Ned is wearing a mask and carrying a gun, Dan deduces that Ned plans to rob the bank.

(A) For this part only, assume the following: Without saying anything to Ned, Dan stands watch outside the bank, ready to warn Ned if the police appear. As it turns out, Dan's help is not necessary, and Ned makes a clean getaway without ever realizing that Dan was standing watch. Ned is later apprehended on robbery charges. The police learn that Dan stood watch. May Dan be convicted of the substantive crime of bank robbery? _____

(B) For this part, assume the same facts, except for the following: As Ned was about to enter the bank, Dan called out, "I'll give you a heads-up if any cops come by." Ned said, "That'd be great," and went in to the bank to commit the robbery. As it turned out, however, Ned made a clean getaway without needing Dan's services. When Ned is later apprehended on robbery charges, will Dan be liable for bank robbery? _____

54. Czar Nicholas wins tickets to a "Tchaikovsky and the Destroyers" concert from a local radio station. Lenin and Trotsky want the tickets, and decide to steal them from Nicholas. Trotsky is not armed, and thinks that Lenin is unarmed. The two hide behind some bushes and jump Nicholas when he walks by. While Trotsky holds Nicholas down, Lenin, instead of grabbing the tickets, whips out his Swiss Army knife and slits Nicholas' throat. Lenin then runs off and leaves the tickets behind. Is Trotsky liable as an accomplice in Nicholas' death? _____

55. Captain Hook, a pharmacist, fills Peter Pan's prescription for fairy dust, a mild hallucinogen, knowing that Peter intends to sell the dust illegally to Wendy. Peter then sells the dust illegally to Wendy.

(A) Assume that Captain Hook charges Peter his regular price, and that all other terms and conditions of the sale are the same as Hook would impose if he did not know that any illegal use was planned. Is Hook an accomplice to Peter's illegal sale to Wendy? _____

(B) Now, assume that the facts are the same, except that Hood charges Peter three times the amount that he would ordinarily charge for filling such a prescription. He does so because he fears that he might be arrested in connection with Peter's plot if things go wrong, and it's simply not worth it to Hood to run that kind of risk for his ordinary prescription-filling rate. Is Hook an accomplice to Peter's illegal sale to Wendy? _____

56. Wellington gives Robespierre some dynamite and encourages him to blow up Josephine's house in order to kill her. Robespierre blows up the house. The explosion kills not only Josephine, but several passersby as well, including Napoleon Bonaparte. Clearly Wellington is an accessory to Josephine's killing. Is he also an accessory to *Bonaparte's* death?

_____

57. King Arthur is charged with murder in the first degree for killing Childric. Merlin is charged as an accomplice for supplying Arthur with the murder weapon, the singing sword, Excalibur, and for urging Arthur to use the sword on Childric.

(A) Assume that Arthur and Merlin are tried in the same trial. Arthur is acquitted by a jury, whose members conclude that the slaying was justified. May Merlin be convicted? _____

(B) Same facts as above, except that King Arthur is acquitted because he was entrapped into committing the crime. No government agents were involved in Merlin's part of the crime. Can Merlin be convicted as an accomplice under these facts? _____

58. A state statute makes it a crime to sell narcotics. Neither that statute, nor any other state statute, makes it a crime to buy narcotics. Sherlock Holmes asks Moriarty to sell him some cocaine. Moriarty does so, and is charged with selling narcotics. Holmes is charged as an accomplice to the sale. Can Holmes be convicted? _____

59. Juliet, age sixteen, seduces Romeo, age twenty-two. A statute makes it statutory rape for a person to have sex with another who is under the age of seventeen, if the defendant is more than four years older that the underage person. Romeo is charged with statutory rape under this statute. Juliet is charged as an accomplice. Can Juliet be convicted? _____

60. Butch and Sundance rob a bank. They tell Etta Place about the robbery. Etta does not report it to the police. Is Etta an accessory after the fact? _____

61. Dostoevsky and Raskolnikov have the same landlady, whom Dostoevsky hates. Dostoevsky urges Raskolnikov to murder the landlady by waiting until she is asleep, and then sticking her nose and mouth shut with Crazy Glue so that she'll suffocate. Raskolnikov thinks that Dostoevsky is a dangerous criminal who must be stopped before he causes someone's murder. Therefore, he says, "No way — you're nuts," and tells the police about Dostoevsky's request. The police arrest Dostoevsky, but need something to charge him with. Because Raskolnikov never even pretended to agree to do what Dostoevsky urged, the police can't charge Dostoevsky with conspiracy.

(A) What common-law crime offers the prosecution's best charge against Dostoevsky? _____

(B) Can the prosecution get a conviction on the offense you listed in part (A)? _____

CHAPTER 8

HOMICIDE, AND OTHER CRIMES
AGAINST THE PERSON

62. Kingsman, holding a lead pipe, walks up to Humpty Dumpty, who is sitting on top of a wall.

(A) Assume for this part only the following additional facts: Kingsman swings his pipe with relatively little force against the side of Humpty's head. His intent is to frighten Humpty into paying his back taxes to the King; Kingsman believes (reasonably) that the pipe will cause only a slight bruise and a little pain, but that it will signify that Kingsman is prepared to get as rough as he has to on later occasions to get Humpty to pay. What Kingsman doesn't realize is that Humpty has an eggshell skull. The tap fractures Humpty's skull, and Humpty dies as a result. Is Kingsman guilty of murdering

Humpty? _____

(B) Assume for this part only that the event happens as described in part (A) with the following differences: Kingsman intends to hit Humpty hard enough that Humpty's skull will be fractured, and he'll be in the hospital for at least a week. He does not intend to kill Humpty, because that would defeat the whole purpose (getting the taxes paid back). Kingsman in fact swings with a force, and in a location, that in most instances would indeed have fractured a person's (or egg's) skull without killing him. In this case, tragically, Humpty's eggshell skull causes the fracture to be so bad that Humpty dies of brain edema. Is Kingsman guilty of murdering Humpty? _____

63. Brutus stabs Julius Caesar, with intent to kill him, on March 15, 44 B.C. Caesar lingers until April 1, 43 B.C., when he dies as a result of Brutus' attack. Under the common law, is Brutus guilty of murder? _____

64. Two thrillseekers, Macbeth and Banquo, set out separately one evening to have a rowdy good time. Macbeth heads off for the countryside. He takes out his gun as he drives along, and fires it into an old abandoned hunting cabin for target practice. Unbeknownst to him, a tramp, Polonius, is sleeping inside; Macbeth's shot kills him. At the same time, Banquo drives through Dunsinane, a heavily-populated residential suburb. He fires his gun into the open window of a dark apartment. His shot kills a person sleeping inside the apartment. Neither Macbeth nor Banquo intended to kill anyone. Macbeth believed the cabin was unoccupied. Banquo believed that the room into which he fired was unoccupied, but believed that there were probably people present elsewhere in the building. Is either of them guilty of murder, and if so, on what theory? _____.

65. Señor Delgato agrees to help Speedy Gonzales rob the Limburger Cheese Factory one night. Delgato lends Speedy his gun, although he doesn't believe Speedy will have to use it; he doesn't want anyone killed just for a stinking piece of cheese. Delgato stands as lookout while Speedy breaks into the factory. Speedy is unexpectedly accosted by the night watchman, who tries to tackle him. To avoid capture, Speedy shoots at the watchman, intending to hit him in the leg to disable (but not kill or seriously wound) him. Unfortunately, Speedy's shot is slightly off, and the watchman bleeds to death from his wound. Is *Delgato* guilty of murder, and if so, on what theory? _____

66. Nero sets a fire to Sabina's house one night, believing (reasonably, based on the facts known to him) that Sabina and her family are away on vacation. In fact, Sabina and her family have returned a day early from vacation, and are asleep inside. The house is soon engulfed in flames. Firemen rush to the scene. One of them, Claudius, is killed while trying unsuccessfully to save Sabina. Another fireman, Maecenas, survives the fire, but is killed when a low-lying tree branch knocks him off the fire truck on the way back to the station. For whose death(s) will Nero be liable under the felony murder rule: Sabina's, Claudius', and/or Maecenas' ? _____

67. Water-Pistol Kelly is robbing the Smalltown Bank. While he is holding the bank manager at gunpoint in the vault, a customer, Kitty Litter, suffers a heart attack and dies in the lobby.

(A) For this part only, assume that at the time Kitty had her heart attack, no one in the lobby, including Kitty, knew that a robbery was underway. Is Kelly guilty of murdering

Kitty? _____

(B) For this part only, assume that just before Kitty had her heart attack, she heard from a teller that someone was holding the bank manager at gunpoint in the vault. Kitty had a nervous disposition, and was frightened (even though others in the lobby were not) that the stickup artist or his confederates might soon threaten her. Her heart attack was brought on by these fears. Is Kelly guilty of murdering Kitty? _____

68. Derevenko slashes Czarevich Alexis in the arm with a dagger, intending only to cut him. In fact, Alexis is a hemophiliac and, as a result of the cut, Alexis bleeds to death. In the jurisdiction, Derevenko's attack with a dagger would constitute aggravated battery, a felony. Is Derevenko guilty of felony murder? _____

69. Aunt Pittypat runs up to Rhett Butler and tells him, "Your wife Scarlett is having an affair with Ashley!" (Assume that a reasonable person in Brett's position would believe, as Rhett does, that Aunt Pittypat is referring to Ashley Wilkes.) In a blind rage, Rhett runs the few blocks over to Ashley Wilkes' house, where he finds Scarlett and Ashley sitting in the living room, sipping tea. Rhett shoots and kills Ashley. In fact, Scarlett has been having an affair with a different Ashley — Ashley Farkus, who lives on the other side of town. What is the most serious crime for which Rhett can be convicted? _____

70. James Bond's wife, Tracy, is gunned down by Fast Eddie Triggerhand as she sits in the front seat of her car next to James. James is heartbroken, but coolly takes her to the morgue. He spends the next few hours looking calmly for clues as to Triggerhand's whereabouts, tracking him down, and finally killing him with his trusty Walther PPK. What is the most serious crime for which James can be convicted? _____

71. Deerslay is an avid, and properly-licensed, deer hunter. During deer season one day, he decides to hunt in a region called Acadia, which was once completely uninhabited, but which (as Deerslay knows) is now immediately adjacent to a sizable development of homes. Deerslay is standing at a point he knows to be about 300 yards away from the closest houses, when he sees a moving flash of brown and white in the direction where the houses lie. He thinks this is a deer. He immediately points his rifle and shoots. Unbeknownst to Deerslay, the flash of brown is in fact Dierdre standing in her back yard at the edge of the woods, wearing a brown fox-fur coat trimmed in white mink. The shot strikes Dierdre in the chest, and she dies immediately.

(A) For this part, assume that Deerslay's actions (hunting so close to the houses, shooting in the direction of the houses, and not verifying that what he saw was a deer) constitute gross negligence, but that his actions do not manifest a depraved indifference to the value of human life. What is the most serious crime of which Deerslay is guilty? _____

(B) Same basic fact pattern as part (A). Now, however, assume that Deerslay is new to the region, and does not know that there are housing developments nearby, in the direction at which he is pointing his gun. Assume further, however, that an ordinarily careful person would have asked questions of hunters who lived in the area, and would probably have discovered that houses were nearby. May Deerslay on these facts be convicted of the same crime which you listed as your answer to the prior question? _____

72. Jerry insults Tom's mother. To retaliate, Tom punches Jerry in the nose. Tom intends only to injure Jerry slightly — the most he hopes or intends will happen is that Jerry's nose will get bloody. Unbeknownst to Tom, Jerry is a hemophiliac. Consequently, Jerry bleeds to death. What is the most serious crime of which Tom can be convicted, and on what theory, in a jurisdiction following the most common approach to relevant matters?

_____

73. Lady Godiva's horse is being re-shoed, so she is forced to drive into town in her car. She let her driver's license lapse several years ago. It is a misdemeanor in the jurisdiction to drive with a lapsed license. On the way into town, she hits a child who runs out into the street, chasing a ball. The child is killed, although Lady Godiva could not have been any more careful a driver. The jurisdiction follows the most common approach to issues of manslaughter. Can Lady Godiva properly be convicted of manslaughter?

_____

74. Mother Goose sends one of her children to Br'er Rabbit with a gift of a bottle marked "medicine." Rabbit drinks the contents, and becomes violently ill. The bottle actually contains a mild poison deliberately mislabeled by Mother. (Mother wanted to make Rabbit slightly sick.) What is the most serious crime that Mother is guilty of?

_____

75. Stolitz Naya is driving a streetcar. He is travelling far faster than his bosses have instructed him to travel, and is under the influence of narcotics. Also, he's not watching whether anyone's on the tracks. Anna Karenina, a pedestrian, is reading a magazine as she crosses the street at a crosswalk. Anna doesn't see the streetcar coming, and it hits her, seriously injuring her.

(A) Has Stolitz committed a criminal assault? _____

(B) Has Stolitz committed a criminal battery? _____

76. Ferdinand, who is very angry at his wife Isabella for funding an extravagant voyage by Columbus, threatens her by pointing a rifle at her and threatening to "blow her in half." Isabella believes that Ferdinand will probably, but not certainly, pull the trigger. Isabella does not know it but the rifle is not loaded. Ferdinand does nothing further. What is the most serious crime of which Ferdinand is guilty? _____

77. Don Juan wants to have sex with Camille. Camille refuses because they are not married.

(A) For this part only, assume that Don Juan gets a friend of his to pose as a minister and fake a wedding ceremony. Thinking she's now an "honest woman," Camille consents to sex with Don Juan. Is Don Juan guilty of rape? _____

(B) For this party only, assume instead that Camille refuses to have sex unless she is at least engaged. Don Juan promises to marry Camille next year, and she consents to have sex with him. In fact, he has no intention of marrying her – next year or ever. Is Don Juan guilty of rape under these facts? _____

78. Clark Kent meets Lois Lane at a singles bar. By the time they meet, it is obvious to Clark that Lois has had quite a few drinks and is seriously drunk. Clark does not buy Lois any additional drinks. Instead, he asks her if she wants to come to his apartment, and she nods, somewhat dreamily. When they get to his apartment, Clark undresses her and begins to make love to her. Lois giggles and makes slurred remarks, which Clark reasonably believes indicate that she is conscious and that she is not objecting. The next day, Lois, now sober, relives the whole episode, and makes a complaint to the prosecutor that she has been raped. Assume that Lois demonstrates to the satisfaction of the court that she would not have consented to sex had she not been drunk, and that Clark knew or should have known that the appearance of consent was due to Lois' drunkenness. May Clark properly be convicted of rape, in a jurisdiction following the Model Penal Code approach?

_____

CHAPTER 9

THEFT CRIMES

NOTE: For all questions in this chapter, assume unless otherwise noted that the common-law definitions of all theft crimes are in effect.

79. Bunter, the manservant of Lord Peter Wimsey, is given certain grooming aids — barber's tools and the like — belonging to Wimsey that Bunter is to use in performing the services of his job. After several years of faithful service, Bunter decides to leave Wimsey's employ and announces that he will be leaving on July 1, following the June 30 expiration of his correct contract. On July 1, having formed an attachment to the tools of his trade, Bunter decides to take the grooming aids with him when he leaves, which he does later that day. What theft crime, if any, is Bunter guilty of? _____

80. Racer X covets Speed Racer's car, the Mach V, which is unattended in Speed's driveway.

   (A) For this part only assume that, succumbing to impulse, Racer X hops in and rolls the car several feet out of the driveway, intending to keep the car until he can sell it. As he is about to start driving down the street, X's conscience overcomes him, and he returns the car to the driveway. Speed Racer, who witnesses the incident from his window, becomes furious, and decides to file a criminal complaint. Is Racer X guilty of common-law larceny? _____

   (B) For this part only, assume the following: Racer X never intends to keep the car or sell it. Instead, he intends just to take it for a little spin, to see how it accelerates. He hops in, drives around the block, and returns the car exactly where he found it. Is Racer X guilty of larceny? _____

81. Pandora leaves her magic box in the cloakroom of a restaurant. Hope leaves her magic box next to Pandora's. After having a few too many cocktails at dinner, Hope returns first and picks up Pandora's box by mistake, even though Pandora's box is somewhat bigger than hers, and a slightly different color. (Assume that Hope's mistake was honest but that a reasonably sober person wouldn't have made the error.) Hope takes Pandora's box home and never looks at it again. Is Hope guilty of larceny? _____

82. Genie loses her black wine bottle at the beach. She puts up signs all over the place offering a reward for its return. Anthony Nelson subsequently finds the bottle.

(A) Assume for this part only that: Anthony, believing the bottle he's found is the one he's seen signs about, picks up the bottle, intending to return it to Genie. However, it sits in his car for a while, and he subsequently decides to keep it. Is he guilty of larceny? _____

(B) Assume for this part only that: Genie never put up the signs, and there are no indications of ownership on the bottle. Nelson finds the bottle and intends to keep it. A couple of days later, during a return visit to the beach, he overhears Genie telling another beachcomber about her lost bottle. He says nothing, and gets in his car and drives home. Is Nelson guilty of larceny? _____

83. T. Pott, presidential advisor to President Warren Harding, has been given a government-owned shredder for his office use. He takes it home one night (to use it to shred cheese for pizza), and never brings it back. Three months later he's fired. What theft crime, if any, has Pott committed? _____

84. Wanda Oceanview is a real estate agent. Charles Foster Kane authorizes her to sell his home, Zanadoo, for $100,000. Wanda sells it for $102,000. She pockets the extra $2,000, honestly believing she's entitled to the extra money as a commission. In fact, however, as a matter of local law governing real estate brokers, Wanda is not entitled to any commission, because she doesn't have a written agreement providing for any commission. An ordinarily prudent real estate broker would know this. As soon as these facts of law are explained to Wanda by Kane's lawyer (two weeks after she deposits the money), Wanda reluctantly refunds the money. Is Wanda guilty of embezzlement? _____

85. Tokyo Rose is the manager of an army base PX during World War II. Silk stockings, which the PX sells for $5 a pair, are in short supply. Rose takes three pair of stockings from the PX, and sells them to civilians for $20 a pair. At the moment she takes the stockings, she intends to put the $5 per pair PX price back in the register as soon as she can sell the stockings and get the cash for them. The next morning, Rose does exactly that, so the PX ends up with the same $5 a pair as if they had been sold in the regular course of business. Is Rose guilty of embezzlement? _____

86. Guido tells Jules that he is going to dredge land from the continental shelf off Florida and build an off-shore casino. He asks Jules to invest, and, with visions of golden poker ships dancing in his head, Jules does so.

(A) For this part only, assume that Guido in fact has no intention of actually building the casino — he plans to invest Jules' funds at the racetrack instead. Under the majority view, is Guido guilty of false pretenses? _____

(B) Same facts as part (A), except that Guido says he's already received the necessary permits to build the casino. In fact, he has not, and has no intention of building the casino. Under the majority view, is he guilty of false pretenses? _____

87. Old Mother Hubbard applies for welfare benefits. Her caseworker asks her if she is receiving funds from any other source. Hubbard says no. Although she receives unemployment benefits, Hubbard believes the question referred to other earnings, not benefits. (Assume that Hubbard's belief about what the caseworker means is honest but unreasonable.) Based on her response to the question, Hubbard receives the welfare benefits. Is Hubbard guilty

of false pretenses? _____

88. Jessie James, a professional criminal, knows that J.P. Morgan, a rich banker, will be away from home for several days. Therefore, at 1:00 a.m. on a Tuesday, Jessie goes to J.P.'s house, jimmies a lock on J.P.'s rear door, and enters the house. At the time of his entry, Jessie's intent is to steal whatever cash and jewelry he can find. However, Jessie inadvertently sets off J.P.'s alarm. Jessie is arrested by police before he has a chance to place any of J.P.'s possessions into the sack that he has brought with him. What is the most serious common-law crime of which Jessie may be convicted? _____

89. Bonnie & Clyde, a crack theft team, decide to try to steal from the First National Bank. They break into the Bank at 10 PM one night, when they suspect no one is there. Their purpose is to steal as much gold bullion as they can from the vault (to which they have previously learned the combination by bribing a bank employee). They break in, and are in fact able to take $100,000 worth of bullion before an alarm rings and frightens them off. Have Bonnie & Clyde committed common-law burglary? _____

90. Prince Charming breaks into his friend Cinderella's home at midnight one evening, intending only to leave a note demonstrating to Cinderella how simple it would be to burglarize her home. While inside, he sees a valuable painting that he falls in love with and decides to make off with it. Is Prince Charming guilty of burglary? _____

ANSWERS TO SHORT-ANSWER QUESTIONS

1. **(A) No.** All crimes require an "*actus reus*" (an act). The act must be a voluntary one. Here, the actus reus requirement is not satisfied, because Seth's act was not voluntary; he was, in effect, Cain's weapon. Since there was no voluntary act on Seth's part, he cannot be criminally liable.

(B) Yes. Here, Seth's actual act was voluntary, even if he wouldn't have done it "but for" Cain's threat. (Note that Seth may be able to defend against criminal charges due to duress, discussed in Chap. 4 (II), although it's doubtful he'd win because duress is generally not available for homicide offenses.)

2. **No.** In order to be criminal, an act must be voluntary – that is, the act must have been committed under the actor's will and control. Where the act is the result of an epileptic seizure, it is not voluntary and thus no criminal liability will attach. (However, an epileptic might become criminally liable for *putting himself in a position* where his potential loss of muscle control is likely to cause serious damage, e.g., by driving a car. Here, the actus reus would be the reckless act of driving while knowingly subject to seizures.)

3. **(A) No.** Crimes that punish status (instead of acts or omissions) are considered unconstitutional, in violation of due process and the prohibition against cruel and unusual punishment under the Eighth Amendment. *Robinson v. Cal.* These include conditions like mental illness and addiction. Note, however, that a state can outlaw, say, public drunkenness – here, it's not one's status as an alcoholic that's being proscribed, but the act of being sloshed in public.

(B) Yes. Statutes outlawing possession of narcotics are valid, provided they require that the person charged knew that he possessed the substance in question. (Note that he does not have to know it is illegal to possess the substance; he just has to know that he has it.) The fact that the possession was the direct result of an addiction, and/or the fact that the possession was for the defendant's own use, makes no difference

4. **(A) No, because she was under no duty to act.** Normally speaking, in Anglo-American law a bystander will not be subjected to criminal liability merely for failing to assist another in distress, even though that assistance could have been given easily and without risk. Only where the bystander has some special *legal duty* to assist can there be liability for failure to assist. Here, nothing caused such a duty to come into existence. India's intense dislike for Ima is irrelevant, since bad thoughts alone are not punishable, and India's bad thoughts did not cause India to have a duty to assist.

(B) Yes. Although normally a bystander has no duty to render assistance, there are some special situations that *will* cause a duty to assist to come into existence. One of those situations is that the defendant *caused the dangerous situation to arise* (whether the defendant acted negligently, intentionally, or even completely innocently). Since India's statement caused the danger to exist — even though India may have behaved non-negligently in making the statement — India then had a duty to render reasonable assistance when Ima started to drown.

5.   No. Intent is a state of mind and, with nothing more, is not criminal. Here, Booth has not yet committed any kind of action designed to bring about the desired result, so his intent cannot by itself give rise to criminal liability. (However, once Booth's intent was combined with some action designed to bring about the desired results, it could become culpable, even though the final act — killing — hadn't yet occurred. As we'll see in later chapters, this is the basis for the crimes of attempt and conspiracy.)

6.   Yes. When courts hold that a crime requires merely "general intent," they usually mean that all that must be shown is that the defendant desired to commit the act which served as the actus reus. Here, the act that served as the actus reus was the placing of the screwdriver against George's throat. Once the prosecution shows that Kramer desired to unlawfully touch George's throat for the purpose of frightening him, the fact that Kramer did not intend to injure George will be viewed as irrelevant.

7.   (A) Yes. State legislatures have the power to enact criminal statutes that do not require a mens rea, particularly where the statutes regulate food, drugs and misbranded articles. Such statutes are known as "strict liability" statutes. The fact that the statute may be violated innocently does not make a conviction (or even a short jail sentence) a violation of the defendant's constitutional due process rights.

(B) No. In a series of cases, the Supreme Court has held set out rules of thumb for determining when a statute was intended as a strict-liability (or as it is sometimes called, "public welfare offense") statute. See, e.g., *Staples v. U.S.* One of these rules of thumb is that if the penalties for violation are relatively severe, it is unlikely that the statute was intended to impose strict-liability. Here, this factor cut strongly in favor of non-strict-liability, since a minimum sentence of 30 days in jail (with a maximum of 1 year) is relatively severe. Therefore, the judge should infer that the legislature intended that at least, the defendant must have behaved negligently in selling the mislabelled product. Consequently, the court should acquit Delilah.

8.   No. Some older cases contain broad statements to the effect that a mistake of fact cannot be a defense unless the mistake was "reasonable." But the Model Penal Code, and nearly all modern statutes, hold that if intent or knowledge is required as an element of a crime, then even an ***unreasonable mistake*** will block conviction if it negated such intent or knowledge. See M.P.C. §2.04(1)(a). Here, Costello's belief in the truth of Abbott's story prevented Costello from having the requisite intent to take another's property or the requisite knowledge that it belonged to another — the fact that Costello was unreasonably credulous is irrelevant. Of course, the more unreasonable Costello's belief in the truth of Abbott's story is, the less likely the judge or jury is to find that Costello *in fact believed* that story. But the facts here tell us that Costello actually believed the story, so this by itself is enough to negate purpose or knowledge.

9.   No, because there is no concurrence between Guy's mens rea and the result. In the case of a crime defined in terms of a bad result, the requirement of concurrence normally means that the mental state must relate to that harmful result, not to some other, quite different, harmful result associated with some other crime. So here, the mental state for public intoxication (intentionally appearing drunk in public) cannot be "transferred" to satisfy the mental-state requirement for some other crime (here, intent to burn). There are some exceptions to this requirement of concurrence (e.g., the felony-murder rule and the misdemeanor-manslaughter rule), but none of those exceptions applies on these facts.

10. **(A) No.** Although Dr. Evil had the mens rea for murder at one point, he did not have it at the time of the act that led to Austin Power's death. The requirement of *"temporal concurrence"* means that the mens rea and the actus reus must exist at the same time, and, indeed, that the mens rea must *"cause"* the actus reus. Here, by the time of the actus reus (the squeezing), the mental state (intent to shoot) was no longer present. Therefore, the requirement of temporal concurrence is not satisfied.

(B) Still no. Although Dr. Evil did intend (eventually) to kill Austin Powers under these facts, his act of shooting was not caused by his desire to kill. For the requirement of "temporal concurrence" to be satisfied, the mens rea must in some way "cause" the act in order. Since that was not the case here, Dr. Evil gets off. That's true despite the fact that Dr. Evil in a sense still possessed the desire to (eventually) kill at the time he squeezed the trigger. (Of course, Dr. Evil might have a hard time convincing the trier of fact that he didn't intend to shoot at the time of the shooting — but if he could do this, he's entitled to an acquittal on the murder charges.)

11. Both Holiday and Earp are causes in fact. Although something that is a "but for" cause will always be a cause-in-fact, the conversely is not true: something can be a cause-in-fact even though it was not a but-for cause. In particular, if two acts are each a *"substantial factor"* in bringing about a result, then each is a cause-in-fact even though the other act would have sufficed. That's what happened here: neither shot was a but-for cause of the death (since the death would have happened anyway without that shot), but each was undeniably a "substantial factor" in bringing about the death. (Each shot contributed significantly to the result — James' death — so that's enough to make it a "substantial factor".)

12. (A) Yes. Under the doctrine of *"transferred intent,"* if a defendant intends to bring about a certain sort of harm and then does bring about that general type of harm, the fact that the victim is different than the intended one will not make a difference. The doctrine applies here: since Yosemite Sam intended to kill someone, the fact that the one who ended up dead was Daffy instead of Bugs won't prevent Sam from meeting the requirements for murder.

(B) Battery against Daffy, and attempted murder of Bugs. First, Yosemite Sam will be guilty of battery against Daffy Duck — Sam's intent to kill Bugs will be transferred to his act of battery against Daffy, even though the crimes are not the same. (Note that this works because battery is sort of a lesser version of murder. If the two crimes were totally unrelated, such as murder and arson, the intent could not be transferred.) Second, Yosemite Sam will also be guilty of attempted murder of Bugs, since he had the intent to kill him (the mens rea) and took an act in furtherance of that goal (shooting towards him). However, Yosemite Sam will *not* be guilty of the attempted murder of Daffy Duck — the doctrine of "transferred intent" does not apply to crimes of attempt.

13. Yes. A case of mistaken identity does not save the defendant. As long as Cheshire Cat had the intention to kill someone, and engaged in an act designed to carry that intention out, the fact that he was mistaken regarding the identity of his victim is irrelevant. A "mistake of fact" will generally only be a defense if it negates the particular mental state required for the crime. That is not the case here, because a correct belief about the victim's identity is not part of the mental state required for murder (or practically any other crime, for that matter.

14. (A) No. When the defendant causes injury or illness, resulting medical treatment will be viewed as a "dependent" intervening cause. A dependent intervening cause will be viewed as *"superseding"* (i.e., as preventing the defendant's action from being a proximate cause) only if that dependent cause was *"abnormal."* Where medical treatment is performed in a grossly-negligent way, that will usually meet the hard-to-satisfy "abnormal" standard. The treatment here was certainly gross negligence — hospitals may commit garden-variety negligence with some frequency (and that ordinary negligence won't be superseding), but giving a patient rat poison because of a labelling error goes way beyond ordinary negligence. Therefore, the rat poison will be treated as a superseding cause. (But if the hospital had acted just a bit negligently, say by not having the most-effective antidote available, or by delaying treatment for 10 minutes because of emergency-room congestion, this would not have been enough to break the chain of causation if Cleo had died, and here Antony's act *would* have the proximate cause of her death.)

(B) No. Where a crime victim refuses to avail herself of medical assistance, most courts hold that the refusal is not a superseding cause. That's true even if the victim's conduct is irrational.

15. No. Ford's conduct is certainly a cause-in-fact of the death. (The death wouldn't have occurred "but for" Ford's conduct, since James wouldn't have been at the spot where the boulder occurred.) But the shooting is not a *proximate* cause. The falling of the boulder was an "independent" intervening event. (That is, the boulder didn't fall because of the shooting.) An independent intervening event will be superseding if it was *"unforeseeable"* (even if it wasn't "abnormal," in the sense of deeply unusual or bizarre). There's no particular reason for anyone to have foreseen a rockfall at the time James passed by (and the facts say that the rockfall was "unexpected"), so the unforeseeable rockfall will be a superseding event.

16. (A) Probably not. Under the *M'Naghten* test, a defendant must show that on account of his mental disease, either: (1) he did not understand the "nature and quality" of his act; or (2) he did not know that his act was wrong. Ripper clearly does not qualify under (1), since he knows that he's killing humans when he slashes throats. The interesting question is whether Ripper qualifies under (2). A court might hold that even though Ripper knew that what he did was legally wrong, his belief that God was commanding him to do the act prevented him from "knowing" that the act was "wrong" in the moral sense. However, it's more likely — in view of the strongly law-and-order approach to insanity followed by most *M'Naghten* jurisdictions today — that a court would say that Ripper's knowledge that the act was legally forbidden prevents him from qualifying under (2).

(B) Probably not. The federal insanity statute essentially follows the *M'Naghten* standard: D prevails only if he shows that "as a result of a several mental disease or defect, [he] was unable to appreciate the nature and quality or the wrongfulness of his acts." Since D would probably lose under M'Naghten, he'd probably lose under the federal rule.

(C) Yes. M.P.C. § 4.01(1) provides that "a person is not responsible for criminal conduct if at the time of such conduct as a result of mental disease or defect he lacks substantial capacity either to appreciate the criminality [wrongfulness] of his conduct or to **conform his conduct to the requirements of the law**." Thus the M.P.C. incorporates both the *M'Naghten* test and a variant of the "irresistible impulse" test — D wins if he satisfies *either* test. Here, the facts make it clear that Ripper is powerless to avoid killing, and that he therefore "lacks substantial capacity … to conform his conduct to the requirements of the law."

(D) Jack as to both. That is, Jack must first come forward with some evidence of his insanity even to make sanity part of the case. (This is true in nearly all states courts as well, by the way.) Then, Jack must prove, by *"clear and convincing evidence,"* that he is insane. (This is one of the ways in which the federal statute makes it much tougher for defendants to win on insanity than in state courts — nearly all states either put the burden of persuasion on the prosecution, or make the defendant prove insanity but only by a "preponderance of the evidence.")

17. It will be a defense to burglary but not to battery. First, let's consider burglary. Voluntary intoxication can be a defense to crimes requiring intent or knowledge (beyond the intent to do the actus reus itself), if the intoxication prevented defendant from forming the mental state necessary. Burglary requires an intent to enter another's dwelling plus an intent to "commit a felony therein." Hansel did not have the intent to enter another's dwelling, and he certainly didn't have any intent (at the time of entry) to commit a felony inside the dwelling. So his intoxication, although voluntary, prevented him from having the mental state needed for burglary.

Battery, on the other hand, is defined quite differently with respect to the required mental state. As the question stipulates (and in this, the stipulation matches the law of most states), battery can be committed either by intending to commit a harmful/offensive contact, or by recklessly committing such a contact. Virtually all states (and the M.P.C.) agree that voluntary intoxication will never negate the existence of recklessness. In a sense, Hansel's recklessness in getting drunk will "carry over" and be deemed recklessness existing at the time of the attack on Witch. Therefore, Hansel meets the mental-state requirement for battery (reckless infliction of a harmful or offensive contact) even though his mistake about whether Witch was a burglar was caused by his intoxication.

18. No. The test for self-defense is an objective one: whether a reasonable, *sober* person would have believed that self-defense was necessary. It is irrelevant that Popeye's intoxication made him believe self-defense was necessary.

19. No. The lesser crime of manslaughter is defined so as to include an *objective* component: the provocation must have been such as would cause an ordinary "reasonable" person in the defendant's position to lose control. The ordinary reasonable person is presumed to be a *sober* one. Therefore, the fact that Othello's intoxication made him unable to rationally process the information won't help him.

20. (A) Duress. The defense of duress is available where D commits a crime on account of a threat by a third person, which threat produces a reasonable fear in the defendant that he will suffer imminent death or serious bodily harm if he does not comply with the third person's demands.

(B) No, because the harm wasn't imminent. Traditionally, courts have required that the harm with which the defendant is threatened must be immediate or at least imminent. Here, the threat is that Clark will be killed if he doesn't take an action during the course of the next week. Although the requirement of imminence is not as iron-clad as it once was, it's still followed by most courts.

(C) Yes. M.P.C. § 2.09 does not impose any requirement that the threatened harm be imminent. All that is required is that the threat be such that a person of "reasonable firmness" would be "unable to resist" it. It seems likely that a person of reasonable firmness would choose to steal rather than die (and would believe Lewis' threat, given his past conduct), so Clark should be entitled to the defense under the M.P.C.

21. **(A) No.** In the vast majority of states today, the defense of duress is available whether the harm threatened is to the defendant himself, or to another. Since Ralph reasonably believed that the threat to Alice was real and immediate (and since the social harm from robbery is less than from murder), his crime will be excused under the doctrine of duress.

(B) Yes, probably. In most states duress cannot be an excuse to commit homicide, even where the defendant reasonably believes that he or his close relative will be killed if he doesn't carry out the homicide. (However, most courts *do* allow duress to be a mitigating factor that reduces a murder charge to manslaughter.)

22. **Not guilty.** Although duress is normally not allowed as a defense to homicide charges (see part (B) to previous question), this is not true where the homicide is felony-murder. In other words, if duress would otherwise be usable as a defense to the underlying felony, duress may be used to prevent the felony from giving rise to felony-murder. Here, if no killing had occurred, Etta would have been entitled to use duress as a defense to her participation in the bank robbery, since the threat that she'd be shot would have been enough to induce a reason-able person in her position to participate in such a robbery. The duress defense thus means that Etta is not guilty of robbery. Therefore, there is no underlying felony on which the felony-mur-der doctrine can operate.

23. **(A) He should assert the defense of "necessity," which will be successful.** Where a person is forced to choose between a violation of law or a greater (and imminent) harm, and he chooses to violate the law in order to avoid the greater harm, he is free of criminal responsibil-ity under the doctrine of necessity. The destruction-of-property situation is, in fact, the classic kind of situation in which the defense is often successful.

(B) Unclear. Courts have generally been extremely reluctant — and in most cases unwilling — to allow the necessity defense when the crime involved is an intentional killing. However, the Model Penal Code allows the defense even in homicide cases, if the killing is necessary to save two or more other lives. Here, since sacrifice of one life was apparently the only way to avoid the likely loss of five other lives, the M.P.C. (and perhaps some courts) would allow the defense.

24. **No.** Dorothy can defend against the charge of trespass by asserting the defense of "neces-sity." The situation here meets all the requirements for the defense: (1) the harm of possibly being killed by the tornado was *greater* than the harm of breaking a window and trespassing; (2) there seems to have been *no lawful alternative method* of avoiding the harm; (3) the harm was *imminent*; and (4) Dorothy didn't *cause the danger* by recklessly or negligently putting herself in a position where the emergency was likely to arise.

25. **(A) No.** To begin with, the facts meet the basic requirements for self-defense: (1) Rambo was resisting the present or imminent use of unlawful force (since the act was completely unprovoked); (2) the degree of force was not more than was reasonably necessary to defend against threatened harm (since the facts say that Rambo realized he probably couldn't repel the act using non-deadly means); (3) deadly force was justified since the threat itself consisted of deadly force (i.e., force that in these circumstances — given Rocky's skills — was likely to kill or seriously injure Rambo); and (4) Rambo was not the aggressor. The question, of course, is whether Rocky was required to *retreat*.

The majority answer to this question is no — perhaps surprisingly, most courts continue to hold that there is no duty to retreat before using deadly force, even where retreat can be accomplished with complete safety. Note, however, that a growing *minority* of courts has held that there *is* a duty to retreat before using deadly force, but even those courts hold there is no duty to retreat where, among other factors: (1) The victim cannot retreat in complete safety, or (2) the attack occurs in the victim's home or place of business, or (3) the attack occurs where the victim is making a lawful arrest. (None of these factors applies here, so in the minority of states sometimes requiring retreat, Rambo is guilty of homicide.)

(B) No. Once the danger of the attack is over, the defense of self-defense is no longer available to the defendant. As soon as Rocky turned and began to leave the scene, Rambo lost his ability to use any sort of force against him. (It would have been different if, say, Rambo reasonably believed that Rocky was leaving just in order to recruit his friends to come back and group-attack Rambo — then, Rocky's leaving wouldn't have been a true withdrawal, and Rocky would have been justified in shooting if there was no other apparent way to prevent a life-threatening group attack.)

26. (A) Yes. In general, the "aggressor" — the one who first committed a battery or other legal infraction against the other party — thereby loses the right to use force in his own defense. Since Butch began the encounter by committing a battery, he thereby lost the right to defend himself, even by the use of what would otherwise have been an appropriate level of force. (The fact that Alfalfa began the hostilities by insulting Butch's mother is irrelevant — insults not accompanied by force or threat of force aren't unlawful, and may not be responded to by force.)

(B) No. These facts illustrate an important exception to the general rule that the aggressor has no right to use force in his own defense: when the victim *escalates* the fight, the aggressor may respond with a level of force appropriate to the escalation. Here, Butch was the aggressor but he started only a minor altercation. Alfalfa, the "victim," is the one who escalated the fight into one involving deadly force. Once that happened, Butch lost his status as aggressor, and was entitled to use self-defense as if he had never been an aggressor. Since a blow to Alfalfa's head was the only way he could reasonably defeat the potentially-deadly chokehold, he was entitled to use that level of force. (Indeed, he would have even been entitled to use deadly force, such as a gun or knife, if non-deadly force would not have sufficed.)

27. No. The defense of self-defense is available only where the threatened force is ***imminent***. Where the threat refers to the future (i.e., a time beyond the "present occasion," in the words of the M.P.C.), physical violence is not necessary, because other means, such as police help, are presumably available. Here, Romeo's words revealed that Juliet was not under an immediate threat of physical violence, so she was not entitled to use physical force, let alone deadly force.

28. Yes, if Fletcher's mistake was reasonable. Even though the defendant is mistaken about the actual need for self-defense, his use of the defense is not nullified so long as his mistake was a reasonable one. Here, the facts strongly suggest that Fletcher's belief was a reasonable, though tragically mistaken, one. If so, Fletcher will prevail with the defense.

29. (A) Yes. A person has the right to defend his property. However, under the M.P.C. (and in many states today), a homeowner may not use deadly force to defend his home or other property from an intruder, unless either: (1) the intruder has used or threatened the use of deadly force; or (2) the owner or his family are exposed to a substantial danger of serious bodily harm. Here, Goldilocks was unarmed and not posing any apparent physical threat to Papa or any of the other Bears. Therefore, Papa was entitled to use only non-deadly force. The baseball bat — especially given Papa's strength — was likely to produce serious bodily harm if swung at Goldilocks' head, so its use constituted deadly force. Consequently, Papa exceeded the bounds of permissible force in defense of his property, and he will have no defense. (He would probably be able to defeat a *murder* charge, because his "imperfect self defense" would entitle him to have the charge reduced to voluntary manslaughter.)

(B) No. As noted in part (A), there is no privilege under the M.P.C. to use force likely to cause death or serious bodily injury if property alone is threatened. But where the threat to property is coupled with a serious bodily threat to the defender, then deadly force can be used in defense, even under the M.P.C. That's what happened here. (The fact that Papa was wrong about what Goldilocks intended is irrelevant — he reasonably believed that she was about to attack him with a knife, and that was enough.)

30.   No. Although a property owner is sometimes privileged to protect his property against intruders by the use of mechanical devices, he may use only non-deadly ones. Under the modern view and the M.P.C., the use of a deadly mechanical device is *never* privileged – even if the homeowner would have been able to use deadly force himself had he been there at the time of the break-in. But even in a jurisdiction following the traditional view on mechanical devices, the device here would not have been privileged: under that view, the mechanical device may only be used under circumstances that would have entitled the homeowner to use deadly force in person. Here, where Goon did not pose a threat of serious bodily harm to anyone, Bunyon would not have been privileged to use deadly force in person, and was therefore not privileged to do so by proxy.

31.   No. Although the common-law view was that an officer could use deadly force to prevent a person escaping the arrest of any felony, the Supreme Court, in *Tennessee v. Garner*, restricted that right. According to *Garner*, use of deadly force to stop a suspect fleeing from a non-dangerous felony is only constitutionally permissible if the suspect poses an immediate threat of serious physical harm, either to the officer or others. Here, Dudley would be violating the Fourth Amendment's ban on unreasonable seizures if he were to shoot Snively, since embezzlement is not a dangerous felony and there's no reason to believe that Snively poses a physical threat to anyone. Given that the shooting would be unreasonable, Dudley would lose his common-law privilege to use force in making an arrest, since that privilege is limited to the *reasonable* use of force. (But Dudley could have used *non*-deadly force, such as parking his car in the middle of the road to block Snively's escape.)

32.   No. A *police officer* gets a privilege to use force (at least non-deadly force) to make an arrest for any felony, and he does not waive this privilege by making a reasonable mistake. But when a **private citizen** uses force (even non-deadly force) to make an arrest, he does not get the benefit of a reasonable mistake, and acts **at his own peril**. Since here, no felony was in fact committed, John cannot escape liability based on his reasonable error. Nor does John get any protection from the fact that he used non-deadly force — a private citizen may not use even non-deadly force based on a reasonable mistake (though John would be protected if the teenager had in fact committed a felony for which John was trying to arrest him).

33.   (A) Yes. Under the majority approach to entrapment, entrapment exists where: (1) the government originates the crime and induces its commission; and (2) the defendant is one who was not predisposed to committing this sort of crime. Here, both elements are satisfied: (1) Bunko came up with the idea of a drug transaction, and by pleading induced Ratso to go along; and (2) Ratso's lack of any prior involvement in narcotics sales indicates that he was not predisposed to commit this sort of crime.

(B) No. Here, Ratso does not satisfy element (2) of the majority rule: his record indicates that he was in fact predisposed to sell narcotics. (But note that under the minority "police conduct" rule for determining entrapment, Ratso might win — under that test, if the government originates the crime and the behavior of the government agents is such that a non-predisposed person would be likely to be induced, the fact that the particular defendant himself may have been predisposed is viewed as irrelevant.)

34. No, because Annie is not a government agent, nor is she working with the police. Entrapment arises as a defense where government agents (or those working under their direction) instigate private persons to commit a crime that they were not "predisposed" to commit. The fact that Annie turned Jessie over to the police immediately after the crime (or even the fact that she always planned to do so) is irrelevant — a private citizen will be deemed to be working with the police, and thus a potential agent for entrapment, only if the police are directing or encouraging the operation while it progresses. (If the police had put a wire on Annie before the sale, that probably *would* be enough to make Annie a government agent for entrapment purposes, in which case Jessie might win.)

35. Yes, probably. In general, crimes of attempt require that the defendant have the specific intention of bringing about the criminal result required for the underlying crime he is charged with attempting. Thus normally, one could not be convicted of attempted murder by recklessly bringing about a near-killing, since the result embodied in the definition of murder is a killing, and for attempted murder one must therefore intend (not merely recklessly disregard the possibility of) a killing. But where the defendant *knows with substantial certainty* that a particular result will follow from his contemplated action, most courts (and the M.P.C.) take the position that this is tantamount to an intent to bring about that result. So here, since Boris knows with substantial certainty that if he carries out his plan people will die (after all, the building is full on a Friday afternoon and Boris knows the building will collapse if there's an explosion), Boris will be deemed to have intended to bring about killings. Consequently, he may be convicted of attempted murder.

36. (A) No. Where a crime is defined in terms of bringing about a certain result, the mental state required for an attempt to commit that crime is normally an *intent* to bring about that result. The mere fact that the defendant had a mental state that would have sufficed for the underlying crime does not suffice. Murder is defined to require, inter alia, a killing of another. Therefore, a person can be convicted of attempted murder only if she intends to kill another. The fact that Hatshepsut may have behaved with a mental state adequate for reckless-indifference murder (a wanton indifference to the value of human life) will not suffice for the crime of attempted murder.

(B) No, for the same reason as in (A). That is, where a crime is defined as recklessly bringing about a certain result (here, a death), there can be no attempt to commit that crime. So the fact that Hatshepsut had the mental state that would suffice for involuntary manslaughter (recklessly causing the death of another) is irrelevant on the attempted manslaughter charge.

37. Yes, because he took a "substantial step" towards committing the crime. As in all jurisdictions, under the M.P.C. a defendant cannot be convicted of an attempt unless he takes some sort of act in furtherance of his criminal plan. Under the M.P.C., that act (or multiple acts) must satisfy two requirements: (1) it constitutes a "substantial step" in a course of conduct planned to culminate in the commission of a crime; and (2) it is "strongly corroborative" of the defendant's criminal purpose. Here, Nero's conduct satisfies both requirements: (1) gathering all the materials needed for a crime will generally constitute a "substantial step" towards commission of that crime, and certainly does so here; and (2) there is no innocent explanation for Nero's gathering activities, so they're "strongly corroborative" of the proposition that he planned to burn down the building. Indeed, M.P.C. § 5.01(2)(f) contains a special provision covering these facts quite precisely: activities shall be considered sufficiently corroborative if they consist of "possession [or] collection … of materials to be employed in the commission of the crime, at or near the place contemplated for its commission, where such possession [or] collection … serves no lawful purpose of the actor under the circumstances."

38. Probably not, because their preparations have not come close enough to success. Courts vary as to how far along the defendants' preparations must have advanced before they give rise to attempt liability. But under virtually any test, it's unlikely that the Ds here advanced sufficiently. Under the popular "dangerous proximity to success" test, for instance, the purchase of the masks did not make the Ds dangerously close to success — there's no evidence that they picked a particular time for the burglary, for instance, and they haven't reconnoitered the scene to determine a point of entry. Even under the relatively easy-to-satisfy 2-part M.P.C. test (summarized in the answer to the previous question), the preparations here probably would not succeed: the purchase of the masks might be a "substantial step" towards commission of the crime (though this is debatable), but it's unlikely that a court would find that the rental of the masks "strongly corroborated" the burglary — the masks might have been rented just for upcoming Halloween, for instance.

39. Yes, probably. The precise analysis will depend on exactly what test is used by the court. Under the "dangerous proximity to success" test, the prosecution's case is probably the weakest, but even here, a court would probably conclude that if hubby had drunk the first cup without complaint, it wouldn't have taken too long for him to consume another six cups on, say, six consecutive mornings. The "probable desistance" approach is almost certain to lead to a conviction, since one who administers one dose of a poison is unlikely to voluntarily abandon the plan. The "equivocality" test is also easily satisfied, since Lucrezia's actions are not the slightest bit equivocal — it's perfectly obvious that one who puts poison in a person's cup wants to kill or at least seriously injure the drinker. Finally, the M.P.C.'s "substantial step" approach is clearly satisfied: administering the first dose of fatal poison is obviously a substantial step towards carrying out the completed poisoning, and it's certainly a step that's "strongly corroborative" of the defendant's ultimate criminal plan (there's no alternative explanation for the poison).

40. Yes, because "factual impossibility" is not a defense. Mickey certainly satisfies the mental state for attempted murder (intent to commit a killing), and has done everything reasonably in his power to bring that result about. The question, of course, is whether Mickey can use the defense of impossibility. Here, the defense would have to be "factual impossibility" — that is, Mickey is claiming that he made a mistake on an issue of fact, such that had he not made the mistake, he would have known that his plan had no possibility of success. The defense of factual impossibility is not accepted by any court. Indeed, the present setting — defendant uses a weapon that malfunctions — is almost the archetypal illustration of the universally-rejected factual-impossibility defense.

41. No. This is a case of *"true legal impossibility."* That is, the mistake is a pure mistake of law — Irving's only mistake is about *how a particular offense is defined.* Even if all the surrounding facts (except for legal definitions) had been as Irving believed them to be, his actions would still not have been a crime, because it is simply not a crime to shoot crows. Therefore, the defense of true legal impossibility — which is accepted in all courts — protects Irving from attempt liability.

42. Yes. Phil could assert a variant of the impossibility defense, namely, what might be called *"factual impossibility related to legal relationships."* But in general, courts reject this defense almost universally now, just as they reject garden-variety claims of factual impossibility. The issue for most courts is whether, had the facts been as the defendant supposed, the defendant would have committed a crime. Here, had the packet really contained cocaine rather than talcum powder, Phil would have committed the crime of drug sale; therefore, he can be convicted of attempting to commit that crime. (In an analogous situation, defendants are convicted every day of "attempted purchase" of drugs, where they buy from an undercover officer what they think is an illegal drug but what is in fact a harmless substance such as sugar.)

Be sure to distinguish the unsuccessful defense of "factual impossibility related to legal relationships," which is what's at issue here, from the successful defense of "true legal impossibility," as in the previous question. Where the defendant's mistake consists of a mistake about how an offense is defined, that's true legal impossibility, and is successful. (For instance, had Phil mistakenly believed that it was a crime to sell talcum powder without a license and then sold what he knew was talcum powder without a license, he'd have a valid defense to, say, a charge of attempted illegal sales of merchandise.) But where the defendant's mistake consists of a mistaken belief about the nature of a particular object, the fact that the mistake relates to the object's legal status doesn't help the defendant. So here, Phil's mistake was a factual mistake about the nature of the bags he was selling (not a "purely legal" mistake about how a particular crime is defined), so he's no different than a person who makes a mistake of fact about some non-legal subject, like whether a gun is loaded — his essentially factual mistake doesn't lead to a valid defense.

43. Probably not. To be guilty of conspiracy, the defendant must be shown to have *intended* to further a criminal objective — it's generally not enough that the defendant merely *knew* that his acts would or might enable others to pursue criminal ends. This rule applies to suppliers: the fact that the supplier knows or strongly suspects that the merchandise may be used for particular illegal purposes is generally not sufficient to make the supplier guilty of conspiracy. There are certain other factors that might change this result as to a particular supplier (e.g., that the supplier has agreed to be paid out of proceeds of the upcoming crime, or is charging much higher prices than are commonly charged in the absence of a criminal purpose, or is selling contraband), but none of these special factors applies here. Therefore, especially when one considers that Sam doesn't support left-wing politics, it's unlikely that a court would find Sam to have had the requisite intent to help commit the overthrow.

44. **(A) No.** A party cannot be guilty of conspiracy to commit crime X unless he has the mental state required for crime X. Conspiracy to commit arson therefore requires the defendant to have the intent to burn the property of another without the other's consent. Here, Crazy Horse believed that the property belonged to Bull and was being burned with Bull's consent. Therefore, Crazy did not have an intent to burn the property without the owner's consent. (Note, by the way, that it wouldn't even matter if Crazy's belief about who owned the property was unreasonable — as long as the trier of fact believed that Crazy honestly, though stupidly, thought the property belonged to Bull, Crazy didn't have the requisite mental state for the completed crime and therefore can't be guilty of conspiracy.)

(B) No. The analysis is the same as for part (A): since Crazy's belief that Bull owns the farm prevents Crazy from having the mental state required for arson, he can't be guilty of conspiracy to commit arson. The fact that Crazy has agreed to commit some other crime (illegal possession of DXM) in preparation for their joint effort is irrelevant — Crazy may be convicted of illegal DXM possession, and even conspiracy to illegally possess DXM, but he can't be convicted of conspiracy to commit arson.

45. **Yes.** Under the traditional view, the definition of conspiracy required that there actually be an agreement between two or more people; under that approach, Penguin couldn't be convicted, because there was no one else who was in actual agreement with Penguin. But the modern and M.P.C. approach applies a *"unilateral"* standard: an individual is guilty of conspiracy if he makes an agreement with another person, even if the other person is merely feigning agreement. So under the modern/M.P.C. approach, it's enough that Penguin thought he had (and attempted to have) an agreement with someone else, and the fact that the someone else was secretly not agreeing at all doesn't make any difference.

46. **(A) Yes.** At common law, a conspiracy is complete once the agreement is made — no further act is required. (It's true that about half the states have *statutes* requiring, in some instances, that some overt act in furtherance of the conspiracy must occur. But the question asks you about the common-law approach.)

(B) Yes. The M.P.C. does contain an overt-act requirement, but it applies only where the object crime is a relatively unserious one. If the object crime is a first- or second-degree felony (and murder certainly falls within that group), no overt act is required under the M.P.C. See Comment 5 to M.P.C. § 5.03(5).

47. **Yes.** In those states that require an overt act, an overt act committed by one member, in furtherance of the conspiracy that all have joined, will be attributable to all. So Ariel's act of loosening the trapeze (which is obviously an act in furtherance of the conspiracy) serves as the overt act for all, not just for Ariel.

48. **Yes.** Virtually all courts would agree with this result, but they might differ in how to get there. Some courts follow the approach of the Supreme Court in the *Pinkerton* case: under that approach, a member of a conspiracy is liable for *any substantive crimes* committed by his colleagues, as long as those crimes are committed in furtherance of the conspiracy's aims. Since Sheena was attempting to further one of the conspiracy's goals (escaping from the bank after the robbery) when she fired the fatal shot, under *Pinkerton* Jane as a co-conspirator will be guilty of the substantive crime of murder, even though she didn't have any interaction with

Sheena or even know of her existence. (As long as all acts are properly viewed as being part of a single conspiracy, as they clearly would be here, the fact that one particular conspirator didn't know of or interact with another particular one won't make any difference.)

Many other courts (and the Model Penal Code) reject the *Pinkerton* view that mere membership in a conspiracy, without more, makes each conspirator automatically liable for any substantive crime committed by any member in furtherance of the conspiracy's objectives. Instead, these courts say that liability for the substantive crimes must depend on the law of *accomplice liability* (aiding and abetting): if, and only if, a particular conspirator can be said to have aided and abetted — i.e., encouraged or facilitated — the substantive crime carried out by another can the former be convicted of that substantive crime. However, even under that rule Jane would almost certainly be on the hook. She has helped bring about the entire conspiracy (it probably wouldn't have happened without a lookout/getaway-driver) and she has at least tacitly encouraged Tarzan's carrying of a gun to the scene and his willingness to use it. A court would therefore almost certainly say that Jane "aided and abetted" Sheena's act, even though she didn't know Sheena and had no direct interaction with her. Once the court decided that Jane aided and abetted the shooting, then ordinary principles of accomplice liability (discussed in the next chapter) make her liable for the substantive crimes carried out by her principal(s) in furtherance of the aided crime.

49. Class B, probably. The question is really whether Minnie will be deemed to have participated in the original $1 million conspiracy between Shellacque and Boodles. Here, this is an unlikely outcome: since Minnie never knew any of the details of the upstream transactions (indeed, never even knew that any upstream transactions occurred), she's unlikely to be found to be part of the overall conspiracy in which Shellacque and Gelt participated. Therefore, although Shellacque and Gelt might be found to have conspired with Minnie (since she furthered their plan of disseminating the counterfeits until they entered the stream of ordinary business), she won't be found to have conspired with them. (Under the modern/M.P.C. approach, upstream members can be part of a conspiracy extending far downstream even if the downstream members are not deemed part of that same conspiracy back to the top. In other words, there can be a "unilateral" approach to determining who the members of a given conspiracy are.)

50. (A) Yes. The traditional rule is that once a conspiratorial agreement occurred, no subsequent act of withdrawal or repudiation by a conspirator could prevent that conspirator from being guilty of conspiracy. The modern / M.P.C. approach recognizes a limited defense of "renunciation of criminal purpose," but even that defense requires that the renunciating conspirator voluntarily ***thwart*** the conspiracy — mere withdrawal is not enough. So since Winken did not prevent the conspiracy's aims from being fulfilled, he'll be guilty even under this more liberal modern view.

(B) No. Most courts hold that if a conspirator withdraws, the withdrawal alone is enough to prevent the withdrawer from being guilty of any substantive crimes committed by the others in furtherance of the conspiracy. That's true even if the withdrawer doesn't try to thwart the conspiracy — however, the withdrawer must bring home to the remaining members that he is in fact withdrawing. So here, once Winken let the other two know he was no longer part of the team, any substantive crime they later committed may not be attributed to him.

51. (A) (i) Wharton's Rule; (ii) yes, probably. Wharton's Rule provides that where a substantive offense is defined so as to necessarily require more than one person, a prosecution for the substantive offense must be brought, rather than a conspiracy prosecution. The Rule is commonly applied to adultery, and thus provides that where a man and woman would be guilty of adultery if they had intercourse, they may not be prosecuted for conspiracy to commit adultery (whether they have sex or merely prepare to have it). Many states would apply Wharton's Rule as a substantive rule on these facts; therefore, regardless of whether the legislature intended to allow a prosecution for conspiracy-to-commit-adultery, in these states the prosecution would not be allowed. In other states, on these facts Wharton's Rule would be treated as a rebuttable *presumption* as to legislative intent; in that situation, the prosecution could try to rebut the presumption by showing (perhaps by legislative history) that the legislature in fact intended to allow conspiracy-to-commit-adultery prosecutions. However, it's unlikely that the prosecution could make that rebuttal showing in an adultery case, because the legislature is unlikely to have even thought about the issue. So all in all, in a state accepting any form of Wharton's Rule the prosecution would probably not be allowed to proceed.

(B) Yes. One well-established exception to Wharton's Rule is that there is no bar to a conspiracy conviction when there are *more participants* than are logically necessary to complete the crime. Here, we have three participants, not merely the two who were logically necessary to commit the crime. Therefore, all three may be convicted even in a jurisdiction that recognizes Wharton's Rule.

(C) No. The Model Penal Code basically rejects Wharton's Rule. See Comment 3 to §5.04(2). The M.P.C. does bar "cumulative" punishment, so that if Bob and Alice had consummated their liaison, neither could have been punished for *both* adultery and conspiracy to commit adultery. But the M.P.C. does not prevent a conspiracy conviction merely on the grounds that both parties would be necessary to the substantive crime, had that crime been committed.

52. (A) Yes. Where two conspirators are tried together in a single trial, and they are the only ones accused of conspiring, all courts agree that if one is acquitted the other must be. (Note, however, that if the conspiracy involves at least three parties and one is acquitted, the others can still be convicted, even if this occurs in the same trial as the acquittal.)

(B) (i) Probably not; and (ii) No. Where the conspirators are tried in separate trials, the community's sense of injustice at inconsistent verdicts is not nearly as great as where the inconsistency occurs in a single trial. Therefore, most courts will not overturn the guilty verdict. M.P.C. § 5.03 agrees that inconsistent verdicts in separate trials do not necessitate overturning the guilty verdict.

53. (A) Probably not. The only way Dan could be guilty of robbery is on an accomplice theory. One who aids and abets another (the principal) in the commission of a substantive crime becomes an accessory, and as such is equally guilty of the crime. However, where a person merely stands ready to give assistance that turns out to be unneeded, and his participation does not in any way encourage or facilitate the crime, the potential assistance will generally not be considered aiding and abetting.

(B) Yes. A person will be considered an accomplice (and therefore substantively liable for the crimes that he aids and abets) if he in any significant way encourages or facilitates the crime. That's true even if the crime would probably have been successfully completed without the aid. Here, the fact that Dan encouraged Ned by letting Ned know he was there for Ned would almost certainly be found to be encouragement and facilitation. (For instance, Ned might have changed his mind about going through with the robbery had he not known that Dan was serving as lookout).

54.   **No.** For a person to be liable as an accomplice to a crime (call it the "target crime") committed by a principal, the accomplice must have the mental state required for the target crime. So for Trotsky to be liable for the intentional murder of Nicholas, Trotsky would have needed a mental state that suffices for murder. Since Trotsky had no intent to kill or seriously injure, he did not have any of the required mental states for murder.

It's conceivable that Trotsky could be guilty on an alternate theory. An accomplice is guilty of additional crimes (i.e., "nontarget" crimes that the accomplice did not expressly aid and abet) committed by his principal if those are a "natural and probable consequence" of the commission of the target crime. However, there are two reasons why this theory probably wouldn't apply here: (1) it's not clear that Lenin committed the nontarget crime of murder *in addition to* robbery, because probably Lenin didn't commit robbery at all (and the theory probably applies only to crimes that are "added-on" to the target crime, not ones substituted for that target crime); (2) more important, it seems very unlikely that a cold-blooded murder would be found to be a "natural and probable consequence" of a robbery like this one, given that the accomplice didn't think the principal was armed and had no reason to think that the principal might commit such a killing, and further given that the killing doesn't even seem to have been in furtherance of the original robbery motive.

55.   **(A) No.** A person will only be liable as an accomplice if he ***intends to assist*** the principal in carrying out the target crime. Mere knowledge that the principal will engage in the crime, even when coupled with some degree of assistance, won't by itself be enough. Therefore, one who as part of an ordinary-course transaction supplies an item to another that he knows will be used by the other in a particular crime won't thereby become guilty as an accomplice to that crime.

(B) Yes, probably. Mere knowledge of a buyer's criminal purpose won't, as explained in part (A), by itself be enough to convert a supplier into an accomplice of the buyer. But if the supplier in some sense takes a "stake" in the buyer's criminal enterprise, this will be enough to cross the supplier over into accomplice territory. The fact that the supplier charges a much higher price on account of the buyer's criminal purpose is likely to be interpreted by a court as his having taken such a stake in the venture.

56.   **Yes.** Where an accomplice aids and abets a principal in the commission of one particular crime (call it the "target crime"), the accomplice will also be guilty of any additional crime that is a "natural and probable consequence" of the commission of the target crime. Here, the other deaths were a natural and probable consequence of the intended explosion. Therefore, since Wellington aided and encouraged Robespierre to blow up the house, all the ensuing deaths will likely be deemed within the scope of Wellington's liability as an accomplice.

57.   **(A) No.** The general rule is that if the principal is acquitted, the accomplice must be acquitted as well. This rule certainly applies where, as here, the two are tried in the same trial — the accomplice cannot be guilty unless the principal committed the target crime, and the verdict here shows conclusively that the principal was not guilty.

(B) Yes, probably. Although the general rule is that the accomplice must be acquitted if the principal is acquitted, there is an exception where the principal has a complete defense to the crime that the accomplice does not share. That is the case here, so Merlin is out of luck.

58.   No. Where an offense is defined so as to logically require two participants, but the statute specifies a punishment for only one of those participants, the other may not be convicted of being an accomplice. See, e.g., M.P.C. § 2.06(6)(b), making D not liable as an accomplice if "the offense is so defined that his conduct is inevitably incident to [the offense's] commission." That's the case here: a "sale" of narcotics can't take place without a buyer, and the state has chosen not to impose specific punishment on buyers; therefore, buyers can't be made accomplices to sales.

59.   No. Where a statute is intended to protect a certain class, a member of the protected class is immune from prosecution as an accomplice. In the case of statutory rape, the underaged person is universally considered to be a victim who is in need of protection. Therefore, Juliet cannot be convicted. Note that the same rule would apply to one who pays ransom to a kidnapper, or pays blackmail money to an extortionist.

60.   No. The crime of accessory-after-the-fact is committed where a person knowingly gives assistance to a felon, for the purpose of helping the felon avoid apprehension following the crime. The accessory must be shown to have taken affirmative acts to hinder the felon's arrest — it's not enough that the defendant merely fails (or even refuses when asked) to give information to the authorities. So Etta's off the hook. (But if Etta took affirmative steps to help the boys — if, for instance, she gave a phony alibi or gave false info about where the boys had gone when they left town — then she *would* be guilty of being an accessory after the fact.)

61.   (A) Solicitation. This crime occurs when one requests or encourages another to perform a criminal act, with the mental state required for that criminal act. The crime is complete at the moment of the request or encouragement.

(B) Yes. The fact that Raskolnikov never agreed with Dostoevsky's proposal (thus making a conspiracy charge not feasible) is no bar to a solicitation charge. Indeed, the scenario of the immediately-unsuccessful request — as well as the scenario of the request which the requestee appears to accept but secretly disagrees with — are the situations in which solicitation is most often charged.

62.   (A) No. Murder in most jurisdictions requires one of the four following mental states: (1) intent to kill; (2) intent to commit grievous bodily injury; (3) reckless or wanton indifference to the value of human life; or (4) intent to commit any of certain dangerous non-homicide felonies (i.e., felony-murder). Here, none of these mental states is present. In particular, (2) is not satisfied, because although Kingsman used a weapon that could be a deadly weapon, he did not use it with intent to commit grievous (i.e., serious) bodily injury — a small bruise, a little pain, and fear, do not add up to serious bodily injury, and that's all that Kingsman intended. So the fact that much worse resulted is irrelevant as far as murder goes — there's no general "you take your victim as you find him" rule in murder, as there is in tort law. (This is, instead, a classic case of manslaughter, perhaps misdemeanor-manslaughter.)

(B) Yes. On these facts, Kingsman has clearly intended to inflict grievous bodily injury. Even if the strictest definition of grievous bodily injury is used (intent to inflict life-threatening injuries), the injuries intended here qualify, since fractured skulls are often fatal. Therefore, Kingsman can be convicted of murder despite the absence of an intent to kill. Alternatively, the brutality and dangerousness of the attack probably qualify for reckless-indifference-to-value-of-life murder.

63. **No.** Under the common-law "year and a day" rule (still in force in many states), a death that occurs more than a year and a day following the defendant's act won't be murder, because the time delay creates a doubt about whether the defendant's act was the proximate cause of the death.

64. **Banquo is guilty of "reckless indifference" murder, but Macbeth is not guilty of any sort of murder.** One of the mental states that will suffice for murder is a *"reckless indifference to the value of human life,"* sometimes called a "depraved heart." Banquo's act of firing into a building that he knew was usually occupied would almost certainly qualify as reckless indifference to the value of human life, even though he thought the particular room was empty — because bullets go through walls, the conduct manifests indifference to the very high risk of death or serious injury. On the other hand, Macbeth had no reason to think his conduct was particularly likely to kill or badly injure someone, so his mental state doesn't meet the "reckless indifference" (or any other) mental state that suffices for murder.

65. **Yes, probably, on a theory of felony-murder coupled with accomplice liability.** First, *Speedy* is guilty of felony murder, because the killing took place during the course of a dangerous felony (robbery). Then, under the rules of accomplice liability Delgato is also guilty of robbery, because by serving as lookout and furnishing a weapon, he encouraged or assisted Speedy's commission of the robbery. The interesting question, of course, is whether Delgato is also guilty of the killing of the watchman. The killing of the watchman was an additional crime beyond the target crime (robbery) that Delgato intended to assist. The rule is that the accomplice will be guilty of additional crimes by the principal if and only if the additional crimes were a "natural and probable result" of the target felony, and were committed in furtherance of that target felony. A court would probably conclude that where an accomplice facilitates what he knows is an armed robbery by the principal, the principal's use of the gun to escape apprehension during the robbery is a natural and probable result of (and is committed in furtherance of) the robbery. In that event, Delgato would be guilty of murder.

66. **Sabina's and Claudius', but not Maecenas'.** When a person commits any of a group of particular dangerous felonies, he will be guilty under the felony-murder rule for any deaths, even accidental ones, that are the natural and probable consequences of the defendant's actions. Arson is universally considered part of this group of dangerous felonies. Therefore, Nero's guilty of any deaths that are the natural and probable consequences of his act of arson. Sabina's death clearly falls in this category: when one sets fire to a dwelling, the risk that the dwelling is unexpectedly occupied is great enough that this occupancy will not be deemed to be a superseding event. Claudius' death also falls into this category: when one commits arson, it is quite predictable that firefighters will respond, and relatively "natural and probable" that a firefighter may die fighting the blaze. On the other hand, death of a firefighter by getting hit by a branch while returning from the fire fight is not very natural and probable: this is not one of the kinds of events that makes fighting fires especially hazardous. So Maecenas' death probably won't be deemed to be a natural-and-probable consequence of the arson, and Nero won't be guilty of his murder.

67. **(A) No, because the requisite causal link is missing.** Even in a felony-murder case, the prosecution must show that the commission of the underlying dangerous felony in some sense was the proximate cause of the death — it's not enough for the death to occur at the same time and place as the dangerous felony is occurring. Here, Kitty's death had nothing to do with the felony.

(B) Yes. Since the heart attack was caused by fear over the felony (the robbery), it's highly likely that a court would say that the felony "caused" the death. That is, although the heart attack was due in some measure to Kitty's unusual fearfulness, the chain of events was not so bizarre or unforeseeable that Kitty's nervous disposition will be viewed as a superseding cause. This case falls within the general rule in felony-murder cases that crime victims' reactions to the crime, unless they are truly bizarre, will be non-superseding.

68.   No, because aggravated battery is not sufficiently "independent" from homicide to be covered by the felony-murder rule. If crimes consisting solely of intent-to-physically-injure could be the predicate to felony-murder, any battery or assault that unexpectedly ended in death would be "bootstrapped" to murder. For this reason, courts universally say that battery and assault cannot be predicate crimes for felony-murder (at least if the battery and/or assault is directed solely at the person who in fact dies.) So here, Derevenko has committed only battery (he didn't intend to kill or even seriously injure Alexis), and this crime can't be the predicate crime for felony murder.

69.   Voluntary manslaughter. What would otherwise be murder will be reduced to voluntary manslaughter if: (1) the defendant acts in response to a provocation that would be sufficient to cause a reasonable person to lose self-control; and (2) the defendant in fact acts with such a loss of control ("heat of passion"). Here, these requirements are satisfied. The fact that Rhett made a mistake of identity will not strip him of the defense, as long as his mistake was in some sense reasonable (and perhaps even if the mistake was careless but genuine, as long as it was not reckless). Some older cases say that "words alone" cannot constitute sufficient provocation, but modern courts recognize that words may be enough if they carry factual information (rather than, say, insults); so Aunt Pittypat's words would probably be held to be enough to cause the kind of lost self-control that voluntary manslaughter is designed to deal with.

70.   He'll be liable for murder, not voluntary manslaughter. That's because one of the requirements for voluntary manslaughter is that the defendant must have in fact been still under the heat of passion at the time of killing. If it's the case either that a reasonable person would have "cooled off" by the time of the killing, or that the defendant himself had actually cooled off (even if a reasonable person wouldn't have), then the defendant can't qualify for v.m. Here, since the facts indicate that James behaved in a quite rational, cool-headed manner, he can't be said to have acted in the heat of passion.

71.   (A) Involuntary manslaughter. One form of manslaughter is "involuntary manslaughter," which is defined in most states as being the ***reckless or the grossly negligent causing of another's death***. It is not necessary for involuntary manslaughter that the defendant have desired to kill, or even that he desired to injure, the victim. It is enough that he behaved in a way that recklessly or grossly negligently disregarded the risk of serious bodily injury or death. Since Deerslay knew that there were houses nearby, in the direction at which he was aiming, it would be quite plausible for a jury to find him guilty of involuntary manslaughter.

(B) No, probably. If the jurisdiction requires "gross negligence" or "recklessness" for involuntary manslaughter, as most jurisdictions do, Deerslay's conduct here probably did not rise to that level. Most courts hold that gross negligence or recklessness is only established where the defendant was ***actually aware*** of the danger, regardless of whether he *should* have been aware of it. Similarly, the Model Penal Code would acquit Deerslay of manslaughter here. The M.P.C. requires "recklessness" for manslaughter, and under §2.02(2)(c), a person acts recklessly only when he "consciously disregards" a substantial and unjustifiable risk.

72. Involuntary manslaughter, under the misdemeanor-manslaughter rule. That rule permits a conviction for involuntary manslaughter when a death occurs accidentally during (and is proximately caused by) the commission of a misdemeanor or other unlawful act. The rule is not in force in all jurisdictions (and isn't recognized by the M.P.C.), but it's part of the law of most states. For Tom to punch Jerry was a battery, which is a misdemeanor. (Jerry's insult does not furnish Tom with a defense — words of insult are never sufficient provocation to entitle the listener to commit a harmful or offensive touching.) Once that happened, any death that was proximately caused by that battery falls within the misdemeanor-manslaughter rule. The fact that Jerry was a hemophiliac won't furnish Tom with a defense — this event (like *any* unusual frailty of the victim) won't be considered so extraordinary that it should be viewed as superseding.

73. No. The only way L.G. could possibly be convicted of manslaughter is if the doctrine of misdemeanor manslaughter applied. We will assume that it does. However, for the doctrine to apply, the commission of the misdemeanor must be the proximate cause of the death. This means at the very least that the death must be attributable to the type of risk that caused the state to make the offense an offense in the first place. It is very unlikely that a court would hold that the state has made driving with an expired (as opposed to, say, a suspended) license a misdemeanor because such driving is especially risky — license renewals are generally required for fiscal and general recordkeeping purposes, not accident-prevention ones. Therefore, the lack of a license wouldn't be considered the proximate cause of the accident.

74. Criminal battery. The crime of battery exists when the defendant causes a harmful or offensive touching of another. The defendant's mental state may be intentional (intent to make the contact), reckless, or criminally negligent. The touching may be direct or, as here, indirect (contact between the harmful "medicine" and Rabbit's body). Thus the fact that Mother did not touch Br'er with her own body is irrelevant. And since Mother intended to bring about the harmful contact, she meets the mental-state requirement.

75. (A) No. An assault occurs only when the defendant either: (1) intends to bring about a harmful or offensive contact with another, and fails; or (2) intends to create in another a fear of an imminent harmful or offensive contact. Here, (1) is not satisfied because it's clear that Stolitz didn't intend to bring about a contact with Anna (he was just reckless in not noticing the risk). And (2) is not satisfied because Stolitz didn't intend to frighten Anna.

(B) Yes. Where a person brings about a harmful or offensive contact with another, he'll be guilty of battery if he acted intentionally or, in almost every state, recklessly. Stolitz' actions — the speeding combined with inattention and driving under the influence — certainly amount to recklessness. Therefore, he meets the mental state for battery. The fact that the contact was in a sense indirect (i.e., the fact that it was the streetcar, rather Stolitz' own body, that made harmful contact with Anna's body) is irrelevant.

76. Assault. One of the ways in which a person can commit the crime of assault is by intentionally putting another in fear of an imminent harmful or offensive contact. That's what happened here: the trier of fact could infer that Ferdinand desired to put Isabella in fear that he would soon pull the trigger and shoot her. The fact that the rifle was unloaded is irrelevant to the sufficiency of Ferdinand's mental state: as long as Isabella didn't *know* that it was unloaded (and as long as Ferdinand was relying on this lack of knowledge), Ferdinand had the requisite mental state, an intent to cause fear of contact. Also, the defendant's present *ability* to actually cause the threatened contact is not one of the elements of assault, so here too the lack of a bullet irrelevant.

77. **(A) No.** Rape is generally defined as unlawful intercourse with one other than one's wife, without consent. Intercourse based on a man's fraudulently persuading his victim that they are married is generally not deemed to be without consent. Fraud can only negate consent in a rape situation if the fraud prevents the victim from knowing the true nature of the act involved ("fraud in the essence") — the existence of a marriage is viewed as instead involving merely "fraud in the inducement."

(B) No. Fraud in falsely promising to marry someone in the future will not negate consent. As with Part A above, fraud can only negate consent in a rape situation if the fraud prevents the victim from knowing the true nature of the act involved.

78. **No.** The question here, of course, is whether there was consent. Clark clearly has not used force or threats. Under the Model Penal Code, Clark would be liable for rape if he had surreptitiously drugged Lois or administered liquor to her without her knowledge. Similarly, if Lois had been completely unconscious, Clark would be liable for rape, since M.P.C. §213.1(1)(c) makes it rape to have sexual intercourse where the female is "unconscious." But nothing in the Model Penal Code makes it rape to have sex with a woman who has become drunk on her own volition, but who remains conscious — the fact that the woman's drunkenness induces her to behave in a way that she might not if she were sober is treated by the M.P.C. as irrelevant. (But some courts would convict Clark here, on the theory that there can be no valid consent where the woman is drunk, even where this state was not induced by the defendant.)

79. **Larceny.** The point of this question, of course, is for you to figure out whether this is larceny or embezzlement. Where at the time of the trespassory taking the defendant is in lawful possession (not just "custody") of the items, the taking is embezzlement; if the defendant is just in custody at that moment, the taking is larceny. Here, had Bunter absconded with the tools during his actual employment, the crime might have been embezzlement, on the theory that Wimsey had given possession (not just custody) of them to Bunter; the case could have gone either way on the issue of possession vs. custody. But by July 1, given that the employment contract had ended, Bunter could not have had more than temporary custody of the tools, not true possession, since he no longer had any job-related reason to have them. At that point, the taking was a taking from Bunter's possession, so the crime was larceny.

80. **(A) Yes.** Larceny is defined at common law as the trespassory taking and carrying away of the personal property of another, with intent to steal. The two interesting issues here are: (1) was there a "carrying away"?; and (2) was there an intent to steal at the appropriate time? (1) is satisfied, because even a very small movement of the goods meets the carrying-away ("asportation") requirement, so rolling the car into the street sufficed. As to (2), the intent to steal must occur at the time of the carrying-away, and need not occur at any other time. Since the facts make it clear that at the moment the car was driven into the street, X intended to keep it and permanently deprive Speed Racer of it, this requirement was satisfied, and the crime was complete. The fact that X changed his mind (and returned the goods) shortly thereafter is irrelevant.

(B) No. Larceny requires the taking and carrying away of another's personal property with the "intent to steal." An intent to steal is generally deemed present only if the defendant has an intent to *permanently deprive* the owner of the property. Since Racer X did not intend to deprive Speed of the use of the car permanently, he hasn't met this requirement. (That's why most jurisdictions have special "joyriding" statutes to deal with this kind of situation.)

81. No, because her mistake was honest. Larceny requires an intent to take the property of another. If a person takes property believing that it is his own, the requisite intent to take another's property is not present. That's true even if the mistake is an unreasonable one. So larceny is in effect a "specific intent" crime — the requisite intent includes a belief about title, and even voluntary intoxication can negate that intent.

82. (A) No. A finder of lost property is only liable for larceny if, at the moment he finds the property, (1) he has reason to believe he can find the owner's identity *and* (2) he intends at that moment to steal the item. Here, (2) is not satisfied, because at the time Nelson found the bottle, he intended to return it. Since his intent to steal and finding the bottle do not coincide, he is not liable for larceny. The fact that Nelson later formed an "intent to steal" is irrelevant, at least under the common law. (But Model Penal Code § 223.5 *does* make it larceny for a defendant to "fail to take reasonable measures to restore [lost or mislaid] property to a person entitled to have it," regardless of whether there was an intent to steal at the time the defendant came into possession. So Nelson *would* be guilty of larceny under the M.P.C.)

(B) No. For larceny to exist, there must be an intent, existing at the time the defendant comes into possession of the property, to deprive the rightful owner of permanent possession. Where property is lost or mislaid, and at the time it comes into the defendant's possession there's no clue to its ownership, the defendant cannot have the requisite intent to "deprive the owner" of it. Therefore, Nelson won't be guilty of common-law larceny, even though he later discovered the owner's identity. (At that later point, he has the requisite intent, but it doesn't coincide with the moment of "taking," so it doesn't count.) (Again, under M.P.C. § 223.5 the result would be different, since by not speaking up Nelson would be "fail[ing] to take reasonable measures to restore [the] property to a person entitled to have it.")

83. Embezzlement. Embezzlement is the fraudulent conversion of the property of another by one who is already in lawful possession of it. That's the case here. The main issue is whether Pott was already in lawful possession of the shredder when he converted it to his own use. Since he was a relatively high-level official, and was given physical use of the shredder for as long as he held the government post, a court would almost certainly hold that Pott had possession, not just temporary custody, of the shredder. That makes his conversion embezzlement, rather than larceny (which could have occurred only if he had custody rather than possession at the time of the conversion.)

84. No. Embezzlement requires the "fraudulent" conversion of another's property by one in lawful possession of that property. The issue here is whether Wanda's conversion was "fraudulent." If a person honestly believes that she has a right to take the property — as where she is taking it in satisfaction of what she believes to be a valid debt — the conversion will not be deemed to be fraudulent. And that's true no matter how unreasonable the defendant's belief in her claim of right is. So the fact that Wanda "should have known better" is irrelevant. (Of course, the more unreasonable the defendant's belief, the more likely the trier of fact is to conclude that the belief was not in fact genuinely held. But if the trier *does* believe the belief was genuine, then its unreasonableness is irrelevant.)

85.   Yes. When a person takes property and intends to replace equivalent property later, that's not a defense to embezzlement. Embezzlement requires only a fraudulent conversion of property by one with lawful possession of the property. Since these elements are satisfied here, Rose will be liable. (Note that this most frequently happens when an employee takes money from his employer to pay off personal debts, intending to replace it later. The "intent to replace" is no defense.)

86.   (A) Amazingly enough, no. False pretenses requires a "factual" misrepresentation. Furthermore, the fact being misrepresented must be a past or present one — a promise that something will or won't happen in the future does not suffice as a factual misrepresentation, under the oft-criticized majority view. And that's so even if the promisor has absolutely no intention of keeping the promise. (But a minority of courts find liability where the speaker never intends to keep the promise.)

(B) Yes. Here, Guido has knowingly made a false representation about a present or past fact: that he has received the necessary permits. Therefore, the transaction meets all the requirements for the crime of false pretenses: (1) a false representation of a (2) material present or past fact (3) which causes the person to whom it is made to (4) pass title to his property to the misrepresenter, who (5) knows that his representation is false, and intends to defraud.

87.   No, because she had an honest belief that her statement was true. False pretenses requires a *knowing* misrepresentation intended to convince the victim to pass title to property. Here, the intent to defraud is missing. Even an unreasonable belief in the truth of one's statement will negate intent, as long as it's an honest belief.

88.   Burglary. The common-law crime of burglary is defined to be the breaking and entering of the dwelling of another at night with intent to commit a felony therein. The "trick" here is that Jessie is guilty of burglary *even though he in fact did not carry out the crime he had intended* (larceny). That is, once Jessie broke into and entered J.P.'s premises at night with an intent to commit larceny, he had already completed the crime of burglary.

89.   No. The definition of common-law burglary requires the breaking and entering of a *dwelling* of another at night. The bank is not a dwelling, it's a place of business. (But many modern statutes have expanded the definition to cover the breaking/entering of any structure, dwelling or not.)

90.   No. Burglary requires breaking and entering the dwelling house of another at night with the intention to commit a felony therein. At the moment Charming broke and entered, he had no intent to commit an act that was a felony therein (since leaving a warning note, even if it's a malicious prank, is not a felony). It's true that Charming later formed an intent to commit a felony (steal the painting), but to count, the felonious intent must exist at the moment of entry. Therefore, Charming is not guilty of burglary (but will, however, be guilty of larceny for taking the painting).

MULTIPLE-CHOICE
QUESTIONS
AND
ANSWERS

MULTIPLE-CHOICE QUESTIONS

Here are 26 multiple-choice questions, in a Multistate-Bar-Exam style. These questions are taken from *"The Finz Multistate Method"*, a compendium of 1100 questions in the Multistate subjects (*Contracts*, *Torts*, *Property*, *Evidence*, *Criminal Law* and *Constitutional Law*) written by Professor Steven Finz of National University School of Law, San Diego, CA, and published by us.

1. On Darr's birthday, his friend Mead gave him a new television as a gift. The following day, when Darr opened the box and began using the television, he noticed that there was no warranty document with it. Darr phoned Mead and asked Mead for the missing warranty document. Mead said, "I can't give it to you because the television was stolen." Darr kept the television and continued using it.

   Darr was guilty of

   (A) receiving stolen property only.
   (B) larceny only.
   (C) receiving stolen property and larceny.
   (D) no crime.

Questions 2-3 are based on the following fact situation.

Tom, John and Sam were teenaged boys staying at a summer camp. One evening Vanney, a camp counselor, ordered Tom and John to go to bed immediately after dinner. Outside the dining hall, Tom and John decided to get even with Vanney. Having seen Vanney take medicine for an asthma condition, they agreed to kill Vanney by finding his medicine and throwing it away. Tom and John did not know whether Vanney would die without the medicine, but they both hoped that he would.

Sam, who disliked Vanney, overheard the conversation between Tom and John and hoped that their plan would succeed. He decided to help them without saying anything about it. Going into Vanney's room, Sam searched through Vanney's possessions until he found the medicine. Then he put it on a night table so that Tom and John would be sure to find it.

As Tom and John were walking towards Vanney's room, John decided not to go through with the plan. Because he was afraid that Tom would make fun of him for chickening out, he said nothing to Tom about his change of mind. Instead, saying that he needed to use the bathroom, he ran away. Tom went into Vanney's room by himself, found the medicine where Sam had left it on the night table, and threw the medicine away. Later that night, Vanney had an asthma attack and died because he was unable to find his medicine.

A statute in the jurisdiction provides that persons the age of Tom, John and Sam are adults for purposes of criminal liability.

2. If Sam is charged with conspiracy, a court will probably find him

    (A) guilty, because he knowingly aided and abetted in the commission of a crime.
    (B) guilty, because he committed an overt act in furtherance of an agreement to throw away Vanney's medicine.
    (C) not guilty, because he did not agree to commit any crime.
    (D) not guilty, because John effectively withdrew from any conspiracy which existed.

3. If John is charged with the murder of Vanney, a court will probably find him

    (A) guilty, because he and Tom agree to throw away Vanney's medicine in the hope that doing so would cause Vanney's death.
    (B) guilty, because he aided and abetted in causing Vanney's death.
    (C) not guilty, because he did not physically participate in throwing away Vanney's medicine.
    (D) not guilty, because he withdrew from the conspiracy before any overt act was committed.

4. Larraby worked as a lifeguard from 5 P.M. to 8 P.M. every night at a public swimming pool operated by the City of Muni. At 8 P.M., Larraby told her boss she was going and left, although the pool had become quite crowded with adults and young children. At 9 P.M., Susan, a nine-year-old child, fell into the pool, striking her head against its edge. Watcher, one of the adults swimming in the pool, saw Susan fall and realized that the child would drown if someone did not rescue her. Watcher had seen Larraby leave and knew that there was no lifeguard present, but made no effort to rescue Susan although Watcher was a strong swimmer and could easily have done so with no risk to herself. Susan drowned. If Watcher is charged with criminal homicide in the death of Susan, the court should find her

    (A) guilty, because she could have saved Susan without any risk to herself.
    (B) guilty, if she knew that she was the only person present who was aware of Susans's plight and who was able to rescue her.
    (C) not guilty, unless she was related to Susan.
    (D) not guilty, because she had no duty to aid Susan.

5. Diller purchased an ounce of cocaine and divided it into fifty packets of about one-half gram each. She was selling them outside the local high school when Gunn, a cocaine user, noticed her and saw the opportunity to get some free drugs. Gunn stepped up beside her. With his hand in the pocket of his jacket, he thrust his finger forward inside the pocket and jabbed her in the ribs with it. Snarling, he said, "I've got a gun. Give me the dope or I'll blow you away." Diller reached into her purse, drew a small pistol which she kept there, and shot Gunn, killing him.

If Diller is charged with the murder of Gunn, she should be found

(A) guilty, because it was unreasonable for her to use deadly force to protect illegal contraband.

(B) guilty, if Gunn was unarmed.

(C) guilty, because Diller was committing a crime and therefore had no privilege of self-defense.

(D) not guilty, if it was reasonable for her to believe that her life was in danger.

6. Anthony was a resident patient at the state mental hospital, where he had been receiving treatment for a mental illness diagnosed as chronic paranoid schizophrenia. As a result of his illness, he believed that the governor of his state was part of a nationwide plot to turn all voting citizens into drug addicts. He felt that the only way to foil the plot was to kill the governor, but realized that the law prohibited such an act. He knew that if he was caught making any attempt on the governor's life he would be punished, but concluded that it would be better to be convicted and punished for a crime than to be turned into a drug addict.

Knowing that the governor visited the hospital every few months, and that when he did he usually ate in the hospital dining room, Anthony volunteered for a job in the hospital kitchen. On the governor's next visit, Anthony placed poison in food he knew would be served to the governor, intending to cause the governor's death. The governor ate the food and died as a result. If Anthony is charged with murder in a jurisdiction which has adopted only the M'Naghten test of insanity, Anthony should be found

(A) guilty, since he knew the nature of his act, and that it was prohibited by law.

(B) guilty, unless Anthony can establish that his mental illness made him unable to resist the impulse to kill the governor.

(C) not guilty, since Anthony's conduct was the result of mental illness.

(D) not guilty, if his delusion was the result of mental disease, and if his conduct was reasonable within the context of that delusion.

7. Ventana was a professional basketball player scheduled to play in an important basketball game on Sunday. On Friday, after wagering heavily on the game, Duggan attacked Ventana with a baseball bat. Duggan's intent was to inflict injuries severe enough to require hospitalization and thus keep Ventana from playing as planned. As a result of the beating, Ventana was taken to a hospital, where he was treated by Dr. Medich. The following day, Dr. Medich injected Ventana with a medicine to relieve his pain. Because of an allergic reaction to the drug, Ventana died within minutes.

If Duggan is charged with the murder of Ventana, he should be found

(A) not guilty, because Ventana's allergic reaction to the drug was an intervening cause of death.

(B) not guilty, if Ventana's death was proximately caused by Dr. Medich's negligence.

(C) guilty, only if Ventana's death was proximately caused by Duggan's attack.

(D) guilty, unless Dr. Medich's conduct is found to be reckless or grossly negligent.

8.   Darrel knew that his neighbor Volmer had a weak heart and that Volmer had suffered several heart attacks in the past. Because he was angry at Volmer, Darrel decided to try to frighten him into another heart attack. He watched Volmer's house and when he saw Volmer leaving through the front door, he ran towards him shouting, "Look out. Look out. The sky is falling," Although Darrel was not sure that this would kill Volmer, he hoped it would. When Volmer saw Darrel running toward him, shouting, he became frightened, had a heart attack and died on the spot.

The jurisdiction has statutes which define first degree murder as "the deliberate and premeditated killing of a human being," and second degree murder as "any unlawful killing of a human being with malice aforethought, except for a killing which constitutes first degree murder." In addition, its statutes adopt common law definitions of voluntary and involuntary manslaughter.

Which of the following is the most serious crime of which Darrel can properly be convicted?

(A) First degree murder.

(B) Second degree murder.

(C) Voluntary manslaughter.

(D) Involuntary manslaughter.

Questions 9-10 are based on the following fact situation.

Angry because her co-worker Ventura had insulted her, Delman decided to get revenge. Because she worked for an exterminator, Delman had access to cans of a poison gas called Terminate which was often used to kill termites and other insects. She did not want to kill Ventura, so she carefully read the use manual supplied by the manufacturer. The manual said that Terminate was not fatal to human beings, but that exposure to it could cause serious ailments including blindness and permanent respiratory irritation. When she was sure that no one would see her, Delman brought a can of Terminate to the parking lot and released the poison gas into Ventura's car. At lunchtime, Ventura and his friend Alex sat together in Ventura's car. As a result of their exposure to the Terminate in the car, Alex died and Ventura became so ill that he was hospitalized for over a month.

9.   If Delman is charged with the murder of Alex, she should be found

(A) guilty, because Alex's death resulted from an act which Delman performed with the intent to cause great bodily harm to a human being.

(B) guilty, because the use of poison gas is an inherently dangerous activity.

(C) not guilty, because she did not know that Alex would be exposed to the poison gas.

(D) not guilty, because she did not intend to cause the death of any person.

10. If Delman is charged with the attempted murder of Ventura, she should be found

   (A) guilty, because Ventura suffered a serious illness as the result of a criminal act which she performed with intent to cause him great bodily harm.
   (B) guilty, because her intent to cause great bodily harm resulted in the death of Alex.
   (C) not guilty, because she did not intend to cause the death of any person.
   (D) not guilty, because the crime of attempted murder merges with the crime of murder.

Questions 11-12 are based on the following fact situation.

Conn had just been released from prison after serving a three year term for aggravated assault. In need of money, he called his old friend Delbert and asked whether Delbert would be interested in joining Conn in the robbery of Perry's Pawnshop. Delbert agreed, but only after making Conn promise that there would be no violence. Upon Delbert's insistence, they carried realistic-looking toy guns and when they entered Perry's Pawnshop, they drew their toy guns and ordered Perry to give them all the money in his cash register and all the gems in his safe. Perry took a gun from the safe and shot Conn, killing him. Perry then aimed the pistol at Delbert, who fled from the store. As Perry ran out into the street with his pistol in his hand, Delbert jumped into the car which he and Conn had left parked at the curb. Speeding away from the scene, Delbert accidentally struck Nora, a pedestrian, who died of her injuries. By statute, the jurisdiction has adopted the felony-murder rule.

11. If Delbert is charged with the murder of Conn, Delbert's most effective argument in defense is that

   (A) Conn was not a victim of the felony which resulted in his death.
   (B) Perry was justified in shooting Conn.
   (C) the use of toy guns made it unforeseeable that the robbery would result in the death of any person.
   (D) Delbert lacked malice aforethought.

12. If Delbert is charged with the murder of Nora, the court should find him

   (A) guilty, because Nora's death resulted from Delbert's attempt to commit a robbery.
   (B) guilty, only if he drove the car in a criminally negligent manner.
   (C) not guilty, if he was in reasonable fear for his own life when attempting to flee in the automobile.
   (D) not guilty, because Nora's death did not occur during the commission of a felony.

13. After looking at a car which Samson had advertised for sale, Berrigan agreed to purchase it for three thousand dollars. Berrigan gave Samson one hundred dollars cash, promising to bring the balance and to pick up the car the following day. In fact Samson was a thief who had no intention of selling the car, and had been collecting

cash down payments from buyers all over the state. As soon as Berrigan left, Samson ran off with the hundred dollars. One week later, Samson was arrested and charged with embezzlement and larceny by trick. He can properly be convicted of

(A) embezzlement only.

(B) larceny by trick only.

(C) embezzlement and larceny by trick.

(D) neither embezzlement nor larceny by trick.

14. Dafton came home from work to find that his wife and two of his children had been slashed and cut and were lying dead in a pool of blood. His third child was also cut and bleeding severely. As Dafton approached, the child said, "Valens hurt Mommy." Dafton said, "I'll kill that son of a bitch." Then he loaded his shotgun and went next door to the home of the Valens. He knocked on the door, and when Valens opened the door Dafton shot and killed him. State statutes codify the common law definitions of voluntary and involuntary manslaughter, and define first degree murder as "the deliberate and premeditated killing of a human being," and second degree murder as "the killing of a human being with malice aforethought."

If Dafton is charged with voluntary manslaughter, the court should find him

(A) guilty, if he intended the death of Valens because he believed that Valens had killed his wife and children.

(B) guilty, because the killing of Valens was deliberate and premeditated.

(C) not guilty, because the killing of Valens was deliberate and premeditated.

(D) not guilty, if Valens was the killer of Dafton's wife and children.

15. Mildred and Bonnie were college students who needed money. One night, Mildred suggested that they hold up a local convenience store. When Bonnie told her that she was afraid to get involved in a robbery, Mildred offered to go into the store alone if Bonnie would wait outside in the car with the engine running so that they could make a getaway after the robbery. Bonnie agreed on condition that they split the take. The following day, they went together to a sporting goods store where Mildred purchased a shotgun. That night, Bonnie drove Mildred to the convenience store and waited in the parking lot with the engine running. Mildred went into the store with the shotgun hidden in a paper bag. Once inside, she pointed it at the store clerk and made him give her the contents of the cash register. Then she ran out to the car. When Bonnie saw Mildred running toward the car, she became frightened and drove away without waiting for Mildred.

Bonnie is guilty of

(A) conspiracy only.

(B) robbery only.

(C) conspiracy and robbery.

(D) either conspiracy or robbery, but not both.

16. A statute prohibited the sale of liquor between the hours of midnight and 8 A.M. When a customer came into Donohue's liquor store and asked to buy a bottle of liquor, Donohue looked at the clock and saw that it said five minutes past eleven, so he sold the liquor to the customer. Donohue believed that the clock was correct and did not realize that the previous day the state had changed from standard time to daylight savings time. In fact, the correct time was five minutes past midnight.

If Donohue is charged with attempting to violate the statute, he should be found

(A) guilty, because he sold liquor between midnight and 8 A.M.
(B) guilty, if he should have known the actual time.
(C) not guilty, unless the statute did not require specific intent.
(D) not guilty, because he believed that the time was five minutes past eleven.

Questions 17-18 are based on the following fact situation.

Dailey and Reavis had been in the same cell together while serving time in prison. Soon after their release, Reavis asked Dailey to join with him in robbing a bank. Dailey refused, stating that he did not want to go back to prison. Reavis then said that he would rob the bank himself if Dailey would provide him with a place to hide afterwards. Dailey agreed that Reavis could hide in Dailey's apartment following the robbery in return for one fourth of the proceeds of the robbery. The following day, Reavis robbed the bank. While he was attempting to leave the bank, a security guard began shooting at him, and Reavis fired back, killing a bystander. One week later, Reavis was arrested at Dailey's apartment where he had been hiding, and was charged with robbery and felony murder.

17. Assume for the purpose of this question only that Dailey was subsequently charged with felony murder on the ground that he was an accomplice to the robbery committed by Reavis which resulted in the death of a bystander. The court should find Dailey

(A) not guilty, because he was an accessory after the fact.
(B) not guilty, if he did not know that Reavis was going to use deadly force to accomplish the robbery.
(C) guilty, only if it was foreseeable that someone would be shot during the course of the robbery.
(D) guilty, because an accomplice is responsible for all crimes committed in furtherance of the crime to which he is an accomplice.

18. Assume for the purpose of this question only that Dailey was charged with conspiracy to commit robbery. The court should find Dailey

(A) not guilty, because he did not agree to participate in the actual perpetration of the robbery.
(B) not guilty, because Dailey's agreement to permit Reavis to stay at his apartment following the robbery was not per se unlawful.
(C) guilty, because he was an accessory to the robbery.

(D) guilty, because he agreed to furnish Reavis with a place to hide in return for a portion of the proceeds of the robbery.

Questions 19-20 are based on the following fact situation.

Okner was the owner of a department store. One day, Okner asked Shafer, who was employed in the store's shoe department, to temporarily replace a sporting goods salesman who did not show up for work. Yule, who was 15 years of age, subsequently entered the sporting goods department and asked Shafer to sell her ammunition for a pistol. Shafer placed a box of ammunition on the counter and said, "That'll be nine dollars, please." Realizing that she did not have any money with her, Yule left the store without the ammunition, saying that she would return for it later. A statute in the jurisdiction provides as follows: "Any person who sells ammunition for a firearm to a person below the age of 16 years shall be guilty of a felony. The employer of any person who violates this section during the course of such employment shall be guilty of a misdemeanor punishable by a fine not to exceed $250. It shall not be a defense to a violation of this section that the defendant had no knowledge of the age of the person to whom the sale was made."

19. Assume for the purpose of this question only that Yule did not return to the store. If Shafer is charged with attempting to violate the above statute, which of the following would be Shafer's most effective argument in defense against that charge?

    (A) Shafer did not know of the statute or its provisions.
    (B) Shafer did not know that Yule was below the age of 16 years.
    (C) Okner should be prosecuted under the statute, since she was Shafer's employer.
    (D) Shafer is customarily employed in the shoe department, and should not be held to the same standard as a person in the business of selling firearms and ammunition.

20. Assume for the purpose of this question only that Yule subsequently returned to the store with money and that Shafer sold her the ammunition. If Okner is prosecuted under the statute, Okner should be found

    (A) guilty, because her employee sold ammunition to a person under the age of 16 years.
    (B) guilty, only if it was unreasonable for Okner to assign Shafer to the sporting goods department without properly instructing him regarding the statute.
    (C) not guilty, unless Okner was present when Shafer made the sale to Yule.
    (D) not guilty, because holding one person vicariously liable for the crime of another violates the constitutional right to due process of law.

Questions 21-22 are based on the following fact situation.

Alice and Bonnie were roommates until they began arguing bitterly. During one argument, Alice moved out of the apartment which they shared. As she left, she said,"I'm going to get even with you for all the grief you've caused me." The following day, Bonnie's friend Frieda told Bonnie that Alice had purchased a gun. Frieda also said that Alice told her that she was going to shoot Bonnie the next time she saw her. As a result, Bonnie began carrying a loaded pistol. Several days later, realizing that she still had the key to Bonnie's apartment, Alice went back to return it. Bonnie was leaving her apartment when she saw Alice walking toward her. As Alice reached into her pocket for the apartment key, Bonnie drew her pistol and shot Alice, aiming to hit her in the chest. The bullet grazed Alice's shoulder, inflicting a minor injury. Alice immediately drew her own pistol and shot Bonnie with it, striking her in the thigh, and inflicting a serious injury.

21. If Bonnie is charged with attempted murder, which of the following would be her most effective argument in defense?

(A) Alice's injury was not serious enough to result in death.
(B) Bonnie did not succeed in striking Alice in the chest as she intended.
(C) It was reasonable for Bonnie to believe that Alice was reaching into her pocket for a gun.
(D) The force which Bonnie used was not deadly.

22. Assume that Alice is charged with attempted murder. If Alice asserts the privilege of self-defense, she will most probably be found

(A) guilty, if it was reasonable for Bonnie to believe that Alice was reaching into her pocket for a gun.
(B) guilty, because Alice's injury was not serious enough to result in death.
(C) guilty, because the fact that Alice was carrying a pistol is evidence of premeditation.
(D) not guilty.

23. Dennison was having dinner in a restaurant with his employer Vale, when Vale left the table to go the restroom. As Vale walked away, Dennison noticed that Vale's wristwatch had fallen off Vale's wrist onto the table. Since it looked like a rather valuable watch, Dennison decided to steal it. Picking up the watch, he put it into his pocket. A few moments later, he began to feel guilty about stealing from his employer, so when Vale returned to the table, Dennison handed him the watch and said, "Here, you dropped this, and I put it into my pocket for safekeeping."

Which is the most serious crime of which Dennison can be properly convicted?

(A) Larceny.
(B) Attempted larceny.
(C) Embezzlement.
(D) No crime.

Questions 24-25 are based on the following fact situation.

Vena was addicted to heroin, and frequently committed acts of prostitution to obtain the money she needed to buy drugs. One night she was out looking for customers for prostitution when she was approached by Dorian who asked what her price was. When she told him that she would have intercourse with him for $20, he said that he would get the money from a friend and see her later. When Vena went home several hours later, Dorian was waiting inside her apartment. He said that he wanted to have sex with her, but when Vena repeated her demand for $20, he said that he had no money. She told him to get out or she would call the police. Dorian took a knife from his pocket, saying that if she did not have intercourse with him he would kill her. Silently, Vena took off her clothes and had intercourse with him.

Immediately afterwards, Dorian fell asleep. Vena tied his hands and feet to the four corners of the bed, and woke him. She said, "Now you are going to be punished for what you have done. I should kill you, but I won't because I want to make sure that you suffer for the rest of your life." Using his own knife, she began to cut and jab him with it, planning to torture but not to kill him. She stabbed and blinded him in both eyes, then cut off his sex organs. She also severed the tip of his nose and made a series of cuts across his face and chest.

24. If Dorian is charged with rape, the court should find him

   (A) guilty, because he overcame Vena's refusal to have intercourse with him by threatening to kill her with his knife.

   (B) not guilty, because Vena's demand for twenty dollars made her resistance conditional and therefore less than total.

   (C) not guilty, because Vena offered no resistance and Dorian did not use physical force.

   (D) not guilty, because of the injuries inflicted by Vena.

25. Assume for the purpose of this question only that Dorian dies as a result of the injuries inflicted by Vena. Assume further that she is charged with first degree murder in a jurisdiction which defines that crime as "the unlawful killing of a human being committed intentionally, with deliberation and premeditation." The court should find Vena

   (A) not guilty, because Vena did not intend to cause Dorian's death.

   (B) not guilty, because Vena was acting in self-defense.

   (C) guilty, because Dorian's death resulted from Vena's commission of a dangerous felony.

   (D) guilty, because Dorian's death resulted from torture.

26. Dingle had suspected for some time that his wife Wilma was unfaithful to him. One night when she came home later than usual, Dingle confronted her, demanding to know where she had been. Tearfully, Wilma confessed that she had been out with a male friend, and that she had sexual intercourse with him. Dingle flew into a rage, striking Wilma repeatedly about the face and head with his clenched fist. The following day, Wilma died as a result of the injuries which Dingle had inflicted.

Dingle was subsequently charged with murder. At Dingle's trial, his attorney asserted that under the circumstances Dingle should not be convicted of any crime more serious than voluntary manslaughter.

Which of the following would be the prosecuting attorney's most effective argument in response to that assertion?

(A) Dingle's conduct indicated an intent to kill Wilma.

(B) Dingle's conduct indicated an intent to inflict great bodily harm on Wilma.

(C) Dingle did not catch Wilma "in flagrante delicto."

(D) In Dingle's position, a person of ordinary temperament would not have become angry enough to lose normal self-control.

ANSWERS TO MULTIPLE-CHOICE QUESTIONS

1. **D**   The crime of receiving stolen property consists of acquiring stolen property with the knowledge that it was stolen and the intent to permanently deprive the owner thereof. Since Darr did not know that the television was stolen when he acquired possession of it, he cannot be guilty of receiving stolen property. **A** and **C** are, therefore, incorrect.

    The crime of larceny consists of the trespassory taking and carrying off of personal property known to be another's with the intent to permanently deprive the owner thereof. Since Darr did not know that the television was the property of another when he took it (i.e., received it from Mead), he cannot be guilty of larceny. **B** and **C** are, therefore, incorrect.

2. **C**   A criminal conspiracy is an agreement to commit a crime and is complete when two or more persons make such an agreement. Although Sam privately decided to assist Tom and John in the commission of a crime, he did not agree with them that he would do so. He is, therefore, not guilty of conspiracy, and **C** is correct.

    One who knowingly aids and abets in the commission of a crime is guilty of that crime as an accessory. For this reason, Sam might be guilty of murder. **A** is incorrect, however, because Sam is charged not with murder but with conspiracy. Some jurisdictions hold that to convict for conspiracy it is necessary to prove an overt act in addition to an agreement to commit a crime. Even in these jurisdictions, however, Sam would not be guilty of conspiracy because he did not agree to commit a crime. **B** is, therefore, incorrect. Co-conspirators are guilty of the crime of conspiracy when their agreement is made and are not rendered innocent by the withdrawal of one or more of them from the conspiracy. **D** is incorrect for this reason, and because Sam was never part of the conspiracy in the first place.

3. **A**   Murder is the unjustified killing of a human being with malice aforethought. Malice aforethought includes the intent to kill, which means the desire or knowledge that the defendant's act will bring about the death of another person. Since Tom threw away Vanney's medicine with the desire that doing so would bring about the death of Vanney and since Vanney died as a result, Vanney was murdered. A criminal conspiracy is an agreement to commit a crime. Since Tom and John agreed to kill Vanney, they were involved in a criminal conspiracy. Co-conspirators are vicariously liable for any crimes committed in furtherance of the

conspiracy. Since the murder of Vanney was committed by Tom in furtherance of his agreement with John, John is vicariously liable for it. **A** is, therefore, correct.

Since John did no physical act which enabled Tom to bring about Vanney's death, he did not aid or abet him in bringing it about. **B** is, therefore, incorrect. **C** is incorrect because the principle of vicarious liability as explained above makes it unnecessary for John to physically participate in the commission of the crime with which he is charged. One who effectively withdraws from a conspiracy before its goal is accomplished may avoid vicarious guilt for the substantive crime, although not for the crime of conspiracy. In order for a withdrawal to be effective, however, the withdrawing conspirator must at least do something which places his co-conspirator on notice of his withdrawal. Since John did not do so, he has not effectively withdrawn from the conspiracy, and **D** is incorrect.

4. **D** In the absence of special circumstances, no person is under a legal duty to render aid to another. Since a failure to act can lead to criminal responsibility only in the face of a duty to act, Watcher's failure to rescue Susan was not a crime.

This is true even though she could have saved Susan without risk to herself, even though she knew that there was no one else who could rescue the child, and even if she was related to Susan. **A**, **B** and **C** are, therefore, incorrect.

5. **D** Self defense is a privilege to use reasonable force to protect oneself against aggression. In determining whether force was reasonable, courts usually balance the danger likely to result from its use against the benefit of using it. If the benefit which would be apparent to the reasonable person in the defendant's situation outweighs the danger which would be apparent to the reasonable person in defendant's situation, the force which the defendant used was reasonable. Since it is generally understood that the reasonable person would consider the benefit of saving her own life to be of greater weight than the danger of killing an assailant, it is usually held that lethal force (i.e., force likely to kill or do serious bodily harm) is reasonable if used by a person who reasonably believes that she is being attacked with lethal force. Thus, if it was reasonable for Diller to believe that her life was in danger, it was probably reasonable for her to use lethal force to protect it.

A is incorrect because Diller was attempting to protect herself rather than the cocaine. Even if Gunn was actually unarmed, Diller's reasonable belief that he had a pistol might have privileged her use of lethal force in self defense. **B** is, therefore, incorrect. A person who is committing a crime has no right to defend herself against a lawful arrest. Since Gunn was not attempting to arrest Diller, however, the fact that she was committing a crime at the time of his attack is irrelevant. **C** is, therefore, incorrect.

6. **A**   Under the M'Naghten test, a person may be found not guilty by reason of insanity only if mental illness prevented him from knowing the nature and quality of his act or from knowing that the act was legally wrong. Since Anthony knew what he was doing (i.e., that he was poisoning the Governor) and knew that it was against the law, he was not insane.

B refers to the irresistible impulse supplement, and is incorrect because the facts indicate that the jurisdiction has adopted only the M'Naghten test. **C** is incorrect because it refers to the Durham rule, which is no longer applied in any jurisdiction. In some jurisdictions, a defendant is insane under the M'Naghten rule if mental disease caused him/her to suffer from a delusion within the context of which the defendant's act would be lawful. **D** is incorrect, however, because even within the context of Anthony's delusion, Anthony knew that killing the governor was an unlawful act.

7. **C**   Murder involves malice aforethought coupled with an act which proximately results in the unlawful killing of a human being. Since malice aforethought includes the intent to inflict great bodily harm, and since it was Duggan's intention to severely injure Ventana, the only issue to be resolved in determining Duggan's guilt is whether Duggan's act was a proximate cause of Ventana's death. If it was, then Duggan is guilty of murder.

Intervening proximate causes of Ventana's death would not prevent Duggan's act from also being a proximate cause, unless those intervening causes could be characterized as unforeseeable or independent. Although Ventana's allergic reaction to the drug was an intervening cause of harm, there is no indication that such an allergic reaction was unforeseeable. Since the drug was given to relieve pain which resulted from the beating, neither its administration nor the patient's allergic reaction to it can be termed independent. **A** is, therefore, incorrect. **B** is incorrect because Ventana's death may have had several proximate causes. The fact that Dr. Medich's conduct was one of them does not mean that Duggan's conduct was not also one of them. Since Ventana's death would not have occurred without Dr. Medich's conduct, Dr. Medich's conduct was a *factual* cause of death. Since Dr. Medich's conduct occurred after Duggan's, Dr. Medich's conduct was an *intervening* cause of that death. But an intervening cause does not break the chain of proximate causation, unless that intervention was unforeseeable. Sometimes gross negligence or recklessness by an intervenor is held to be unforeseeable. This is not an inflexible rule, however. Under some circumstances, even reckless conduct or gross negligence has been held foreseeable. For this reason, a finding that Dr. Medich's conduct was reckless or grossly negligent — without an additional finding that it was unforeseeable — would not be sufficient to result in the conclusion that Duggan's conduct was not one of the proximate causes of Ventana's death. **D** is, therefore, incorrect.

8. **A** A killing is intentional if the defendant desired or knew to a substantial degree of certainty that it would result from his act. A killing is deliberate and premeditated if the defendant was capable of reflecting upon it with a cool mind and did in fact do so. Since Darrel hoped for (i.e., desired) Volmer's death, the killing was intentional. Since he reflected on it in advance with a cool mind, it was deliberate and premeditated.

Since first degree murder is the most serious crime listed, **B**, **C** and **D** are incorrect. Voluntary manslaughter is an intentional killing resulting from extreme emotional disturbance or in the mistaken belief that it is justified. **C** is also incorrect because there is no indication that Darrel was emotionally disturbed or mistakenly believed that his act was justified. Involuntary manslaughter is an unintended killing which results from criminal negligence. **D** is also incorrect because Darrel intended the death of Volmer.

9. **A** Murder is the unjustified killing of a human being with malice aforethought. Malice aforethought includes the intent to cause great bodily harm to a human being. A defendant "intends" a particular consequence if she desires or knows to a substantial degree of certainty that it will occur. Since Delman desired and/or knew that exposure to Terminate was likely to result in great bodily harm to Ventura, she intended to cause great bodily harm to a human being. Since Alex died, Delman may be found guilty of his murder. **A** is, therefore, correct.

B is incorrect because engaging in an inherently dangerous activity is not equivalent to malice aforethought. **C** is incorrect because Delman's intent to cause great bodily harm to any human being is sufficient to make her guilty of murder in causing the death of Alex. Although the intent to kill is a form of malice aforethought, **D** is incorrect because the intent to cause great bodily harm is also a form of malice aforethought.

10. **C** A person is guilty of a criminal attempt when, with the specific intent to bring about a prohibited result, she comes substantially close to doing so. Thus, all attempts are "specific intent" crimes. This means that although murder does not require a specific intent to cause the death of a person, attempted murder does. Since Delman did not intend to cause the death of a human being, she lacks the intent required to make her guilty of attempted murder.

A is, therefore, incorrect. The death of Alex does not satisfy the specific intent requirement unless Delman intended to bring it about. For this reason, **B** is also incorrect. Although the attempt to murder a person may merge with the actual murder of the person, **D** is incorrect because Ventura did not die, and so could not have been murdered.

11. **B**   Many jurisdictions hold that the defendant will not be guilty of the murder of a co-felon under the felony murder rule if the co-felon's death resulted from a justifiable attempt by the crime-victim to prevent the crime. Although this is not the law in all jurisdictions, it is the only argument listed which would provide Delbert with any defense at all.

  A is incorrect because the felony murder rule is applied to deaths which occur during the commission of a felony, even though the person killed is not the intended crime-victim. **C** is incorrect because the normal reactions of victims, bystanders, and police, make violence a foreseeable result of any robbery. **D** is incorrect because jurisdictions which apply the felony murder rule regard the intent to commit a felony as a form of malice aforethought.

12. **A**   The felony murder rule provides that the intent to commit a felony is malice aforethought, and that a death which results from the perpetration of a felony is, therefore, murder. For this purpose, the perpetration of a felony continues during the defendant's attempt to escape to a place of seeming safety. Nora's death thus occurred during the perpetration of a robbery, and Delbert could be convicted of murder even if he was driving carefully at the time it occurred.

  B, **C**, and **D** are, therefore, incorrect.

13. **D**   Embezzlement is the conversion of personal property known to be another's with the intent to defraud, by a person in lawful possession of the property. Since Samson's possession was the result of fraud and therefore not lawful, he is not guilty of embezzlement. **A** and **C** are, therefore, incorrect. Larceny by trick is committed when the defendant fraudulently induces the victim to deliver *temporary possession* of personal property to the defendant. If the victim transfers title to the property involved, the crime of larceny by trick has not been committed. Since Berrigan's intention was to make Samson the owner of the money, he transferred title to the money, and **B** and **C** are incorrect. The crime actually committed by Samson was false pretenses, since Samson knowingly made a false representation to Berrigan to induce Berrigan to part with title to the money.

14. **A**   Voluntary manslaughter is committed when the defendant, with the intent to cause death or great bodily harm, causes the death of a human being under circumstances such that the defendant is acting in the "heat of passion." The belief that Valens brutally murdered his family probably is sufficient to furnish the heat of passion which reduces the crime from murder to manslaughter.

  B is incorrect for two reasons: first, deliberation and premeditation require a mind which is capable of thinking coolly and rationally, and under the circumstances Dafton's probably wasn't and, second, deliberation and premeditation are not elements of voluntary manslaughter. Since voluntary manslaughter is a lesser offense included in first degree murder, Dafton could be convicted of voluntary manslaughter even if he were guilty of first degree murder. **C** is incorrect because it suggests that guilt of first degree murder would prevent a conviction for voluntary manslaughter. Convicting and sentencing for crime are functions of the court, not of the family of the crime's victim. **D** is incorrect because it suggests a law of vendetta (i.e., that if Valens was the killer Dafton could punish him without incurring criminal responsibility).

15. **C** One who intentionally aids or facilitates the commission of a crime is guilty of the crime as an accessory. Robbery is larceny committed by force or threat of force. Although Bonnie did not point a gun and demand money, she aided and abetted Mildred by operating the getaway car. She is thus guilty as an accessory. Conspiracy is an agreement to commit a crime made by two or more people who have specific intent. Bonnie and Mildred committed the crime of conspiracy when they agreed on the commission of the robbery.

   A, **B** and **D** are incorrect because the crime of conspiracy is separate from and does not merge into the substantive crime which the conspirators agreed to commit.

16. **D** A person is guilty of a criminal attempt when, with the specific intent to bring about a result which is criminally prohibited, he comes substantially close to accomplishing that result. Since Donohue believed that the time was five minutes past eleven, and since it would have been lawful to sell liquor at that time, he did not have the specific intent to bring about a result which was criminally prohibited. For this reason, he could not be guilty of attempting to violate the statute.

   A and **B** are, therefore, incorrect. Attempt always requires specific intent, even where the substantive crime does not. Thus, even if the statute did not require specific intent, Donohue could not be guilty of *attempting* to violate it without specifically intending to sell liquor after midnight. **C** is, therefore, incorrect.

17. **C** One who intentionally aids, abets, or facilitates the commission of a crime is criminally responsible for the crime as an accomplice. In addition, an accomplice is criminally responsible for all the foreseeable consequences of the crime which he facilitated. Since the use of Dailey's apartment to escape detection was part of Reavis' plan in preparing for the robbery, Dailey's agreement to permit Reavis to use it facilitated the robbery, making Dailey an accomplice to it. As such, Dailey may be guilty of felony murder in the death which resulted from the robbery, but only if it was foreseeable that such a death would occur.

   One who becomes an accessory after a crime has been committed (i.e., accessory after the fact) by knowingly harboring the person who committed it is not criminally responsible for prior acts committed by the person harbored. A person who facilitates the commission of a crime by agreeing in advance that he will harbor the perpetrator after the crime is committed is guilty as an accomplice (i.e., accessory before the fact), however. As such he is criminally responsible for all foreseeable consequences of the crime to which he was an accomplice. **A** is, therefore, incorrect. Since an accomplice is criminally responsible for those consequences which were foreseeable, the fact that Dailey did not actually know that Reavis would use a gun does not protect him from liability if Reavis' use of a gun was foreseeable. **B** is, therefore, incorrect. A conspirator is criminally responsible for all crimes committed by co-conspirators in furtherance of the subject of the conspiracy. **D** is incorrect, however, because an accessory is criminally responsible only for consequences which were foreseeable.

18. **D**   A conspiracy is an agreement by two or more persons to commit a crime. Ordinarily, one who agrees to furnish services to another which the other will use in committing a crime is not guilty of conspiracy merely because he knows the purpose to which the services will be put. Where, however, the supplier has a stake in the criminal enterprise, his agreement to furnish services may constitute a conspiracy to commit the crime. Since Dailey knew that Reavis would be using his apartment as a hideout following the robbery, and since Reavis' promise to compensate Dailey by paying him a percentage of the loot gave Dailey a stake in the criminal enterprise, Dailey may be guilty of conspiracy.

   A is, therefore, incorrect. **B** is incorrect for two reasons: first, Dailey's agreement probably was per se unlawful, since he knew that Reavis would be hiding in his apartment to escape detection (i.e., that he would be harboring a felon); and, second, Dailey had a personal stake in Reavis' crime. The crime of conspiracy to commit robbery is complete when the defendant agrees with another to commit the robbery, and is a separate crime from the robbery itself. Thus, the fact that a defendant is guilty of robbery is not relevant to the issue of whether he conspired (i.e., agreed) to commit it. For this reason, **C** is incorrect.

19. **B**   A person is guilty of a criminal attempt when, with the specific intent to bring about a criminally prohibited result, he comes substantially close to bringing about that result. Thus, while certain crimes may be committed without intending the prohibited consequences, criminal attempt always requires the specific intent to bring about the prohibited result. Although Shafer could be convicted of violating the statute if he actually sold ammunition to Yule who was under the age of 16, he could not be convicted of attempting to violate the statute unless he knew that Yule was under the age of 16 and intended to sell her the ammunition.

   For obvious practical reasons, there is usually an irrebuttable presumption that all persons know the law. Ignorance of the law, therefore, would not provide Shafer with a defense. **A** is, therefore, incorrect. The fact that Okner is vicariously liable under the statute would not furnish Shafer with a defense, since the statute imposes liability on both employee and employer. **C** is incorrect for this reason, and because the statute imposes vicarious liability on the employer only if the employee actually makes a sale, which Shafer did not do. **D** is incorrect because the statute does not make knowledge or experience an element of guilt.

20. **A**   Some cases have held that the imposition of a prison term on the basis of vicarious liability for a strict-liability crime committed by a defendant's employee is a violation of due process. It is generally understood, however, that the imposition of a fine on this basis is constitutionally valid. Since this statute makes an employer vicariously liable for the payment of a fine if an employee sells ammunition to a minor, and since Okner's employee sold ammunition to a minor, Okner may be convicted.

     B and **C** are incorrect because of the specific language of the given statute: **B** because the statute imposes strict liability, and does not make negligence or unreasonable behavior a basis of guilt; and **C** because the statute does not make the employer's presence an element of guilt. **D** is incorrect because it is overinclusive: there are many situations in which the criminal law may validly impose vicarious liability for the crime of another (e.g., co-conspirators are vicariously liable for each other's crimes committed in furtherance of the conspiracy).

21. **C**   A person is privileged to use reasonable force to protect herself from what she reasonably believes to be a threat of imminent bodily harm. Potentially lethal force is reasonable when used in response to what the defendant reasonably perceives to be a threat of potentially lethal force. Thus, if Bonnie reasonably believed that Alice was reaching for a gun, her use of a gun in response may have been reasonable, and therefore privileged. While it is not certain that a court would come to this conclusion, the argument in **C** is the only one listed which could possibly provide Bonnie with an effective defense.

     A person is guilty of a criminal attempt when, with the intent to bring about a criminally prohibited result, she comes substantially close to achieving it. **A** is incorrect because the fact that a death did not actually occur will not prevent a conviction for attempting to cause one. If Bonnie had the intent to kill Alice when she aimed her pistol at Alice's chest, she would be guilty of attempted murder if she came subsequently close to causeing Alice's death. this might be so even if she did not strike Alice in the chest, or even if she did not strike Alice at all. for this reason, **B** is incorrect. **D** is incorrect because deadly force is force which is likely to result in death or great bodily harm. The use of a pistol thus constitutes deadly force even though the harm which it actually causes happens to be slight.

22. **D**   A person is privileged to use reasonable force to protect herself from what she reasonably believes to be a threat of imminent bodily harm. Since Bonnie fired a pistol at Alice, and was (or appeared to be) capable of firing it again, it was reasonable for Alice to believe herself threatened with imminent bodily harm, and was probably reasonable for her to respond with deadly force.

     If Bonnie's belief that Alice was about to shoot her was a reasonable one, Bonnie's use of force may have been privileged. **A** is incorrect, however, because, although an aggressor has no right of self-defense against a reasonable response to her initial aggression, Alice committed no act of aggression until after Bonnie fired at her. Self-defense may privilege the use of deadly force in response to what is reasonably perceived as deadly force. Even though the force used by Bonnie had not yet caused death or serious injury, it was capable of doing so, and can, therefore, be regarded as deadly force. **B** is, therefore, incorrect. **C** is incorrect because even a premeditated killing may be privileged by self-defense.

23. **A**   Larceny is defined as a trespassory taking and carrying off of personal property known to be another's with the intent to permanently deprive the owner thereof. A trespassory taking is an acquisition of possession contrary to the rights of the owner and without the owner's consent. Since Dennison acquired possession without Vale's permission, he committed a trespassory taking. A carrying off occurs when the defendant moves the property, even slightly, with the intention of exercising dominion over it. Since Dennison moved the watch from the table to his pocket with the intention of keeping it, he carried it off. Since he knew that the watch belonged to Vale and intended to keep it for himself, he had knowledge that the property was another's and intended to deprive the owner of it. He, therefore, committed a larceny, making **A** correct.

A person is guilty of a criminal attempt when with the specific intent to bring about a criminally prohibited result, he comes substantially close to bringing it about. Although Dennison is probably guilty of attempted larceny, **B** is incorrect because larceny is a more serious crime. Embezzlement is defined as a criminal conversion of personal property by one in lawful custody of that property. Employees who steal property from their employers while in custody of it because of the employment relationship may be guilty of embezzlement. **C** is incorrect, however, because Dennison did not come into possession of the watch as a result of his employment relationship with Vale. **D** is incorrect because Dennison is guilty of larceny for the reasons stated above.

24. **A**   Rape is committed when the defendant intentionally has sexual intercourse with a female not his wife without consent. Although it is necessary that the victim be unwilling, it is not necessary for her to put up a fight if it would be futile for her to do so or if she reasonably believes that resisting will cause her to sustain serious injury. Since Vena's refusal was overcome by a threat which would have led a reasonable person in her place to fear for her life, the intercourse was without her consent.

If her resistance had been overcome by payment, the intercourse would not have been against her will. But the fact that she was willing to accept payment does not mean that she consented to intercourse with one who did not offer payment, or even with one who did. **B** is, therefore, incorrect. **C** is incorrect because Vena's resistance was overcome by Dorian's threat of physical force. Since Vena inflicted the injuries after the intercourse occurred, her conduct in inflicting them could not possibly relate to whether she consented to the intercourse. **D** is, therefore, incorrect.

25. **A**   Since the statute requires intent, and since Vena did not intend Dorian's death, she is not guilty of first degree murder under the statute.

B is incorrect because once Dorian was asleep (and certainly once he was tied to the bed), Vena was no longer in danger and therefore not privileged to use force in self-defense. Although some first degree murder statutes include deaths resulting from the commission of dangerous felonies, this particular statute does not. **C** is, therefore, incorrect. Many first degree murder statutes include death resulting from torture, but this one does not. **D** is, therefore, incorrect.

26. **D**   Voluntary manslaughter is the killing of a human being with the intent to kill or inflict great bodily harm, under circumstances of extreme emotional distress (or mistaken justification). Frequently, the rage which accompanies a discovery of infidelity by a spouse has been held to be sufficient emotional distress to reduce an intentional homicide from murder to voluntary manslaughter. Most jurisdictions apply an objective standard, however, in judging a defendant's emotional distress. Thus, if a person of ordinary temperament would not have lost self-control, Dingle's emotional distress would not have been sufficient to result in a reduction of his crime from murder to manslaughter.

A and **B** are incorrect because although a killing with the intent to kill or inflict great bodily harm *may* be murder, extreme emotional distress may reduce it to voluntary manslaughter even though the defendant intended to kill or inflict great bodily harm. Although anger which results from the defendant's catching his spouse in *flagrante delicto* (i.e., in the act) may justify reducing a murder charge to one of manslaughter, **C** is incorrect because there is no requirement that defendant's emotional distress result from this particular circumstance.

ESSAY EXAM QUESTIONS AND ANSWERS

ESSAY EXAM
QUESTIONS & ANSWERS

The following questions were asked on various Harvard Law School First-Year Criminal Law examinations. The questions are reproduced as they actually appeared, with only slight modifications. The sample answers are not "official" and represent merely one approach to handling the questions.

QUESTION 1

QUESTION 1: Sapo and Crapaud agreed to commit a holdup at the First County Bank, in which Badger worked as a teller. They obtained her cooperation in the plan. The three of them agreed that Sapo and Crapaud would enter the bank and carry out the "holdup" at Badger's window. She would give them the money, apparently under the threat of the holdup. Later the three of them would meet and divide up the money. It was agreed that the plan would be carried out on January 12.

On January 9, Badger became frightened. After thinking about it, she called the apartment where Sapo and Crapaud lived together. Someone who was cleaning the apartment answered and said that neither Sapo nor Crapaud was at home. Badger asked the person to leave a message for them saying, "Can't go through with it. Sorry. Badger." The person on the telephone misunderstood (!) and left a note saying that someone had called and left the message, "Aunt Flo threw a fit. Sorry. Alger." When Sapo and Crapaud came home, they saw the message, concluded that someone was playing some sort of silly joke, and thought no more about it.

On January 12, as planned, Sapo and Crapaud went on foot to the bank and entered, brandishing guns. Sapo ordered everyone to stand still. Crapaud went to Badger's window and, pointing a gun at her, demanded money. As he did so, he winked at her. Startled that the "holdup" was taking place despite her message and frightened that her part in the plan would be discovered, Badger passed over the money. Crapaud grabbed it and he and Sapo ran out of the bank. Badger fainted.

As they ran onto the street, Sapo bumped into Wale (who knew nothing about the holdup) and knocked him to the sidewalk. Sapo and Crapaud kept running. Furious at Sapo's rudeness, Wale pulled out a gun and fired. The shot hit Sapo in the heart and killed him instantly.

Crapaud kept running and turned a corner. He bumped into Gark who had heard the shots (but knew nothing about the holdup). "What's the matter, friend?" Gark shouted.

"Oh, help me, they're after me," Crapaud shouted. He kept running.

"They are, are they? I'm with you, friend," Gark said.

As people from the bank came running around the corner after Crapaud, Gark tackled the first of them, who was named Dasher. As he did so, he said to Dasher, "Leave that poor man alone, friend."

The people behind Dasher tripped over the bodies of him and Gark and there was great confusion. In the melee, Dasher shouted at Gark, "You idiot, that was a bank robber."

"And I'm the king of diamonds. Relax, friend," Gark said, and pushed Dasher down again. Dasher fought back. Haley, one of the bank people who was behind Dasher concluded that Gark was one of the holdup men and that Dasher was trying to capture him. He grabbed Gark around the neck from behind, and tried to pull him off Dasher. Thinking that he had fallen among a gang of dangerous thugs or lunatics and thoroughly frightened, Gark grabbed a brick lying on the pavement and reached around and hit Haley in the head with it. Haley fell to the ground and lost consciousness.

The police arrived and restored order. Haley was put in an ambulance to be taken to the hospital. Speeding through an intersection with the siren sounding, the ambulance was struck by an automobile driven by Leek, who had heard the siren but paid no attention to it because he was preoccupied by an argument he had had with his boss earlier that day. By the time another ambulance arrived at the scene of the accident, Haley had died from head injuries.

In the meantime, Crapaud had boarded a bus and escaped. He arrived home and found that he had $5,742 of bank money. He spent $42 on a floral wreath, which he sent anonymously to Sapo's funeral, and put the remainder in his desk.

So far as you can tell from these facts, what crimes were committed by Sapo, Crapaud, Badger, Wale, Gark, Dasher, Haley, and Leek? Explain your conclusions, where that is necessary.

ANSWER TO QUESTION 1

Conspiracy by Sapo, Crapaud and Badger: Sapo, Crapaud and Badger have all agreed to commit the crime of larceny (and perhaps the crime of robbery). Therefore, they are guilty of ***conspiracy*** to commit those crimes.

Badger might argue that she has not agreed to do anything unlawful; she has simply agreed to hand over money to gunmen, which is probably in accord with the policies of the Bank anyway. However, she has clearly agreed to be party to a crooked scheme, and will receive money if all goes well; this should suffice for conspiracy liability.

Badger may also argue that she ***withdrew*** from the conspiracy. However, the common law does not recognize a defense of withdrawal from a conspiracy at all. Some states, and the Model Penal Code, might recognize withdrawal as a defense, but even these require that the conspiracy be thwarted. It is not sufficient that Badger took action which could reasonably be expected to thwart the robbery, if this did not happen.

Robbery by Sapo, Crapaud and Badger: Sapo and Crapaud (and perhaps Badger) are guilty of robbery, which is defined as theft from the person or presence of another, by force or intimidation. Since Badger was originally part of the plan, it is not clear whether force or intimidation should be deemed to have been used against her. Also, the facts indicate that she passed over the money not out of fear of violence, but fear that her part in the plan would be discovered. In any event, if it can be shown that anyone else in the bank was placed in fear, robbery would exist, since the property would have been taken from the "presence" of these others.

Badger may also be liable for robbery, as an ***accomplice***. She certainly gave aid and encouragement at the beginning, which would be enough for accomplice liability. But she may be able to raise the defense of ***withdrawal***. Less is required for withdrawal by an accomplice than by a conspirator. However, even an accomplice must bring home his withdrawal to the other conspirators, which Badger has not done. A court might, however, hold that her attempt to do so sufficed. Alternatively, Badger could argue that she cannot be an accomplice to the robbery of herself; this argument might be rebutted by showing that other persons present were placed in fear of the gun.

Larceny and embezzlement by Sapo, Crapaud and Badger: Sapo and Crapaud have committed either larceny or embezzlement. If Badger is regarded as still having been part of the plan when she handed over the money, the crime is probably embezzlement by all three, since modern embezzlement statutes cover an employee who appropriates property already in her lawful possession. (Sapo and Crapaud would be viewed as accomplices to Badger's embezzlement in this situation.)

If, on the other hand, Badger is not regarded as part of the theft, the crime by Sapo and Crapaud is larceny, since they took the property unlawfully from the possession of Badger and the bank.

Battery by Sapo: Sapo may be guilty of battery. He did not intend to collide with Wale, but it may suffice that he was ***criminally negligent*** in doing so. Alternatively, Sapo, since he was in the process of committing an "unlawful act" (the robbery), might be guilty on that ground alone, by analogy to the misdemeanor-manslaughter rule. If Sapo were guilty of battery on either of these theories, Crapaud might be liable as an accomplice.

Murder or manslaughter by Wale: Wale is almost certainly liable for some kind of homicide in the death of Sapo. He might argue that he acted in self-defense or in order to apprehend the felon, but both of these defenses require that the actor have been aware of the necessity for them. The factors indicate that Wale did not know anything about the holdup at the time he did the shooting.

Wale may be able to get the charge reduced to ***voluntary manslaughter***; a more-than-trivial battery is generally considered to be sufficient provocation. However, it is not clear that there was a battery, and even if there was, the court might hold that only a battery which Wale could reasonably have regarded as intentional should suffice. Nor, of course, will Wale be entitled to have his own highly excitable temperament taken into account in determining whether the provocation was sufficient

Felony-murder of Sapo by Crapaud: Arguably, Crapaud may be liable for the felony-murder of Sapo, since Sapo's death occurred "in the commission of" the robbery. However, many courts now refuse to apply the felony-murder doctrine where the person killed is a co-felon, on the theory that the doctrine only covers the death of innocent persons. Also, some courts have refused to apply the doctrine to a shooting by a bystander. A felony-murder conviction is even less likely here, since the shooting by Wale was not even in resistance to the robbery, or done in an attempt to apprehend Sapo.

Battery by Gark against Dasher: Gark is probably guilty of battery against Dasher. Gark had the necessary intent, since he intended to make the bodily contact, even though he may have been mistaken as to other facts.

Gark could raise the defense that he was defending another (Crapaud). His success depends in part on whether the jurisdiction is one which follows the "alter ego" rule; if it does, Gark has no defense, since Crapaud would not have been privileged to use force against his pursuers. If the "alter ego" rule is not in effect, and Gark can show that his mistake as to who was the aggressor was reasonable, his defense will probably be valid, at least as to the first tackle. But it is unlikely that his second pushing-down of Dasher is justifiable, since here, a reasonable man would probably have believed Dasher's statement about Crapaud's being a bank robber, and would therefore have known that force against Dasher was not lawful.

Battery by Haley against Gark: Haley has committed a battery against Gark, unless he can establish the defense that he reasonably believed Gark to be one of the robbers, and was trying to prevent his escape. Escape prevention is a grounds for use of reasonable force, provided that the belief in the need for it is either correct or reasonably mistaken.

Battery by Gark against Haley: Gark is guilty of a battery (and perhaps manslaughter) against Haley, unless he can establish ***self-defense***. It is usually held that one may use force to defend against only if the latter is ***unlawful***. Since Haley's use of force against Gark may have been lawful (if Haley reasonably believed Gark to be one of the bank robbers), this requirement for self-defense would not be met. However, a court would probably allow self-defense if Gark showed that his mistake as to the lawfulness of Haley's motives was in turn a reasonable one. But since Gark was already on notice that this was a bank robbery, he might be unable to make this showing.

Even if Gark is able to show a reasonable mistake, it may nonetheless be held that he used a greater degree of force than necessary in the circumstances. The use of the brick to hit Haley in the head might even be considered ***deadly force*** (force intended or likely to cause serious bodily injury), so that in some states Gark would have had a duty to retreat if he could have safely done so.

Involuntary manslaughter of Haley by Leek: Leek may be guilty of involuntary manslaughter of Haley. This will depend on whether Leek was reckless or criminally negligent (depending on the jurisdiction). It seems doubtful that mere inattention to a siren would constitute anything more than ordinary civil negligence. But if Leek is held to be reckless or grossly negligent, he can try to raise the defense that he was not the proximate cause of death, since the death occurred from head injuries inflicted by Gark. However, it is surely a foreseeable consequence of failing to pay heed to an ambulance siren that a collision may result and that the patient may die because he cannot receive treatment for his pre-existing injuries. This would seem to be an extension of the rule that one takes one's victim as one finds him.

Alternatively, if Leek's failure to pull over at the sound of the siren constituted a violation of traffic laws, this might trigger application of the ***misdemeanor-manslaughter*** rule. In that event, Leek's proximate cause argument would have even less chance of success, since proximate cause is often virtually suspended in misdemeanor-manslaughter cases based upon *malum in se* violations.

Murder or manslaughter by Gark: Gark may be liable for the murder of Haley, since murder may be based upon an intent to do serious bodily injury, or a "reckless indifference to the value of human life." Gark can, of course, raise self-defense, but this will not necessarily succeed (as discussed above in the context of the battery of Haley). Gark may also claim that his blow was not a proximate cause of Haley's death, because of the intervening traffic accident. However, assuming that the head injuries which proved fatal to Haley were from the blow (rather than the collision), the proximate cause defense is unlikely to work, since the case will probably come within the rule that a third party's failure to act will never be a superseding cause. That is, the ambulance driver's failure to get Haley to the hospital cannot absolve Gark of liability. (However, Leek's act of affirmative negligence might be sufficiently abnormal and unforeseeable so as to be held to have broken the chain of causation).

If Gark's proximate cause defense fails, but he is not shown to have had the requisite intent for murder, he will probably be liable for involuntary manslaughter. This might be founded on the fact that he committed a battery, triggering the misdemeanor-manslaughter rule. It is not clear whether the death occurred "in the commission of" the battery. But since the blow itself is what finally killed Haley, the requisite link between the battery and the death probably exists.

Felony-murder by Crapaud: It is possible that Crapaud is liable for the felony-murder of Haley. However, this is unlikely, since: (1) the killing was not from the hand of Crapaud or his co-robbers; and (2) the chain of events leading from the robbery to Haley's death is quite bizarre and unforeseeable.

QUESTION 2

Your boss has asked you to write a memorandum outlining the legal issues in the following case:

A 22-year-old heiress of a wealthy family was kidnapped by a small band of revolutionaries, who held her captive in a closet for several weeks, and repeatedly threatened to kill her unless she sent taped messages to her family. After 10 days of such threats and abuse coupled with deprivation of food and sleep, the heiress [hereafter H] heard a commotion and several shots in the room adjoining her closet. Fearing that she would be killed, she opened the closet door and observed the following scene: a member of the revolutionary group [hereafter M] was lying in a pool of blood; another member of the group [hereafter A] was standing over him with a smoking pistol. Seeing that H had emerged from the closet, A pointed the pistol at H and said, "Now you'll have to die, because you can pin the murder on me. I won't kill you now, since you're still valuable to us. But you'll never leave here alive; we can't afford to let you go now; we will kill you eventually — maybe next week, maybe next month, maybe next year. There's only one way out for you. M is dying, but he's not dead yet. If you kill him, I will be able to trust you. What'll it be? Do you kill him or do I kill you? M has only 5 or 10 minutes to live, so you have two minutes to make up your mind." Fearing that she would be killed, H said she would kill M. She was then given a pistol and told it had one bullet in it. Still covered by A's pistol, she was told to shoot M — through the head, which she did.

Over the next several weeks H became convinced that she was guilty of first degree murder and she began to identify more and more with the group. Soon she was allowed out of the closet. A month after the shooting of M, the police received an anonymous telephone tip that H was being held in the house where she was, in fact, being held. The police — without a warrant — surrounded the house and burst through the front and back doors with their guns drawn. H was sitting at a table with A when the raid took place; nobody else was in the house at the time. As the police came through the door, A handed H one of the two sub-machine guns that were under the table, shouting, "It's the pigs; they're going to kill us; we have to protect ourselves!" H and A began shooting and one policeman was killed before A and H were subdued and taken prisoner. The bullet that killed the policeman came either from A's gun or from H's gun but it cannot be determined from which, since the guns were mixed up in the excitement. After A and H were arrested, handcuffed, and removed from the building, the police — without a search warrant — conducted a search of the entire house, claiming that they were looking for other members of the group. In the process of searching for other members, they opened closets, drawers and cabinets, and seized numerous papers, including a diary kept by A from the beginning of the kidnapping and a diary kept by H beginning the day after the shooting of M. A's diary reveals that on the morning of the shooting of M, A discovered that M was an undercover agent for the F.B.I. Deciding that M had to be killed, A contrived to have H kill him. A knocked M unconscious and spilled animal blood around his body and then fired two shots into the air. H then killed M as A had planned (as previously described). A's diary also revealed that he had put LSD into H's drinking water the day before the killing of M. H's diary revealed that she did not know that M was an informant, and that she believed that M was alive but dying at the time she shot him. It also reveals that she did not think that A would kill her immediately if she refused to shoot M, but she did think there was a good chance she would be killed at some future time. The diary also reveals that H hated M because M had constantly threatened to rape and kill her in the early days of her kidnapping and that H felt pleasure when she shot M. There is a statute, enacted just before the kidnapping of H, which provides for a mandatory sentence of death for the first degree murder of a law enforcement official.

You are an assistant either to the prosecuting attorney or the defense attorney for H (pick either one). Your boss has asked you to write a memorandum outlining the issues in the case, including the crimes that the defendants (both H and A) can reasonably be charged with and the defenses they can reasonably raise. If any facts are unclear or if facts that you deem critical are not stated, indicate what they are and how they would affect your analysis.

ANSWER TO QUESTION 2

CRIMES BY A

Murder of M as accomplice or principal: A is probably guilty of the murder of M, either as accomplice or as principal. A has obviously aided and abetted H's shooting of M, so he is potentially liable as an accomplice. However, it is usually required that, for accomplice liability, the principal be guilty. As is discussed below, H may have a defense to murder (perhaps duress); if so, A may escape accomplice liability. However, a modern tendency has been to allow an accomplice to be held guilty even though certain defenses are available to the "principal".

Alternatively, A may be guilty of murder as a ***principal***. A court might take the view that H was merely an innocent agent, whose conduct was controlled by A. See, e.g., *R.v. Cogan*. If A is found to have been a principal to murder, it might well be held to be first-degree, since A was aware that M was a law enforcement official.

Alternatively, A may be liable for ***felony-murder***. That is, the killing of M might be viewed as having been in furtherance of the kidnapping scheme. But it seems to me that A can successfully argue that the killing of M was unrelated to the kidnapping, and was not a "natural and probable" result of it.

Conspiracy to murder M: A may be guilty of conspiring to murder M. However, it seems probable that there has been no "agreement" between A and H, but rather, duress used against H. If H's duress defense is found not to be valid, perhaps the necessary agreement would exist.

Battery of M: A is clearly guilty of committing a battery on M, since he knocked M unconscious.

Battery of H: A, by placing LSD in H's drink, may be guilty of committing a battery against her. Battery is the intentional causing of bodily injury, and administering of a hallucinogenic drug would probably qualify. It is not necessary that the injury be caused directly (e.g., by a blow).

Murder of policeman: A is probably guilty of murdering the policeman, either as an accomplice or as a principal. Obviously, if the prosecution can show that the fatal bullet came from A's gun, he is liable as principal. But even if this cannot be shown, A clearly aided H in the shooting (by giving her the gun). This would be enough to make A an accomplice to murder. Under modern procedural rules, it is probably not necessary that the prosecution specify in the indictment whether A is charged with being an accomplice or a principal, so long as enough facts are stated to allow A to defend himself.

Conspiracy to murder the policeman: A may also be guilty of conspiring to murder the policeman, since there was probably a tacit agreement (even though very hurriedly reached) between A and H to shoot at the policeman.

CRIMES BY H

Murder of M: H is probably guilty of the murder of M. She had the necessary intent to kill, despite the fact that she believed that M was already dying; it is probably enough that one intends to hasten the already inevitable death of another. (Certainly H's shot would have been the "cause in fact" of M's death even if he had actually been dying prior to the shot).

H may be able raise the defense of ***duress***. However, the court might very well hold that the duress defense is not available where the charge is murder as a principal, which the threatened shooting of H by A was not. However, the Model Penal Code would not impose such a requirement, provided that a person of "reasonable firmness" would have been "unable to resist" the threat; in view of H's deprivation of food and sleep, and the previous abuse directed to her, the Model Penal Code's test might be met.

Assuming that H can overcome these hurdles to a duress defense, the defense is probably not lost by the fact that H hated M, and took pleasure in killing him. These factors would, of course, have some evidentiary bearing on whether H really acted out of duress, but as long as duress was the principal motivation, the other facts would probably be disregarded.

It is conceivable that H may be able to raise the defense of ***involuntary intoxication***, based on A's having given her LSD. However, H would probably have to show that the drug contributed materially to her shooting of M; that this was the case is not indicated by the facts as given.

If the duress and intoxication defenses fail, the murder will probably be *first-degree*. Assuming that one of the purposes of the statute imposing severe penalites on killings of law enforcement personnel is to protect such personnel, the killer's lack of knowledge that an officer was involved would probably be irrelevant. The problem is similar to that posed in *U.S. v. Feola*, where the Supreme Court held that one could be guilty of conspiracy to assault a federal enforcement official without knowledge that the victim was an official.

H may be able to get the charge reduced from murder to *voluntary manslaughter*. She might argue that M's mistreatment of her brought her to a rage, of the sort that would have provoked a "reasonable man." However, since M's misconduct occurred early on in the kidnapping, a "cooling off" period may have passed. Alternatively, a manslaughter verdict might be justified by a theory of "imperfect" duress, since H was obviously acting under a fair amount of coercion.

Conspiracy to murder M: H may also be guilty of conspiring to murder M. Again, however, it is not clear that she has made the necessary "agreement." Also, she can raise the same defenses against the conspiracy charge as against the murder charge.

Murder of policeman: If it cannot be determined whose gun the bullet that killed the policeman came from, H can probably escape liability for murder. H can assert that the bullet came from A's gun. On that hypothesis, H would probably not be an accomplice to the killing, since there is not much evidence that she aided or abetted A's conduct. (However, the prosecution might succeed in arguing that merely by virtue of H's participating in the shoot-out with A, she gave him encouragement, thus making her an accomplice.)

Felony-murder of policeman: Since the killing of the policeman took place in the course of an assault on a group of police, the felony-murder rule might apply. The assault, since it was made with a deadly weapon, was probably the felony of aggravated assault. However, H can argue that the assault here was included in the killing, and that the requirement of an independent felony is therefore not met. But the prosecution can counter that several police were being assaulted, and that a felonious assault against the ones other than the dead officer can support a felony-murder conviction.

Conspiracy to murder policeman: Finally, there is a small chance that H might be liable for conspiring to murder the policeman, again on the grounds that she participated in the shoot-out and thereby acted in concert with A.

QUESTION 3

Foyle and Pierce went to Smitty's Novelty Shop to buy masks that they intended to use in a holdup of the Lightheart Liquor Store, which was a few hundred yards away from Smitty's, in the same block of stores. While he was waiting on them, Smitty overheard Foyle say Pierce, "We can hit Lightheart at night, when there are no customers. They'll have the whole day's receipts then too." Smitty concluded that the two women planned to hold up the liquor store. He sold them masks. He said nothing about the holdup. He decided that he would watch to see when the holdup took place and that if he had an opportunity to help Foyle and Pierce he would do so, in hope of sharing in the loot.

Three nights later, Foyle and Pierce, wearing masks, entered the Lightheart Liquor Store. They displayed revolvers and ordered Bear and Wolf, two clerks, to go around to the back of the counter with their hands up. Foyle opened the cash register, which was empty. Wolf said, "There's no money there. The store is closed today because we are taking inventory." Pierce ordered the clerks not to leave the store, and both women ran out. When they got outside, they found that their "getaway" car (which was a stolen car) was blocked by another car illegally double-parked beside it, in which Driver was sitting. Pierce shouted at him, "Move that car."

"Take it easy, lady, you got a roast in the oven?" Driver responded. Angered, Pierce shot him.

"You fool," Foyle shouted to Pierce. "There was't supposed to be any shooting." They both started to run down the street.

Smitty had heard the shot and guessed what was happening. As Foyle and Pierce ran by his shop, he opened the door and said, "In here." The women ran into his shop. He led them through the back of the shop to an exit onto an alley. They ran out. Smitty shouted after them, "Don't forget me now."

As they came out of the alleyway, Lindsey, who was carelessy not looking where he was going, crashed into Foyle and knocked her down. "Oh, I'm terribly sorry, madam," Lindsey said, and bent down to help her up. Foyle punched Lindsey in the face. He fell down.

"That's dumb," said Pierce. They ran up the street.

A policeman who had seen Foyle punch Lindsey (but knew nothing about the preceding events) ran after them. When they failed to stop in response to his shouted command, he fired his pistol twice, both times aiming high with the intention of firing over their heads. He failed to reckon sufficiently on the steep upward incline of the street. One shot hit Foyle in the leg. The other shot hit the tire of a car.

The car was being driven by Sport, whose license had expired ten days previously, as he knew, and had not been renewed. The tire burst. The car careened and hit Morton, who was crossing the street against the traffic light, which constitited jaywalking, a minor traffic offense for which the maximum fine was $5.00. Morton was crushed under the car and died instantly.

Driver died in the hospital the next day, from the bullet wound. Lindsey recovered from his fall and went home, which was several blocks away. He was in a disturbed state. After he told his wife about the incident, he lay down on a couch. Two hours later, his wife discovered that he was breathing badly, and called an ambulance. He died that night. The attending physician said that he had suffered a heart attack.

In the Lightheart Liquor Store, Wolf took the opportunity afforded by the excitement to remove a bottle of brandy from the shelf and place it in his coat pocket. He took the brandy home without paying for it and drank it that night to calm his nerves. What crimes were committed, and by whom?

ANSWER TO QUESTION 3

Conspiracy to rob by Foyle and Pierce: Foyle and Pierce are clearly guilty of *conspiracy to rob* the liquor store. They have obviously reached an agreement to commit the robbery, and have met any overt act requirement.

Conspiracy to rob by Smitty: It is not so clear whether Smitty has joined this conspiracy. A person who sells non-contraband items with knowledge that they will be used for criminal purposes will not usually be held to have joined a conspiracy, if he does not actively desire a criminal result. However, Smitty's additional intent to assist if he can do so may be enough to give him the required mental state. As there has been no agreement by Smitty on the one hand and Foyle and Pierce on the other that Smitty will help them, Smitty might escape conspiracy liability.

Attempted robbery by Foyle and Pierce: Foyle and Pierce have committed *attempted robbery*, regardless of what test is used to determine the sufficiency of their acts. They might try to raise the defense of "factual impossibility," but this defense is extremely unlikely to succeed — the situation is not very different from that of a pickpocket who finds that his victim is not carrying a wallet; the pickpocket would certainly be guilty of attempted larceny.

Attempted robbery by Smitty: Smitty might be liable for attempted robbery as an *accomplice*. Such accomplice liability for an unsuccessful attempt seems allowable in principle. However, Smitty has not directly aided or encouraged the attempt (as distinguished from the escape) except by selling goods. It is questionable whether his sale of goods, coupled with his knowledge that the attempt would take place, and intent to render assistance in the future, if needed, add up to accomplice liability. Certainly the sale of the goods with knowledge is not by itself sufficient.

Robbery by Foyle and Pierce: Foyle and Pierce are not guilty of robbery, because that crime requires an underlying taking of property, and nothing was taken from the liquor store.

Murder of Driver by Pierce and Foyle: Pierce seems clearly guilty of murdering Driver. She might try to get this reduced to ***voluntary manslaughter*** on the theory that Driver provoked her, and she acted in a heat of passion. However, words of harrassment or abuse are almost never accepted as the sort of provocation that will cause a "reasonable person" to lose his temper.

Foyle may be liable for the ***felony-murder*** of Driver. Pierce committed the killing while attempting to commit a dangerous felony (robbery), and the killing could be viewed as "in the commission of" the robbery. Foyle might then be an accomplice to Pierce's felony-murder. However, since Pierce killed out of anger, and not directly in furtherance of a felony, Foyle might be able to show that the killing was not the "natural or probable" result of the robbery. But this case seems a lot like *U.S. v. Carter*, where the accomplice was found guilty of felony-murder, despite his disapproval of the killing.

It is conceivable that Smitty might also be found guilty of the felony-murder of Driver. However, it is not even clear that he was an accomplice to the robbery, so the connection between him and the death of Driver is probably too attenuated for liability.

Accessory after the fact by Smitty: Smitty is probably an accessory after the fact to attempted robbery. Although he did not know the precise details of the robbery attempt, or that it had failed, he probably still had the requisite knowledge of the essential elements of the crime. He might also conceivably be guilty of attempted compounding of crime, since he was hoping to receive money from the robbers for his help.

Murder or manslaughter of Lindsey by Pierce and Foyle: Foyle might conceivably be guilty of murdering Lindsey, based upon an intent to do ***serious bodily injury***. However, it would probably be found that Foyle intended to commit merely a minor battery, rather than serious bodily harm.

Alternatively, Foyle may be guilty of ***felony-murder*** in Lindsey's death. The episode took place while the two were attempting to escape, and this might be viewed as having been part of the "commission" of the attempted robbery. However, the requisite causal relationship between the punch and the heart attack may be lacking. If Lindsey would have had a fatal heart attack exactly when he did, even without the punch in the face, the punch is not a "cause in fact" of death. If, however, the heart attack occurred earlier than it would have (even if it would have happened eventually) the punch is probably both a cause in fact and a proximate cause of the death. This is an application of a "pre-existing weakness" rule.

Foyle may, alternatively, be liable for ***misdemeanor-manslaughter*** in the death of Lindsey. She has committed a battery, which will suffice for misdemeanor-manslaughter liability. Again, however, the necessary causal relationship between the blow and Lindsey's death may be lacking; this is likely to be determined in essentially the same way as causation in the felony-murder context (discussed in the preceding paragraph).

Whatever homicide Foyle is found liable for in Lindsey's death, Pierce may have the same liability on an ***accomplice*** basis. However, she can argue that neither the collision between Lindsey and Foyle, nor Foyle's punch, was the "natural and probable" consequence of a robbery attempt, and that accomplice liability should therefore not apply. This issue is similar to the question of whether Foyle is liable as an accomplice to Pierce's killing of Driver.

Battery and manslaughter liability of Policeman: If Policeman is found to have been grossly negligent or reckless in the way he shot towards Foyle and Pierce, he may be liable for battery of Foyle. This is because intent is not necessary where gross negligence or recklessness exist. He may be able to raise the defense of ***attempted arrest***.

However, as far as Policeman knew, Foyle was merely a misdemeanant; ***deadly force*** may not be used against misdemeanants. The court would probably find that firing a gun constitutes use of deadly force, even if the intent is to shoot over the target's head. (The Model Penal Code would make the shooting deadly force if the gun was fired "in the direction" of another person, which Policeman seems to have done.)

Policeman might also claim that Foyle and Pierce were in reality *felons*, and that he was therefore permitted to use deadly force against them. However, it does not seem likely that the fact that they were, unbeknownst to Policeman, felons, will shield Policeman; for instance, self-defense may not be claimed where one was not aware of the danger until later.

Policeman may also be guilty of ***manslaughter*** in the death of Morton. He may have ***misdemeanor-manslaughter*** liability, if his using his gun against persons believed to be mere misdemeanants constitutes a misdemeanor (perhaps assault or, in the case of the shot which hit Foyle, battery). Alternatively, he may be guilty of ordinary involuntary manslaughter, if his failure to take the steepness of the hill into account constitutes recklessness or gross negligence (whichever the jurisdiction requires). Some jurisdictions may require an actual awareness of the risk on Policeman's part, in which case he will probably not be liable. Policeman might also try to show that his shot was not the proximate cause of Morton's death, since it was somewhat unlikely that the shot would puncture the tire, and lead to a traffic accident. However, this chain of events is not completely "bizarre" or "abnormal", and the necessary causal relationship may well be found.

Finally, Policeman may rely on the same "attempted arrest" defense as he will use on the battery charge. However, even assuming that the other requirements for the defense are met (which, as noted, is questionable), the defense only exists if his act presented no unreasonable danger to persons other than the fleeing criminals.

Misdemeanor-manslaughter by Sport: Sport might conceivably be liable for misdemeanor-manslaughter in the death of Morton. Sport's failure to renew his license is probably a misdemeanor. However, it is *"malum prohibitum"* rather than *"malum in se."* No matter which of the three tests for proximate cause is used, it is hard to see how Sport's failure to renew his license has any direct causal relationship to the accident (except for the fact that had he not been driving at all the accident would not have occurred). Therefore, Sport will probably escape liability.

Larceny or embezzlement by Wolf: Wolf has probably committed either larceny or embezzlement. He was probably not entrusted with "possession" of liquor sitting out on the shelves, so his taking is probably larceny (i.e., an unlawful taking from the liquor store's possession). However, he will not be guilty of larceny if, at the time he took the liquor, he intended to pay for it subsequently. This is true regardless of whether he ultimately changed his mind and decided not to pay. If he did not intend to pay at the time he took the liquor, he might try to claim the defense of necessity or duress, since he used the liquor to calm his nerves. However, these defenses are available only where there was no third, non-criminal alternative. Since Wolf was free to pay for the liquor, these two defenses seem not to apply.

TABLE OF CASES

This table includes references to cases cited everywhere
in this book, including in the various Exam Q&A sections.

Ake v. Oklahoma, 67

Blaue, Regina v., 65

Carter, U.S. v., 280
Coker v. Georgia, 126

Enmund v. Florida, 126

Feola, U.S. v., 101
Ford v. Wainwright, 69
Foucha v. Louisiana, 68

Gebardi v. U.S., 108
Goetz, People v., 80, 81
Gregg v. Georgia, 126

Iannelli v. U.S., 107

Jones v. U.S., 68

M'Naghten's Case, 66, 163, 164, 228
Martin v. Ohio, 83
McCleskey v. Kemp, 126

Medina v. California, 68
Mitchneck, Commonwealth v., 143
Montana v. Egelhoff, 71

Pinkerton v. U.S., 178, 236, 237

Ratzlaf v. U.S., 57
Redline, Commonwealth v., 123
Reid, People v., 142
Robinson v. Cal., 225

Schoon, U.S. v., 75
Shaw v. Dir. Pub. Prosec., 102
Stamp, People v., 64
Staples v. U.S., 54, 226

Taylor, People v., 114
Tennessee v. Garner, 87, 88, 232
Thabo Meli v. Regina, 58
Thomas, U.S. v., 96

Wilson v. State, 95
Woodson v. North Carolina, 126

SUBJECT MATTER INDEX

This index includes references to the Capsule Summary
and to the Exam Tips, but not to Q&A or Flow Charts

ABANDONMENT
See ATTEMPT, CONSPIRACY, 52

ACCESSORY AFTER THE FACT
Offense defined, 109, 116, 182

ACCESSORY BEFORE THE FACT
    See ACCOMPLICES, 109

ACCOMPLICES
    Generally, 109-117
Accessory after the fact, 109, 116
Accessory before the fact, 109
Act requirement, 110-111, 181
        Assistance attempted, but no crime
                occurs, 111
        Assistance given but not needed, 111
        Conspiracy as meeting, 111
        Failure to intervene, 110
        Presence at crime scene, 110
        Words alone, 110
Additional crimes by principal, 113-114, 182
        Felony-murder cases, 114, 183
        Intentional murder, 114
        Misdemeanor-manslaughter cases, 114, 183
        Model Penal Code limits liability, 117, 121
        "Natural and probable" crimes, 113, 182
Mental state, 111-113, 181
        Drunk driver, car lent to, 112
        Intentional aid, 111
        Knowledge of criminal result, without
                intent, 112
        Mens rea of underlying crime, 112
        Recklessness and negligence, 112
        Strict-liability crime, 92
        Ulterior motives, 119
Misprision of felony, 117
Principal in first degree, 109
Principal's guilt required, 109, 114
        Conviction not necessary, 114
        Principal lacks required mental state, 111-
                113
Victim, no liability of, 116
Withdrawal as defense, 114

ACT
Committed under hypnosis, 50
Omission
        See OMISSION TO ACT
Possession as, 49

Reflex or convulsion, 49
Requirement of, 49-60
Status as, 49
Unconsciousness, 50
Voluntary requirement of, 49, 165
Words as, 49

ACTUS REUS
See also ACT
Defined, 49, 157

ARREST
    Generally, 86-88
By private citizen, 88, 169
Rules for making, 87-88, 167
Use of deadly force to make, 87-88, 167
        Dangerous felon fleeing, 88, 169
        Misdemeanor fleeing, 87, 170
        Model Penal Code view, 83
        Non-dangerous felon fleeing, 82, 170

ASSAULT
    Generally, 133-134, 192
Aggravated forms of, 134
Attempted-battery variety, 133, 192
Conditional, 133
Intentional-frightening variety, 133, 192

ATTEMPT
    Generally, 91-98, 172-175
Act, generally, 91, 172
        Equivocality test, 93
        Mere preparation not sufficient, 93-94
        Model Penal Code "substantial step"
                test, 93, 94
        Proximity to success, 93
Assault, attempt to commit, 97, 172
Attempt-like crimes, 97
Broadening of liability for, 91
Conviction of despite proof of completed
        crime, 98
Conviction of on charge of completed crime, 98,
        175
Impossibility, generally, 94-96, 173-174
        Factual, 94-95, 174
        Inherent, 96
        Mistake of fact governing legal relation, 95-
                96
        Model Penal Code view, 96
        True legal, 96, 174

Mental state, generally, 91-92, 172-173
    Intent usually required, 91-92, 172
    Knowledge of likely result, 92
    Recklessness and negligence, 92, 172
    Strict-liability crime, 92, 172
    Surrounding circumstances, 92
Rationale for punishing, 91
Renunciation, generally, 96-97, 179-180
    Voluntariness requirement, 96-97, 180

AUTOMATISM
See also ACT
    Generally, 69
Low blood sugar as basis for, 69
Post-traumatic stress disorder, 69
Premenstrual Syndrome, 69

BAD CHECKS
Statutes punishing writing of, 148

BATTERY
    Generally, 133-134, 191-192
    Aggravated forms of, 133
    Mental state for, 133

BLACKMAIL
See EXTORTION

BURGLARY
    Generally, 149-150, 199-201
    Breaking, 150, 199
    Dwelling of another, 150, 200
    Entry, 150, 200
    Intent to commit felony within, 150, 200
    Nighttime, 150, 200

CAUSATION
    Generally, 60-66, 160-163
Cause in fact, generally, 60-61, 160-161
    Shortening of victim's life, 61
    Substantial factor in producing harm, 60
    Victim dead before act, 61
Intervening acts, 61, 162
    By defendant, 61, 162-163
    By third person, 60, 65
    By victim, 65, 162
    Crime of negligence or recklessness, 62
    Dependent, 162
    Felony-murder cases, 64
    Independent, 64, 162
    Misdemeanor-manslaughter cases, 64
    Negative act, 70
    Poor medical treament as, 65
    Suicide by victim, 65
    Victim attempts to escape, 65
    Victim refuses medical aid, 65
Legal Cause *see* Proximate Cause, this entry
Manner of harm unintended, generally, 63-66

Direct causation, 63-64
    Pre-existing weakness of victim, 63
    Recklessness and negligence crimes, 62, 166
Proximate cause, generally, 61-66, 161-163
    Model Penal Code approach, 61
    Unintended victim, 62, 161
    "Year and a day" rule in homicide, 62, 161
Substantial factor in producing harm, 160
"Transferred intent" rule, 62, 161
    Victim completely unforeseeable, 62
Unintended victim, 62, 161
    Crime of recklessness or negligence, 62
    Defenses assertable against, 62
    Mistake of identity, 62, 161
    Resulting crime is more serious to, 62
    "Transferred intent" rule, 62, 161
Victim dead before act, 160

CAUSE IN FACT
See CAUSATION

COMMON-LAW CRIMES, 54

CONCURRENCE
    Generally, 57-60
Different crime than intended, 58
Mental state must cause act, 58
Mind and acts, 58
Mind and results, 58-60
Same harm as intended but different degree, 59-
    60

CONFLICT OF LAWS, 167

CONSPIRACY
    Generally, 98-109, 176-180
Abandonment by all parties, 106, 179-180
Accomplice liability, distinguished from, 103
Acquittal of other conspirators, 108
Agreement, 99-100, 176-178
    Circumstantial evidence as proof of, 99
    Feigned, 100
    Implied, 99
    To commit object crime, 100
Aiding and abetting of, 99, 177
"Chain", 104
Corporations, 108
Duration of, generally, 105-106
Feigned, 177
Hearsay, admission of, 98-99
Husband and wife, 107
Identity of others, knowledge, 104
Impossibility, defense of, 103
Inconsistent disposition at trial, 108
    Different trials, 108
    Same trial, 108
Joint trial of persons accused of, 98
Legislative intent to punish only one party, 108
Mental state, generally, 100-101, 177
    Attendant circumstances, 101

Goods and services supplied, 101-102
Intent to commit crime, 100-101
Recklessness and negligence, 101
Strict-liability crimes, 101
Objective of, 102-104, 177
Non-criminal aims, 102
Organized crime, 74
Overt act, requirement of, 103, 178
Party who joins late or leaves early, 105
Punishment of
Merger with completed crime, 109, 180
Rationale for punishing, 89
Substantive crimes, liability for, 103-104, 180
Wharton's Rule, 107, 180
Merely presumption, 107, 180
Model Penal Code rejects, 107, 180
"Wheel" or circle, 104
Withdrawal from, 106
As defense to conspiracy charge, 106

CONTRIBUTORY NEGLIGENCE
By victim, 89
In manslaughter case, 131

DEFENSE OF OTHERS
Generally, 84-85
Mistake as to who is aggressor, 84
Retreat, requirement of, 84

DEFENSE OF PROPERTY
Generally, 85-86, 169
Chattels, recapture of, 86
Deadly force, use of, 85, 169
Dwelling, defense of, 85
Dwelling, defined, 169
Mechanical devices, use of, 85
Real estate, right to retake, 86

DEPOSITIONS
Request for production of documents, 163

DIMINISHED RESPONSBILITY
Generally, 69
Definition of, 69
First-degree murder negated by, 69
Insanity defense as superseding, 69
Murder reduced to manslaughter, 69

DIMINISHED RESPONSIBILITY
Generally, 165
Insanity defense as superseding, 165
Murder reduced to manslaughter, 165

DISCIPLINE
Force used to maintain, 88
By parents, 89
By school teacher, 88

DURESS
Generally, 73-74, 171
Death or serious bodily harm, requirement of, 73

Elements of defense of, 73
Homicide cases, use in, 73, 171
Imminent harm, requirement of, 73
Mistake, effect of, 77
Third person, harm directed at, 74

EMBEZZLEMENT
Generally, 142-144, 197-198
By one in lawful possession, generally, 143-144
Employees, 143-144
Finders of property, 144
Conversion, 142
Fraudulent taking, 144
Claim of right, 144
Collection of debt, 144
Intent to repay, 144
Intent to repay, 198

ENTRAPMENT
Generally, 90, 171
Evidence of, 90, 171
Falsehood about legality of act, 90
Rationales for, 90
Tests for, 90

ERIE V. TOMPKINS, 167

EXTORTION
Generally, 152
Attempt to recover property, 152
Model Penal Code, 152

FALSE PRETENSES
Generally, 145-148
Concealment and non-disclosure, 145
False promise, 146
Gullibility of victim no defense, 147
Larceny by trick, distinguished from, 148
Mental state, 147
Pecuniary loss, no requirement of, 147
Property
Nature of, 147
Of another, 147
Related Crimes, 148
Reliance by victim, 146
Title passing, 146

FELONY-MURDER
See MURDER

FORGERY, 148

HYPNOSIS
Act committed while under, 50

IGNORANCE OR MISTAKE
Generally, 56-57

Belief conduct not illegal, generally, 56
    Official statement of law relied on, 57
Bigamy, mistake as to existence of, 57
Defense based on, 57
    Ambiguous statute, 57
Effect on justification or excuse, 72
Law, mistake as to, 57
    Concerning collateral fact, 57
"Lesser crime" theory, 56
"Moral wrong" theory, 56
Reasonableness, 56

IMPOSSIBILITY
See ATTEMPT, CONSPIRACY

INSANITY
    Generally, 66-69, 163-165
At time set for execution, 69
Commitment following acquital, generally, 68
    Burden of proof, 68
    Mandatory, constitutionality of, 68
    Release from, 68
    Telling jury about, 68
Diminished responsibility *See* DIMINISHED RE-
    SPONSIBILITY
Fitness to stand trial, 68
"Irresistible impulse" test, 67, 164
M'Naghten test, 66, 163-164
Model Penal Code test, 67
Procedures for presenting defense, generally, 67-
    68
    Constitution does not require recognition, 67
    Role of jury, 68
    When raised, 67
Psychiatric exam as basis for, 67
XYY chromosome defense, 68

INTENT
    Generally, 51-52, 184-186
Different crime than intended occurs, 58
Intentional act, 52
Intoxication, effect of, 52, 184
"Malicious" conduct, 119
Motive, distinguished from, 52, 184
Presumption of, 53
Purposely, 52-53
Same harm as intended but different degree, 59-
    60
Specific, 51-52
    Distinguished from general intent, 51-52
    Negatived by intoxication, 52

INTOXICATION
    Generally, 69-72, 165-166
Alcoholism and narcotics addiction, 71
Defense in rape case, 71, 165
First-degree murder negated by, 70
Insanity, relation to, 71, 166
Intent negatived by, 70
Involuntary, generally, 71, 166

Murder reduced to manslaughter because of, 71,
    166
Negligence, does not negate, 52
Recklessness, does not negate, 71, 166
Voluntary manslaughter, 71, 165

KIDNAPPING
    Generally, 136, 193

KNOWLEDGE
As meeting intent requirement, generally, 112,
    201

LARCENY
    Generally, 137-142, 193-197
Asportation, 140, 193
By trick, 139, 196
Definition, 137, 193
Employee, taking by, 138, 196
Finders of lost or mislaid property, 139
Intent to steal, generally, 141-142, 196
    Claim of right, 141
    Collection of debt, 141, 195
    Concurrence of taking and intent, 141
    Intent to permanently deprive, 141, 195
Property, 140
    Nature, 196
    Of another, 140
Taking from owner's presence, 141
Trespassory taking, 137-140, 193

LAW ENFORCEMENT
See ARREST, PREVENTION OF ESCAPE,
    PREVENTION OF CRIME

LOST PROPERTY
See LARCENCY, EMBEZZLEMENT

MAIL FRAUD, 148

MANSLAUGHTER
    Generally, 127-133, 188-191
Criminal negligence, generally, 130-131
    All circumstances considered, 130
    Awareness of risk, 131
    Contributory negligence of victim, 131
    Inherently dangerous objects, 131
    Model Penal Code's negligent
        homicide, 131
    Proximate cause, 132
    Vehicle homicide, 131
"Heat of passion," generally, 127
    Adultery as provocation, 129
    Battery as provocation, 128
    Cooling off, actual, 128, 129
    Cooling off, reasonable time for, 128, 129
    Intoxication, effect of, 130

Mistake, effect of, 129
Model Penal Code's subjective test, 130
"Reasonable man," characteristics of, 129
Reasonable provocation, 128-129
Requirements for, 127
Words alone as provocation, 129
Involuntary, generally, 130-133, 189-191
Misdemeanor-manslaughter, 131-132, 183
   Battery as basis for, 132
   Proximate cause, 132
   Traffic violation as basis for, 132
Other extenuating circumstances, generally, 130
   Imperfect coercion or necessity, 130
   Imperfect crime-prevention, 130
   Imperfect defense of others, 130
   Imperfect self-defense, 130, 189
   Intoxication, 130
   Mercy killing, 130
Voluntary, generally, 130

MAYHEM, 133

MENS REA
See also INTENT, KNOWLEDGE, MENTAL
   STATE, NEGLIGENCE, RECKLESS-
   NESS, STRICT LIABILITY
Defined, 51, 157

MENTAL STATE
Ambiguity as to, 91, 172
Intent, 91-92, 172
Negligent, 92
Reckless, 92, 172
   See also Names of individual crimes

MISTAKE OF FACT
See IGNORANCE OR MISTAKE

MISTAKE OF LAW
See IGNORANCE OR MISTAKE

MURDER
Generally, 118-127, 183-193
Death penalty for, 125
   Non-intentional killings, 126
   Non-murder cases, 126
   Racial prejudice, 126
Depraved heart, generally, 52
   Awareness of risk, 120
Elements of crime, 119-120
Felony-murder, generally, 122-125, 186-188
   Accomplice liability of other felons, 124,
      188
   After felony, killing occurring, 125
   Arson cases, 125, 186
   Assault as basis for, 122, 191
   Battery as basis for, 125, 191
   Bystander killed by robber, 123, 187
   Bystander killed by robbery victim or
      police, 123
   Causal relation between felony and

death, 123-124, 187
   Dangerous felonies, limited to, 122, 186
   Death must be "natural and probable" conse-
      quence of felony, 123, 187
   Distinguished from "depraved heart"
      murder, 123
   Escape, killing occurring during, 125, 188
   Felon killed by co-felon, 124, 188
   Felon killed by victim or policeman, 123,
      187
   "In the commission of" felony, 125, 188
   Manslaughter as basis for, 125
   Model Penal Code rejects, 125
   Robbery as basis for, 125, 186
First-degree, generally, 126
   Intoxication as negating, 127
   Premeditation and deliberation, 126
Intent-to-kill murder, generally, 120-121, 184-
   186
   Deadly weapon as evidence of, 120, 158
   Substantial certainty of death, 120, 184
Intent-to-seriously-injure murder, 121, 185
   Knowledge that injury is highly likely, 121,
      185
   Model Penal Code rejection of, 121
Non-intentional killings, 126
Proximate cause of, 123
Reckless indifference to value of human life, *see*
   Depraved Heart, this entry
Second-degree, 127

NECESSITY
Generally, 74-75
As meeting mental state requirement, 130
Choice of evils, 74
Civil disobedience, 75
Homicide cases, use in, 75

OMISSIONS TO ACT
Generally, 50-51
Based on special relationship, 50
Based on statute, 50
Based on undertaking to act, 51
Duty to act, generally, 50
   Based on contract, 50
Liability limited, 50

POSSESSION
As meeting act requirement, 49, 193

PRESUMPTIONS
Of knowledge, 53

PREVENTION OF CRIME
Use of force to achieve, 130

PREVENTION OF ESCAPE
Use of force to achieve, 87

PRINCIPAL IN THE FIRST DEGREE
See ACCOMPLICES

PRINCIPAL IN THE SECOND DEGREE
See ACCOMPLICES

RAPE
Generally, 134, 192
Consent lack of, 134
Homosexual, 135
Intercourse, requirement of, 134, 192
Mistake as to consent, 135, 193
Spousal exemption, 134, 189
Statutory, 135, 192

RECEIVING STOLEN PROPERTY
Generally, 148, 201-202
Knowledge of theft, 149, 201

RECKLESSNESS
As meeting mental state requirement, 91, 166

RENUNCIATION
See ATTEMPT

ROBBERY
Generally, 150-152, 197
Aggravated forms of, 151
Definition, 150, 197
From person or presence of another, 151, 197
Violence or intimidation, 151

SELF-DEFENSE
Generally, 75-83, 167-169
Aggressor, rights of, 75, 168
    Withdrawal by, 75, 168
"Battered child" and, 82
"Battered women" and, 81
Burden of proof, 83
Bystander, injury to, 82
Deadly force, use of, 75, 167
    Retreat, requirement of, 76, 79
"Imperfect" self-defense, 83, 189
Mistake, effect of, 80-81
    "Imperfect" self-defense, 83, 189
    Unreasonable error, 80-81, 189
Non-deadly force, use of, 82
Requirements for, 75
Resisting unlawful arrest, 75
Unlawful force requirement of, 76

SERVICE OF PROCESS, 157

SOLICITATION
Generally, 117, 183
Communication not received, 117
Defenses to, 117
Relation to attempt, 117

SPECIFIC INTENT
See INTENT

STATUTORY RAPE
Mistake as to age, 135, 192

STRICT LIABILITY
Generally, 54
Constitutionality of, 54
Model Penal Code treatment of, 54

THEFT
Consolidation of three crimes into one, 137, 148
    Model Penal Code, 139, 148

TRANSFERRED INTENT, 62, 161

VEHICULAR HOMICIDE, 118

VICARIOUS LIABILITY
Generally, 54, 178-179
Automobile owner, 55
Constitutionality of, 55
Employer, 55

WHARTON'S RULE, 107, 180

XYY CHROMOSOME DEFENSE, 68

"YEAR-AND-A-DAY" RULE, 62, 120, 161

The Emanuel Law Outline Series

Each outline in the series is the work of Steven Emanuel.
Each is packed with features that take you from next-day
preparation to night-before-the-exam review. Outlines are
available for all major law school subjects and many are
revised annually. This year, Steve will prepare new editions
of Evidence, Constitutional Law, Torts, Criminal Procedure
and Property.

Available titles
Civil Procedure
Constitutional Law
Contracts
Corporations
Criminal Law
Criminal Procedure
Evidence
Property
Torts (General Edition)
Torts (Prosser Edition)

Law In A Flash Series

Flashcards add a dimension to law school study which
cannot be matched by any other study aid, and these
are the acknowledged leader in flashcards. They mak
legal issues and answers stick to your mind like glue.
Each Law In a Flash card set contains 350-625 cards
arranged to give you black-letter principles first. The
they teach you all the subtleties by taking you through
series of hypotheticals filled with mnemonics and
checklists. Excellent for exam preparation.

Available titles
Civil Procedure 1
Civil Procedure 2
Constitutional Law
Contracts
Corporations
Criminal Law
Criminal Procedure
Evidence
Federal Income Taxation
Future Interests
Professional Responsibility
Real Property
Sales (UCC Article 2)
Torts
Wills & Trusts